"I am convinced beyond a doubt, based on Mr. Dear's investigation that I have been privileged to follow, that the Los Angeles police department had overlooked a major suspect, one that should have been considered a suspect from the very beginning."

—Dr. Harvey Davisson, Psychologist, Texas

"Unlike preceding books on this subject by others, Mr. Dear's new book, to me, offers a 'strong suspect.'"

—Hugh Aynesworth, *The Washington Times*

"An outstanding piece of investigative work that should shock everyone once they read Mr. Dear's book."

—J. F., retired, FBI

"I was fascinated with what your investigation came up with. I am in complete agreement. I always had the opinion that the LAPD did not have enough evidence in the Simpson case and they fixated on one suspect and one suspect only. This book will be like an H-Bomb!"

—Alan Blozis, retired Police
Lieutenant Commander, NYPD

"As an investigator in the state of Texas, Mr. Dear's book into the murders of Nicole Simpson and Ron Goldman can be described as an outstanding investigative piece of work, I'm convinced."

—B. Madding, Chief Deputy, Fairfield, Texas

"Mr. Dear's investigation and former theories and new facts in this book make it extremely plausible and believable."

—James Cron, former Commander,
Dallas County Sheriff's Crime Scene Unit

"I couldn't put it down; I told members of my staff, 'Oh my God, it all makes sense now.' "

—Sheriff Dick Wagman, retired, Texas

"While these alleged crimes are not within the apparent jurisdiction of a Texas state court, were these events to have taken place here, with Bill's investigation which I have read in detail, the matters would seem to perhaps warrant, at minimum, a grand jury investigation, or even the convening of a rarely used Court of Inquiry procedure, under our law."

—Judge R. M., Texas

O. J.
IS INNOCENT

AND I CAN PROVE IT!

THE SHOCKING TRUTH ABOUT THE MURDERS
OF NICOLE BROWN SIMPSON AND RON GOLDMAN

by WILLIAM C. DEAR

SKYHORSE PUBLISHING

Skyhorse Publishing books may be purchased in bulk at special discounts for sales promotion, corporate gifts, fund-raising, or educational purposes. Special editions can also be created to specifications. For details, contact the Special Sales Department, Skyhorse Publishing, 307 West 36th Street, 11th Floor, New York, NY 10018 or info@skyhorsepublishing.com.

Skyhorse® and Skyhorse Publishing® are registered trademarks of Skyhorse Publishing, Inc.®, a Delaware corporation.

www.skyhorsepublishing.com

10 9 8 7 6 5 4 3 2 1

Library of Congress Cataloging-in-Publication Data is available on file.

ISBN: 978-1-61608-620-6

Printed in the United States of America

To my parents, James and Lucille Dear, who are with me in spirit.
Mom . . . Dad, I never gave up.

To my sons,
Michael and Adam Dear,
daughter-in-law Missy, and my two gifts from God,
Macy and M. J.

To a very special person in my life, Marty Koch.

Special thanks to John McCready, Phil Thompson, and Courtney
Foley.
Without them, this book would never have come to fruition.

A very special thanks to all the men and women in law enforcement
who take their job so seriously.

To Justice, which sometimes works so slowly.

To Nicole's children, who are now grown, her parents, and to the
Goldmans.

DISCLAIMER

The factual information presented herein was obtained from court proceedings and other documents of public record associated with the criminal case: State of California vs. O. J. Simpson, except for new information recently discovered by the author.

All the people and events depicted are real. Only a few names have been changed for the protection of the individual.

However, the conversations reported within the text are written from memory. They represent the author's best recollection. The author makes no claim that the words spoken during those conversations are accurately recorded herein. He apologizes in advance for any omissions or errors in content or meaning. In essence, these recollections are not intended to be statements of material facts, but rather his opinions of what was said and his interpretation of what those words meant.

CONTENTS

Introduction   xv

Foreword   xviii

A Prediction That Has Come True   xxiii

Prologue: Dan Rather of CBS   xxiv

1 Reasonable Doubt   3

2 If Walls Could Talk   11

3 In My Mind's Eye   32

4 Freedom to Pursue   42

5 Delving Deeper   54

6 Driving Force   64

7 Trial of the Century   77

8 The Quest Continues   89

O. J. IS INNOCENT

9 Anticipating Answers   102

10 Cry for Help   111

11 Complete Understanding   120

12 "Going to Rage"   124

13 Airtight Alibi?   134

14 Wearing Blinders   145

15 Enlisting Expertise   169

16 Disbelief   184

17 Encouragement   196

18 Denial   218

19 Divulging the Dark Side   231

20 Dr. Jekyll/Mr. Hyde   243

21 Tunnel Vision   256

22 Reflection   265

23 Accumulating Evidence   281

24 "Dear Jason"   286

25 Alibi Extinguished   289

26 Loose Ends   293

27 "Bubbling Up"   300

28 "He's Sick . . . He's Sick"   304

29 Reiterating Concerns   308

CONTENTS

30 Handwriting on the Wall 315

31 Overview of Mayhem 325

32 He Has a New Job 327

33 Waiting for the Phone to Ring 333

34 Crucial New Evidence 337

35 Disaster and Disappointment 343

36 Conference and Jeep 345

37 Brian Douglas Evidence 353

38 Jason Simpson Diaries 361

39 The Possible Murder Weapon: the Knife 363

40 The Nonexistent Subpoena 368

41 The Phone Call 372

42 The Roommates 375

43 Alibi Questioned 379

44 The Bloody Socks 382

45 O. J. Fails Polygraph Test 385

46 Dr. Henry Lee 387

47 Dr. Vincent J. M. Di Maio 400

48 My Peers/the Markle Symposium 412

49 The Drawn Blood 416

50 The Knit Cap/the Bindle of Hairs 422

51 Dr. William Flynn   424

52 What Did the LAPD Email Say?   429

53 Denise Brown   432

54 If I Did It   434

55 Las Vegas Arrest: the Setup   437

56 Who Really is Christie Prody?   445

57 Film Festival   450

58 Attorney General's Meeting   455

59 Freedom of Information Act Requests   463

60 Justice or Publicity   471

Author's Closing Statement   477

Red Flags   480

Jason Lamar Simpson: Why He Should Be
Considered a Major Suspect   484

O. J. Simpson Is Innocent but Likely
at the Crime Scene After the Murders   498

Juror's Ballot   502

Acknowledgments   504

About the Author   506

Works Cited   509

Index   512

Like most Americans, I believe O. J. probably was involved in the slayings, but I don't think he did it alone. He must have had help. And it could be that Simpson was not the person wielding the knife. The physical evidence—the multiple footprints at the crime scene, the lack of blood at the crime scene, the forcefulness with which the crimes were committed, the time restraints during which the crimes were committed—strongly supports the theory that there was a second attacker involved.

—Cyril H. Wecht, Greg Saitz, and Mark Curriden, *Mortal Evidence: The Forensics Behind Nine Shocking Cases*

Introduction

ALMOST EIGHTEEN YEARS AGO, I began assembling a team consisting of my own agency and its resources, along with an international group of distinguished experts in the investigative fields of forensics, pathology, and crime scene to look into the brutal murders of Nicole Brown Simpson and Ronald Goldman on the night of June 12, 1994.

The legal process of this case had left me with more questions than answers and a feeling, shared by many, that justice had not been served and the truth had not been uncovered, in spite of two "trials of the century" that consumed endless man-hours, millions of taxpayer dollars, and the riveted attention of most of the nation.

My purpose in what became a long journey was not just to write another O. J. book but to seek the truth, just as I have done in every other murder case I have investigated, even though I was aware I would be fighting odds stacked heavily against me. My experience over the past forty-five years has been that when facts in a case are uncovered which could disprove the original theory, no one wants to admit they could have been wrong. Too many interests are vested in preserving the original conclusions. So I knew I would face many challenges.

I am a private investigator who had to take the road back into the murders the hard way. I am neither a police officer nor a member of the district attorney's office. I do not have the power of subpoena, the right to take depositions, or the right to arrest. That's why my methods sometimes have to be unorthodox. I have had to follow twisted paths and employ some of the same clandestine and controversial evidence-gathering tactics as those used by investigative journalists.

Beyond the wide-ranging expertise and experience of my team and my own determination, the crucial equipment I possess—more gift than tool—is my ability to enter, intuitively, into the mind of a killer. I had successfully solved other "unsolvable" murder cases in this way and I felt certain it could be helpful in this case. This ability to intimately understand—to experience the killer and his acts—is a double-edged sword, because as the investigator moves deeper into the killer's mind, a pit can open into the darkness, alienation, and pain. This kind of journey is a high-risk endeavor, precisely because of the need for that intuitive leap, and because the intricate maneuverings and elusiveness of the target can draw the investigator toward preoccupation. More than once on the journey, I had to resist that pull.

It also requires a laser insight into the complexity of human relationships . . . into the intricate ties of friends and lovers, of marriage and parenthood that bind people in mysterious, profound ways. To begin my investigation I made a list of all the suspects whom I felt could possibly be involved. From this, I narrowed, gradually and painstakingly, my investigation down to a single major suspect. If I am wrong, it is not out of any intent or malice. The road to truth was a hard one, and many times I wanted to quit, especially as I drew closer to the end. You see, it was not, nor has it ever been, my intention to hurt anyone. However, sometimes the search for truth leaves no alternative.

I have been asked why I did not turn over my investigative report to the proper authorities once it was completed. I tried many times to pursue justice through full disclosure to the appropriate officials, as you will read. But due to the sensitivity of the information uncovered, along with the potential embarrassment it might bring to those involved in the O. J. Simpson murder trial, I felt my findings might well wind up buried in the political labyrinth of the legal system.

My years of experience as a private investigator taught me, in this particular case, it would now be prudent to release this new information to the general public, allowing you to decide the merits of the investigation without bias. I hope that your support of my investigative report, along with a completely new approach to the tragic events of June 12, 1994, offered by evidence our team has uncovered, can serve as a catalyst to the reopening of the investigation into the murders of two vital young people.

It is my personal goal that the information I have brought to light will lead to the convening of a special grand jury, an arrest, and a conviction for these senseless murders.

At the original trial, you had no way to voice your opinions. If you are convinced, as I am, that this new information supports a reopening of the case, I urge you to rally behind me. Go to our website, www.ojisinnocentandicanproveit.com, and cast your ballot. Do not take this lightly. With your help, justice could prevail and finally bring the truth to the families and friends of Nicole Brown Simpson and Ronald Goldman, thanks to you.

Remember this, in my seventeen-year investigation into the murders I do not hesitate in making this statement:

"O. J. is innocent—I can prove it!"

I leave it up to you, as a reader and now a juror, to make a decision.

How do you find O. J. Simpson?

Guilty or not guilty?

William C. Dear
Mount Calm, Texas
2012

Foreword

A TALL, TAN, VERY DISTINGUISHED gentleman in cowboy boots and Stetson hat called out, "Dr. Harper?" I knew immediately that this was Bill Dear, a fellow Texan and a world-renowned private investigator. I had invited him to be a keynote speaker at my conference on Lessons Learned from Famous Cases. Dr. Henry Lee, who was thoroughly familiar with Bill's hypothesis that an "overlooked suspect," and not O. J. Simpson, was responsible for the murders of Nicole Brown Simpson and Ron Goldman, had strongly recommended him as a speaker. I had read his book and knew that an audience of 600 police officers, investigators, forensic scientists, and criminal justice students were in for a real surprise when they heard his conclusion that O. J. was innocent! Everyone believed that O. J. got away with murder, but here was Bill Dear, one of the most famous and seasoned private investigators in the world, proclaiming his innocence. This was going to get real interesting, I thought, especially with police officers who, once they are convinced they've got their man, are very difficult to persuade otherwise. Everyone, especially the police, *knew* O. J. did it.

As the lights in the auditorium dimmed, I walked to the podium to introduce Bill. It was a real pleasure to talk about his many fascinating cases, his great accomplishments, his several books, and his extensive media history. Bill began his career as a police officer in Miami but soon transplanted himself to the Lone Star State where he began his own investigation agency, William C. Dear & Associates, in 1961. When he began to speak, he mesmerized the entire audience, including me. He told the story of his investigation into the deaths of Nicole and Ron and then how he began to suspect that O. J. was not the killer. He turned to the "overlooked suspect" as a potential suspect and then laid the foundation of an overwhelmingly convincing case that this suspect could be the killer! When he reached into his briefcase and pulled out the large hunting knife he obtained from the suspect's possessions, the audience gasped! Wow! How did he get this knife? Was it really the knife that slit Nicole's throat? Is Ron Goldman's blood on the blade? My head was spinning with a thousand questions about the significance of what Bill was holding in his hand. When he finished, he asked the audience a second time for a show of hands by those who believed that O. J. committed the murders. The first vote, before Bill laid out the case that someone else killed Nicole, was almost unanimous that O. J. was guilty. Having heard and seen Bill's evidence, the audience, including the seasoned police officers, had almost unanimously agreed that O. J. was not guilty! It was an incredible demonstration of the power of marshaled evidence, systematically and objectively presented, to prove the truth: O. J. is innocent!

Since that day more than five years ago, I have visited Bill on his ranch outside of Waco, Texas, where he raises Texas Longhorns and other exotic cattle and maintains his training academy for law enforcement officers and private investigators. This is also where Bill writes and where he securely curates and preserves evidence he has collected from seventeen years of investigating Nicole Simpson's and Ron Goldman's murders, including the suspect's boot knife, diary, and psychiatric records. I emphasize *securely*, because the perpetrator of their murders has not been convicted, and someday the evidence that Bill Dear so carefully curates will hopefully be used in court to bring their killer to justice. On my first trip to the ranch, my wife, Janet, and I drove in through the iron gates of the Triple D ranch to Bill's Wild West town and training academy, where he keeps his office. Bill was anxious to show us the evidence, including the "overlooked suspect's" Jeep, which once may have had Nicole and Ron's blood on the console. How Bill came by this evidence is part of a fascinating account of his investigation recounted in this new book, *O. J. Is Innocent, and I Can Prove It.*

Bill Dear has spent seventeen years on the trail of Nicole and Ron's killer, during which time he has amassed overwhelming evidence that O. J. was not their killer. It is critical to understand that Bill's interest in the case is not that he has some connection to or fascination with O. J. Simpson; in fact, I know that they have never met, and if they did, Bill wouldn't give a damn about O. J. Bill's devotion to the case stems from the fact that the real perp is free and O. J. is behind bars.

O. J. Is Innocent is the saga of Bill's long and difficult struggle to convince the Los Angeles authorities of the error of their ways. Justice has not been done for Nicole or Ron, and Bill Dear is the only person interested in righting this tragedy. He started working on the case at his own expense shortly after the murders. Over the years, he has spent countless hours on the streets of Los Angeles, diving into dumpsters to find and collect physical evidence, tracking down witnesses, and charming statements out of the reluctant ones, all while spending hundreds of thousands of dollars of his own money. Just to be fair, Bill did eat in some pretty fancy restaurants along the way, and he does share some very interesting restaurant reviews, but that hardly makes up for the time, effort, and expense of conducting this investigation by himself.

What impresses me most about *O. J. Is Innocent* is the way Bill allows the reader to see into his thought processes as he plans and executes his investigation. Sometimes he plots his next move with calculated methodology. Other times, he responds instinctively to seize any opportunity or evidence that will help his case. Most of all, Bill demonstrates that a good investigator "never assumes, always verifies." He avoids the common problem of "tunnel vision" which plagues many police investigations when officers fail to follow the scientific method of crime scene investigation. Rather than formulating a hypothesis and then collecting physical evidence and witness statements to test the hypothesis objectively, police investigators are often guilty of deciding who must have committed the crime and focusing the entire investigation only on that suspect. If the evidence doesn't fit, then just ignore it or worse, make it fit.

This, of course, is exactly what happened in the investigation of Nicole and Ron's murders. From the very outset, long before any physical evidence was analyzed, the LAPD and district attorney's office had jumped to the conclusion that O. J. must have committed the murders. Had the investigation been conducted properly, all relevant evidence collected, and all suspects interviewed, there would never have been controversy over who killed Nicole and Ron. The blood of Nicole's killer was found on her shoulder but was never collected. Detective Vannatter carried the tube of O. J.'s blood around in his pocket for hours. The bloody socks from O. J.'s bedroom were contaminated with EDTA, a blood preservative. But we knew all of these facts and other shortcomings of the investigation at the time of the trial in 1996. What we didn't know was that the "overlooked suspect" was never considered as a suspect, nor was his alibi that he was working that night ever verified, nor any of the many other reasons why this individual should have been a major suspect in the investigation. Never assume, always verify.

Bill's investigation, in stark contrast to that of the LAPD, was a model investigation. He hypothesized every possible party as a suspect until evidence proved the hypothesis wrong and the suspect eliminated. Systematically, he considered and rejected multiple hypotheses until he was left with a single suspect, the "overlooked suspect." The scientific method of crime scene investigation at work! Bill then used his remarkable investigative skills to collect more and more evidence that the suspect was the person most likely to have killed Nicole Simpson in a fit of rage, and Ron Goldman, who was simply in the wrong place at the wrong time. Systematically, Bill collected the suspect's personal history of rage attacks on girlfriends, his psychiatric records and drug use, his work history, his photographs, and his diary—all of which paint a portrait of a highly disturbed young man, a veritable Jekyll and Hyde, in the suspect's own words. I won't give away the ending, but it is the most compelling compilation of eighty-four reasons why the "overlooked suspect" should be considered the major suspect. Don't be tempted to turn ahead: savor the delightfully intriguing tale of investigation, told so expertly by Bill, before you turn to the end. The read is worth the wait, and you don't have to wait long because the book is a real page-turner.

In his quest for justice for Nicole Brown Simpson and Ronald Goldman, Bill Dear has done an amazing job of pointing to the "overlooked suspect" as a major suspect who was never considered by the police. To the dismay of the many who presumed O. J. did it, O. J. was found not guilty after a trial by jury of his peers, but that is the very strength of our system of criminal justice. The suspect should be afforded all of his constitutional protections to the presumption of innocence that O. J. did not receive. The suspect is not currently under investigation by the LAPD, he has not been charged with any crime. The suspect has not been tried and found guilty beyond a reasonable doubt of killing Nicole and Ron. Until that day, the "overlooked suspect" is and deserves to be considered an innocent man, but he must, nonetheless, as Bill Dear so deftly demonstrates, be considered a major suspect.

—Dr. Albert Harper
Lenox, Massachusetts

A Prediction That Has Come True

JOSEPH BOSCO WAS A freelance crime writer who, in 1996, wrote a book about the O. J. Simpson trial titled *A Problem of Evidence*.

In Chapter sixteen, titled "Life with Mark and Marsha," on page 194 of his book, the second paragraph reads::

> This is not to say the ridiculed possibility that O. J. Simpson had nothing to do with the murders will not reveal itself someday to be a fact. In the past few years, my preoccupation with murder, murderers, and the criminal justice game has taught me never discount the impossible.

Joseph Bosco died on July 8, 2010, at the age of sixty-one. He died in Beijing, China, where he had been living and working as a professor.

Now, sixteen years later, it is too bad that he is not still alive to read *this* book and to realize his prediction has come true.

Prologue
DAN RATHER OF CBS

TWO WEEKS AFTER DAN Rather had made his last appearance on the CBS News, I was driving on Highway 31, headed back to Dallas, when I received a call from my close friend John McCready.

"Stay off your phone for a few minutes," he said.

"Why?" I asked him, as he knew I would.

"Just do it," he replied and hung up.

Less than five minutes later, as I approached Hubbard, Texas, my cell phone rang. I answered it and heard a very recognizable voice on the other end of the line asking to speak to me. I suddenly realized who it was. I pulled over to the shoulder of the road and stopped the car.

"This is Dan Rather," he said. "I'm in New York."

Dan went on to tell me that he and his wife had seen a rough cut copy of my O. J. documentary. Before viewing the documentary, Dan's wife had said that no one was ever going to change her mind about O. J.'s guilt, but she reluctantly agreed to watch it with him. "Ninety minutes later," said Dan, "my wife turned to me and said, 'I can't believe what I've just seen.' Bill, this is one of the finest investigative pieces I have seen in many years."

"Coming from you, that's a great compliment," I said.

"When the murders broke and the stories were all over the news," he continued, "I told some friends and associates at CBS that I felt O. J. may very well not have committed the murders and that someone else could have, and perhaps did."

What Dan Rather had just shared with me, made my seventeen years of investigative work worthwhile, proving to me I was not wasting my time. Maybe thanks to his assistance in this prologue the real story will someday appear on CBS, not with Dan Rather at his desk, but someone else who will have the opportunity to announce:

"Ladies and Gentlemen, we have interrupted to bring you a news bulletin from Los Angeles. New evidence proves O. J. Simpson is not guilty in the murders of Nicole Simpson and Ron Goldman. Stay tuned for the complete story."

O. J.
IS INNOCENT

AND I CAN PROVE IT!

1

REASONABLE DOUBT

"**NEVER ASSUME. ALWAYS VERiFY.**" Every detective, public defender, and investigative reporter should have those four words tattooed in black ink on their foreheads. Then every time they look at themselves in the mirror they would be reminded of the great responsibility they have to themselves and to the public to check their facts before jumping to conclusions. Lives are on the line—and not only those of the falsely accused.

It is with this in mind that I ask you to step back and reexamine the many assumptions that have been made regarding the murders of Nicole Brown Simpson and Ronald Goldman on June 12, 1994. I want you to try to forget the many newspaper articles, books, and television shows you may have read or seen about this case; try not to think about the "mountain of evidence" presented to jurors in what has been termed the "trial of the century"; try to ignore the role that racial prejudice may have played in the trial; and try not to speculate on the alleged conspiracy of one or more officers of the LAPD to frame a national sports legend.

Most importantly, I want you to step back to the afternoon of June 17, 1994, the day when millions of people throughout the world jumped to the same conclusion that homicide detectives, prosecutors, and the press had already reached during the first critical hours of their four-day-old investigation. That was the afternoon when O. J. Simpson, Heisman Trophy-winning halfback, television spokesman, millionaire celebrity, and now a fugitive from justice, became the one and *only* suspect in the brutal double murders on Bundy Drive.

On that day, June 17, I happened to be in St. Louis, Missouri, where I had been invited to give a lecture at the National Conference of Investigative Reporters and Editors. The subject of the lecture was "How the Gumshoes Do It: Tips from Private Eyes." Given the fact that the Nicole Simpson and Ron Goldman murders were front-page news, and that I was being billed at the conference as the modern-day Sherlock Holmes, it was no surprise that the press asked for my opinions.

Like most people who only knew about the murder case from what they read in the newspapers or watched on television, I too was tempted to convict O. J. based on the seemingly overwhelming circumstantial evidence against him. And so, on the morning of June 17, just hours before the historic car chase that would result in O. J.'s arrest, I candidly told reporters exactly what I believed to be true: "O. J.'s blood is at the Bundy Drive crime scene. Nicole's blood is at the house on Rockingham. And Ron Goldman's blood is in O. J.'s Ford Bronco. This looks exactly like what it is: O. J. is guilty."

I regretted what I said almost as soon as I said it. After all, I had no personal connection to the case and knew from firsthand experience that the press is not always an accurate purveyor of details regarding homicide investigations. In fact, I was already disturbed by the eagerness of the journalists covering this story to focus their attention on O. J. and not on the facts of the case. Later that same day, my worry became outright concern when I joined reporters in front of a wall of television monitors in a crowded hallway at the St. Louis Convention Center to watch the now historic "slow-speed" car chase.

In all my years of following the coverage of murder cases, I had never seen such a spectacle as the one I was witnessing on CBS, CNN, ABC and NBC. Fugitive O. J. Simpson and his devoted childhood friend, A. C. Cowlings, led a caravan of twenty-five or more police squad cars on the slow-speed, five-lane car chase through Orange County, just south of Los Angeles. Seated in the back seat of Cowlings's white Ford Bronco, O. J. was holding a Magnum pistol to his head. As Cowlings drove up the freeway, cameramen in helicopters provided a live television feed while commentators filled in the missing details. Television audiences were reminded of the circumstantial blood evidence linking O. J. to the Bundy Drive crime scene and were provided tantalizing details of his rocky marriage to Nicole and his presumed history of spousal abuse.

Then there was Robert Shapiro, O. J.'s attorney, describing his client as emotionally "frail" and "fragile." And Robert Kardashian, O. J.'s longtime friend from the University of Southern California, publicly pleading with police and the press to help save O. J.'s life. Kardashian read from what was described as a suicide letter Simpson had left behind. In O. J.'s letter, the sports star proclaimed his innocence. Yet, he ended by saying, "Don't feel sorry for me, I've had a great life, great friends. Please think of the real O. J. and not this lost person."

Listening to Kardashian read from the letter, I couldn't help but wonder who this "lost person" was, why he would kill the mother of his children, and what possible real connection he or Nicole might have had to Ron Goldman, a waiter in a Brentwood restaurant where Nicole and her family had dined earlier in the evening of the murders. Having spent the better part of my career psychologically profiling suspected murderers, I tried to put myself into the "mind" of the killer and asked myself if this "lost person" who had once been the "real O. J." could indeed be a vicious killer on the run from justice?

As the car chase continued, along with the play-by-play coverage by reporters, people whom O. J. had never met and who had no direct connection to the case, began to participate in the unfolding story. Radio disk jockeys begged O. J. to surrender. Hundreds of onlookers jammed the overpasses, or cheered O. J. from embankments along the shoulder of the freeway. All kinds of so-called experts, Simpson family members, and many others made cameo appearances. It was no wonder the car chase utterly dominated the airwaves, disrupted the telecast of a championship basketball game, delayed meals in restaurants, and nearly shut down shopping malls as people rushed home to turn on their television sets to see what would happen next.

The longer I watched the unfolding drama, the more mystified I became. Helicopters hovered overhead as Cowlings drove the white Bronco into Los Angeles County. The Bronco, followed by a caravan of police, exited the freeway at Sunset Boulevard, where the city streets were as strangely deserted as the freeway had been. The police had apparently known, or suspected all along, that O. J. was headed for his home on Rockingham Drive in the upscale and trendy neighborhood of Brentwood and had cleared traffic from the streets just as they had cleared the cars off the freeway. The press too had been tipped off. Television viewers were treated to a behind-the-scenes look at O. J.'s Rockingham estate as police sharpshooters and negotiation teams took up positions in the bushes and around the driveway. Onlookers were ushered away from the house. A vehicle assault team was dispatched from the LAPD's Parker Center.

Minutes later, A. C. Cowlings would pull his Bronco into the cobblestone driveway. As if on cue from an off-camera director, O. J.'s twenty-four-year-old son, Jason Simpson, made a desperate dash from a neighbor's house through the police line and to the side of the Bronco. He was finally blocked by Cowlings, who shoved Jason away and into the waiting arms of the police. Apparently they didn't want the young man to be caught in the crossfire if shooting erupted.

O. J. was sitting by himself, trapped in the back seat of the Bronco. His only companions were the revolver, his rosary, and two framed family photos that he had taken with him. He appeared to be confused and overwhelmed as LAPD negotiators urged him not to take his own life. It hardly mattered that viewers couldn't hear what was being said between O. J. and the detectives. LAPD was obviously treating O. J. as they would a man poised to jump off the ARCO Tower in downtown Los Angeles. He was being told that he had friends who understood what he was going through and was urged to think of his children and the many people who loved him.

Finally, hours after the chase had begun, O. J. put down his gun, picked up the framed photos, and stepped out of the Bronco. Police didn't rush forward to put him in handcuffs but instead embraced him at the entrance to his home. He was permitted to walk inside. And once inside, they allowed him to use the bathroom, drink some orange juice, and call his mother. O. J. then walked back outside where he calmly apologized to the police.

"I'm sorry for putting you guys out," he told officers. "I'm sorry for making you do this." He shook a few hands, graciously smiled for the cameras and waved, as if taking a last curtain call before making his exit to LAPD's Parker Center.

The only thing missing from the television drama I had just seen was the closing credits. As it was, it seemed more like the conclusion of a live sporting event than a news story. But that was not ultimately what came to bother me. It was the reaction of the journalists and others standing beside me in St. Louis that had me worried. As O. J. finally gave himself up, the top investigative reporters in the country began to applaud. Total euphoria swept the room. I couldn't be sure if the crowd huddled in front of the television monitors were clapping because O. J. had finally been apprehended, or because this was the conclusion of a national television event.

The truth soon became abundantly clear. Nearly everyone watching television that night had been pulled into the drama that was unfolding. They were completely engrossed by what they had seen and emotionally moved by it. Their applause was an emotional response to the events taking place: relief that O. J. had done the right thing and "behaved" as he should. Although guilty, he had shown true character and inner strength by giving himself up rather than taking his own life and bringing more hardship on his family or his many fans and television viewers. In many respects, the press, the LAPD, and O. J. himself appeared to be getting exactly what they wanted.

I couldn't have been more baffled by what I had seen or the reaction at the convention center. It's not that I am callous or was unsympathetic to the plight of the fallen hero; I just didn't believe for an instant that what I was seeing on the screen represented the truth. There were too many unanswered questions to convince me that the "lost person" in the suicide letter was the same man now giving himself up to police. To my mind, O. J. appeared to be in control of the situation, not the LAPD or the media.

Foremost on my list of unanswered questions was why police allowed O. J. to become a fugitive from justice in the first place. If indeed the LAPD had solid incontrovertible blood evidence linking O. J. to the murders, and if reports were true that his bloody glove had been found at the crime scene and his shoe prints led from the victims to the alley behind Bundy Drive, it seemed inconceivable to me that the LAPD hadn't already arrested him or, at the least, known where he was at all times.

Furthermore, I had to ask myself why the highway patrol didn't stop the Bronco in Orange County, where it was first reported seen. Even if A. C. Cowlings hadn't willingly pulled the Bronco over, the highway patrol could easily have set up a blockade or laid down a strip of metal tire tacks in the roadway that would puncture the Bronco's tires and disable the vehicle. As a former Miami policeman and highway patrolman, I knew this was the accepted procedure. Instead, the LAPD gave the entire freeway to the fugitives as they would for a visit from the president of the United States.

Nor did the LAPD appear to be in any rush to get O. J. handcuffed when he did reach his Rockingham estate. He was permitted to leave his car, enter his house, use the bathroom, telephone his mother, and shake hands with family and friends before being taken into custody. Rather than arrest him back in Orange County ten minutes after the Bronco was spotted on the freeway, police and prosecutors permitted the drama to last all day and into the evening.

The activities of O. J. himself raised even more questions in my mind. Had he truly been a family man, as suggested by the loving manner in which he cradled the framed pictures in his lap, he surely would not have desired to kill himself on network television, or worse still, in the driveway of his own home in full view of his friends and family. Nor would he have led the police and press on a slow-speed freeway car chase if he truly desired to make a run across the border. He would have gone underground and undoubtedly had enough contacts so he could remain hidden for quite some time. And if he really was running from the law because he was guilty, and truly was on the verge of a nervous breakdown, as the police and practically everyone else appeared to believe, there was the question of his innocence. Despite the evidence against him, he repeatedly claimed he was innocent of the murders. Here was a man who volunteered to be interviewed by the police, gave the crime lab samples of his blood and, as I later would learn, willingly agreed to take a polygraph test.

These were not the actions of a guilty man.

My initial reaction to this prime-time drama was to think that the car chase had been concocted ahead of time by O. J.'s attorneys in preparation for a plea of insanity, or to lay the foundation for an appeal based on jury prejudice or bias. This well might have been the case. However, it was also possible that O. J. was telling the truth. He may not have minded giving blood samples, cooperating with the police, or taking a polygraph test because he knew in his heart that he wasn't guilty of killing Nicole Simpson or Ron Goldman and wouldn't ultimately be convicted of the crimes. Thus his action might be viewed as those of a man whose aim was to draw attention to himself in order to shift suspicion away from the real killer.

The longer I thought about what I had seen, the more skeptical I was that O. J. was guilty. I couldn't help but feel that I was being manipulated into viewing the murder case against this man in a certain way, and that everything I had seen and much of what I had read had been carefully orchestrated to present a certain point of view, much as a director manipulates the audience in a Hollywood movie. It wasn't that I believed there was a grand conspiracy taking place, but rather that it somehow seemed to be in the collective interest of the police, the media, and perhaps even O. J. himself, to lead the public in a particular direction.

O. J. IS INNOCENT

Except for the initial comments I gave to the press on the morning of June 17, I chose not to communicate my concerns to the journalists and editors who had invited me to St. Louis. Perhaps I didn't wish to embarrass myself before a panel of people who were so convinced that O. J. was guilty that they had already begun making the creative leaps it would take to convict the man. It was also equally true, however, that I had no real insights of my own and no first-person connection to the case. I knew only what had been reported.

In retrospect, I regret not having been more candid. I was already disturbed by the eagerness of the journalists covering this story to focus their attention only on O. J. By not speaking up, or at least voicing serious concern, I now believe I was contributing to the problem facing anyone investigating or writing about the crime. From the moment O. J. made headline news there was a distinct lack of critical thinking taking place. The right questions were not being asked because everyone assumed he was guilty. It was merely a question of tunnel vision—finding proof for what they believed to be true and ignoring the rest.

I would no longer remain silent about this case. However, before I risked challenging the status quo, I had to study the case from every conceivable angle and check the facts. I had solved the majority of crimes in my career by doing just that. In one of my more recent high-profile investigations, that of sporting-goods mogul Glen Courson, I conclusively proved Courson had been murdered and had not committed suicide as police believed. In that case, the Irving, Texas, police department had failed in the most fundamental way: No one had taken the time to examine the murder weapon closely enough to see that the breech-block firing mechanism was in a closed and locked position and not partially open as it would have been after being fired. Dead men don't eject spent shell casings.

I suspected that the LAPD had overlooked such details in their own rush to judgment. The only way for me to find out for sure was to visit the crime scene and check the facts out for myself.

2

IF WALLS COULD TALK

TWO WEEKS AFTER WATCHING O. J. Simpson's slow-speed car chase on television, I purchased two round-trip plane tickets for Los Angeles. The first was for me. The second was for Chris Stewart, a good friend, my chief investigator, and the man whom my staff had nicknamed Dr. Watson.

Like me, Chris tells it as he sees it. He is proud to be a Texan, stands over six feet tall and weighs over 250 pounds. He too watched the chase on television, but less from a detective's point of view than out of mere curiosity.

That I needed him with me was no mere indulgence, however. I was in great physical pain, the result of a car accident I had sustained prior to my speaking engagement in St. Louis, for which I would soon be undergoing back and neck surgery. I needed him to carry my suitcase, shoot photographs, and help me do the fact checking that is our investigative agency's stock in trade. Most importantly, I would be depending on his good judgment, for he, like everyone else in our office, not to mention greater Dallas County and the rest of the country, hadn't the slightest doubt that O. J. was guilty of premeditated murder.

"You've surprised me before," Chris had told me when I asked him to accompany me to Los Angeles. "But this isn't going to be one of those times. O. J. is guilty, and he'll go to prison. Don't waste your time and money getting involved in something that's already been solved. Let justice do its job."

I didn't know whether or not I would be able to convince Chris to see things from my point of view, but I was determined to try. If I failed to convince him that there was a great deal more to the murder story than the LAPD and O. J. himself was admitting, I would stop nosing around in police business and occupy my free time with what Chris considered "more constructive" endeavors.

The first stop on our planned itinerary was O. J. Simpson's home on North Rockingham Avenue in the exclusive residential suburb of Brentwood. Leaving the airport and exiting onto Sunset Boulevard near the construction site of the J. Paul Getty Museum, I had the distinct feeling of having traveled this route before. Indeed I had, along with millions of other television viewers on the now famous slow-speed car chase from Orange County. The house had been photographed from every conceivable angle as it had been turned inside out by the LAPD and the media for the whole world to see.

I had selected the Rockingham house as our first stop because this was where everything had begun for O. J. and Nicole. I didn't presume to know what had gone on behind their closed doors, or what exactly it was that made O. J. allegedly "snap," but I suspected the answer had to be at Rockingham and not at the Bundy Drive crime scene, for it was here that the dynamics of O. J.'s and Nicole's relationship took shape, and where it ultimately ended. No matter who had conveniently or accidentally dropped the bloody glove behind O. J.'s guesthouse, the underlying truth of what had occurred on Bundy Drive lay behind O. J.'s tall wrought-iron gates at North Rockingham.

Like Chris, I knew the milestones in O. J.'s relationship with Nicole. O. J. was still married and playing football when he met the statuesque seventeen-year-old blond waitress, twelve years his junior, at a small Los Angeles restaurant called The Daisy. That he was black, and she white, naturally created tension for many of O. J.'s fans and her friends, but nothing could be done to pull them apart. By all accounts, they fell head over heels in love. In fact, most of the people who knew them agreed that Nicole and O. J. just couldn't get enough of each other. Nicole herself had confided to friends that they sometimes made love five times a day. And it stayed that way for fourteen years.

I knew considerably less about O. J.'s personal life prior to Nicole. He had married Marguerite Whitley, a childhood girlfriend, with whom he had three children: Arnelle, the eldest; Jason, two years her junior; and Aaren, the youngest. O. J.'s marriage and subsequent family, however, hadn't stopped him from carrying on a number of highly publicized affairs. One woman just didn't seem enough. As Marguerite once confided to reporters, "I have been shoved out of the way, pushed and stepped on by more than one beautiful woman [in O. J.'s life]." O. J. himself, at the time, was more contrite, believing that he could sustain his marriage in spite of his philandering. "My wife knows I'm under control."

O. J. had just separated from Marguerite after fourteen years of marriage when twenty-three-month-old Aaren, their daughter, accidentally drowned in the swimming pool at Rockingham. That single tragic event marked the dissolution of O. J.'s marriage more than his many affairs or Nicole's arrival on the scene.

O. J. and Nicole naturally sought to put the past behind them. They married, proceeded to renovate Rockingham and then raise a family of their own. Shortly after their wedding, Sydney Brooke, a daughter, was born, and then, three years later, a son, Justin. This was arguably the happiest period in their lives together. The couple had been separated and divorced in 1992, a little over two years before Nicole's death, not counting an occasional tryst and reconciliation. Nicole got custody of their two children, Sydney and Justin, along with $24,000 a month spousal support (eventually to be reduced to $10,000 a month), and a three-quarters-of-a-million-dollar home and car. Though separated and living in two homes—he on Rockingham and she on Gretna Green, then later on Bundy Drive—O. J. saw or spoke to Nicole and the children on almost a daily basis, whether it was birthday parties at Rockingham or games of Monopoly at Bundy Drive.

Chris and I didn't have to read the numbers on the otherwise quiet, tree-lined road to know we had arrived at O. J.'s home. Camera-toting tourists and an automobile gridlock at the corner of Rockingham and Ashford Street were all we needed to see. A traffic cop on the corner waved us through as there were so many other people looking for parking places. We had to drive nearly a quarter of a mile before we could park the car and then hike all the way back to Rockingham.

Like Chris, I had already begun to question the sense of coming all the way from Dallas to be herded along with other tourists to see the outside of a house. This didn't fit the picture of what I had had in mind. Still, Chris took his camera and reluctantly joined me as we followed a parade of people along Rockingham to peer through one of the two green wrought-iron gates that opened onto the circular driveway. Not only were reporters here, but there were street peddlers as well, hawking maps to the homes of movie stars and souvenir postcards of O. J. in his football uniform. Business looked brisk.

The press had repeatedly called the Simpson house an "estate." That was something of an exaggeration, for it conjured up Fantasy Island images of a helicopter pad or acre-size lawns dotted with Italian statuary. This wasn't an estate on those terms. It wasn't a showplace mansion trying to call attention to itself or of the kind to be featured on the cover of a trendy magazine. This was a family home that Nicole and O. J. had decorated and landscaped together, with plenty of bushy trees, a cobblestone driveway, and patches of green lawn for dogs and children.

I could imagine O. J. chipping golf balls here, Nicole grilling steaks on the barbecue, and their children playing on the rock waterfall slide near the pool. Not that it didn't have those special things that separate the rich from the poor: a swimming pool and a tennis court. The Simpson children had their own playground complete with jungle gym and playhouses. And there was the main house, a spacious Cape Cod-style with a great sloping wooden-shingle roof and river-rock chimneys. The garage was to the right of the house. Behind that, and connected to the main house by a covered walkway, were the guest quarters. Arnelle Simpson, O. J.'s eldest daughter by his first marriage, lived in one of the three guest suites; Gigi, O. J.'s housekeeper, lived in a second; and Kato Kaelin lived in the third. Kaelin was a friend of Nicole's who had in turn become a friend of O. J.'s, and he promised to be an important witness for both the prosecution and the defense.

I couldn't get any closer to this property than to peer through the gates, so I had to content myself with making mental pictures as Chris shot photographs. And, as I would frequently do in the days, months, and years ahead, I tried to put myself in O. J.'s place, trying to re-create his activities on that fateful day, nearly three weeks earlier, when the murders had taken place.

In my mind's eye, I imagined O. J. loading his golf clubs into the back of his white Bronco for his regular game of golf at the Riviera Country Club. That day—the morning before the murders took place—he had joined a group of men with whom he had been playing golf for some seven to eight years. Afterward, they sat in the clubhouse and played cards.

I pictured O. J. returning later that afternoon, climbing the stairs to his spacious bedroom with its oriental carpet and selecting his clothes for the evening. O. J. always dressed immaculately and was perfectly groomed. His bedroom, like his closets and desk drawers, were impeccably maintained. Nothing was ever out of place. He showered, perhaps for the second time that day, dressed, and then left for his daughter Sydney's dance recital at Paul Revere Middle School. Along the way he stopped to buy flowers, which he presented to his daughter when the recital ended at 6:30 PM.

Next, I pictured O. J. returning in the early evening, making a few telephone calls, and packing for the trip he was to make later that night to Chicago, where he was scheduled to attend a function for Hertz Rent-A-Car, for whom he had once done commercials, and for whom he was now a celebrity spokesperson and media consultant.

The LAPD claimed that O. J. might also have used this time to plan the murders, which would occupy him later that evening. All that is known for sure was that he and Kato Kaelin left in O. J.'s Bentley to buy dinner at McDonald's and returned at approximately 9:30 PM. His activities between this time and 11 PM, when he left with a limo driver for the airport, were the critical ninety minutes in question.

I pictured, in my mind's eye, the events that the LAPD claimed had taken place: O. J. in his upstairs bedroom, putting on a pair of black sweatpants, dark sweatshirt and expensive, size 12, Bruno Magli loafers. He pulls a knit cap over his head, slips on a pair of brown Isotoner gloves and removes a Swiss Army knife from the top drawer of his dresser. Either that or he takes an equally deadly stiletto switchblade that he had purchased a year or more ago while shooting a movie in downtown Los Angeles. O. J. then sneaks quietly out of his house and into the garage where he selects a shovel, collects a carefully prepared black plastic bag and loads these into his white Ford Bronco, which he had earlier parked out on the street so Kato Kaelin would not hear him leaving. He starts the engine and drives out into the night, in the direction of Bundy Drive, where Nicole lives.

The events that allegedly took place at Rockingham later that evening were a bit more difficult to envision because I couldn't see through the Rockingham or Ashford gates beyond the garage and main house. I had no real idea what the guesthouse, or the back of the guesthouse, looked like. I imagined, as the LAPD claimed, O. J. returning in his white Bronco between 10:45 and 11 PM. There is a drop of blood just above the Bronco's door handle and more drops of blood inside the vehicle, but they are too small for him to notice. In order not to raise the suspicion of the limousine driver who is already parked out on Ashford Street, O. J. leaves the Bronco on Rockingham, and using the cover of darkness to hide his movements, enters his neighbor's yard and climbs over the fence behind his own guesthouse.

In the darkness, O. J. stumbles into the air conditioner sticking out of the wall at the back of the guesthouse. He is dizzy, momentarily stunned, and accidentally drops the bloody glove that LAPD investigator Mark Fuhrman will find the next morning. Moments later, O. J. quietly sneaks out from behind the guesthouse and into his own house, where he showers, changes his clothes, and then comes outside to meet with Kaelin and the limo driver, who was parked in the driveway.

To my mind, the most obvious glitch in the LAPD scenario was the ease with which O. J. allegedly left Rockingham without Kaelin having heard him drive away in the Bronco, and the limousine driver's failure to hear or see his return. As anyone who has ever driven a Bronco can attest, this is not a quiet vehicle. It's a high-powered four-wheel drive vehicle. The LAPD must have known this, as they must also have known that the "plastic bag" which O. J. allegedly took from his garage—presumably to bury evidence—was identical to the spare tire cover which Ford Motors includes as standard equipment on the Bronco. O. J. didn't put the plastic bag in the vehicle—it was already there—as was the shovel, which O. J. frequently used as a pooper-scooper to clean up after his dogs.

I also had a question about the blood on the driveway, allegedly left when O. J. returned to Rockingham. There didn't seem to me to be any point to O. J. slipping through his front gate and walking up the driveway—where he allegedly left behind the three drops of blood—and then turning around to hop the gate into his neighbor's yard and, finally, running along the back gate to the guesthouse—where he allegedly dropped the glove—only to exit into the driveway and enter the front door to the house. If he were truly interested in not being seen by the limo driver and Kaelin, he would never have entered through the Rockingham gate at all, but would have chosen the most convenient and logical route. He would have run directly through the neighbor's yard from Rockingham Avenue, hopped the rear fence, and entered the house through the kitchen or pantry door. He wouldn't have had to run the risk of disturbing Kaelin at all and wouldn't have been seen by the limo driver. O. J. certainly knew this route existed because he had once caught his son Jason using it when trying to sneak into the main house undetected.

I also had questions about the glove, the knife, and the bloody clothes. If O. J. had buried his bloody clothes and the knife, he certainly would have also buried the glove that police later recovered behind the guesthouse. The LAPD had no real explanation for this except to suggest that he might not have had time to bury the knife and the bloody clothes but brought these things with him back to Rockingham and then either dumped them into a trash bin at the airport or took them on to Chicago, where he safely disposed of them. That made perfect sense except for the fact that O. J. apparently didn't think to take the right-hand glove, which was found behind the Rockingham guesthouse, and the left-hand glove and knit cap, which were found at the Bundy Drive crime scene. This would have been exceptionally poor planning on the part of a premeditated murderer, or for that matter, a man like O. J. Simpson, who sat on the board of several multimillion-dollar corporations. No matter what anyone said about O. J., he wasn't that stupid.

It also didn't seem conceivable to me that a man as compulsive about cleanliness and neatness as O. J. would have selected a stiletto or folding pocketknife for a murder weapon. A man who didn't park under trees because sap or leaves might fall on his car, who didn't permit smoking in his house, who compulsively cleaned his fingernails and who—according to at least one person who knew him well—allegedly wouldn't even bait his own fishhook for fear of getting blood on his hands, simply wouldn't choose a weapon which would bring him into direct contact with blood. Rather, he would have used one of the many guns he was said to have owned.

The sound of the Bronco's engine, O. J.'s failure to collect his glove, and his selection of a knife for the murder weapon were relatively minor issues for me at this point, as were the position and number of the bloodstains found in the Bronco or at the Rockingham house. The important question for me was O. J.'s state of mind on the night of the murders. As a keen observer of human behavior and a longtime student of criminal pathology, I could well understand O. J. having an emotional outburst which resulted in murder. Yet the evidence just didn't support such a conclusion.

There was no evidence O. J. had been stalking Nicole earlier that night, or that he had been drinking or doing drugs that afternoon, as is frequently the case when people "lose control." Nor was there evidence to suggest he was engaged in any other obsessive or destructive behavior that day. Just two hours before the murders, he was on the phone making a date with Gretchen Stockdale, a *Playboy* "Playmate of the Month." And prior to that, he took time out of his busy travel schedule to buy flowers and to attend his daughter's dance recital. O. J. simply wasn't in the "frenzy" that the police and the press were suggesting.

As Dr. Lenore Walker, the foremost expert on domestic violence and spousal abuse, would later say after a lengthy examination of O.J, he "did not fit the profile of a batterer who murders . . . He has good control over his impulses . . . He appears to control his emotions well."

Furthermore, Simpson's alleged history of abuse, by medical standards, did not fit a pattern that would culminate in murder. O. J. and Nicole had frequently resolved conflicts peacefully during their seventeen-year relationship. Nor were the alleged incidents of domestic violence building to any recognizable "crescendo." The one documented occasion that the LAPD and the prosecution focused upon was five and a half years before the murders, and no one had yet been able to document an incident of O. J. laying a hand upon her since.

To my mind, there was even less likelihood that O. J. had premeditated the murders.

Perhaps I had been brainwashed by the sports legend, Hertz commercials, and the *Naked Gun* movies, but I just couldn't fathom why a devoted father, a man truly proud of his previous accomplishments, and with a promising future, substantial bank account, and an adoring public, would plan and execute the cold-blooded murder of the woman he loved. That O. J. and Nicole's relationship ran hot and cold was not in question, nor was the fact that he was capable of physical violence. However, no one could claim that he didn't have a deep and abiding love for Nicole. They had been together for seventeen years, and though divorced, had slept in the same bed only a few months earlier, the two of them contemplating moving back in together.

I knew from reading the press reports that as late as May 10, when Nicole had come down with pneumonia, O. J. had sat by her side and nursed her back to health. And though the police and the press made much of the fact that Nicole had filed reports of domestic violence, it was also true that O. J. had never once been arrested for assault and battery, nor spent a single day in jail. He had pled guilty, on one occasion, to lesser charges. In my professional opinion he didn't fit the profile of someone who reached for a knife to settle domestic differences. A fist, perhaps, but not a knife.

Equally important—given alleged premeditation on the part of O. J.—was his apparent failure to adequately protect himself from being connected to the murders. Never mind the bloody glove and the bloodstains. He would surely have known ahead of time that he would be the logical suspect in any investigation of the crime, yet prior to the murders he openly stated, "I'll kill Nicole" and made references to friends and family of his desire "to kill Nicole."

O. J. also made no secret that he had been spying on Nicole. He had purchased at least one of the knives presumed to have been the potential murder weapon in front of numerous eyewitnesses. The company that made Swiss Army knives, on whose board of directors he sat, had given the other to him. O. J. also didn't think to dispose of a set of keys he had allegedly stolen from Nicole's condo. And after the murders, he had given hair and blood samples, which ultimately linked him to the cap and bloody gloves. Nor had he established a convincing alibi. He had no better explanation for his activities during those ninety minutes than a vague story about napping and chipping golf balls on the lawn, which were proven to be lies when he later took, and failed, his own private polygraph test. He had scored a minus 22, which meant that he had failed every single question put to him about the murders.

These facts suggested to me that indeed O. J. had visited the crime scene, but his actions that night and the next day were not those of a man prepared to be questioned about the murders of Nicole Simpson and Ron Goldman. It made me wonder whether O. J. was trying to hide something or possibly protect someone.

After an hour or two spent strolling up and down the street and chatting with neighbors, Chris and I headed back to our rented car. I can't say that I learned much, or had any serious questions laid to rest, but at least I now had a better mental picture of what was presumed to have occurred and why the LAPD murder scenario didn't make sense, given the layout of the house and O. J.'s natural interest in keeping his activities a secret. The one certain insight I did come away with was that I had dressed entirely wrong for investigating crime in Brentwood. I would have to exchange my monogrammed, ostrich-skin cowboy boots and black suit for white running shoes and a jogging outfit.

The next stop on our itinerary was Mezzaluna Trattoria, where Nicole and her family and friends had dinner on the night of the murders, and the place where Ron Goldman had worked as a waiter. I was especially interested in stopping here because I believed that this restaurant had more significance to the case than the press or the LAPD knew or were willing to acknowledge. I had reached this conclusion based on something I had heard back in Dallas from a well-respected surgeon who once had a serious cocaine addiction. Distrustful of buying his drugs in Dallas, where he was easily recognizable, he would fly to Los Angeles and visit Mezzaluna. "They had the finest cocaine I ever had," he said. "That's why the 'in crowd' ate there. It's what kept the restaurant in business." This same claim was later substantiated by a psychologist who is a well-known "therapist to the stars."

When questioned about Mezzaluna's reputation as a place to score coke, Pat McKenna, one of O. J.'s private investigators, was quoted in *A Problem of Evidence* as saying, "Without a doubt." The concept of buying your drugs at a restaurant and carrying them home in a take-out bag was an entirely new idea for me. Then again, I could see how attractive that might be for someone like a doctor, an actor, or a business person, who wasn't the kind of man to visit the home of a drug dealer or have a drug dealer visit him. I had this in mind as Chris and I drove east on Sunset Boulevard, south on Cliffwood Avenue, then again east, this time on San Vicente Boulevard. From there it was a short drive to Gorham Avenue, where the restaurant's large white-canvas awnings were visible at the first intersection, in the heart of Brentwood's Parisian-style shopping area. Even from a distance, Chris and I could see that the same tourists who had flocked to Rockingham had also come to stand in line for lunch at Mezzaluna.

Once we had parked, Chris shot a few photos while I made my way into the restaurant through the line of tourists. Along the way I noted the Mexican flowerpots and the crisp cream-colored linen on ten tables outside and the twenty or more tables inside. But what caught my immediate attention were the clouds on the ceiling. Artists had painted them in white and blue. There were other nice touches too. All the waiters and waitresses wore elegant bistro-style outfits: black slacks, white shirt, and a knee-length white apron. No doubt Nicole, who liked seeing and being seen by the "in crowd," also appreciated the fact that there were windows on three sides, along with the tables right out on the street.

I picked up a menu, knowing that without reservations Chris and I weren't likely to get in, as indeed we did not. The food on the menu was what might be termed Italian prepared California style. That meant smaller portions, more color, and fewer calories. The prices ranged from $10 on up to $16—high priced by most restaurant standards, but moderate for Beverly Hills and Brentwood. However, as my friend the surgeon had mentioned, food wasn't the only thing on the menu.

Glancing at the faces of the tourists who now crowded through its doors, I knew that this side of the business—if indeed drugs had been sold here—would not continue for long. With the heightened scrutiny of Mezzaluna by everyone and everybody, the regular customers who would normally think nothing of leaving a $200 or $300 dollar tip for that extra little service, weren't likely to feel safe doing business as usual.

It is unlikely that drugs had been on Nicole's mind when she and her family dined there on the night of the murders. It was a party of seven, which included Nicole, her two children, one of Nicole's three sisters, their parents, Lou and Juditha, along with Sydney's friend Rachael, who was going to have a sleepover at the Bundy Drive condo that night. The Brown party sat down for dinner at 7:30 PM. Ron Goldman, whom Nicole had gotten to know, hadn't been waiting on them that night but did stop by their table at one point to say hello. Within an hour they had finished their meal and were ready to leave. The bill came to $179.95, which Nicole paid for with a credit card and added a $34.00 tip.

That's all that the LAPD determined had happened there, except for the fact that Juditha Brown, Nicole's mother, had dropped her prescription sunglasses at the restaurant when she was leaving. Juditha had called later on that night and asked one of the waitresses to see if she could find them. They found the glasses outside on the curb, and apparently Ron Goldman volunteered to drop them at Nicole's Bundy Drive condo on his way home from work that night.

Chris and I didn't stick around to wait our turn to eat a late lunch but pushed on, this time continuing our tour on foot. Our destination was Ron Goldman's apartment building, which was just two blocks up Gorham Avenue on the left-hand side. His small apartment, at the back of an unimposing building on the north side of the street, didn't have much going for it except a Brentwood address. Dull gray paint was chipping off the carports out front. Empty milk cartons lay strewn on the ground in front of the building. Here there was no manicured front lawn or iron gates, just cement steps leading to twenty or more single and double apartments that were no doubt as drab inside as they were outside. Ron had lived in apartment number three.

I didn't have anything particular in mind when Chris and I began to climb the rear steps. However—as I pointed out to Chris—I had my doubts that Ron Goldman truly happened to be "in the wrong place at the wrong time" on the evening of the murders, as the press had reported. I believe there was more to it than that. He had volunteered to bring the glasses to Nicole. But before doing so, he had run home, showered, changed his clothes, and put on cologne. As would later become known, he had borrowed a friend's car, which he parked up the street from Nicole's condo and presumably entered her property through the rear gate. He hadn't just pulled up at the curb and jumped out of his car with the intention of giving Nicole her mother's glasses. It appeared he intended to stay, for a while at least.

Nicole too had apparently freshened up. She had on a black, knee-length summer dress. The lights in the house were turned off, except for candles that lit the living room and bathroom. New Age mood music was playing on the stereo, and a hot bath had been drawn. It appeared that this was not just a matter of accepting her mother's glasses—unless, of course, Nicole intended to entertain someone other than Goldman that night.

Chris and I stood for a few minutes looking at the door to Goldman's apartment. Louvered blinds on the windows to the left of the door prevented us from seeing inside. On a whim, I knocked. I didn't know exactly what I would say if someone actually opened the door, but I was sure to think of something. And in the meantime, I would get a glimpse into the apartment, though already I was taking mental snapshots of what lay behind the door.

Ron was only twenty-five years old. He aspired to a career as a fashion model and had enjoyed a bit of success, appearing in a fashion spread for a Giorgio Armani print ad. He looked the part: six-foot-two, well-muscled, healthy, and with that overly suggestive catch-me-if-you-can smile. Not many people remembered him from the ad, but he was pleased to have been in it and the experience had whetted his appetite for more. In the meantime, he had to earn a living. Being a waiter in L.A. was the right choice for him. He not only could earn $400 or $500 a week, but also it gave him time in the mornings to work out at the gym, study martial arts, give a private tennis lesson or two, or just hang out at Starbucks, where he had originally met Nicole. After work, he would go out and party, which is apparently what he intended to do that evening, for he had arranged to meet a friend for drinks around midnight.

My preliminary research also revealed that although Goldman lived alone at the time of the murders, he hadn't always lived alone. According to one report—which had neither been confirmed nor denied by the LAPD—his last roommate, who had been a waiter at the Dragonfly in Los Angeles, had his throat cut in what was being called a drug-related death.

This, and the curious fact that Goldman had filed for bankruptcy on November 10, 1992—with $12,216 owed on credit cards—were the kind of details I believed couldn't be ignored.

No one answered my knocks on the door to Goldman's apartment. Chris and I turned and walked back to our car. We proceeded to what was our primary destination that day—Nicole's condo on Bundy Drive. This time we drove straight down Gorham Avenue until it intersected with Bundy.

Again, there was no need to consult a map or read street addresses. To Chris's amusement, and my dismay, the atmosphere resembled a street carnival. A huge crowd of tourists had convened in front of Nicole's condominium, along with motorcycle police doing crowd control, LAPD patrolmen, reporters, and the ever-present street ped-dlers selling maps to the homes of movie stars.

Chris and I parked on nearby Dorothy Street and joined the parade of onlookers milling about Bundy Drive. People were animated, freely sharing their own theories and insights into the murders, content to listen to the theories of others or to be photographed standing in front of the bloodstained Spanish paving stones that marked the entrance to Nicole's elegant condo. Despite my intense dislike of crowds and the fact that I had to wait my turn before I could reach the police line blocking tourists from entering the crime scene, I was able to gain an overall positive impression of the neighborhood. This was a nice place to live. Though it wasn't the high-income section of Brentwood—where O. J. lived—the narrow streets were lined with large palms and shade trees. The walled and gated homes and condominiums were tasteful and well maintained, and many contained small private gardens.

Nicole's residence was a classical two-story Mediterranean townhouse, covered in pale-pink stucco with a sloping red-tile roof. The homes on either side had the same pastel colors and sloping roofs, giving the impression of a safe, private, walled-in community.

The reason for the walls and the gates became immediately apparent to me. Bundy Drive, I could see, was a heavily traveled cross street, surrounded by hundreds of private homes, condominiums, and apartments within a very small radius of Nicole's home. However, this was not like the residential part of Beverly Hills, where people live behind high walls and seldom leave their property unless driven by car. Here in Brentwood, people walked their dogs, jogged, or casually strolled the shopping area around San Vicente Boulevard on their way to shops or restaurants. As Chris and I would confirm later that night, people drove or walked along Bundy Drive at all hours—not just in the daytime. That's how Nicole's and Goldman's bodies were actually discovered: Nicole's unleashed dog, a Japanese Akita, Kato, named after Kato Kaelin because, as she said, Kato was always lounging around—was found at about 11 PM on Bundy Drive by a neighbor out walking his own dogs. This was not the kind of remote location that a premeditated killer would select to ambush his victim or victims.

Chris also noticed, as I did, how close Nicole's property was to the neighboring house. Only a thin masonry wall separated the house next door from Nicole's, and that neighbor's upstairs window looked directly down onto the crime scene. Furthermore, there was no nearby thicket of trees or tall shrubs between Bundy Drive and Nicole's condo to offer a six-foot-two marauder any protection. Rather, there was an assortment of shade trees and palms planted evenly along the street, and then a neatly planted flowerbed atop a gentle grassy slope. Lavender and lilies are as lovely to look at as they are to smell, but offer no place for someone to hide.

This point was important to both Chris and me, for in most press accounts the underlying assumption was that O. J. had stalked Nicole on Bundy Drive and that this was where he allegedly ambushed her and Ron Goldman. I didn't know where the police, or the press, were getting their information, but there was no possible way for O. J. or anyone else to have hidden here without Nicole or Goldman seeing them. And if O. J. had been parked and waiting on Bundy Drive in his easily recognizable Bronco or his even more obvious Bentley, they would have known that too. There just was no place to hide. And even if there had been, O. J. was alleged to have been on a very tight time line. He couldn't afford to have waited for her to come outside on her own volition.

The only logical conclusion I could draw from what I had read, and now what I had seen, was that O. J. would not have hidden on Bundy Drive but would have used the keys he was said to have possessed to enter the property through the metal gate at the entrance to Nicole's condo. Nor was there a place to hide here because that spot, according to the police reports, was only ten feet by ten feet square. I couldn't, at this time, verify the size because the police had placed a row of potted plants in front of the gate to keep people from getting too close or looking over the top to the spot where the murders actually had been committed. The only things visible here, beside the mailbox and call box, were the Spanish tiles, five rows deep. Dried blood, still visible on the tiles closest to the gate, was the only evidence of the gruesome murders that had taken place.

I had to confine myself, for the time being, to just imagining that perhaps it was possible for O. J. to have stood here in the shadows cast by the Bundy Drive street lights, waiting for the right moment to jump out at his two unsuspecting victims. However, even with the metal gate to shield the killer, there were only a few feet between the gate and the curb, and then only a few more feet to the street. The point I made to Chris was that this was simply not a location that a premeditated killer would select to attack his victim or victims.

Anyone driving along the street or standing on the sidewalk could have seen or heard the commotion taking place.

The LAPD wasn't about to let anyone off the street inspect Nicole's three-thousand-square-foot condo, so I had to be content to point out the important features to Chris that I had learned from reading the press accounts. To the rear of the two-unit, three-story condo, backing onto an alley, was the garage where Nicole parked her white Ferrari. Adjacent to the garage was a guest bedroom and large kitchen with marble countertops and subzero refrigerator. Closer to Bundy Drive were her two-story sunken living room and den, tastefully decorated in whitewashed pine and low-to-the-ground white sofas. Three bedrooms were upstairs. One, which contained a Jacuzzi, belonged to Nicole and was where the LAPD had found more lit candles. Here also, it should be noted, the television had been found turned on, tuned to the Prime Sports cable station. Nearby were the bedrooms of Nicole and O. J.'s children, Sydney and Justin, who had been asleep when the murders took place. This fact alone—that the children had been home—to my mind, offered one of the most convincing reasons of all why O. J. had either not premeditated the murders, or why O. J. hadn't committed the murders at all.

I believe that, to anyone who has children, it stretches the imagination to believe that a man who loved his children and, by all accounts, desired that his family be reunited, would risk stabbing his former wife with their children in close enough proximity to see it happen, or to hear their mother's anguished cries for help.

And then there were all the possible variables, which potentially could have interfered with any premeditated murder plan.

"For all O. J. knew, the children were not asleep," I told Chris. "And what he did know was that Sydney had invited a school friend, Rachael, over to the house that night for a sleepover. The two girls could have been up until all hours of the night."

I went on to point out to Chris that all O. J. would have known about the whereabouts of Nicole and the children after the dance recital was that they were headed off to dinner. He couldn't have known, for example, that Nicole was going to stop with the children for ice cream on the way home, or that the parents of Sydney's school friend had actually come to pick up their daughter that night, or that Nicole's sisters or parents hadn't decided to spend the night—as they often did. For all O. J. knew, Sydney was still up watching television.

I left Chris to take pictures and ponder these issues while I walked to the intersection of Bundy Drive and Montana Avenue, then continued up Montana to see if I could look down the alley behind Nicole's condominium. There were no tourists here or police, only an empty alley. Police had apparently not put up a barricade because residents needed access to their parking garages. Looking down the length of the alley, I could see where Nicole had parked her black Jeep Cherokee on the night of the murders. I could also see where O. J. had presumably parked his white Bronco.

I casually walked the length of the alley, pausing momentarily at the locked, seven-foot metal gate which opened onto the rear of Nicole's condo. It was here, police claimed, that the killer exited. Bloody footprints, believed to have been O. J.'s, had been found both coming and going along the narrow, 120-foot walk leading to the rear of the condo. This evidence suggested that O.J—if indeed the Bruno Magli shoe prints belonged to him—had left the front of the condo where the murders had taken place, then returned, perhaps to try and recover his knit cap and glove.

The footprints, like the cap and glove, were certainly compelling circumstantial evidence that O. J. had been at the crime scene. However, I couldn't conclude from this same evidence that he committed the murders. Not only had other unidentified shoe prints been found at the crime scene, but investigators had also reported finding blood and skin under Nicole's fingernails—suggesting she had fought or clawed at her attacker—along with blood drops on her back that didn't match those of her ex-husband. And though the LAPD had found nine sets of fingerprints at the crime scene, none belonged to O. J.

Furthermore, had O. J. been engaged in a vicious fight-to-the-death that left one victim's head dangling from her neck, and the other victim bleeding from twenty-two wounds in his feet, hands, and torso, O. J. would have literally been drenched in the blood of his victims. That blood would have soaked through his slacks and shirt, dripped off the knife handle into his hair, and run down his arms. Yet all the blood that was recovered from O. J.'s Bronco, from his Rockingham home and his clothing, could have fit onto the end of a grown man's thumbnail.

Police investigators never adequately explained this lack of blood except to suggest that O. J. had changed and possibly disposed of his bloody clothes before returning to his Rockingham home, then showered and scrubbed himself clean. This, however, assumed that he had a place to change them in the first place. He certainly didn't change his clothes on the bloody cement walkway in front of Nicole's condo. Nor would it have made sense for O. J. to have changed his clothes in full view of passing pedestrians on Bundy Drive, or in the well-lit back alley at the rear of the condo. Had he changed in the Bronco, bloodstains would have been found on everything from the gas and brake pedals to the carpet on the floor—not just a few isolated drops. And if O. J. had indeed showered upon his return to Rockingham, blood evidence would undoubtedly have been found in the drainpipes. No blood was found there, despite the fact that the LAPD had literally dismantled the plumbing.

Finally, there was the curious matter of the bloody left-hand glove. LAPD seemed to be suggesting that the glove had somehow fallen off during the three- to ten-minute knife fight, at which point O. J. had been cut on the hand. I didn't know how such a thing was possible. Gloves just don't fall off a person whose hands are as large as O. J.'s, particularly this type of gloves which are designed for a very snug fit. And if he had indeed been cut on the hand during the knife fight, there surely would have been evidence of a cut on one or both of the gloves. Lack of a cut or abrasions on the gloves suggested to me that O. J. had perhaps arrived at the crime scene during the fight or immediately afterward. These thoughts accompanied me out of the alley and back to Bundy where I found Chris snapping pictures of the people gathered in front of the crime scene. He had enough of what had become Brentwood's biggest tourist attraction.

"If we leave right now," he said, "we can be back in Dallas before midnight."

I told him, "I want to come back tonight, around 10 PM."

Chris knew exactly what I had in mind. I didn't have to spell it out for him. I intended to return to the crime scene at the exact hour the murders had been committed and then do what I do best: enter into the "mind" of the killer, and then build a logical sequence of events that complements the known material and forensic evidence. I had employed the same technique to solve the notorious Dean Milo murder case in Akron, Ohio. By visiting the crime scene and acting out the parts of both the victim and his killer, I was able to build a case that ultimately resulted in the arrest and conviction of eleven people for murder. I was determined to try this technique again, only now on Bundy Drive.

3

IN MY MIND'S EYE

IT WAS JUST BEFORE 10:30 PM when we arrived back at Bundy Drive that night. The moon was high and a cool breeze blowing in from the ocean tugged at the tops of the emerald-green palm fronds and turned what had been an unusually hot day into a chilly, star-filled night.

Chris let me out in front of Nicole's condo and then parked the car on Dorothy Street in virtually the same place where Ron Goldman had parked his car on the night of the murders. As I watched Chris pull over to the curb and cut the engine, it occurred to me that he, like Ron Goldman, had chosen that spot for a particular reason. The natural and most convenient place for anyone visiting Nicole to have parked would have been beside her black Jeep Grand Cherokee in the alley behind her condo. And yet, Goldman had not parked there. Like Chris, he parked a full block away, on Dorothy Street, at a spot which was close enough to comfortably walk to the condo, but not so close that his car might be noticed by someone looking for it next to Nicole's house. Perhaps Goldman didn't wish his car to be seen, or more likely, Goldman couldn't or didn't wish to park beside Nicole's car in the alley because someone else—possibly the killer—was already parked in that spot.

This thought was foremost in my mind as I stood on the sidewalk looking across the police line at the front entrance to Nicole's condo.

I was immediately glad we had come, for all the tourists, street hawkers, and police had left. At least I hoped the police had left. I saw no one except a man walking two dogs, and he barely paid any attention to me as I walked to the corner, turned up Dorothy Street, and then headed down the alley toward the rear gate to Nicole's condo, which is where I intended to begin my real work for the evening.

Chris, who sat patiently in the car waiting for further instructions, knew exactly where I was headed. He also knew from years of experience that I couldn't discuss exactly what I was going to do until after the fact. That way, if he was questioned, he could honestly deny complicity in my activities.

I had made my second pass through the alley when I approached Nicole's back gate with the intention of climbing over it. My heart began to pump as I mentally rehearsed what I was going to do. Put my hands on the top, bend knees, jump, turn shoulders and put my left leg over the top. I knew this had to be done in the correct order and without pausing. Even the slightest hesitation as I climbed over the gate would draw attention to me. In four more steps I would be there.

I had taken three of those four steps when a pair of headlights cut through the darkness behind me. Instead of taking that fourth step, the one that would bring me to the gate, I continued down the alley, looking as innocent as a six-foot-three man in cowboy boots and a black suit could look. At that moment I also began mentally preparing what I was going to tell the LAPD if they stopped to question me or, worse still, if I climbed the metal gate and got caught on the other side. The lights on the car behind me steadily increased until the car drove right past me, not even slowing down.

I took two deep breaths and continued on toward the end of the alley, planning to make a right turn down Montana Avenue, along Bundy and Dorothy and then back up the alley to make another try for the gate. I didn't get that far. Another pair of headlights greeted me at the alley's end. Then a second pair appeared behind that one. I was certain my scouting mission was over. No doubt a neighbor, already on the alert for potential trespassers, had called the police about a suspicious character in the alley.

The car in front of me slowed and then stopped, its headlights shining directly on my face. Then, just behind the first car, a second car pulled up. Only this one didn't stop in front of me as the first one had. The driver pulled over to the side, at a right angle to the first car, so that the second car was also pointing directly at me. I was blinded by all the headlights and cornered in the alley. This was, I knew, standard police procedure, and gave me all the more reason to be apprehensive.

Squinting into the lights, I knew I was fortunate at least to have been stopped before I made the climb over the gate and into the crime scene. Then I would have had some serious explaining to do. At least here, out on the street, I could be just a tourist. That wouldn't, however, explain the fact that I had a pistol strapped to my ankle, and another gun in the rented car parked on Dorothy. The guns would take a bit more explaining.

The driver of the first car got out. Silhouetted in the glare of the headlights, I could see a middle-aged man dressed in a raincoat. The driver of the other vehicle, who got out next, was a woman. Both stood staring at me for a moment before the man called over to me, asking what I was doing in the alley.

"I'm meeting a friend," was all I said.

They stood for another moment or two looking at me, then turned, got back in their cars and disappeared down Montana Avenue. To this day I don't know who they were, but I suspect that they weren't LAPD or they would have questioned me further. However, I wasn't about to test my luck yet again the same night, so I returned to Dorothy and told Chris that we were calling it quits for the night.

Chris was ready to head back to Dallas. It wasn't that I had convinced him of O. J.'s innocence, because I hadn't. All I had accomplished so far was to plant a reasonable doubt that the full truth of the story hadn't yet been revealed. He also knew, or had begun to suspect, that I was willing to take some personal risks to answer some of the lingering questions that disturbed me about this case. And of course, he was right. Risk taking was part of what I did. I wouldn't have lasted thirty-five years in this business if I weren't willing to take some calculated risks. In other words, Chris knew, and I knew, that it was only a matter of time before I would climb the back gate to begin making a real examination of the crime scene and to "enter into the mind" of the killer.

The opportunity came the next day, July 2. Again, I chose to come in the evening, at 10:30 PM, because that was around the time when the murders had been committed. I also left the guns behind in our hotel room. Chris again remained in the car on Dorothy Street as I made one quick pass along Bundy to see that the coast was clear; I then retreated around back to the alley.

Like the night before, the path appeared clear. There was not a sound as I casually strolled toward Nicole's rear gate, then glanced to my left and right to see that no one was about. I stepped up to the gate and, just as I was about to reach for the top, headlights cut through the shadows and I heard the dull roar of a car engine. Cursing silently to myself, I pressed my back to the wall and prayed that whoever was driving along the alley wouldn't look in my direction. The car, a white sedan, drove past. In answer to my prayer, the driver didn't turn her head.

In one adrenaline-pumping jump I was perched precariously on the top of the gate, pain shooting down my neck and back. The car accident from a year before had come back to haunt me. I was in agony, but I couldn't back down now. I swung my leg over the top, leaned forward and, in a split second, was standing in the dark on the opposite side of Nicole's gate. Other than the pounding of my heart and my deep breaths, I could hear nothing. Not a sound. For the moment, I was safe. There were no police or night watchmen waiting for me . . . no embarrassing explaining to do. I took a few more deep breaths and then started down the narrow, unlit walkway toward the scene of the crime.

Experience had taught me there is no substitute for a personal inspection of a crime scene. Photographs are deceiving. Diagrams don't adequately evoke the environment. I wanted to see and smell that ten-foot square of concrete behind the metal gate, to stand where the killer had stood and to imagine the killer actually standing there. I know that sounds old-fashioned in an age when many patrol cars come equipped with video cameras and crimes are solved with DNA scanners. But that's just how I like to work. I go to a crime scene and let what I hear and feel wash over me like I'm taking a hot shower. And here at the back of Nicole's condo, my heart still pounding from the anticipation of meeting an LAPD officer or night watchman at each step, I was now feeling that sensation of "being there." The killer must have felt much the same as I did; not knowing what was going to happen next or whom he or she might meet in the narrow corridor.

It was much darker than I imagined it would be. The only light came from the distant yellow street lamps on Bundy and from the pale blue quarter moon high overhead, filtered through the green leaves of the palm trees. To my surprise, I discovered that the walkway was not level. A flight of stairs led down, and then back up the other side, preventing anyone at the rear gate from seeing what was taking place at the front gate. I carefully and quietly took the steps one at a time, and with each new footfall, I pictured in my mind's eye what the killer must have experienced on that cool, moonlit night of Sunday, June 12.

Letting my intuition be my guide, I reached for my imaginary knife. It's long and it's sharp and gives me a sense of power. I'm holding it out in front of me as I move forward to the small cement square in front of Nicole's front door. I try to step back, to hide in the shadows, except there is no place for me to hide. Directly above me is a neighbor's window. I'm now wondering if anyone is home next door, if the neighbors will see or hear me.

Had Chris been there he most assuredly would have stopped me from knocking on Nicole's door. But he wasn't, and I was so wrapped up in trying to act out the part of the killer that I could no more keep myself from knocking than I could put the imaginary knife I held in my hands away.

I knocked on the front door, just as the killer must have done. In my mind's eye, the door opens, and tall, shapely Nicole Simpson stands framed in the doorway in her short, black summer dress. She has rings on her fingers and her long blond hair cascades to her shoulders. Behind her, candles are burning in the living room; music drifts from a distant stereo. Nicole is expecting someone, but she's not expecting me. She's planning on seeing one of her boyfriends. Her surprise turns to anger when she realizes who I am. But she's not frightened. That's important. That's why she opened the door in the first place.

There is something I have to say to her, something that I must communicate, only Nicole doesn't give me a chance to speak. Nicole scolds me, points her finger, and demands to know why I've come. She orders me to leave. I take a step backwards, toward the front gate that opens onto Bundy. I'm telling her, "No, I'm not going. *I need you to listen to me.*"

Now she steps away from the door, closing it behind her. She doesn't want to wake up the children. Only she doesn't close the door all the way. Kato, the dog, is nosing his way outside. The dog is not alarmed because he knows me. But he senses something isn't right.

Nicole is coming at me, yelling at me, cursing me, telling me she is going to call the police if I don't leave. Now I'm thinking what a cold-hearted, ungrateful person she is to threaten calling the police on me. I can't believe it! *I'm getting angry.*

Nicole keeps coming at me, pushing me, just enough that I lose my balance on the steps. Now I'm wedged in the corner between the closed metal gate on Bundy and the neighbor's house.

"Listen to me, listen to what I've got to say," I'm telling her. But she's not listening. The only thing on her mind is having me leave before her boyfriend gets there. Nicole keeps pushing me back, pointing at me with her finger.

I tell her to lower her voice. But she doesn't listen. She keeps coming at me, even after I've shown her the knife.

I'm really getting pissed. I don't understand why she won't stop cursing and coming at me. Her words are ringing in my ears. And now I'm beginning to lose it. I'm thinking that I have to do something to shut her up—make her listen.

I'm holding the knife tightly in my fist. *I don't want to do this*, I'm telling myself. *Make her quit! Make her shut-the-fuck-up!*

All at once I hear someone hollering at me. "Hey! Hey! Hey!"

Now I know she must be *made* to shut up. I take the handle of the knife and slam it down on top of her head. That will shut her up.

Nicole drops to her knees, clawing at me with her fingernails. All I can see is the mass of her blond hair in my face, and then the man running toward me. I'm thinking that I've never seen this man before in my life. He's shouting at me as he's coming toward me. He must think I'm raping Nicole. I'm telling him to stay away, but he keeps coming at me.

I've got to get out of here. I'm backing up. I've backed up as far as I can go. My back is to the gate, and I can't get out. I'm trapped.

This guy—this big hulk of a man—knows he's got me trapped. He keeps coming at me, all hands and feet. He's dangerous. He's going to attack me. He's going to hurt me.

I can't stand by and let this guy hurt me. I *have to* defend myself. I have no choice. He's *making* me defend myself. That's when I threaten him with my knife. I don't have a choice. He's given me no choice!

I slash him in the arm. He keeps coming at me. Then I get him in the hand. Now I'm really slashing away. I cut him across the chest, and then his neck, but he still won't quit. Again and again he keeps coming at me. I don't want to hurt him, but I have to. I have to stop him. He thinks I've hurt Nicole.

I must have hit him twenty or more times before he falls back, blood covering his face. He's down and he's not going to get back up.

Oh God, I've killed him! I tell myself.

His eyes are open. He's lying against the gate. He's dead. I know he's dead. This son-of-a-bitch gave me no choice.

Now Nicole is beginning to moan. She's trying to raise her head off the ground. *How could this be happening to me?* I'm asking myself. *I only came to talk to her, but she wouldn't listen. What the hell am I going to do? I have to do something.*

Nicole has given me no choice. She is the only person who can identify me!

I don't remember pushing Nicole back down on the pavement. I don't remember putting my foot on her back. I don't remember pulling her head up by her blond hair. I don't remember slashing her throat. All I remember is that this was what I had to do. Nicole knew who I was. I *had* to keep her from screaming. I *had* to kill her.

I heard the dull roar of a car's engine in the alley behind Nicole's condo, which suddenly restored me to reality. I understood, in real time, how fast I was breathing, how really worked up I was. I had just knocked on the door of Nicole's Bundy Drive condo. Thank God no one answered. I looked down, and I suddenly realized I was standing in blood. It hadn't all been cleaned up. There was still a crimson pool of dried blood at my feet, in the grass, on the pavement, even it seems, on the leaves.

That's the moment when I realized beyond any shadow of a doubt what had happened here—the reason that I had to see the crime scene for myself. Nicole Simpson had been hit on the head at least once. Her throat had been slashed. Ron Goldman had been stabbed twenty-two times. And nearly three pints of blood had been spilled. No matter what spin the prosecution would put on this evidence, Nicole Simpson's and Ron Goldman's deaths were decidedly not the work of a cold-blooded killer who had planned and executed the murders in a rational, premeditated state of mind. This was the work of one man, a deranged individual, who had hit and slashed his victims in a mad, bloody and uncontrollable rage. This was definitely a rage killing!

I had now been at the crime scene for about the same length of time as the killer may have been there. It was time for me to leave, and I knew it. I'd pressed my luck. The killer must have known it too. Without so much as looking back, I walked briskly to the rear gate, listened for a moment to make sure no cars were headed up or down the alley, and then climbed back over the gate. Even then I felt certain the LAPD was on the other side, waiting to grab me. But when I landed, to my great relief, no one was there. I was alone. I retraced my steps to Dorothy Street and, still breathing hard, climbed back into the car beside Chris.

I remained silent for much of that night, unable to share with him what I experienced. It wasn't until the next day, on a long walk at the beach in Santa Monica and during lunch on the pier, that I explained to him my conviction that there was only one explanation consistent with the crime scene.

To my mind, this was a rage murder committed by a deeply disturbed individual who had known and perhaps desired to frighten Nicole on the night of the murders. O. J., I believed, was not that man. Had he possessed those psychotic tendencies, there would have been evidence throughout his career, as those tendencies would be very difficult to conceal for a celebrity who has been in the spotlight for the last twenty-five years. However, that didn't mean O. J. hadn't been at the crime scene. I had become convinced more than ever before that he had. That's the only thing that would explain both the material evidence found by the LAPD and his behavior. He kept proclaiming his innocence, repeatedly kept saying how "sorry" he was to the Goldman and Brown families, yet he seemed to know more than he was saying.

This started me thinking that if I was right, O. J. had to have a strong motive to go to Nicole's house that night. What could possibly have made him take that chance?

I could only conclude O. J. Simpson had been called to the crime scene by someone he knew and who knew him. O. J. had arrived at Bundy Drive knowing full well that Nicole was dead or at least fearfully expecting it. Either that or he had left for her house because he believed her life was in danger and was going to warn her. He must have grabbed his cap and gloves because he didn't want to be recognized or leave fingerprints. Even then, he obviously wouldn't have been prepared for what he was to see.

I could picture him kneeling, peeling off his glove to feel for Nicole's pulse. He would have reached down through the knot of her bloody blond hair. And that's when it must have hit him. He would have been looking into the empty eyes of the woman he had loved and who had loved him for seventeen years, making the sudden and horrible realization that her head was barely attached to her neck. In fact, she was nearly decapitated. Her blood was everywhere.

Then he would have looked up to see the dark shape of a man stretched out on the ground, blank eyes staring back at him. Like Nicole, he too was dead. He too was drenched in blood.

Frightened, O. J.'s temperature shot up. His heart pounded. His hands shook. He didn't know what to do. Kato, Nicole's dog, was now beginning to howl. He knew he had to get back to Rockingham and get on that plane to Chicago or the police would surely arrest him for murder.

I didn't have to play the rest of the scenario out for Chris. He got the message. More important to me, he believed it. The only problem now was what we were going to do about it.

4

FREEDOM TO PURSUE

PRIVATE INVESTIGATORS ARE GENERALLY not welcomed by the police, especially in high-profile murder cases. The police will not open their doors to them. It is also true that private investigators don't have to follow the same rules as the police. They have the freedom to pursue any line of inquiry they choose without having to ask permission, file reports, or answer to anyone except their clients. I decided to open my own investigation into the Brown-Simpson and Goldman murders. Details of the LAPD investigation were already part of the public record, and soon nearly all of it would be readily accessible. Perhaps equally important to my investigation, I also had no client. That gave me the luxury to develop leads and delve into areas otherwise unexplored, to take the time to make a thorough investigation, to speak to whomever I chose and answer to no one but myself.

I began the Brown-Simpson and Goldman investigation as I did all other homicide cases: by establishing a dedicated work space in my 7th-floor office suite on Stemmons Freeway in Dallas, holding a meeting of office personnel to discuss our objectives, and then putting people to work. As it turned out, everyone in my office wanted to be part of the investigation.

I assigned Chris Stewart the initial task of building a time line of known and verifiable events, while Joe Villanueva, a surveillance expert and undercover operative who had worked for me for the past nineteen years, compiled fact files and collected photographs. Herman King, another veteran investigator and former Dallas County deputy sheriff, put together background information on the principal players and, along with Donna Roland, my secretary, tackled the time-consuming task of collecting and organizing the mass of published information that this case generated on an almost daily basis. Donna also ran computer operations. In this investigation, however, she also kept tabs on various Internet chat rooms devoted to discussions of O. J. Simpson or the murders. I supervised everything from behind my desk in our Dallas office, while juggling the four or five other cases that were paying the bills. But most importantly, I put together a master list of potential suspects.

Determined not to make the same mistakes as the LAPD, I included everyone even remotely connected to the case on my suspect list, from O. J.'s former all-pro friend Marcus Allen, to Ron Shipp, whom O. J. leaned on for favors at the LAPD. Donna repeatedly reminded me that I could save time and money by using more discretion in choosing my list of suspects, but I think the decision to include anyone and everyone proved to be a good one. It enabled me to get to know the case through the eyes of all of the participants. And it was only through developing an understanding of what went on behind the scenes that the greater truths, however implausible they might at first appear, would become clear.

The first and most important "behind the scenes" suspect in our investigation was Allen "A. C." Cowlings, a man who supposedly would do anything for "The Juice" and in whose white Ford Bronco O. J. had become a fugitive from the law with the famous car chase from Orange County. Cowlings had been at the wheel, and in his pocket he carried nearly $10,000 in cash, along with O. J.'s passport. Another thing that made Cowlings suspicious in our eyes was his reputed underworld connection to Joey Ippolito, a known Mafia kingpin alleged to have been operating a heroin and cocaine distribution business in New Jersey and Los Angeles. This didn't, of course, make Cowlings a cold-blooded murderer, but it did suggest he may have been part of some larger drug- or mob-related conspiracy that involved O. J., Nicole, and possibly Ron Goldman. O. J. could have simply asked A. C. to frighten Nicole and the situation got out of control. I couldn't dismiss this possibility for one important reason. If there was anyone in O. J.'s small circle of friends for whom O. J. might risk going to jail to protect, or who would risk going to jail to protect O. J., that man would be Cowlings.

Research indicated that the bond between O. J. and the 225-pound Cowlings had been forged as much off the football field as on. They had grown up together on Potrero Hill, the San Francisco ghetto, had been members of the same street gang that routinely pelted rocks at passing buses and shoplifted from grocery and liquor stores, had attended the same high school and colleges, dated the same women, and played on the same football teams.

The best known tale from their childhood centered on a day when they were caught shooting dice in the school bathroom. O. J., Cowlings, and another student were marched into the principal's office. No sooner had they entered the room then O. J. turned to leave. When the principal asked where he was going, O. J. replied that he had only been asked to bring the other two guys into the office. He—Orenthal James Simpson—hadn't been gambling.

O. J. had turned the tables on Cowlings that afternoon as he had on another day when Cowlings sent O. J. as an intermediary to talk to Cowlings's girlfriend, Marguerite Whitley, about an argument they'd had. O. J. had been sent to make amends on Cowlings's behalf. Cowlings later realized the big mistake he had made when O. J. began dating Marguerite, whom he eventually married.

After high school, Cowlings joined O. J. at San Francisco City College, and then again at the University of Southern California. They were both first round draft picks—one year apart—for the Buffalo Bills. That Cowlings was a defensive end and O. J. the star running back made them a natural pair, and stories told about them contributed to the popular mythology of the sport.

Cowlings played a trick on O. J. once at training camp. Cowlings had led O. J. to believe that he was just as exhausted as O. J., and then bet him $100 he could beat O. J. in a mile-long running race. Cowlings played his part to the hilt, dragging his feet, just barely keeping up with the fleet-footed running back. But then, in the last quarter of the race, when O. J. was running out of "Juice," Cowlings sprinted far ahead and stood at the finish line waiting to collect his reward.

They continued to play together during the early 1970s; then their paths finally split when Cowlings was traded to Houston. But their careers would cross paths again when both were nearing retirement from pro-ball. They played their last games for the San Francisco 49ers, back in the hometown where it had all started.

During the early seventies they allegedly shared not only women but drugs too. According to one account, O. J. had become addicted to barbiturates and amphetamines. He used uppers to keep him running and downers to put him to sleep. He was also alleged to be using cocaine. One reported drug source was Butch Sucharski, the owner of a popular sports bar that O. J. and Cowlings frequented back in Buffalo. Sucharski figures into the story only marginally, though he was worthy of our attention since he was known to have visited Los Angeles only two weeks before the Bundy Drive murders and was himself gunned down, along with two female companions, in Miramar, Florida, two weeks after the murders. However, like so many other leads that suggested drug involvement in the lives of O. J. and Cowlings, I was unable to find a single clue that would link those connections directly to Bundy Drive.

After retirement, O. J.'s and Cowlings's careers went in radically different directions. Unlike O. J., who used his charm and savvy business skills to forge a career for himself in the entertainment industry, Cowlings drifted from one job to the next and allegedly became hooked on cocaine, which was said to have ended a budding romance with singer Dionne Warwick. From what little Herman King and Joe Villanueva were able to cull from newspaper accounts and the recollections of other retired players, Cowlings got mixed up with a number of unsavory characters in Los Angeles, where he became a bouncer and a bill collector for loan sharks. O. J. apparently offered Cowlings jobs through his contacts at Hertz, but Cowlings was too proud a man to take help from his friend. He made his own way, joining Joey Ippolito's team of bill collectors who hung out in a pair of nightclubs Ippolito operated in Santa Monica. Cowlings remained a steadfast friend of O. J., however, and was drawn even closer to the Rockingham family when he began to date Nicole's oldest sister, Denise Brown. That there were still drugs involved in their nightly activities can only be inferred by a number of unsubstantiated stories describing O. J., Nicole, Denise, and Cowlings snorting cocaine. All that could be said with any certainty was that the four of them had met and kept company with Ippolito and also with another known mob figure, Tony "The Animal" Fiato, and that a large number of telephone calls were made between Ippolito-owned restaurants and O. J.'s Rockingham house.

Though the FBI briefly looked into the possible connections between O. J., Cowlings, and various mob figures, the only direct evidence linking them together was through a drug bust involving Tracy Hill, a thirty-two-year-old stripper from Santa Monica. According to the documents that Herman King and Joe Villanueva were able to obtain, Tracy Hill, a.k.a. Amanda Armstrong, was having an argument with her boyfriend while riding a train in Northern California when she grabbed her suitcase and tossed it out the door of the train. The suitcase turned out to contain forty pounds of cocaine. Police linked it to her because of an electronic organizer found in the suitcase. Included in the organizer were the names and private home telephone numbers of Cowlings and Simpson. That might have been ignored altogether had police not also found a vial of pills in Hill's purse. They were prescribed to Cowlings.

I didn't know what possible connection, if any, Cowlings's drug connections might have to the Bundy Drive murders, but it was enough to warrant adding Joey Ippolito's name to our suspect list and having our detective team put together fact files on him—something that wasn't difficult to do since he had been the object of at least two FBI investigations.

From what we were able to gather from sources, Joey Ippolito was second generation Mafia, one of several powerful successors to Meyer Lansky. A former speedboat racer, he headed for California in 1988 after completing a prison sentence for marijuana smuggling. There, he opened Cent'Anni, a fashionable Italian restaurant in Malibu, and distributed cocaine in Santa Monica and Brentwood. In the early 1990s he undertook a major expansion of his drug network, and his influence in the cocaine trade was said to have reached as far as New Jersey, Miami, and Philadelphia, as well as Los Angeles.

The FBI tapped Ippolito's phones, followed his cars, and put together a solid case against him. But when they went to arrest him, he couldn't be found. Agents burst into Ippolito's apartment and instead found A. C. Cowlings. Not only this, but the attorney who eventually represented Ippolito when the FBI did arrest him, Donald Re, was also Cowlings's attorney. No charges were brought against Cowlings, but Ippolito was later convicted and sentenced to ten years in prison. He did not, however, serve more than a few months of his sentence. In May of 1994, less than one month before the murders, he escaped from prison.

As interesting as this material was to study, the path leading from Cowlings to Ippolito seemed to dead-end, and no one in my office could find a single link that would put Ippolito or one of his men on Bundy Drive. Nor did the killings themselves suggest a drug connection. These were rage murders. The killer was not trying to exact "justice" or revenge, but venting great anger.

I also had come to believe that Cowlings himself could not have been directly involved in the murders. However convincing he might have been as a bouncer and bill collector, he was never implicated in a crime involving knives or a gun. He consistently put O. J. and Nicole's interests over his own, as evidenced by his willingness to play chauffeur to O. J. during Simpson's short-lived flight from the law. He had never bad-mouthed Nicole as O. J. often did, and Nicole knew it.

That's why she invited him to family functions and routinely assigned him the role of doorman at her parties. Nicole trusted and liked him. And if Nicole or one of her friends had a drug-related problem, he certainly would have tried to solve it before Nicole, O. J. or their families were in any danger. He had the contacts to deal with any drug-related problem before any blood was spilled.

The only other way I could imagine Cowlings fitting into a possible murder scenario was in his role as a protector. Perhaps O. J. had asked Cowlings to go to Bundy Drive and scare Ron Goldman, whom he suspected of having an affair with Nicole. He might well have had a knife with him, though in all honesty, a man as large and ferocious as a Buffalo Bills defensive end doesn't need a knife to get his message across. That and his airtight alibi was what eventually took Cowlings off my list of suspects. On the night of the murders he had been attending a birthday party for his friend Bubba Scott's daughter. There were upwards of twenty people who saw him at the party between 9:30 PM and 11:00 PM, the time when the murders took place.

I next focused my attention on Marcus Allen, another football player and behind-the-scenes participant who figured into the murder story because he was strongly suspected of having an affair with Nicole. In fact, nearly everyone connected to O. J. and Nicole—except Marcus himself—said that he and Nicole were secretly meeting. He became an even more likely suspect when Nicole's Bundy Drive neighbor, Tom Lange (not to be confused with the detective), reported to police that he had seen a well-dressed black man in an expensive car—not O. J.'s—parked in front of Nicole's condo around 10 PM on the night of the murders. Lange told police that Nicole, wearing only a bathrobe, was standing out on the curb and then leaned inside the car to kiss him. The suggestion here was that O. J., who trusted and mentored Marcus, may have caught the two together and became enraged. Ron Goldman, in this scenario, was just a bystander, a man who truly was in the wrong place at the wrong time and whose possible interference in a domestic squabble cost him, and perhaps Nicole, their lives.

Unlike Cowlings, Allen had no lifelong bond with O. J. Marcus was more the young protégé whose own rise as a sports star was as dramatic as Simpson's was. Throughout a lengthy and celebrated career, which had begun as a schoolboy all-star in San Diego, Allen had exhibited the same cool demeanor and powerful legs that catapulted O. J. to success. He, too, was a Heisman Trophy winner, and his credits matched, if not surpassed, those of Simpson. He had been an NFL Rookie of the Year, All-Pro and Super Bowl MVP. It was only natural, given Allen's credentials, that the older Simpson should offer a hand up to Allen and that Allen would pay homage to this older superstar. That he, too, had married a beautiful blonde was just one of the many things that bore comparison.

Allen and O. J. played tennis together, traveled, golfed, shot baskets, visited nightclubs, and attended intimate dinner parties. They also became partners in a thoroughbred racehorse, which they named "Reiterate." Allen had come up with the name after a speaking engagement he and O. J. had attended together. Talking with a group of youngsters, O. J. had reportedly gotten hung up on the word *reiterate*, using it a number of times in a speech to a group who Allen felt were too young to understand its meaning. Afterward, Allen had kidded him and it had become a standing joke between them.

Exactly how close Marcus Allen and Nicole were to one another was a matter of speculation. According to Allen, he didn't so much as flirt with Nicole, let alone entertain the notion of carrying on an affair with her. In deference to O. J., Nicole was strictly off limits. This was not, however, the opinion of O. J.'s niece Terry Baker, A. C. Cowlings, and Nicole's best friend, Faye Resnick. According to Resnick, the handsome, debonair, eloquent, and articulate Allen "put the moves" on Nicole every time O. J. left the room, and it was for him, Resnick suspected, that Nicole had lit the candles found burning in her condo on the night of the murders.

In Resnick's tell-all book about Nicole, *Nicole Brown Simpson*, she described the "need" Nicole had for someone like Allen after her separation from O. J. The white men whom Nicole had been dating just couldn't give her the quantity and quality of the sex that she had become accustomed to. Not only was O. J. reported to be a literal "sex-machine," but also to be exceptionally well-hung. According to Resnick, O. J.'s only real competitor in the field was Allen, a man who was alleged to be so well-endowed that Nicole compared him to a huge piece of driftwood she found on the beach. Resnick claimed that all she had to do to get a rise out of Nicole was to say the word "drift-wood."

Though Allen vehemently denied Resnick's claim that the two were any more than just friends, O. J. himself told police Nicole had confessed to having a relationship with Allen. That was why police suspected it was Allen whom neighbor Tom Lange saw outside Nicole's apartment on the evening the murders took place. The LAPD apparently also suspected that Allen's presence that night may have been what set O. J. off into the blind rage that resulted in the murders.

The only problem with this scenario was that Marcus Allen, like Cowlings, reportedly had an airtight alibi. At 10 PM on the night of the murders, Allen and his wife Kathryn were boarding a plane at LAX, en route to the Cayman Islands, where Allen and a few other high-profile players were filming a show to be called *The NFL Super Bowl of Marlin Fishing*.

Ron Shipp, a former member of the LAPD and a frequent visitor to Rockingham, was also added to my list of suspects. Though he didn't have the same close and trusted relationship with O. J. as did Cowlings and Allen, nor would O. J. be likely to have covered up for him, Shipp had access to and from the Rockingham house, had a history of alcoholism, and perhaps most important, had the requisite skills and opportunity to frame O. J. for the murders. Shipp and O. J. could have had a serious falling out that resulted in a vendetta, which in turn resulted in Shipp committing the murders and directing the blame to O. J.

It was not difficult to compile a background report on Shipp. He had been with the LAPD for fifteen years, during which time he worked seven years in a patrol car, and then as an undercover operator before becoming an instructor at the LAPD Police Academy. His special training, coincidentally, was domestic violence, a subject he lectured on at the police academy. Like O. J., Shipp was vilified in the black community for abandoning his African American roots by marrying a white girl and moving to a predominantly white upscale neighborhood, Santa Clarita, which is just north of Los Angeles. Shipp's tenure at the LAPD was cut short when he took an early retirement due to "job-related" stress and unspecified incidents related to alcoholism. After leaving the LAPD he worked briefly as an actor in a movie produced by one of O. J.'s friends, tried unsuccessfully to start his own security company, and then took a position in an L.A. property management company.

There was no record of when he and O. J. first met, though they had known one another since O. J. moved to Rockingham, some two decades before the murders. It is entirely likely that Shipp was dispatched to the Rockingham house on a routine call, and struck up a friendship with O. J. Later, when O. J.'s marriage to Nicole was on the rocks, Shipp referred Simpson to a Santa Monica psychologist, Dr. Burton Kittay, whom Shipp himself had seen during his rocky last months at the LAPD, and whom both Nicole and O. J. eventually also began seeing.

It was clear from the dynamics of their relationship that both O. J. and Shipp stood to gain something by knowing one another. O. J. routinely autographed footballs for Shipp to give to his friends and permitted Shipp and his friends to come to Rockingham to play tennis, swim in the pool, or use the Jacuzzi. In return, Shipp did favors for O. J., everything from being the security guard at O. J.'s parties to running license numbers for him through the LAPD computer, before he retired from duty. According to the source I talked to, the reason O. J. had wanted Shipp to run computer searches was quite benign: O. J. would spot a pretty girl driving in a fancy car and then use Shipp to obtain an address on her. Shipp may also have covered up for O. J. with the LAPD, since Shipp was said to have been one of the police officers who was called to Rockingham during an alleged January 1989 incident of domestic violence.

That the relationship of O. J. and Shipp had taken a turn for the worse in the months leading up to the murders was well documented. The reason is easy to understand. O. J. had little real need of him once Shipp left the LAPD, for he no longer had access to their computer system nor could he help O. J. steer clear of trouble.

Immediately prior to the murders, O. J. reportedly had gotten annoyed at Shipp for arriving at Rockingham unannounced, hopping the Ashford gate, and then freely using the pool and Jacuzzi. The last time Shipp was known to have done this was on or around June 5, just one week before the murders. Shipp allegedly woke O. J. up from a deep sleep and requested that he open the gate for him so Shipp and his blond-haired neighbor, Lisa Madigan, with whom Shipp was attending acting school, could use the Jacuzzi. He also asked that O. J. furnish them with a bottle of wine and urged him to "play" with them. He described Madigan as a "blond Nicole type," whom O. J. would "like," and perhaps should "check out" for a part in his next movie. O. J. let Shipp and his date into Rockingham that night, gave them the wine, but went back to sleep.

Having been with the LAPD, and having known O. J. for as long as he did, Shipp was indeed capable of framing him. He could have stolen a pair of Bruno Magli shoes from among the forty or more pairs in O. J.'s closet. He also could have taken the Isotoner gloves. Further, he could conceivably have obtained a sample of O. J.'s blood and would have known how to plant this forensic evidence at the Rockingham house and at the crime scene without raising the suspicion that a conspiracy existed to frame O. J. There was still, however, the problem of motive and alibi. No matter how annoyed O. J. might have been with him, no matter how seriously Shipp may or may not have had a vendetta against him, Shipp was never part of "O. J.'s family" in the way that Cowlings and Allen were, and thus didn't have much to gain or to lose by committing the murders. He may indeed have been upset by his deteriorating relationship with O. J., but it taxes the imagination to think he would have gone to such lengths to "get back" at him. And according to a source, Shipp, like Cowlings and Allen, had an airtight alibi: he was at home with his wife Nina and their sons on the night of the murders. This, to my mind, ruled Shipp out as a serious suspect.

In studying Shipp, I became further convinced that the killer was someone close enough to the family to have access to both Bundy Drive and Rockingham, and at the same time, had some special or "visceral" connection to Nicole. Indeed, even Mark Fuhrman had been rumored to have disliked O. J., but he had no access to Simpson's house until the night of the murders. My study of the crime scene indicated that the acts of violence on Bundy Drive were directed at Nicole, not Goldman. And though some of the evidence suggested premeditation, the murders themselves were clearly committed in a wild and uncontrollable rage, suggesting that the killer had a secret passion, obsession, or unrequited love for Nicole.

5

DELVING DEEPER

MADE NOTES TO double-check Marcus Allen's, A. C. Cowlings's and Ron Shipp's alibis, and then directed my attention to the more recent friends of Nicole and O. J., who, I believed, could have also played an important behind-the-scenes role in the murder story. Unlike Cowlings, they had no long-term commitment to the couple but arrived at a particularly vulnerable period in O. J.'s and Nicole's life together, when O. J. had become despondent about his relationship with Nicole and when she had entered life in the Brentwood fast lane. Foremost among these recent arrivals was Kato Kaelin.

Though I couldn't imagine what possible motive Kaelin might have to commit the murders and doubted that he was even capable of such a brutal and overt act of violence, he couldn't be ruled out as a potential conspirator in a murder plot since he was in such close proximity to everyone involved. Kaelin had once been a friend and housemate of Nicole's on Gretna Green, before he moved into O. J.'s house on Rockingham, where he was living rent-free at the time of the murders. That made him privy to family secrets. He was also the closest O. J. had to an alibi, or lack of one. And considering that his statements to police about something hitting the outside wall of the Rockingham guesthouse led Mark Fuhrman to discover the bloody glove, Kaelin unwittingly contributed more than anyone else to providing evidence that put O. J. behind bars. There had also been a rumor, which had long circulated around Hollywood, that Kato had omitted an important feature from his testimony regarding the night of the murders. According to the rumors, which were circulated on the Internet, Kato had seen O. J. Simpson, stripped naked, standing behind his guesthouse shortly before Simpson was scheduled to leave for Chicago. "If you ever tell anyone about this, I will have you killed," Simpson reportedly told him.

Most television and press reporters portrayed Kaelin as little more than a self-serving groupie of the rich and famous, a deadbeat dad, loafer, and bleached-blond gadfly who walked the dogs, turned on the sprinklers, and cleaned the pool for O. J. There was, we discovered, a certain amount of truth to this. He did many of these things, first for Nicole, and then for O. J. The rest of his story, however, got lost in the shuffle.

Thirty-six-year-old Brian Gerard Kaelin, "Kato," was seldom unemployed. My research revealed that Kaelin had worked hard since dropping out of college to pursue an acting career in Hollywood. He had been a singing waiter, deliveryman, cable television talk-show host, stand-up comedian, and an automobile pitchman. Along the way he had married a waitress at one of the restaurants where he worked, fathered a daughter, and gotten divorced. And yet, throughout all his ups and downs and his unsuccessful attempts to break into the movie business, he kept his $300-a-month child support payments current and seldom missed a scheduled visit with his daughter, Tiffany, who lived with her mother and stepfather in Riverside, California. There was also nothing in his past to suggest emotional instability or criminal behavior. It was just the opposite. He appeared to be quite responsible and kept to a strict dietary and exercise regime that included running an hour each day. He was also anti-drugs, which was one of the reasons that Nicole and O. J. came to trust him with their children.

Kaelin first met Nicole at a Christmas party in Aspen, Colorado, in 1992. By this time, Nicole had been separated and divorced from O. J. for almost a year and was in the process—her friends said—of building a new life for herself without the "The Juice." That next January, when Kaelin was in Los Angeles trying to set up a temp agency for movie and television extras, Nicole invited him to a party at her house on Gretna Green. They got to talking and he asked her about the vacant guesthouse at the rear of the property. Nicole agreed to rent it to him for $500 a month on the condition that he would be available to babysit and do other odd chores, payment for which he could deduct from his rent.

This was no "free ride," as the tabloids characterized the relationship that developed. Kaelin paid his way, and Nicole increasingly relied on him to watch the children and take care of the house while she began dating other men and living the life of a single woman. The arrangement worked out especially well for Sydney and Justin, who greatly enjoyed playing games with Kaelin and eventually came to think of him as part of the family.

A year later, in January 1994, when Nicole moved to the Bundy Drive condo, there was no separate guesthouse and she invited Kato to live in the house with her. He could stay in the spare bedroom adjacent to the garage, pay the same rent, and continue babysitting and doing odd jobs for her. Although it was clear that the relationship between Kato and Nicole was strictly platonic, O. J. objected to Nicole living with a man other than himself and during their brief reconciliation, did all he could to run other men out of her life. Perhaps as a means of keeping Kato "in the family" for the sake of Sydney and Justin, or possibly just to prevent him from moving into the Bundy Drive condo, O. J. offered Kato free housing in one of his guesthouses in exchange for being the caretaker at Rockingham and occasionally babysitting the children. Much to Nicole's disappointment, Kato moved in with O. J. that same day. Nicole justifiably felt betrayed, for up until this point, he had been *her* friend, and she didn't want Kato reporting her activities to O. J.

The question I had to ask myself was whether or not Kaelin would betray Nicole by covering up for O. J., or conversely, becoming part of some conspiracy to plant evidence that would convict O. J. There was no good reason to think he had done either. Kaelin testified at length, during which he didn't appear to either embellish or under-play the incidents he had personally witnessed, and everything he described would be later verified. Nor did he appear to have fueled O. J.'s temper in regard to Nicole.

The LAPD, like the press, seemed to ignore the fact that on the night of the murders, Kaelin had urged O. J. to get on with his life and had provided him with telephone numbers for people he thought O. J. ought to date, among them, *Playboy* "Playmate of the Month" Traci Adell and another *Playboy* bunny, Gretchen Stockdale. Kaelin's testimony to police about the timing of personal telephone calls he made to friends that night and his own activities, were also corrobo-rated by Allan Park, the limousine driver, and O. J. himself. I also knew that Kaelin had demonstrated both compassion and good faith in the months after the murders. At a time when Faye Resnick—whom Nicole and O. J. did not trust with their children—was giving interviews and writing a tell-all book, Kaelin was turning down numerous opportunities to cash in on his story. To my mind, this was decidedly not the behavior of a man who selfishly acted only in his own interests or had deep secrets to hide. He appeared to be truly sorry about what had happened and what was happening to the people he cared for.

As for the rumor about Kato covering for O. J., which circulated on the Internet, there seemed to be no credible reason to believe it. No one had actually come forward to corroborate the story, and it just didn't seem in character for Kato not to have told the truth about what had happened that night.

Faye Resnick, Nicole's best friend and another suspect on my list, demonstrated no such character or good faith. Though she too had an airtight alibi and I couldn't imagine that she was capable of com-mitting the murders any more than Kaelin, I couldn't dismiss her as a possible conspirator because there were so many unanswered ques-tions about her and Nicole's activities prior to the murders. Her tes-timony to the police about her last telephone call to Nicole—just minutes before the murders—did not stand up under scrutiny. And perhaps most significant, to my mind, was Resnick's history of drug abuse and the potential she had for drawing Nicole into a drug-related intrigue, which could have resulted in the Bundy Drive murders.

Like Kaelin, Resnick was a recent arrival in Nicole's life. They first met in the spring of 1990 through a mutual friend, Kris Jenner, who was, at the time, in the midst of divorcing Robert Kardashian, O. J.'s longtime friend. However, it wasn't until 1992, when Nicole had separated from O. J., that their acquaintance developed into a friendship. By that time Nicole was living on her own at Gretna Green, and Faye, herself three times divorced, was engaged to a fourth man, Christian Reichardt, a respected Los Angeles chiropractor.

Exactly what Nicole and Faye saw in one another was not difficult to ferret out. In Faye, Nicole had access to the jet-set Brentwood lifestyle she had been denied during her marriage. Faye wasn't afraid of staying out all night, going off on wild adventures, or keeping company with the handsome "playthings" who hung out at the Starbucks on San Vicente Boulevard, partied in Aspen, or danced through the night at the Monkey Bar and other Los Angeles nightclubs. And in Nicole, Faye found a rich and beautiful companion, happy to validate and underwrite that jet-set lifestyle, and whose perfect body and celebrity status as O. J.'s ex-wife opened doors that were otherwise closed. There were trips to all the hot spots: Aspen, Las Vegas, New York, and Cabo San Lucas. And then there were the boys. After seventeen years of monogamy, Nicole, urged on by Faye, took one lover after the next, including her hairdresser, the law clerk from the firm which handled her divorce, a handsome Italian Beverly Hills waiter, the director of operations at Mezzaluna Restaurant, and also Faye herself, if Resnick's tell-all book is to be believed. If Kaelin had been a moderating force in Nicole's life, Resnick appears to have been just the opposite.

In the ten months leading up to the murders, Nicole's lifestyle had changed so dramatically that practically everyone who knew her was worried about her well-being. Kris Jenner told police that she "never knew in the morning where you'd find her." Another friend, Cora Fischman, said Nicole's life was "spinning out of control," and that Nicole and Faye were involved in three-way-sex parties. O. J. clearly knew at least some of what was going on. And according to O. J., he urged Nicole to free herself from what he saw as a circle of parasites that surrounded her and to think of her responsibilities as a mother and homemaker. "These people are losers, they'll eat you up," he allegedly warned her.

Resnick didn't deny that barhopping and visiting nightclubs played a major role in their activities together but pointed out it was not all "fun and games." According to her, she and Nicole were planning on opening their own coffee shop or restaurant, something along the lines of a Starbucks. Faye and Nicole did, in fact, look into opening a Starbucks, but when they discovered that it was not a franchise, they decided to design their own place, which they were going to call the Java Café.

Like others who delved into this aspect of Nicole's life with Faye, I couldn't help but think it was more than just coincidence that Ron Goldman, whom Nicole had met at the Starbucks on San Vicente Boulevard, shared this same dream of opening a coffee shop and restaurant. He, however, had gone so far as to have blueprints and menus drawn up. Though it was not clear whether or not all three of them would participate together in such a venture, there is no question Nicole and Goldman had discussed the possibility.

According to Faye, the coffee shop that she and Nicole planned to open would be jointly financed. Each would contribute several tens of thousands of dollars. At least that's what Faye told police. Only Faye, as it was later revealed, didn't have that kind of money. No matter what she initially told Nicole, or the police, Resnick was virtually bankrupt and in the month before the murders, had begun selling such high-ticket items as her fur coat, had defaulted on her medical insurance, and had to temporarily move in with Nicole because she apparently had no other place to live. The $12,000 a month Faye received from spousal support from her last husband and another

$1,000 a month child support she received for her daughter Francesca, were being spent before the checks arrived.

There was no question in my mind where Faye's money was going. She was freebasing cocaine. Faye didn't deny her problem, but merely said she hadn't used drugs until two weeks prior to the murder, at which point she admitted to becoming addicted to a $20-a-day habit. However, Christian Reichardt, her boyfriend, put that figure significantly higher, to the tune of $1,000 a day. And no matter how costly her habit might have become, and how long she had had it, she and her friends considered it serious enough to admit her to Exodus House, a drug rehab clinic in Marina Del Rey. Already a two-time graduate of the Betty Ford Clinic in Palm Springs, she knew the routine.

Faye and Nicole remained in communication throughout that time, and Faye was the last known person Nicole spoke with prior to her murder. Faye reported that Nicole had sounded "happy, confident, and upbeat" and that their talk had been "full of hope for the future." However, ten-year-old Sydney Simpson told police she heard her mother "fighting and crying" with "Mommy's best friend." Justin also apparently heard Mommy crying. "Mommy was crying and upset with her friend," he confided to another police officer.

If Sydney and Justin's memories were accurate, then the extent of Resnick's problems may have been considerably more serious than Resnick acknowledged and may truly have had something to do with the events on Bundy Drive that night. Faye denied such speculation as being absurd. However, Private Investigator Barry Hostetler, a member of the Simpson "Dream Team," believed that both Faye and Nicole "were over their heads with some dope dealers" and that the restaurant that Nicole, Resnick, and Goldman intended to open would also sell cocaine.

I didn't have any evidence one way or the other to support such a theory, but I knew I couldn't dismiss the notion out of hand. Drugs seemed to be entering into the Brown-Simpson and Goldman murder story at every turn. Only now there was a direct connection to Bundy

Drive through Faye, a known addict. At this point in my investigation, I didn't know who Faye's cocaine contact was.

I added another name to my ever growing list of suspects: Keith Zlomsowitch, the manager of the company that not only operated the Mezzaluna Restaurant in Brentwood, but also a restaurant by the same name in Aspen, along with the popular Los Angeles nightclub called the Monkey Bar. Zlomsowitch might have been a potential investor in Faye and Nicole's plan to open the Java Café. I couldn't dismiss this possibility because he and Nicole were known to have had an affair in April and May of 1992. And like his partners in Colorado, Zlomsowitch's business dealings, which took him to Mexico, Miami, New York, Aspen, and Los Angeles, appeared to be as suspicious as those of Joey Ippolito.

A few details of Keith Zlomsowitch's affair with Nicole Simpson became part of the public record when the prosecutors in the Simpson murder case suggested that it might have contributed to the emotional breakdown that resulted in O. J. committing the murders. They pointed to one incident in particular, when O. J., arriving unannounced at Nicole's house on Gretna Green, looked through a window into the living room and saw his ex-wife giving Zlomsowitch oral sex. According to O. J., and later corroborated by Faye Resnick and Zlomsowitch himself, O. J. rang the doorbell and then left. A few days later, O. J. visited the Mezzaluna Restaurant to talk to Zlomsowitch. He did not threaten or try to intimidate him but merely shook Zlomsowitch's hand and said that his "beef" was not with him, but rather with Nicole, for allowing them to be seen in such a compromising position, especially with the children in the house. Nothing more was said between O. J. and Zlomsowitch, and apparently that was the end of the matter.

How the prosecution and LAPD intended to use this incident to discredit the defense was a mystery to me, for to my mind, O. J. actually demonstrated remarkable restraint, as had been the conclusion of various domestic violence experts who studied the case.

The deeper I delved into Zlomsowitch, the more convinced I became there indeed was far more to the Keith Zlomsowitch story than the LAPD had yet uncovered. Computer database checks on him and his partners only confirmed these suspicions. Both he and the president of the company he worked for were foreign nationals, having only recently emigrated to the United States. And though Zlomsowitch, like his counterpart in Aspen, was known to drive a Mercedes and a Porsche, among other vehicles, and had lived in exclusive resort condominiums in Miami, Aspen, New York, and Los Angeles, he owned no property, used no credit cards, and paid for everything in cash. Equally suspicious was an undeniable pattern of violence surrounding his restaurants and those belonging to his partners and friends. The most notable example involved Brett Cantor, who ran a Hollywood nightclub called the Dragonfly.

From what Herman King was able to learn from newspaper and LAPD sources, the Dragonfly was one of the places where Ron Goldman had worked before coming to Mezzaluna's, and it may have been on Cantor's recommendation that Zlomsowitch had hired him. Ron had also gone dancing at the Dragonfly with Nicole and Faye. On July 30, less than a year before Ron and Nicole's murders, at a time when Cantor was suspected of turning state's evidence against a known drug dealer, he was slashed to death in a knife attack. The killer had approached Cantor from behind, stabbed him in the lower side of his neck and then sliced up and to the right. And, as with both Ron and Nicole, the knife used had a long blade, as experts determined from the wounds.

Another friend of Ron Goldman, and a fellow restaurant colleague, had his car torched in 1994 in Corona Del Mar, California. A third friend and former roommate was murdered in Aspen. Two other waiters at Mezzaluna have disappeared altogether.

However, like A. C. Cowlings, Marcus Allen, Kato Kaelin, and Faye Resnick, Keith Zlomsowitch had an airtight alibi. And no matter how drugs figured into the Nicole Simpson and Ron Goldman story, I felt positive the Bundy Drive murders were committed in an act of blind rage, not the cool and calculated contract killings that might have been ordered by the likes of a Joey Ippolito or a Colombian team of hit men. Except for isolated incidents—when a hired killer is dispatched to send a clear message to the friends and family of a potential witness, as was believed to have been the case with Brett Cantor—contract killers murder their victims with guns. Knives are the weapon of choice for psychotics with a blood fetish or someone who has been professionally trained to use them.

This led me to investigate two other potential participants in the murder story, Arnelle and Jason Simpson, O. J.'s children by his first marriage. Both, according to the LAPD, had airtight alibis. Both also had histories of problem behavior, access to the Bundy Drive crime scene and the Rockingham house, and a personal connection to Nicole.

6

DRIVING FORCE

INFORMANTS OFTEN TELL PRIVATE investigators things they don't
confide to police. That's because it is less likely their names will go on
the public record or that they will later be called to testify. And it was
due to such an informant, a Los Angeles limousine driver, that I began
to focus my attention on Arnelle and Jason Simpson, the least visible
members of O. J.'s family.

At this point in my investigation I had spent nearly a year running
down leads on Cowlings, Allen, Shipp, Kaelin, Resnick and Zlomsowitch and keeping careful notes on the trial, which was just getting
under way in downtown Los Angeles. Most of my team of investigators had since been reassigned to other cases pending any new devel-
opments. I, too, had to devote an increasing number of hours to other
cases in order to meet the agency's payroll and was now clearing my
calendar for the neck and back surgery I had been putting off for over
a year. I hadn't anticipated devoting any more hours to the Bundy
Drive murder case. Nor was I prepared for the new direction my
investigation would take when I accepted an invitation to fly to Los
Angeles to be a guest panelist on a nationally syndicated television talk
show in July 1995.

The subject I would have preferred to discuss on my hour-long
television appearance was O. J. Simpson and the Bundy Drive murders, but the topic I was invited to discuss that night was teenage

violence and the need for greater parental involvement. This subject I was competent to address, not only because I was raising my two children, but also because I had solved a notorious missing persons case in which the victim—a brilliant young college student—had become involved in a sinister real-life version of the popular Dungeons & Dragons game.

The fact that I didn't have a television audience with whom to share my theories on the Bundy Drive murders didn't keep me from discussing the case with whomever I came into contact, whether it was a source at the LAPD or the travel agent who booked my flight into Burbank. Thus it was only natural that I struck up a conversation with the limo driver who was taking me to the studio. In most instances, casual conversations such as these don't amount to much more than a rehashing of what has been said on the evening news or heard on the ever-present rumor mill that is a staple of the Hollywood entertainment industry. In this case, however, the driver truly did have something important to contribute to my investigation.

Like so many Los Angeles limo drivers, that friendly young man was an aspiring film producer. He was starting from the ground up, or in this case, the parking lot up. Had I been in the film business, he no doubt would have tried to pitch me a script. But since I was a private detective, he regaled me instead with his own insights into the murder trial in progress. I didn't mind, for he enjoyed talking about the case as much as I did, and he too believed there was much more to what happened on Bundy Drive than was coming out in the press or the trial.

"I know the Simpson family," he said. "At least I knew Jason, O. J.'s son by his first marriage."

He now had my full attention, for I knew little if anything about O. J.'s eldest son, or for that matter, Arnelle, Jason's older sister. I didn't know what either did for a living, whether or not they were still in school or what he and his sister's relationships were like with their mother and father.

All I knew about Arnelle and Jason was that they both had temporarily lived with Nicole and their father in the house on Rockingham

Avenue after O. J.'s divorce from their mother, Marguerite. Arnelle played a key role in the subsequent investigation because she had greeted detectives Fuhrman, Vannatter, and Lange when they arrived at Rockingham at 5 AM on June 13, 1994, from the Bundy Drive crime scene. Jason's single appearance in the media coverage of the murder case, came at the end of O. J.'s and Cowlings's much heralded "slow-motion" car chase from Orange County to Brentwood. Jason, who was a massive twenty-four-year-old, stood almost as tall as his father but weighed considerably more, had broken through the police line, vaulted over a police squad car, and sprinted across the driveway toward Cowlings's white Bronco. In the back of my memory I also had a recollection that Jason, like his father, had played football at USC.

The driver confirmed as much. "He played for at least a season or two, but he couldn't keep it together. He just wasn't the athlete his dad was. Either that or he wasn't driven to perform like O. J., nor was he any kind of student, for that matter. That's why he dropped out of school. I think the only reason they kept him on as long as they did was in deference to O. J."

The limo driver went on to describe Arnelle as an alcoholic who was suffering from deep-seated emotional problems stemming from the dysfunctional relationship between O. J. and her mother, Marguerite. According to him, Arnelle had had numerous run-ins with the law, mostly in connection with her alcohol use. However, it was Jason, according to the limo driver, who had the most psychological problems.

"He was just never right in the head. Everyone knew it. Always getting into fights or some kind of trouble. But the press never caught on because his dad kept bailing him out, keeping everything quiet. The only reason I know is because I went to USC with him."

The more he told me, the more intrigued I became. According to the driver, Jason had a drug and alcohol problem throughout his short tenure at USC and may have had related problems in high school or even earlier. Once, when Jason went on a drug binge at USC, his father showed up on campus asking all kinds of questions. O. J. had allegedly raised "Holy Hell" and demanded to know who was supplying Jason with drugs.

"I wouldn't have wanted to be in that dealer's shoes," the limo driver said.

As he continued to talk, I recalled articles I had read indicating that Jason apparently had trouble with his mother, Marguerite. The two had had such intense arguments that Jason eventually went to live with his dad and Nicole. But that hadn't worked out either, at least after Sydney was born. Nicole just didn't want Jason in the house. The apparent reason was that Jason allegedly also suffered from depression and was known to have tried to hurt himself and possibly others when under the influence of alcohol, cocaine, or other drugs.

The driver didn't know much about what had become of Jason after he left USC, but had heard that he had worked as a busboy and then as a cook. He had also heard rumors Jason had gotten into serious trouble with the police.

Minutes later we arrived at the studio. I thanked the driver, took his card, and wished him the best of luck on his future in the entertainment business. The receptionist at the studio ushered me upstairs to meet with the host of the show, then sent me to the makeup room to have my nose and forehead powdered. I can't say I remember much about doing the show except for the fact that I got to meet Jay Leno in the greenroom, and he told me he thought I would make an interesting guest on *The Tonight Show*. When the show ended, a different driver took me back to the airport, and within the hour I was on a plane for my return trip to Dallas.

As the plane lifted off the tarmac, I found myself again preoccupied with the Bundy Drive murders. Only now I was also thinking about an important point I had made during the television taping—how necessary it is for parents to be intimately involved in all aspects of their children's lives. The physical and psychological dangers facing young people are many. All too frequently problems develop, which are later complicated by drug and alcohol abuse. And if a troubled child got mixed up with those things, and if they didn't get help, problems in the home became even greater when that child became an adult and left home to fend for himself or herself.

I couldn't help but wonder whether Arnelle and Jason Simpson were such children. It certainly wouldn't have been the first time the offspring of a celebrity had gotten deeply into drugs or tried to commit suicide. Nor was it unusual for a celebrity parent—or any parent for that matter—to repeatedly try to bail their children out. I knew from personal experience that bailing children out of trouble often resulted in creating even greater problems down the line. It had apparently been more of a problem for Jason than it had been for Arnelle, and it was on him that I eventually focused my attention.

The new question in my mind was not whether or not Jason was "mixed up" enough to take his own life, but whether the child, now an adult, could have gotten "mixed up" enough to murder someone. Jason may have become infatuated with Nicole. By divorcing O. J., she was, in a sense, betraying both father *and* son. Perhaps this had triggered some kind of psychotic episode.

Had Jason been the one to kill Nicole, this might also explain O. J.'s strange behavior after the murders, and why he would be willing to put his life and career in jeopardy. O. J.—a martyr rather than a murderer? Could he have taken the rap for his son? Was this the ultimate bailout? That theory made much more sense to me than a conspiracy among drug dealers or a love triangle between retired football players and a divorced Brentwood mother.

As I gave more thought to this possibility, I went back to the night I had climbed the rear gate at Bundy Drive and imagined how the killer had confronted Nicole. I had no hard evidence to support my conclusions, but there was no doubt in my mind that Nicole had opened her door to someone she knew. Nor had she apparently been concerned for her own safety. Jason may have had something he desperately needed to tell her. Nicole may have turned her sharp tongue on Jason, as she was known to have lashed out at O. J. and others. As Faye Resnick had said, when Nic was "pissed," she was "short, cold and deadly."

I kept remembering how Jason had seemed on television the evening his father was arrested. Jason had run from the neighbor's yard and jumped onto and over one of the police cruisers parked on Rockingham. Like a football fullback breaking through a defensive line, Jason kept going. He was determined to reach his father, desperate to tell him something. I couldn't help but wonder what he so urgently needed to say to him.

In the confusion that erupted with Jason's sudden entry onto the scene, police drew their guns. They had no idea who he was or why he was there until Robert Kardashian, O. J.'s friend, shouted for them to hold their fire. "That's his son! That's Jason!" By that time, it was already too late for the police to keep Jason away from the Bronco.

Cowlings, still sitting in the front seat of the car, rolled the window down. "Get away from here!" Cowlings yelled as he pushed Jason back with his left hand. "Get the fuck out of here!"

But Jason, as large and strong as Cowlings himself, kept coming. "I just want to talk to my dad!"

Jason threw himself against the car window, where O. J. sat in the back seat holding a revolver to his head. "Dad, you can't do this," Jason pleaded. "Dad, put the gun down. You can't do this."

Before Jason even had a chance to hear his father's reply, or get a real view of him through the Bronco's dark-tinted windows, two policemen dragged him away from the car. I don't know what happened to Jason after that as television reporters were naturally focusing all of their attention on O. J. However, it was clear from the newspaper and television reports that followed O. J.'s arrest and prosecution that Jason had not been considered a suspect in the case.

Upon my return to Dallas I was already thinking that, with the enormous publicity, we might never find the real truth. I put my team of investigators back to work on the case, this time researching Jason and his sister Arnelle. Herman King was dispatched to the library to find what he could from newspaper and magazine archives, while Chris Stewart put in calls to people who may have known O. J.'s children from school. Donna Roland ran a computer search to see what background and asset information we could pull up. I took on the more delicate task of calling my associate who had contacts in the LAPD. He wasn't directly connected to the Brown-Simpson and Goldman case, but he had enough clout to call someone who was, and who could find out if Jason had been questioned in connection with their investigation, or whether or not he had ever been considered a suspect.

Herman King had no difficulty referencing Arnelle's and Jason's names in an assortment of articles and newspaper stories and magazine interviews that had been written over the past twenty or more years. The first and earliest reference was immediately prior to daughter Arnelle's birth in Los Angeles on December 4, 1968, which was coincidentally the same night that O. J. received the Heisman Trophy at the Downtown Athletic Club in New York. The expectant father was quoted as saying, "It just has to be a boy!"

Two years later, on April 21, 1970, O. J.'s "prayers" were answered with the birth of Jason. There was no evidence the proud father was on hand for Jason's birth because he was living in Buffalo, while Marguerite was living in Los Angeles in a small house off Mulholland Drive. All we were able to find out was that A. C. Cowlings was Jason's godfather.

The next reference we could find was in a lengthy article in *Sports Illustrated*, after the family had been reunited in Buffalo. The article focused almost exclusively on O. J.'s football career, but there was a brief reference to Jason having a problem at school. According to the reporter, Jason was prone to "acting up" and had once gotten into a fistfight and been punched in the face. The suggestion was that Jason was either trying to defend his father's honor and had picked the fight, or was being picked on because he was O. J.'s son.

Another article, which appeared three years later in *Parents Magazine*, suggested that O. J. was considering giving up his career with the Buffalo Bills and moving to Los Angeles so he could spend more time with Marguerite, Jason, Arnelle, and the youngest member of the family, newborn Aaren Simpson. I supposed there was at least an element of truth to such a claim because O. J.'s relationship with his wife and three children was stretched to the breaking point. The article didn't say this, but rather painted a picture of domestic bliss. However, I knew it was not true because it was less than a year later, in 1978, when Jason was eight years old, that his parents separated. They would divorce a year later, the same year when twenty-three-month-old Aaren, Jason's sister, would accidentally drown in the family swimming pool at Rockingham.

The part of the article that particularly interested me concerned Jason, who was described as one of the main reasons for O. J. giving up the life of a pro football player. Asked what his chief concerns were, O. J. had this to say: "[Jason] is sometimes headstrong and smart-alecky . . . He may think he's smarter than adults are and if a grownup says something that Jason thinks isn't too bright, even though he's not in the conversation, he'll butt in and correct the person. In school he tends to be so quick to blurt out the answers, without giving other kids a chance, that the teacher kept him close to her desk for a while to control him." Arnelle, in this same article, was characterized as being "loving and trusting."

There were fewer references to Jason and Arnelle in the years to come. The most notable was an account of the drowning of Aaren. According to family friends, O. J. was playing football in San Francisco when the toddler drowned. Arnelle and Jason were standing in the driveway at Rockingham, washing the family van. Aaren was standing beside them watching. While Marguerite was occupied paying a babysitter, Aaren wandered away from the van, opened a side door leading from the front of the house to the rear, fell into the swimming pool and drowned. A. C. Cowlings arrived on the scene and took the baby to Saint John's hospital in Santa Monica, but it was too late to save her.

Marguerite would later say that O. J. showed up in the hospital that night screaming at her, "You murdered my baby!"

That was the final straw in the marriage. As part of her settlement, Marguerite obtained custody of Arnelle and Jason, in addition to a financial settlement. O. J. got the Rockingham house, but not without a struggle. On the day he took formal possession of Rockingham, which was the same day he had the locks changed, Marguerite refused to leave the house. She allegedly threatened physical violence when he tried to remove her.

The custody arrangement was by no means amicable. O. J. tried and failed to gain custody of Jason. No mention in the court documents suggested that he demanded the same for Arnelle and, in fact, just the opposite might have been true. A letter from Marguerite's attorney to O. J.'s attorney, sent in 1980, stated: "There is a distinct favoritism shown toward Jason. This has had an effect on Arnelle which, combined with the death of her sister Aaren, has created a serious emotional problem of adjustment. Arnelle is in need of love and recognition, to the same extent as Jason. O. J. should give her such consideration."

Though O. J. did not ultimately gain custody of Jason, he—and Nicole—did "win him over" emotionally. While Arnelle experienced what some family friends described as "difficulties" with her father and Nicole and went to live with her mother, Jason felt an immediate affinity for Nicole and came to live with his father and Nicole at Rockingham. The older Jason got, the closer he and Nicole became. As Jason later told television reporter Katie Couric, "It seemed like we have a common wavelength—we liked the same songs, the same TV shows, we were friends." The same, however, was not necessarily true between Jason and his father. Though Jason apparently desired to be close to his father, O. J. allegedly had high, almost unreasonable, expectations for him, which Jason apparently did not live up to, however hard he tried.

Jason reportedly entered a variety of public and private day schools. Though by most accounts he was a sweet, likeable boy, he didn't do well enough for his father in Little League or in an early acting debut. In a commercial that one of O. J.'s friends used Jason in, he had difficulty catching a football. As another one of O. J.'s friends reported, "Jason seemed always to be floating around on the perimeter, trying to be a part of things. I think when you have a famous father you have to do one of two things: either be as good as he is or accept the fact that you're not."

Eventually Jason was transferred to Crossroads, a small private school in Santa Monica, in 1985. In the middle of that same academic year, when Jason was fourteen, he experienced what Ron Shipp described as the first serious behavioral outburst. The incident occurred when O. J., Nicole, and infant Sydney were away on vacation. Late that night, Rolf Baur, O. J.'s caretaker at Rockingham, found Jason—seemingly inebriated or high on drugs—swinging a baseball bat at the life-sized black bronze statue of his father in the garden. Rolf was seriously concerned, for one of his jobs as caretaker was to spray O. J.'s much loved statue with an oily compound used to keep it nice and shiny. Jason was discovered whacking at the statue so hard that its bolts came out and it was starting to topple off its pedestal.

"I hate my father! I hate my father! I hate my father!" Jason kept shouting as he swung the baseball bat.

Ron Shipp, called in by the caretaker, tried to calm the distraught young man. Shipp also promised not to tell O. J. what happened, although he didn't keep his word. O. J. allegedly "beat the hell out of Jason" when he found out what he had been doing.

Later that year, Jason allegedly was experimenting with drugs and had to be rushed to the hospital. This apparently was the incident that prompted O. J. to send Jason away to boarding school at the Army and Navy Academy in Carlsbad, near San Diego. The Academy had a reputation for being able to handle the "problem children" of celebrities. The strict and regimented academic and living structure of the military academy must have been good for Jason, since he remained at this school until graduation, three years later, when he distinguished himself by becoming the vice president of his class and breaking various track and field records. A call to the Army and Navy Academy confirmed as much: Jason had been a model student and twice recipient of the school's most valuable player award.

I was not able to find out much about what happened to Jason after that. The last formal education he received was at USC, where he had been enrolled for two semesters and then only part of a third, just as my Los Angeles limousine driver had said.

Our research on various computer databases helped us to fill in a few details of his life after USC. Jason had been spending his summers and school vacations at the Rockingham house during the mid-1980s. At least that was where Jason was receiving his mail up until he dropped out of USC in 1989. In the 1990s he appeared to be living on his own in a series of different apartments with a girlfriend, identified only as DeeDee.

We found at least five different addresses for Jason and Arnelle during the four years leading up to the murders. The most frequently used was an apartment on South Orange Avenue, near La Brea, where neither Jason nor Arnelle apparently had to pay any rent. This mystery was cleared up when we discovered that the building was owned by their mother, who had taken possession of it as part of the divorce settlement.

Records indicate that Jason, in the fall of 1990, was employed at the Atlas Bar and Grill for approximately seven months. After that he took a job at the Border Grill in Santa Monica, where he remained employed for three to four months before moving on to the Bravo Cucina in Santa Monica. He lasted there for about a year. In December of 1992, he took employment at the Revival Café, and then in January of 1994, at Jackson's Restaurant, on Beverly Drive. That added up to five different jobs in less than four years. By this time, he had stopped going out with DeeDee and was dating another girl, Jennifer Green, a receptionist at a Beverly Hills hair salon with whom he was going out when the murders took place.

The databases consulted also revealed an equally enlightening documentation on Jason's history. There was no way to know what bills, if any, his father and mother were paying, but they hadn't covered his telephone, utilities, or medical bills during these three years. Bill collectors and collection agents had come after him at least nine times. The amounts he owed were minor, ranging from an $87 telephone bill to a bounced check for $280. All the bills together totaled little more than $1,000. The medical bills were unusual in that they were all from a single hospital, Cedars-Sinai, which Jason appeared to have visited on numerous occasions. This could, perhaps, have been related to drug or alcohol problems, but there was no way for us to know for sure because the hospital business office would neither confirm nor deny that Jason had ever been a patient.

The last or most recent reference we found on Jason was in an article in the *Los Angeles Times* on October 11, 1994, four months after the Bundy Drive murders. According to this article, Jason had been charged in connection with a hit and run incident that occurred at 2 AM on October 9, in which he rammed the rear end of a Nissan pickup truck with the front end of his Jeep. A bystander took down his license plate number, and Jason was later charged with leaving the scene of an accident and driving with a suspended license. Here again, there was the distinct possibility drugs or alcohol might have been involved, but we couldn't know for sure because it was impossible for us to access California DMV records without going through official channels. However, the fact that his license was suspended in the first place, and he had left the scene of the accident, raised a red flag for me.

Arnelle's record, by comparison, was tame. At the time when Jason seemed to be getting in the most trouble, Arnelle had stayed in school. First she attended the University of Colorado, and then Howard University, where she eventually graduated. She had done some modeling, but her real interest seemed to be in film production. Around the time of the murders she was working as an assistant to a producer, who was reportedly pleased with her work. However, she too had apparently had alcohol problems as evidenced by at least two serious traffic violations, one of which occurred on May 7, 1994, little more than a month before the murders took place.

Studying this material, it seemed highly likely that what the limo driver had told me could be correct, and Jason, and maybe his sister too, was worth looking into. Here indeed were individuals within the family circle with a history of instability, especially Jason, witness his attack on his father's statue.

My interest was further piqued, when I read what Joseph Bosco reported in *A Problem of Evidence*:

> The day after the murders of Nicole Brown Simpson and Ronald Goldman, a real top-gun criminal-defense attorney in the African-American community, specializing in death-penalty cases, *was retained for Jason by O. J.* Carl Jones confirms without hesitation that he was retained to "protect Jason's interests in the investigation" of the double homicide [Bosco's emphasis].

Why?

To me this was a red flag. Why would O. J. Simpson hire a criminal attorney to represent Jason Simpson, who, from what we could learn, was not even a suspect at the time in the murders of Nicole Simpson and Ron Goldman?

Arnelle had been dismissed as a suspect on the night of the murders when it was confirmed she had been out with friends. Jason Simpson, or his attorney, Carl Jones, had not been questioned in connection to the Bundy Drive murders because Jason also had an airtight alibi. His employer, restaurant owner Alan Ladd Jackson, himself the son and grandson of well-known Hollywood celebrities, had allegedly told police that Jason had been employed as a chef in his Beverly Drive restaurant on the night of the murders.

"Jason couldn't have been on Bundy Drive that night because he was cooking in front of several hundred paying customers," my source said. "That's about as tight an alibi as you'll find."

7

TRIAL OF THE CENTURY

EVEN ON MY BEST behavior I am a lousy patient. I can't sit still for very long. I think best standing on both feet, pace when I'm under pressure, and use my hands when I want to get my point across. Friends and family knew this before I submitted myself for surgery. I had to understand that this was a major procedure in which they opened my throat, removed bone from my hip, and placed it in my spine through my throat. For the next six months I had to be extremely careful, with all my activities limited as I've never been before.

In retrospect, I can only say my behavior might have been much worse had I not been able to follow the Simpson murder trial on television and in the press. During my one week confined to a hospital bed, and then the three months spent recovering in my overstuffed leather recliner in my living room, I occupied the better part of each day watching television or dictating notes into a Dictaphone for later transcription by Donna Roland. I tuned in to the trial, watched previous telecasts on videotape, or poured over the commentary in the supermarket tabloids and the array of magazines and newspapers.

This is not to say, however, that I enjoyed everything I watched or read. I didn't. The inflexible and obviously biased manner in which Christopher Darden and Marcia Clark presented their case, and defense attorney Johnnie Cochran's relentless hammering away at the standard of police work, consistently raised my blood pressure. The long-winded and mind-numbing discussions of forensic and DNA evidence nearly put me to sleep. However, I was able to make at least one important observation by the conclusion of each day's testimony and had the added bonus of being able to see many of the people whom I had only read about.

Like millions of other television viewers, I became caught up in the vexing legal questions presided over by Judge Lance Ito, along with the childish melodrama of the attorney spats and the simmering juror revolts that sometimes threatened to end the trial before a verdict had been reached. That O. J. might be found guilty or acquitted was important to me. In attempting to learn the truth, I had gathered as much information about the murders as I could, or so I thought.

The LAPD and the prosecution had already leaked so much of their case to the press that I felt it was almost anticlimactic when Christopher Darden presented his opening arguments. He described how O. J. had beaten his wife, spied on her, struggled to control her, and had then been rejected by her. He told jurors about the safe deposit box in which Nicole had kept her will and a photo of herself battered at O. J.'s hand. Nicole was, Darden said, "Leaving you a road map to let you know who will eventually kill her."

I commended Darden for his use of the "road map" analogy, and half expected him to produce a graph or other visual aid to support it, but none was forthcoming. Nor would it be, for although the prosecution repeatedly claimed there existed an ever-increasing record of abuse, I knew from my own study of the case that the history of that abuse didn't necessarily reach the crescendo that a clinical psychologist would claim necessary to "light the fuse" that set O. J. off.

Also anticlimactic was the opening argument of Darden's fellow prosecutor, the cavalier Marcia Clark, who employed a series of elegantly integrated photographs, slides, and charts to make her presentation. Picking up the story on the night of the murders, Clark told jurors about the incriminating "trail of blood" leading from Bundy Drive to Rockingham. I couldn't disagree with Clark that the blood evidence pointed to the defendant's presence at the Bundy Drive crime scene. However, as I had told Chris Stewart and later visitors who stopped by to chat with me at home, the trail of blood may have put O. J. at the murder scene, but it didn't necessarily make him the murderer. Neither the prosecution nor later the defense ever appeared willing to address this.

After all the flourishes and exhortations by Darden and Clark, Johnnie Cochran Jr. made his appearance, radiating righteous indignation at the remarks previously made by the prosecution. Had there been any question what place race would play in the defense of O. J. Simpson, Cochran settled the issue almost immediately by invoking Dr. Martin Luther King and Malcolm X. This trial, Cochran said, amounted to a "search for truth," and it was just that search for truth, he claimed, that couldn't be found in the lies generated by the LAPD. "Garbage in, garbage out," he exclaimed. That phrase, along with "Something's wrong," which was later invoked by Forensic Scientist Dr. Henry Lee, became the defense mantra.

Cochran's contention, as would soon become apparent, was that Fuhrman, a racist police officer, along with his no-good buddies, had planted much of the evidence against O. J. Bungling criminologists and inept technicians had contaminated the rest. Between the frame-ups and the incompetence, all the evidence collected was garbage. This meant that all the DNA test results were garbage too.

"This case is about a rush to judgment," Cochran asserted, "an obsession to win at any cost and by any means necessary."

As the trial got under way, Darden painted a grim picture of the abuse Nicole had suffered at O. J.'s hands. I couldn't argue with the presentation or the evidence. Nicole had been battered and abused by O. J. However, none of the witnesses who took the stand could convincingly explain the fact that the LAPD had not pursued a spousal abuse case against O. J.

The truth, as soon became clear, was that the LAPD treated celebrities differently than they did the general population. As prosecution witness Ron Shipp would explain, members of the LAPD were constantly using the pool and tennis courts at Rockingham, and O. J.

routinely appeared at LAPD Christmas parties where he autographed footballs. As would also be revealed, the pistol which O. J. held to his temple during the slow-speed car chase, was actually registered to a police lieutenant at the LAPD! However satisfying this explanation might have been to the jury, it had the cumulative effect of highlighting the very same type of conspiracy Johnnie Cochran was suggesting at each turn: that the LAPD couldn't be trusted.

Denise Brown's testimony ended the domestic violence part of the prosecution's case, leaving Marcia Clark to call a series of witnesses to build the "mountain of evidence" that would implicate O. J. Cochran and the other defense attorneys didn't go on the attack until Clark called patrol officer Robert Riske, the first member of the LAPD on the crime scene.

To my mind, Riske didn't actually have much to say. He reported finding the bodies and then going into the house, where he found Sydney and Justin asleep in their upstairs bedrooms. Despite the rather innocuous nature of his testimony, Cochran ripped into Riske for ignoring ice cream melting in a Ben and Jerry's cup and for permitting the candles to continue to burn in Nicole's living room and bedroom. As a private investigator, I seriously doubted that any relevant information could have been obtained from the candles or melting ice cream, but I could see what Cochran was doing. By repeatedly emphasizing what the LAPD could have and perhaps should have done, Cochran was highlighting their deficiencies. He did so with Riske, and turned up the heat when he cross-examined Tom Lange, the co-lead detective, along with his partner, Philip Vannatter.

I was impressed by Lange, despite the hoops Cochran put him through. He was blasted for failing to promptly call in the coroner, for not having requested that a rape kit be used to determine whether or not Nicole had had sex prior to the murders, for failure to preserve blood on Nicole's back, and for also spreading a blanket taken from Nicole's house over the bodies, thus potentially contaminating the crime scene with old hairs and fibers. Under cross-examination, he was grilled about members of the crime lab who had allegedly "trampled" the crime scene, possibly obscuring footprints.

I doubt that I myself could have withstood Cochran's questioning any better than Lange. Had Mark Fuhrman, the next witness, conducted himself in such a professional manner, the LAPD might actually have been able to maintain a degree of integrity in front of the jury. This was not to be.

Fuhrman began testifying on stable ground. Tall and chiseled, with keen blue eyes and Marine Corps posture, he not only looked like a policeman out of central casting, he spoke like one. He told the jurors about his own background as a soldier in Vietnam, how he had started with the LAPD and how he had eventually been assigned to the Brentwood area. He then described being called to respond to a domestic violence call at the Rockingham house, when O. J. had allegedly shattered the window of his own Mercedes-Benz with a baseball bat.

At this point in Fuhrman's testimony, Clark apparently sought to put the jury at ease about certain "personal" and unspecified issues relating to Fuhrman by referring to "side issues" that were not directly pertinent to the case. Questioned by Clark, Fuhrman presented himself as nothing less than an earnest civil servant. Demonstrating her confidence in Fuhrman, Clark had him deny what would become a major focus during the trial: his blatant racism.

F. Lee Bailey had a field day cross-examining Fuhrman. The defense attorney questioned him on a number of issues; suggesting Fuhrman had found a second glove at Bundy Drive and secretly planted it at Rockingham, along with much, if not all, of the blood evidence. These assertions stretched the imagination. But that was exactly what Bailey aimed at doing. He was preparing Fuhrman for the moment when he asked if he had ever used the word "nigger." Like many other police officers or former police officers who were undoubtedly watching the exchange on television, I pleaded with Fuhrman to confess. "Tell the truth!" I shouted from my armchair. "Get it over with."

The fact that he didn't confess to using the word *nigger* opened him up to the attack I knew would later be a problem for him. I didn't suspect, at the time, how serious a problem it would become, but I knew trouble lay ahead. Bailey was like a snake waiting for the right moment to strike.

Marcia Clark went on to question Kato Kaelin, with whom she appeared to display great impatience, almost treating him as a hostile witness. Despite this, I believe Kaelin conducted himself well. Clark handled herself more appropriately with Allan Park, the limo driver, who told of seeing a shadowy figure resembling the defendant walk across the driveway and into the dark house at about the same time when Kaelin heard someone or something behind the Rockingham guesthouse. Park also testified to O. J.'s demand that he be the only person to handle a particular knapsack that was part of the luggage being brought to Chicago that night, and to O. J.'s curious request that the rear windows on the limousine be kept open on their drive to the airport despite the fact that the air-conditioning was on and that it was unseasonably cool outside that evening.

Cochran appeared to have no serious complaints with either Kaelin or Park, at least to the degree that he attacked virtually every witness who came next.

The forensic-evidence portion of the case began with the testimony of Dennis Fung, a soft-spoken criminologist, who, along with his junior colleague, collected evidence from both Bundy and Rockingham on the morning after the murders. Prosecutor Hank Goldberg questioned Fung without much enthusiasm or creativity. Goldberg obviously didn't know what he was up against when defense advocate Barry Scheck began his cross-examination. It proved to be an embarrassing mistake, because Scheck, the Dream Team's least known attorney, who had built his career challenging DNA evidence, came at Fung with a brilliantly researched and ultimately devastating attack. He had Fung flustered. Using both police and news media photographs of the crime scene to drive his message home, Scheck convincingly showed that Fung had neglected his duties. Fung hadn't picked up a piece of paper near Goldman's feet. Nor had he removed the envelope holding Juditha Brown's glasses until Ron Goldman's body was literally dragged over them by the coroner.

After days of questioning, Fung conceded that he hadn't changed his rubber gloves as frequently as he should have, that he may, in fact, have handled some of the evidence without gloves, that he should have taken larger samples of blood from O. J.'s Bronco, that he hadn't noticed any blood on Simpson's socks when he first picked them up at the foot of O. J.'s bed at Rockingham. To me, and apparently to the jury, Fung emerged from a heated cross-examination looking like an incompetent amateur, confirming my suspicion the LAPD hadn't done its homework.

Next was the coroner. In my opinion, prosecutor Brian Kelberg could have won an Emmy for his dramatic use of a ruler to slash the air in a demonstration of the killer's possible technique and then submitted his own neck for a graphic simulation. However, even this demonstration was no match for the research done by the defense.

Even by the prosecution's tally, the coroner's office made at least thirty errors. Nicole Simpson's stomach contents were not saved and neither victim's hands were bagged correctly to preserve evidence. Nicole Simpson's dress and panties were stored in the same envelope, violating yet another procedure. And the examiner had mislabeled or overlooked some of the wounds on both victims.

Prosecutors presented their most compelling evidence in the "trail of blood," which stretched from the bodies to the socks on O. J. Simpson's bedroom rug. The LAPD had found the black socks, which contained both Goldman's blood and that of Nicole.

Five drops of blood at the crime scene—to the left of the size 12 footprints—matched O. J.'s genetic characteristics. I couldn't help asking myself if those same genetic characteristics might match those of his son, Jason, and whether Jason, like his father, wore a size 12 shoe? I also wondered if Jason, who had lived at the house on Rockingham, might have been given the Bruno Magli shoes, and perhaps even the gloves?

Prosecutors continued to paint the trail of evidence to Nicole's back gate, where a bloodstained fingerprint, picked up three weeks after the murders, matched O. J.'s DNA. From there, prosecutors traced Simpson's blood *to* his Bronco *to* his driveway and *to* his foyer.

In the trial's most startling statistic, Robin Cotton of Cellmark Diagnostics laboratory told jurors that only one person in several billion could be a source of the blood she pegged as Nicole's. Blood with genetic markers matching Nicole and Ron Goldman turned up in O. J.'s Bronco—a bit of evidence prosecutors considered especially damning because Goldman did not know Simpson. Blood matching that of both victims appeared on the leather gloves.

FBI Special Agent Doug Deedrick followed the DNA analysis with a science lesson on hair shafts and clothing fibers. Hair resembling O. J.'s appeared in the knit cap at the crime scene and on Ron Goldman's blood-soaked shirt. A hair matching Nicole's turned up on the Rockingham Avenue glove. Mysterious blue-black cotton fibers popped up at the crime scene as well, and prosecutors hinted that they might have come from the dark sweat suit O. J. was alleged to be wearing on the night of the murders.

The prosecution, indeed, had made a strong argument.

However, I knew from personal experience as an expert witness in similar high-profile murder cases that such evidence wasn't infallible. The blood, hair and clothing fibers, like the Cellmark tests, were only as good as the integrity of the criminologists who collected the evidence, the laboratory personnel conducting the tests, and the technical advisors brought in to interpret the findings. In other words, a bank is only as safe as its employees are honest, and in the Nicole Simpson and Ron Goldman investigation, I had every reason to believe the LAPD had conducted a haphazard, hasty, and sloppy search of the crime scene. Using Nicole's own blanket from inside her house to cover her body and drawing the blanket over her could have dispersed in the air the hair and clothing fibers from O. J.'s prior visits. In one of the most dramatic criminal investigations of my own career, I had successfully proven in a Toronto courtroom, in the Dan

Beckon murder case, that so-called "tamper-proof" specimen bottles used to collect and store forensic evidence hadn't been "tamper-proof" at all. The Simpson defense, I believed, could and ultimately would attack the prosecution in much the same way.

Having presented their witnesses and the scientific evidence, the prosecution obviously believed they had proved that O. J. was at the crime scene and had the motive and opportunity to kill. Their only major blunder—except perhaps for Fuhrman—was the matter of O. J.'s gloves.

Darden had unthinkingly requested that the accused try them on. Everyone realized the blunder when they discovered the gloves wouldn't fit over O. J.'s hands. I knew, or thought I knew why. They had either shrunk or O. J. simply wasn't trying very hard to get them on his hand. In either event, this image—more than any of the others—appeared to characterize the prosecution's case against O. J. As Cochran would say, "If it doesn't fit, you must acquit!"

Cochran obviously decided to play it safe when he opened the defense's case by trotting out the greater Simpson family: daughter Arnelle, sister Carmelita, and O. J.'s mother, Eunice, but not Jason.

Why?

I naturally wondered at the time how different the presentation might have been had Jason Simpson been called to testify.

Following the Simpson family came various witnesses, all of whom testified to O. J.'s state of mind around the time of the murders. All of them naturally testified that O. J. had behaved appropriately. Clark went after them with much the same aggressiveness that Bailey had shown Fuhrman, but to little advantage. Clark just didn't have the facts to rebut them. Again, the LAPD hadn't done its homework. They had merely assumed O. J.'s guilt.

Next, Cochran began to build his argument that there simply wasn't time for O. J. to have committed the murders—at least according to the prosecution's time line. Foremost among these witnesses was Robert Heidstra, who testified to hearing a commotion in the area of Nicole Simpson's condo at around 10:40 PM, approximately a half hour after the prosecution declared that the murders had taken place, when Heidstra was walking his dogs. He heard two voices, one indistinct, and the other quite clearly shouting: "Hey, Hey, Hey!" His testimony supported three other witnesses put on the stand, who claimed they had been in the immediate vicinity earlier that night, at approximately 10:15, and hadn't heard or seen anything out of the ordinary.

The defense raised the racial flag with Dr. Michael Baden, the first witness who testified on the medical evidence. Defense attorney Robert Shapiro, the founding father of the Dream Team, brought to the predominantly black jury the fact that Dr. Baden had come of age in Harlem, and that he had served on a congressional committee formed to investigate the death of Dr. Martin Luther King. In actuality, Dr. Baden didn't have much to contribute to the case except to say that the coroner who had previously testified had employed far too much guesswork in his reconstruction of the crime.

I put much more stock in the testimony of Dr. Henry Lee, who, I believe, is arguably the foremost forensic expert in the country today. Like Dr. Baden, he too is considered an expert in his field. Under examination in the Simpson case, Lee claimed that LAPD criminologists had reached improper conclusions and had missed finding a shoe print at the crime scene that clearly could not have belonged to Simpson. In what I considered his most revealing observation, he said: "Too much blood . . . Killer would have been covered in blood." I particularly liked this statement because it coincided precisely with the conclusion I had reached.

To my surprise, Lee also made the point that the depth of the knife wounds suggested that two knives, not one, may have been used in the slayings. In other words, the knife that had been used to kill Goldman may not have been the same one used to slit Nicole's throat. This was a departure from what I had long felt to be the case, so that I later went to the trouble and expense of having two independent crime scene experts verify Lee's finding. Indeed, I was told, not one, but two knives may have been used to commit the Bundy Drive murders.

This, of course, suggested to me several possibilities. The killer had brought two knives with him, or could it have been a double-bladed knife, or two people with two different knives had committed the murders, and in a small confined area such as the ten-foot by ten-foot rectangle of concrete where the murders took place, I did not see how it was possible for four people to be engaged in a knife fight. If this had been the case, the murder scene would have been more spread out. The possibility of two knives was something the LAPD had apparently chosen to ignore in their one killer, one knife, and one suspect scenario, and was clearly also something I would have to take under careful consideration as I pursued my own investigation.

Just as Darden and Clark had been humiliated by the defense when O. J. tried and failed to put the gloves on, it was now the prosecution's turn to embarrass the defense. The opportunity occurred when Shapiro called Dr. Robert Huizenga to the stand to testify about O. J.'s inability to physically be capable of committing the murders. According to him, O. J. suffered from "a whole array of typical post-NFL injury syndromes," that included bad knees, a problem ankle, and severe arthritis. Brian Kelberg effectively cross-examined the witness, but he literally destroyed Huizenga's argument when he showed the jury a clip from an exercise video that had been shot less than a month before the murders. In the seventy-minute video clip, O. J. stretches, marches, bends his knees and does push-ups and sit-ups.

The joy the prosecution took was short-lived, for it was only a few days later when screenwriter Laura Hart McKinney was asked to testify and portions of the "Fuhrman Tapes" became public record. Though the damage to the prosecution could have been considerably worse had Judge Ito permitted the tapes to be played in their entirety, what *was* played struck an irreparable blow to Fuhrman's credibility and to that of the LAPD. Having denied ever using the racial epithet *nigger*, Fuhrman was exposed, in excerpts from his own taped interviews, deriding minorities in the crudest of terms, and bragging about beating suspects and evading discipline after engaging in conduct most unbecoming an officer. "The only good nigger is a dead nigger," Fuhrman had told Laura Hart McKinney.

To my mind, Cochran could have rested his case at that moment. He instead trooped out more witnesses to prove Fuhrman a liar, and finally, in perhaps the most curiously cinematic and colorful presentation, he invited brothers Larry and Tony "The Animal" Fiato to the stand. They came complete with earrings, dyed hair, and accents out of a Robert DeNiro movie. These two witnesses played the card that I had expected to see right from the start: They testified to detectives Lange and Vannatter's decision to leave the murder scene and go to O. J.'s house on Rockingham. They claimed Vannatter had said, "We didn't go up there with the intention of saving lives. He [O. J.] was the suspect."

Marcia Clark called LAPD officer Keith D. Bushey to the stand to refute the Fiato brothers by stating that the true reason Lange and Vannatter had gone to Rockingham was to notify O. J. of his ex-wife's death. I don't know what the jury thought about this witness, but his truth seemed clear to me. As Clark herself would later admit in her book, *Without a Doubt*, O. J. Simpson had indeed been the "sole suspect" in the Bundy Drive murders.

I didn't have to listen to the closing arguments to know the verdict. Just as I imagined, the jury, after deliberating for slightly over three hours, dismissed a case that nine prosecutors and seventy-two witnesses had taken ninety-nine days to build. Clark herself spoke in court more times than any other lawyer in the recorded history of jurisprudence. It still wasn't enough. And not because the prosecution hadn't done their best. Except for Fuhrman's lies, and LAPD's bumbling, I think they had done remarkably well. The root of their problem lay in the false assumptions that had been made before the trial had ever gotten under way.

8

THE QUEST CONTINUES

THAT NOVEMBER I HAD to bury my father. He died in my arms after a long and painful heart condition that had left him bedridden. For my family and me, his passing brought home the uncertainty of our short lives together. And though we were grateful for the many blessings his presence had brought us, his death also left a tremendous void in our lives.

I filled that void with long days at the office. Even then, with all the funeral arrangements, the huge task of putting my father's papers in order, and the greater task of catching up new business after my long absence from my investigative agency, it was a full nine months before I could again give my undivided attention back to the Brown-Simpson and Goldman murder case. It would not be until February 21, 1996, that Chris and I were able to return to Los Angeles to begin checking out our suspects' alibis. Among the many other leads we hoped to pursue, investigating Jason Simpson was foremost. Dinner for two at Jackson's Restaurant, his last known place of employment, seemed the logical place for us to start.

Chris and I had no luck meeting Jason on this, our fourth trip to Los Angeles. Upon entering Jackson's, a quiet and small, elegantly furnished restaurant on Beverly Boulevard, just east of Beverly Hills, I inquired at the reception desk if Jason was to be our chef that night. "No, he's no longer with us," came the reply. "He hasn't cooked for us for over a year."

I pressed the hostess for more information, but she didn't seem all that knowledgeable about Jason. All I could get from her was that our chef for the evening was Jason's former employer, Alan Jackson, the restaurant's owner. The hostess pointed him out in the open kitchen at the rear of the room. He was standing behind the steam table and grill, wearing a white waist-length chef's jacket.

Like Chris, I tried not to let my excitement show, for although it was clear we would not get to meet Jason, one of the most promising suspects on our list of potential killers, in front of us stood Alan Jackson, the man who had apparently provided Jason with an alibi on the night of the murders. And now that we had actually seen the restaurant where Jason was said to have been cooking for "several hundred" people on that Sunday night, I had two big reasons for wanting to question Jackson about that alibi.

The first stemmed from the fact that the sign on the front door of the restaurant clearly indicated the restaurant wasn't open on Sunday nights. There was always the possibility the hours of operation had been changed since the murders or that Jason had been cooking for a private party at the restaurant that night, but it was also possible that Alan Jackson—our chef for the evening—had lied to the LAPD, if indeed they had even spoken to him.

My other question for Jackson stemmed from the fact that this intimate dining room and bar, with its open kitchen and serving area, could not seat 200 people. I suspected this was true the moment we walked inside, but I couldn't be certain until I counted the tables while Chris and I waited to be seated. At most, Jackson's could seat seventy to eighty people, unless Jackson's had been recently renovated, or there had been some kind of special engagement taking place on the evening of the murders.

"Perhaps it's just as well Jason's not cooking tonight," I whispered to Chris after we had been seated at one of the booths at the front of the restaurant. "Alan Jackson is the person we ought to be talking to."

Moments after our arrival at the table, a pretty, young waitress wearing a black vest and white bistro-style, knee-length cotton apron took our drink order and told us the chef's specials for the evening. She handed me a wine list and on her recommendation I ordered a bottle of Merlot. I went on to order my favorite meal, a porterhouse steak medium rare, and mashed potatoes. Chris ordered grilled rack of lamb.

In an effort not to draw any undue attention to ourselves, Chris and I maintained a low profile throughout our meal. However much we would have liked to discuss Jason and his activities at the restaurant, we completely avoided the topic and instead engaged our waitress in a brief discussion about the history of the restaurant.

Jackson's, I learned, had been open for business for the past three years and catered to intimate groups of two and four, mostly people in the entertainment industry who preferred privacy and a gourmet meal over comparably priced but more crowded "see-and-be-seen" eateries, such as Le Dome or Spago. As I could see for myself, patrons had plenty of elbow room, and except for the four tables in the middle of the room, seating consisted of discreet high-backed booths. The lights were kept low and the linens, like the flowers on the bar, were a pale gold.

Having once owned my own Dallas steak house, I knew the success of an upscale restaurant like Jackson's rested almost entirely on the reputation of its chef and the personality and charm of its owners. In Jackson's case, where the head chef and the owner were one and the same, Alan Jackson was the star of the show. This was obviously the reason for the open kitchen, where patrons could watch him prepare their meals. Like Benjamin Ford, son of Harrison Ford, who was the chef and owner of a restaurant in neighboring Beverly Hills, Alan Jackson clearly had an advantage in his ability to trade on the family name. Being the grandson of actor Alan Ladd, and the son of radio talk-show host Michael Jackson, added to the charisma of the restaurant. That he knew how to cook was also in his favor, as evidenced by the excellent meals he prepared for Chris and me.

I had hoped Jackson might come to our table and introduce himself. Doing so would have been good for business and perfectly in keeping with the personal service diners received at small upscale bistro-style restaurants where dinner for two, with wine, cost in the neighborhood of $100. Jackson, however, remained in the cooking area, even after I had complimented the waiter on the fine meal.

Determined not to leave without meeting him, I briefly ducked into the men's room at the back of the restaurant, and on my way out, casually stood in front of the cooking area to watch Jackson and his prep chef preparing meals. The restaurant was not all that crowded at this point in the evening—perhaps twenty patrons altogether, many of whom had already eaten—so there was no particular urgency on the part of Jackson or his assistant.

"Dinner was superb," I told him.

Jackson, who bore a striking resemblance to his grandfather, only a bit stockier, graciously accepted the compliment. "I hope you'll come again."

"You can count on it."

In an attempt to engage Jackson in further conversation, I told him about the restaurant I had once owned in Dallas and how I had come to the inevitable conclusion that there were some businesses in which the owner or investors didn't necessarily have to be part of the daily operations, but restaurants weren't one of them. "I had to learn that the hard way," I told him.

In all honesty, I truly did learn that painful lesson. Buffalo Bill's, my Dallas steak house, had drained my entire savings before I called it quits, vowing never again to try and run two businesses at the same time, especially a restaurant. Jackson nodded in sympathetic agreement but didn't contribute to the conversation. Nor did he respond to a question I asked about Jackson's not being open on Sundays. All I could get out of him was that business was traditionally slow in all Los Angeles restaurants on Sundays. The big nights were Fridays and Saturdays.

The only thing Jackson showed any genuine interest in was cooking and meal preparation. I could plainly see that he was extremely meticulous, and like any top-notch chef, was as concerned about how his meals looked as how they tasted. Another thing I noticed was his set of knives. They appeared to be extremely sharp and came in various lengths and designs. Having spent a certain amount of time in my own restaurant, I knew that all good chefs, like mechanics, have their own set of tools. It's a badge of honor.

I asked Jackson about his knives, and whether or not they belonged to him or the restaurant.

"No, they're mine."

I resisted the urge to ask if Jason owned such a set of knives and whether or not he had them with him on the night of the murders. To my mind, that might reasonably explain how the killer, if indeed Jason Simpson was that man, might arrive at the scene of the crime with not one, but two knives. In fact, he may have had an entire set. It would also explain the choice of weapons for Jason, a chef.

Unwilling to reveal the real reason for my visit, I instead concentrated on the most important task at hand: establishing a rapport with Jackson and his staff. Perhaps on a return visit I could engage Alan or one of his staff in a more specific conversation about Jason. Better still, a peek into the reservation book at the reception desk to confirm what I already suspected to be true: that on June 12, 1994, Jackson's Restaurant didn't serve 200 people.

Learning what we did at Jackson's gave added incentive to our activities over the next three days. I sought to obtain any police files, criminal reports, or DMV records that the state of California or the city of Los Angeles might have on Jason. I knew that some records and files existed because of the hit and run accident he had been involved in. However, the challenge was obtaining them. In Texas, as in many other states, DMV and criminal reports can be accessed by anyone with a legitimate reason or a good contact at the police department, but in California, privacy laws make it difficult for anyone—even the police—to access records without a court order.

Chris and I struck out at each turn. City clerks in Newport, Redondo Beach, and Hollywood—where we knew Jason had lived—gave us the brush-off. The DMV wouldn't even talk to us. Then, on our third day of navigating our way through the top-heavy bureaucracy which Los Angeles is famous for, we went directly to the Criminal Courts Building on Temple Street in the heart of downtown Los Angeles. This building we knew to be the central clearinghouse for most, if not all, county records.

Like Chris, I was struck by the irony of coming all the way from Dallas to visit the same building where, a few months before, Judge Ito had presided over O. J.'s trial. Only we weren't pursuing O. J.'s records, but those of his son.

The records, we knew, were housed on the 17th floor. No one requested identification or authorization from us as we stepped inside the modern twenty-five-story office building, passed through the metal detectors, and then took the elevator upstairs. A minute later we arrived at room 713, which a sign over the door informed us was the Records Unit. Chris took a seat outside in the hall, while I nonchalantly approached the reception desk.

The greatest challenge, I knew, was to look like I belonged—which was one of the things Sherlock Holmes did best. This wasn't difficult for me to do because I had been around courts long enough to know what was expected in terms of posture and attitude. All I had to do was strike an arrogant pose and act as if no one else in the room mattered. This, coupled with my dark suit, diamond rings, and expensive ostrich-skin briefcase, gave me everything I needed to act the part. And no doubt this is what the clerk thought when I stood in line behind attorneys, file clerks, and assorted police detectives collecting or returning files for ongoing cases. In an effort not to draw suspicion to myself, I didn't immediately ask for Jason's records. Instead, I gave her the file number on a case being tried the next morning downstairs, which I had noted on a docket posted on the courtroom door. I jotted this case number on a request slip and passed it on to the file clerk when I reached the head of the line.

The clerk, a young Hispanic woman, took the request without looking up at me, disappeared down a hall and returned a few minutes later with a thick manila envelope, which she handed to me for review.

I thanked her, stepped away from the desk and stood for a few minutes flipping through its pages.

I then got back in line. This time, when my turn came, I casually asked if she could pull files on J. Lamar Simpson, DOB 4-21-70. I gave her Jason's social security number, which I had obtained from the computer profile my secretary, Donna Roland, had run on Jason the year before. The clerk didn't hesitate. She typed the information into the computer terminal beside her, wrote a few numbers on a request slip, and then disappeared again down the hall to the file room. A few minutes later she returned with a two-inch-thick file folder that she handed to me, just as she had done earlier. I took the file, stepped out of line and proceeded to read it. There was no mistake: the file had Jason's correct date of birth, his social security number and, among the various addresses listed inside, his father's house on Rockingham.

Jackpot! I said to myself as I read the details of Jason's first arrest. But before I had a chance to enjoy the moment, another file clerk appeared beside me. The woman carried herself with an imperious air of authority, which suggested her rank as a supervisor.

"Are you an attorney or a member of the court?" she asked sternly.

I had to reply honestly. "No I'm not."

"Then you can't read those files."

Before I could protest, she snatched the folder out of my hands, stepped back to the reception desk and handed it back to the original file clerk who had given it to me. I couldn't hear exactly what she told the clerk, but the look on the woman's face indicated she had just been severely reprimanded. The supervisor then returned to me and stated—in no uncertain terms—that only members of the court and attorneys working on a particular case had access to confidential criminal records.

I protested, declaring that I had every right to read them. "Under the Freedom of Information Act I am entitled to look at these files."

The clerk only looked at me more sternly. "You don't have any right to read these files, and you're not going to read them unless you have a court order."

I stood up to my full height and looked down at the clerk. "Listen, lady," I told her, "I certainly do have a right to read these files."

"I don't think so," she said. Then, without warning, she raised her hand and snapped her fingers to alert a security guard. He came over to our desk, asking if there was a problem.

At this point I realized I was not going to be able to bluff my way to these files, at least not on this particular day.

Frustrated, Chris and I left the building. Though we still had not accomplished our mission, we had learned one important thing. Given the thickness of the file folder, there was much more to Jason's police record than the single Hollywood hit and run. And with persistence I knew I would get it. At least I would try.

We spent the next two days running down other leads before I sent Chris back up to the Criminal Courts Building. This time he went at lunch hour, just when the stampede of civil servants were heading for the underground parking lot across the street. If we got lucky, the supervisor would be gone. And since she hadn't associated Chris with me, and we now knew the actual case numbers, Chris's request might slip through unnoticed. It was worth a try.

Chris went directly to the window, filled in the request form, and handed it to one of the file clerks. There was no sign of the supervisor. The clerk disappeared down the hall. Instead of returning with the files, she arrived back at the reception desk with the chief of security and the division head of criminal records. Chris was questioned and then threatened with arrest. Only this time, he was grilled about the reason he wanted to see the files on Jason Simpson. He admitted to the supervisor that he was a private investigator, a response that might have landed him in jail. Luckily for us, they let him go after his promise not to return.

Again frustrated, but unwilling to give up when we had come so close, I put another plan into action. This time I hired a legal research service to see if they could access the files. Their couriers were known to the file clerks and supervisors and might not be questioned the way Chris and I had been. For all the clerk at the Criminal Courts Building would know, the research service was merely collecting a copy of the reports.

In the meantime, Chris and I had one more dinner at Jackson's Restaurant, where I wanted to be seen as frequently as possible. Again, I spoke to Alan Jackson, complimenting him on the fine dinner. The next day Chris and I paid another visit to the Bundy Drive crime scene before returning to Dallas.

I was informed that the research service had acquired Jason's criminal records. Soon I received a manila envelope in the mail—the same size and weight as the folder of records I had briefly handled on my first visit to the criminal courts building.

My hands trembled with anticipation as I opened the envelope. Inside were four cases, the most recent being the hit and run violation I had read about in the *Los Angeles Times*. It was the three others I was most curious about.

The earliest record of arrest that I received was a Los Angeles driving-related incident when Jason's car had been pulled over by El Camino College campus police near Redondo Beach, where we knew he had lived at one time. On July 21, 1990, he had been charged with one misdemeanor count of driving under the influence of alcohol and drugs in a vehicle, and a second misdemeanor count of driving under the influence of alcohol of .08% or more on a highway. Jason was scheduled for arraignment on August 15, and appeared without counsel. The arraignment was then rescheduled for August 16, and Jason's counsel, Charles English, appeared in court requesting a continuance, but Jason was not present. A continuance was granted for August 30, in which Jason and English appeared and entered a not guilty plea, and a trial was set for October 3, 1990. On October 3, Jason's attorney appeared in court again without Jason and requested another continuance. The continuance being granted until October 10, at which time Jason and his attorney appeared in court. Jason waived his rights to trial by court and trial by jury and entered a plea of guilty. At the conclusion, Jason was put on summary probation for forty-eight months and received restricted driving privileges for 365 days, limited to driving to and from work, during work, and to and from the required alcohol education program. In addition, Jason was required by law to receive treatment for ninety days, fined $1,015.50, required not to drive a motor vehicle without a valid California driver's license, not to operate a motor vehicle with any measurable amount of alcohol in his blood system, not to refuse to take a chemical/breath test when requested by a peace officer, and to obey all laws and orders of the court. A blood alcohol deposition, of which he was convicted, showed Jason's alcohol level registered .12 percent. Legally, he was blind drunk at the time of the arrest.

A follow-up court date was set for February 7, 1991 to show progress reports from his psychologist Dr. Burton Kittay for twenty-five sessions at his own expense as well as two IBARS to be performed. On that date, Jason presented his progress report from Dr. Burton Kittay but asked for an extension for the two IBARS. Jason was also required to pay fines totaling $1,047.50 on February 7, 1991. Apparently other fines had accrued.

Jason's second arrest had occurred on May 26, 1992, when he was again stopped for a traffic violation. This time there was no evidence he was driving under the influence. He pleaded guilty to driving with a suspended license and failure to keep a current registration card in his vehicle. Jason had warrants out twice on this case and put up bail on July 30, 1992, for $958.00 and on March 5, 1993, for $1,098.00, for not appearing in court, twice. The final case action summary showed he was fined $448.00.

The records of Jason's third arrest consisted of more pages than any of the other three put together. A warrant had been issued on January 7, 1993, over an incident that occurred on December 6, 1992, which, I knew, was after Jason had left USC. According to the charges brought against him, Jason—then working at the Revival Café—had attacked Paul Goldberg, the restaurant's owner and manager. Like the other three cases in the file, the report contained actual police records on the case, along with all the records pertaining to the documentation and disposition of the charges. The reports were enough to leave me speechless.

B2   TUESDAY, OCTOBER 11, 1994   ★

Metropolitan Digest

LOS ANGELES COUNTY NEWS IN BRIEF

WEST HOLLYWOOD

Simpson's Son Questioned in Hit-Run Accident

O.J. Simpson's 24-year-old son could face misdemeanor charges for allegedly driving away from the scene of an accident in West Hollywood, a Los Angeles County sheriff's spokesman said Monday night.

The crash occurred about 2 a.m. Wednesday on Santa Monica Boulevard, Deputy Matthew Rodriguez said. Jason Simpson, who is not a licensed driver, ran his Jeep Wrangler into the rear of Olga Claveria's 1994 Nissan pickup, Rodriguez said.

"The Jeep then sped away without stopping and was pursued by a witness who wrote down its license plate number," Rodriguez said.

Deputy Rich Erickson said Simpson "met with our investigators at West Hollywood Station on Sunday, and during that discussion he admitted that he was driving the Jeep at the time the collision took place.

"What we're looking at so far are charges of hit-and-run and driving as an unlicensed driver in the state of California, both of which are misdemeanors," Erickson said.

Jason, then working as a prep chef at the Revival Café, had assaulted Paul Goldberg with a deadly weapon. There were three counts of assault and battery lodged against Jason, along with separate civil charges associated with the same incident.

On February 2, 1993, Jason pleaded not guilty, and a trial was scheduled for March. On March 19, Jason waived his right to a jury trial and pleaded no contest to a reduced charge of "disturbing the peace."

There was no way to know from the record what had caused the charges to be reduced, but the logical assumption was Paul Goldberg hadn't appeared in court or wasn't willing to press his rights in the civil or the criminal case. However, the court thought the incident serious enough to issue a judgment that Jason must stay away from Paul Goldberg and the Revival Café and that he not annoy, harass, or molest any person or witness involved in the case. He was sentenced to ten days community service and put on twenty-four months' probation.

I could only read between the lines, but the evidence seemed clear. Jason had attacked his boss with a kitchen knife, the kind a prep chef might use to carve meat or cut vegetables. Even though the charges had been dropped, the fact remained that at the time the Bundy Drive murders took place, twenty-four-year-old Jason Lamar Simpson was on probation for assault with a deadly weapon.

```
            IN THE MUNICIPAL COURT OF L.A. - HOLLYWOOD JUDICIAL DISTRICT,
                 COUNTY OF LOS ANGELES, STATE OF CALIFORNIA
    23H00132                                      PAGE NO.  1
THE PEOPLE OF THE STATE OF CALIFORNIA    VS.      CURRENT DATE 02/24/97
DEFENDANT 01:  JASON SIMPSON

             DOB    DLN     VIN
AW ENFORCEMENT AGENCY EFFECTING ARREST: LAPO - HOLLYWOOD AREA

BAIL: APPEARANCE   AMOUNT      DATE     RECEIPT OR  SURETY COMPANY    REGISTER
      DATE         OF BAIL     POSTED   BOND NO.                      NUMBER

CASE FILED ON 01/14/93.
COMPLAINT FILED, DECLARED OR SWORN TO CHARGING DEFENDANT WITH HAVING
COMMITTED, ON OR ABOUT 12/06/92 IN THE COUNTY OF LOS ANGELES, THE FOLLOWING
OFFENSE(S) OF:
    COUNT 01: 245(A)(1) PC MISD - ASSAULT W DEADLY WEAPON/INSTR.
    COUNT 02: 242-243(D) PC MISD - BATTERY ON A PERSON W/INJURY
    COUNT 03: 242 PC MISD - BATTERY.
NEXT SCHEDULED EVENT:
    02/02/93    900 AM  ARRAIGNMENT   DIST L.A. - HOLLYWOOD DIV  077

ON 02/02/93 AT  900 AM  IN L.A. - HOLLYWOOD DIV  077

  CASE CALLED FOR ARRAIGNMENT
PARTIES: COMR ROBERT SANDOVAL (JUDGE)  DAVID YAGUCHI  (CLERK)
         RICHARD W. MATZKUS  (REP)     PAM DOUGLAS  (CA)
DEFENDANT PRESENT, AND REPRESENTED BY REBECCA KATZ WHITE
DEFENDANT ADVISED OF THE FOLLOWING RIGHTS VIA AUDIO CASSETTE:
DEFENDANT ARRAIGNED AND ADVISED OF THE FOLLOWING RIGHTS AT MASS
  ADVISEMENT:  SPEEDY PUBLIC TRIAL, TRIAL WITHIN 30/45 DAYS, RIGHT
  TO REMAIN SILENT, SUBPOENA POWER OF COURT, CONFRONTATION AND
  CROSS EXAMINATION, JURY TRIAL, COURT TRIAL, RIGHT TO ATTORNEY,
  SELF REPRESENTATION, REASONABLE BAIL, CITIZENSHIP, EFFECT OF
  PRIORS, PLEAS AVAILABLE PROBATION.
A COPY OF THE COMPLAINT AND THE ARREST REPORT GIVEN TO DEFENDANTS COUNSEL.
DEFENDANT DEMANDS COUNSEL.
COURT REFERS DEFENDANT TO THE PUBLIC DEFENDER.
PUBLIC DEFENDER APPOINTED.  REBECCA KATZ WHITE
DEFENDANT WAIVES FURTHER ARRAIGNMENT.
DEFENDANT PLEADS NOT GUILTY TO COUNT 01, 245(A)(1) PC - ASSAULT W DEADLY

  WEAPON/INSTR.
DEFENDANT PLEADS NOT GUILTY TO COUNT 02, 242-243(D) PC - BATTERY ON A PERSON
  W/INJURY.
DEFENDANT PLEADS NOT GUILTY TO COUNT 03, 242 PC - BATTERY.
DEFENDANT RELEASED ON OWN RECOGNIZANCE
NEXT SCHEDULED EVENT:
    03/16/93    900 AM  JURY TRIAL   DIST L.A. - HOLLYWOOD DIV  077

ON 03/16/93 AT  900 AM  IN L.A. - HOLLYWOOD DIV  077

  CASE CALLED FOR JURY TRIAL
PARTIES: COMR ROBERT SANDOVAL (JUDGE)  DAVID YAGUCHI  (CLERK)
         JULIE WELCH  (REP)     MARK LAMBERT  (CA)
DEFENDANT PRESENT, AND WAS REPRESENTED BY REBECCA KATZ WHITE DEPUTY PUBLIC
  DEFENDER
DEFENDANT RELEASED ON OWN RECOGNIZANCE
NEXT SCHEDULED EVENT:
```

101

9

ANTICIPATING ANSWERS

DRUG AND ALCOHOL ABUSE are rarely the root cause of dysfunctional behavior in young people but rather a symptom of mental illness or unresolved childhood emotional problems. I had suspected this to be the case with Jason back when I had spoken to the Los Angeles limo driver who had known him at college. Having now read Jason's police records, I felt certain that mental illness or some deep-seated emotional problems had contributed to his checkered employment history, his hit and run traffic accident, and his felony arrest for attacking his employer with a kitchen knife. I could also imagine how such an illness, or the irrational behavior that resulted from it, might have played a central role in Jason's activities on the night of the murders.

Eager to prove my theory one way or the other, I reviewed my investigative files for potential sources of medical information or psychiatric records on Jason. The name that appeared in my files with the most frequency was Dr. Burton Kittay, Jason's psychologist, whom he had begun to see following his first drunk-driving arrest. I could only assume, however, that because of doctor and patient confidentiality agreements, Kittay would be no more forthcoming about his patient's personal life than would Carl Jones, Jason's Pasadena attorney. There was also one other medical-related reference in my investigative files. Jason had been a patient at Cedars-Sinai Medical Center, in Los

Angeles. I knew this to be true because hospital collection agents had hounded him for three years for overdue bills. This information could prove to be an important part of my investigation into the murders of Nicole Simpson and Ron Goldman.

I was now faced with the more formidable challenge of obtaining Jason's medical information. Hospitals are notoriously careful about releasing any information at all, let alone medical records for a patient who is the offspring of a major celebrity.

I dispatched Herman King, one of my assistants, to Los Angeles to give me a rundown on the layout of Cedars-Sinai Medical Center as well as what might be available under the Freedom of Information Act.

Herman had only been in Los Angeles for a few days when he called me with a brief update. Cedars-Sinai Medical Center, he reported, was a huge complex consisting of ten or more buildings covering three square city blocks between 3rd Street and Beverly Boulevard, near the huge blue glass building called the Pacific Design Center. All hospital medical records were centrally located in the archives on the plaza level of the South Tower of the main building.

"There are ways to obtain the records that you want," Herman told me, "but it's going to be expensive. I know you like to do things by the book, but in this instance I don't think you're going to have any alternative."

He could tell I was reluctant.

""Look," he said, "I have a lot of contacts in Los Angeles. Give me a week and let me put the word out as to how important it is to obtain these documents and where I'll be staying. You never know, something might just come up."

Ten days later, disappointed, Herman returned to Dallas. It was now time for me to return to Los Angeles. I had made arrangements to keep the same room Herman had been in, just in case.

My plan was actually quite simple and perfectly in keeping with how Sherlock Holmes might have tackled the challenge. I would let the staff of Cedars-Sinai assume that I was a doctor, and when the timing was right, request the records department to make me a copy of the files. At least this way, no matter what happened, only *I* would be responsible. The system had left me with no choice. I was investigating two unsolved murders and I needed this information.

A white jacket, along with a metal clipboard, notepad, and a bouquet of red roses that I would pick up in Los Angeles, were all the props I thought I would need. The rest I would improvise as I went along.

Thus began what became a two-week undercover operation. For legal and security reasons, no one at the office knew where I was staying in Los Angeles or the details of my trip. Nor did anyone at the hospital know what I was up to. At least I *hoped* no one did. I wanted to appear to be merely one of the many hundreds of physicians, medical practitioners, and researchers who casually passed through the Cedars-Sinai lobby on any given day, without actually identifying myself as such.

Each morning I carefully dressed in my white jacket, took my clipboard, and punctually made my rounds up and down the halls on the plaza level of the South Tower. I greeted the security officers at the desk with a smile, bought coffee for the nurses at the commissary and, most importantly, smiled at the file clerks who came and left from the records department. That no one stopped to question me gave me growing confidence to finally walk into the records room carrying my bouquet of flowers.

I flashed the clerk at the desk a wide smile as I held the flowers up for her to see. "These are for you," I announced. I leaned forward and read her name tag and handed the flowers to her.

"They're for you, Maria," I said. "I want you to have them. You're the backbone of this hospital. If anyone deserves flowers it's you."

Maria [not her real name], a young woman in her early thirties, looked surprised at first and then returned my smile. Obviously pleased, she took the flowers from my outstretched hands.

"Thank you . . . Doctor," she said as our eyes met. "It's so very nice to be appreciated for a change."

I was elated by her response, for it didn't seem to bother her that I had no security identification tag clipped to my pocket.

Now that my initial gambit had worked and I had her undivided attention, I played my second card. "If you ever need a job, I could use a good record keeper like you in my office," I said. "Good people are hard to find these days."

"I'm very happy here, Doctor," she said, blushing.

I had to keep reminding myself *Do not identify yourself as a doctor.* Over the many years of being an investigator, I had to learn to portray many parts, some of which saved my life and solved a number of murder cases. But in this case I had to continue to remember *I am not a doctor!* If they wanted to assume otherwise that would be to my benefit.

That was my first appearance in the records department. Perhaps I was being overly cautious, but I knew I had to do everything I could to make the clerks comfortable with my presence.

From then on it was easy to breeze in just to say "Hi" and smile.

But it wasn't until three days later, when no records had shown up at my hotel, that I felt I was being left with no alternative.

I had begun to feel confident enough to approach Maria with my request for Jason's files. The flowers I had given her were prominently displayed in a vase on the table. I took it as a good omen. She looked up and smiled when I approached her desk.

"I need a copy of all the records you have on a patient, J. Lamar Simpson," I said with a smile.

She hesitated and then asked how soon I would need them.

"I'm in no rush," I replied. "Just get to it when you have the time."

Maria seemed pleased and not the least bit suspicious. "I could have the files copied by tomorrow morning," she said.

"That would be great, thank you."

I left the office, walked down the hall and out into the courtyard situated below the clerk's office window. Casually glancing back in through the enormous plate glass windows, I could see the clerks in the central records office, but Maria was busy with bookkeeping and other matters. No one appeared to be concerned or preoccupied with the request I had just made.

Late the next afternoon I came back into the same office; this time wearing a conservative business suit. I walked quickly up to the reception desk, smiling but looking hurried. To my disappointment, Maria was not there. A different woman was seated at her desk. Taken off guard, I asked if Maria was on duty. Apparently this new receptionist recognized me, though I didn't remember seeing her before.

"No, Doctor," she said. "Maria's off today."

I said thank you and quickly turned and left. I didn't want to press my luck by asking her when she would be back, or whether or not my files had been copied. I walked out of the hospital disappointed and suspicious. This new receptionist recognized me but I didn't recognize her. Already, I had begun to fear that this might be a setup.

Later that day, back in my hotel room, I decided that it would be best for me to pack my bags and leave. No papers or records had changed hands. It was best to leave well enough alone and go back to Dallas without Jason's records, no matter how important they could be. These were the thoughts that were on my mind as I fell asleep that night.

Before I knew it, I was walking back into Cedars-Sinai Hospital. Again, I was wearing my white jacket and walking through the corridor toward the medical records. Maria wasn't there—the same woman I had spoken to the day before was sitting behind the reception desk.

"Is Maria back?" I asked.

The woman shook her head, asking if she could help me.

"I'm sure you can," I said. "I requested some medical records on J. Lamar Simpson."

"Yes sir, I have them right here."

"How much do I owe you?"

"$43.20," she said. "Do you want me to bill it to your office?"

"No, I might as well pay you right now."

My heart was beating fast as I pulled out two twenties and a five, telling her I would need a receipt. She put $1.80 on the counter and started making up the receipt. "Who do I make this out to, Doctor?" I immediately came up with the name of William Eubanks. She handed me the receipt and slid over a thick manila envelope.

"Tell Maria thanks for all of her help."

"I certainly will, Dr. Eubanks."

I had to get out of there. As I was turning and starting out the door, I could see some small cubicle offices off to the left. Starting to turn right, I saw two uniformed guards standing in the cubicles, then heard a voice say, "Dr. Eubanks, wait a minute."

It was a setup. I began to panic, and heard myself shouting, "Oh My God!"

As I sat bolt upright in my bed, sweat beading my forehead, I realized this had all been just a dream.

In most cases I worked on, I was usually up against the crooked and the lawbreakers. Here I was up against the law-abiding establishment and truly frightened at the prospect of going in to get Jason's records. However, I still had a job to do. I needed to see them. I needed to know. It was not my intention to hurt him or anyone but to seek the truth. Someone killed Nicole Simpson and Ron Goldman. If it wasn't O. J., I needed to know whether Jason's records would assist me in finding the truth.

That next morning I entered the hospital, knowing for certain that I was not dreaming. It was about half an hour before the records division would change shifts and hopefully Maria would be back on duty. I went into the commissary, ordered a small breakfast, and sat down. I prayed to God the dream of the night before would remain just that. I did not want to see my thirty-five-year career end in the Los Angeles County jail, maybe in the cell next to the one O. J. had occupied.

As I walked back up to the lobby, I was beginning to feel more confident, trying hard not to let my dream influence my decision-making process. I had certainly done riskier things before. Only a few years back I had lain in between a railroad track and did what was called trestling at Michigan State University, as a train lumbered toward me. I had done it in an attempt to experience the emotions of a young man who had supposedly disappeared in the tunnels of Michigan State University while playing a game called Dungeons and Dragons. The thought of the risks I took in that investigation made me smile and I began chuckling to myself.

"Doctor . . . Doctor. . . ."

All of a sudden I heard a man's voice from behind me, "Doctor."

I stopped, and then started to turn.

My heart seemed to skip a beat. I was face to face with a uniformed security guard. Had my dream actually been a warning, a warning which I ignored?

"Doctor, Maria told me if I saw you to tell you the records are ready."

"Oh, thanks," I stammered. "Thanks. You have a nice day. Thank you, sir."

Twice in twenty-four hours was too much for me.

As I walked into the records division, there was Maria, smiling, "Doctor," she said, "your files are ready."

"That's fine," I said hurriedly. "Faster than I imagined."

I then hesitated and as I did, my cell phone rang, startling me. "Just a minute, Maria."

I opened the flap on the cell phone and the voice on the other end said, "Dad, it's Adam."

It was my son.

"How are you?" he asked.

"I'm fine, Son. I'm fine."

"I love you, Dad."

"I love you too, Adam. Can I call you back, Son?"

"Sure."

I closed the flap on my phone and realized how lucky I was. I had nearly made a serious mistake.

"Maria, I've got to run. I'll be back."

I rushed out and hurriedly walked to my car. In doing so, I pulled off the white jacket. I had nearly done something that I probably would have regretted. That phone call meant more to me than anything. It brought me back to the realization that no investigation was worth losing my sons, my freedom, and a business that I had worked at for over thirty-five years.

I kept walking, trying hard to resist the urge to run. Then, farther down the hall and still bracing myself for the moment when someone would call out my name or come rushing out of the records office shouting for security, I could see the glass doors of the exit. As I continued on, out into the late afternoon sun, I still expected I would be stopped at any minute. But no one came after me. Nor was there anyone waiting in the parking garage. I hurriedly climbed into my rented car and pulled onto San Vicente Boulevard. I checked my rearview mirror and then looked ahead. The path was still clear.

Breathing hard, my heart pounding, I moved out into traffic, again checking my rearview mirror. Now all I was thinking about was putting as much distance between me and the hospital as I possibly could. That I was soon lost in the tangle of rush-hour traffic hardly mattered to me as I headed back to the hotel.

I parked the car and entered the elevator from the basement, bypassing the front desk on the main floor. I wanted to get to my room.

As I opened the door, I felt relieved but upset because I still did not have the records I needed. I couldn't believe I was so *damn* close, yet— because of the laws— so far away, in hopefully seeking the truth. I was disappointed in myself but mostly with the system, especially the LAPD not being there to help me.

I took off my boots and lay on the bed. Suddenly there was a knock at my door. I jumped!

"Who is it?" I said.

"It's Mark, from the front desk. I have a package for you. I thought it might be important."

I opened the door.

Mark handed me a large unmarked brown package.

"Do you know where this came from?" I asked.

Mark shook his head. "I just came on duty. I asked Jimmy who worked the earlier shift if there was a card or envelope along with the package and he said no. The man who dropped it off didn't want to leave his name or number either. Jimmy said he was black, about in his late thirties, wearing a sport coat and sunglasses." Mark smiled. "We all know what kind of business you're in, Mr. Dear, so we try not to ask too many questions."

Then, and only then, did I breathe my first sigh of relief and . . . begin to smile.

As I reached into my pocket, I thanked Mark as I tipped him $5. I felt the first rush of joy and exhaustion, the kind of feeling an athlete must experience when he or she knows they have scored a major victory. Had I? I would only know once I opened this package, hoping it contained what I needed so badly in this investigation.

I locked the door behind me.

My breathing became erratic and my hands were shaking as I approached the couch. I sat down and carefully removed the brown paper wrapping on the large package.

After removing the paper, I noticed it was a white, eight-and-a-half by eleven box about the size that would hold three reams of paper. I wanted to open it without being disappointed. Working on as many murder cases as I have in the past, I have received plenty of anonymous packages. Someone would believe in what you were doing but did not want to get involved.

As I lifted the lid I found that this, again, was the case!

10

CRY FOR HELP

THE DOCUMENTS DIDN'T APPEAR to be in any particular order. I could see at first glance, however, these went well beyond what I had learned from the police records.

Jason Simpson had been a frequent visitor to Cedars-Sinai Hospital and had been treated for some form of psychiatric disorder for which he was being given Depakote, a drug frequently prescribed to prevent seizures, also prescribed for manic episodes in larger doses.

Paging through the documents I counted at least five hospital visits over a three-year period. All five had been to the emergency room. I was no physician, so I couldn't interpret all I was reading, but it seemed clear to me that at least two of his five visits were the result of suicide attempts.

Jason's first attempt had been a self-inflicted stab wound to his abdomen on March 17, 1991. This was, I knew, an extremely unusual and painful means of taking one's life. Jason's second attempt at suicide was on October 12 of that same year, when he had taken a drug overdose. I could also tell from the documents that after both of these suicide attempts the hospital recommended he undergo psychological testing and evaluation.

I turned the pages eagerly, reading and then rereading passages of Jason's background. Combined, they formed the tragic picture of a young man crying out for help.

O. J. IS INNOCENT

That Jason had' been a frequent visitor to Cedars-Sinai Medical Center came as no surprise. I just didn't know his visits had begun as early as 1984.

Fourteen-year-old Jason had been admitted to the hospital with an injury to his right hip. I could only presume, based on the few scant pages documenting this visit, that he had sustained the injury playing football. I couldn't be sure, since no history of the patient had been recorded and medical treatment apparently consisted of painkillers and a recommendation that he stay off his feet until he felt better. His father had checked him into the hospital, and his father's insurance through the Screen Actors Guild had covered the bill, which was paid in full.

Though the visit was nothing out of the ordinary—given Jason's early promise as an athlete—I did think it was interesting to note that reports of later visits to the hospital revealed that his hip injury had continued to cause him pain and that two years later, while a student at the Army and Navy Academy in Carlsbad, he would undergo surgery at a different hospital. This, presumably, could have been one of the reasons Jason ultimately gave up football for good. I also knew from the profile that Herman King and Chris Stewart had helped put together, Jason hadn't wanted to play football anyway but desired to go into an entirely different field. He wanted to become a chef. According to the Los Angeles limo driver I had spoken to, Jason had talked about opening his own restaurant as early as high school. But, instead of pursuing his dream, he had gone on to play football at USC, following in his father's footsteps.

Jason had, of course, eventually secured a job in a restaurant. That we already knew, and it was further verified by his next two visits to Cedars-Sinai, in December and January of 1989 and 1990. Twenty-year-old Jason, then working as a prep chef at the Bravo Cucina Restaurant, at 1319 3rd Street in Santa Monica, cut his right thumb on a meat slicer and had to be taken to the emergency room. The wound wasn't deep and required no stitches. A follow-up visit consisted of a checkup to see that the wound had healed properly, which it had. These visits were paid for by the Bravo Cucina's workers' compensation policy.

Jason was back in the hospital on March 18, 1991, for a far more serious injury, this time a suicide attempt. Now age twenty, Jason had walked into the emergency room assisted by his girlfriend, DeeDee, after having twice stabbed himself in the abdomen with a pair of scissors. He was treated by physicians, given a battery of physical tests, and kept overnight for observation.

According to the report of the psychiatrist who interviewed him on the night of his arrival, Jason had had an argument with his live-in girlfriend, DeeDee, whom he had been dating for approximately eight months. All Jason would initially say about the argument was that it was about "truth." Exactly what this meant was not clear, but the logical assumption, based on later statements he made to other Cedars-Sinai psychiatrists, was that one or both of them had accused the other of lying or having been deceitful. Jason apparently refused to give any more specific information, only that he and DeeDee had been drinking tequila that night, and that he "felt frustrated that she would not pay attention [to his concerns]." At this time Jason denied having any history of emotional illness or previous suicide attempts.

The attempt had actually occurred the night before, around midnight, after they had given up arguing and had gone to bed. Jason, if he slept at all, slept not more than a few minutes. When he got up out of bed, he and DeeDee began to argue again, at which point Jason impulsively grabbed a pair of scissors and stabbed himself twice in the lower right side of his abdomen. As later examination would reveal, the wounds were not deep and consequently were not considered life-threatening by the two paramedics who were called in to treat him.

It was DeeDee who had called the paramedics and who had pleaded with Jason to go to the hospital. He declined, saying he didn't want to alarm the neighbors and that he would go by himself to the hospital the next day. According to Jason, he and DeeDee reconciled their differences and went back to bed.

The next morning Jason called his father. Apparently he didn't tell O. J. what he had done, only that he and DeeDee were not getting along and he wanted to move back into Rockingham. The record did not reveal whether or not he actually did so. It was clear, however, that the wounds in his abdomen had caused him a great deal of pain later the following day, when he and DeeDee had finally gone to the emergency room.

Jason appeared not to be forthcoming about his own medical or psychological history when he was initially interviewed in the emergency room. It was not until the next day, when he was questioned by a psychiatrist and another psychologist and they asked him to voluntarily remain at Cedars-Sinai for further observation, that he admitted to having a history of psychological counseling and treatment.

He admitted that he had been attending therapy sessions once a week for the previous eight months with Dr. Burton Kittay, and that DeeDee had also been seeing Kittay at Jason's suggestion. The reason Jason gave for these visits was "problems with his relationships with his mother and girlfriend."

Further, Jason initially denied use of drugs or heavy drinking, but did confess on later questioning that he had used LSD, cocaine, and mushrooms in the past and that he sometimes had "audio hallucinations." In other words, Jason sometimes heard voices.

However, potentially the most significant revelation to my mind, and something that quite possibly had more to do with his suicide attempt than anything else, concerned Jason's confession to having undergone testing and treatment at the UCLA Neuro-Psychiatric Institute. According to Jason, he had last visited the Institute three months before. Jason told his attending Cedars-Sinai physicians that he had been diagnosed at UCLA as having juvenile mycological epilepsy, a condition for which he was being treated with Depakote, an anti-seizure medication. He was to take Depakote three times each day.

Not being a psychologist myself, I didn't know exactly what juvenile mycological epilepsy was, but after speaking to contacts I had back in Dallas, I learned it meant that Jason suffered from an occasional malfunctioning of the neurotransmitters in his brain, which could cause various degrees of impairment, anything from a brief loss of consciousness to an inability to control coordination of his arms and legs—what psychologists called "overactive psychomotor activity."

Jason had allegedly suffered from this neurological condition since childhood, though it had only been later in life that his illness had been diagnosed and treated. Unfortunately, no other information about Jason's "epileptic" condition was provided, nor was there a description of how such a "seizure" affected him.

These documents did, however, make one extremely interesting and potentially significant note in the record. They diagnosed Jason as suffering from what they described as an "unknown psychiatric illness," which manifested itself as "impulsive behavior." According to the psychiatrist who interviewed Jason, it was stated: "In the past the patient has been impulsive when he was drinking. He would punch the wall, break a glass . . ." This suggested to me that perhaps the "seizures" for which Jason was being given Depakote could be triggered by alcohol or drug use, and were not necessarily those of someone who blacked out or suffered uncontrollable spasms, as those with epilepsy are known to do. It resulted in impulsive or uncontrollable behavior—such as beating a statue of his father with a baseball bat. From what I've been able to learn, this type of rage behavior is typical of only a very small fraction of those who have epilepsy and is not at all common among the vast majority of people who have epilepsy.

Jason was strongly urged to remain at the hospital and also to attend therapy sessions at the Cedars-Sinai drug and alcohol abuse center. However, since his stomach wounds were not considered life threatening and there was no proof he would harm himself or others, he could not legally be forced to remain under their care. He asked to leave the hospital and declined to attend their recommended therapy sessions. It is no surprise that he also refused the physician's recommendation that both his parents and Nicole be notified. He told them he would tell them himself, in his own way.

Interesting to note, Jason was not released from Cedars-Sinai, at least in the formal sense. He simply walked out of the hospital on March 19 at 3 PM, before the nurse had arrived with the instructions on how to care for his wounds and a physician's formal written recommendation that he undergo psychological testing and therapy.

There was no evidence in follow-up reports that Jason had undergone any additional therapy other than his weekly appointments with Dr. Kittay. Jason's next visit to the emergency room was on October 12, 1991, seven months later, following a second suicide attempt. This time, twenty-one-year-old Jason Simpson, now unemployed and suffering from depression, had taken an overdose of Depakote.

According to the findings, Jason had begun feeling depressed over unspecified "personal problems" relating to his father. At 3 AM on the morning of October 12, after having drunk beer and tequila, he swallowed thirty tablets of Depakote, which amounted to well over ten times the recommended dose. Immediately after taking the drug, Jason had called his mother's house and left a message on her answering machine. "No matter what," Jason told her, "I really love you."

The records further described how Jason's mother, Marguerite, after hearing the message later that night, went to her son's apartment. He did not answer the door. Concerned, she had the apartment manager let her into his room, where she found him in a semiconscious state. Paramedics were called and he was taken to the hospital. Emergency room physicians induced vomiting, and he was treated with charcoal to prevent any remaining drugs in his stomach from entering his bloodstream. A few hours later, Jason was conscious, and though feeling sick, was clearly out of danger.

As in his earlier visit to the emergency room, Jason was not immediately forthcoming about the reasons for this suicide attempt. Initially, he also denied ever having attempted suicide before. Physicians either didn't believe him, or had already looked into his previous records, for this time he was legally forced to remain at the hospital for a precautionary seventy-two-hour hold. During this time, psychiatrists would evaluate his mental condition. His mother, along with his aunt, was present.

Based on Jason's statements, he had lost his job at the restaurant and was now being supported by his father, who had also given him a car to drive. It was clear that he still suffered from what he called "seizures," though he now did not specifically identify this disorder as an epileptic condition.

Upon further questioning by hospital psychiatrists and physicians, Jason had finally revealed his previous suicidal tendencies. Only this time he described yet another attempt, the previous June, for which he had been treated in another hospital.

The June suicide attempt, according to Jason, had occurred when he and DeeDee were breaking up and DeeDee was moving to New York. The record was not clear as to exactly what happened; only that he discovered that DeeDee was seeing an old boyfriend. Angry and upset, and presumably high on drugs and alcohol, Jason had punched his fist through the window of the apartment where DeeDee was living. With a shard of broken glass jutting out of the broken window, Jason had slashed his wrist. The only other details Jason gave were that he subsequently received seventeen stitches in his arm.

As he had done earlier, Jason denied having any history of emotional illness, though he was more forthcoming about family problems. He said his entire family was alcohol dependent, and his maternal aunt was a recovering alcoholic. Pressed for more details on his reason for suicide, he said it was an attempt or gesture to call attention to himself because he was unhappy about family matters and about his relationship with his ex-girlfriend. He also said he had serious and unresolved differences with his father, felt distant from him, and blamed him for many of his own problems.

O. J. was contacted by telephone in New York. A transcript of the conversation was not made, but the psychiatrist who made the call reported that O. J. admitted his son had a "chaotic past, involving unstable relationships, alcohol dependence, [and] drug use . . ." He also said that Jason "has been involved in psychotic incidents in the past."

O. J. IS INNOCENT

```
        SAINT JOHN'S HOSPITAL AND          PT:    SIMPSON, JASON
               HEALTH CENTER               MR#:   870278
            1328 - 22nd STREET             PHYS:  GERALD ROZANSKY, M.D.
     SANTA MONICA, CALIFORNIA   90404      ADMIT DATE:       10-15-91
                                           DISCHARGE DATE:   11-01-91
```

DISCHARGE SUMMARY

DISCHARGE DIAGNOSIS: Major depression, with suicide attempt; and
                     alcohol abuse.

HISTORY AND HOSPITAL COURSE: This was the first Saint John's Hospital
Mental Health unit admission for this 21-year-old man who was referred
from Cedars Hospital because he had taken an overdose of Depakote, his
anti-seizure medication, in an attempt at suicide. He stated that he
had felt in a state of despair, and felt depressed over the past year,
and had attempted suicide on two other occasions. When he gets
depressed, he may try and get drunk.

Of significance in his past history, his mother and father are divorced,
and he had a sister who died, drowning, when he, the patient, was eight
years old.

PHYSICAL EXAMINATION: Physical examination revealed seizure disorder.

LABORATORY DATA: General laboratory studies were not done, in that he
had been transferred after a work-up at Cedars of Lebanon Hospital, and
it was not felt that further testing was necessary, other than a routine
urinalysis, where urine for Depakote was found to be lower than the
therapeutic level.

HOSPITAL COURSE: Treatment consisted of individual and group
psychotherapy in the East Psychiatric Unit, and involvement in the dual
diagnosis program. He was also again placed on Valproic Acid, anti-
seizure medication. The patient progressed in the unit; and with
improved mood and open sharing with his family, he began organizing his
life so that he might go back to work and return to his apartment.
Although Recovery House was recommended, he did not feel the need for it
at this time, but recognized it as an alternative.

DISCHARGE DIAGNOSES:
1. Major depression.
2. Seizure disorder.
3. Overdose of Depakote in an attempted suicide.

DISPOSITION: The patient will continue in treatment with me, and will
have full range of activities and a regular diet.

                                   GERALD ROZANSKY, M.D.

DD: 11-21-91
DT: 11/25/91
GR/gm

                                  1   DISCHARGE SUMMARY

118

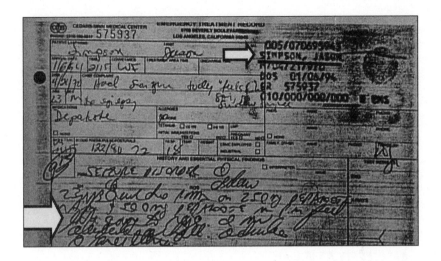

It was noted, however, that upon the request of his parents, three days after being admitted, Jason was transferred by ambulance out of Cedars-Sinai on October 15, 1991, to a mental ward at St. John's Hospital in Santa Monica.

Jason would make only a few more visits to Cedars-Sinai.

On January 20, 1993, while Jason was awaiting trial for attacking his employer with a kitchen knife, the twenty-two-year-old prep chef would arrive at the emergency room, presumably in a panic, claiming to have run out of his medication, Depakote. His prescription was refilled. As the file revealed, he was now being prescribed a much larger dose of the medication. Almost another year later, on January 6, 1994, just six months prior to the murders, Jason again ran out of his Depakote and went to the emergency room. He needed his Depakote, he told them, because he felt as if he was "going to rage."

11

COMPLETE UNDERSTANDING

JASON FELT AS IF he was "going to rage." Could that same "rage" have resulted in the brutal murders of Nicole Simpson and Ron Goldman just six months later?

Jason, I learned, had visited St. John's hospital twice. The first visit had occurred on September 27, 1984. I was shocked to learn that Jason, then age fourteen, had been brought into the emergency room having suffered what appeared to be a classic epileptic seizure. The seizure had apparently been triggered by a quantity of cocaine he had ingested while attending a party. No mention was made of where the party had taken place, only that paramedics had been called in to take him to the hospital after he blacked out. According to the report, Jason had been partying with his friends until the early hours of the morning. No mention was made of where his father was, whose "stash" Jason and his friends had gotten into, or if the "party" had been at Rockingham. All that was revealed was Jason's reaction to taking the cocaine. His arms and hands began to shake uncontrollably, and his eyes rolled back in his head. This lasted approximately three minutes. By the time paramedics arrived to take him to the hospital, he appeared to be back to normal again.

The doctors at St. John's administered a series of diagnostic tests, including a CAT scan of his skull, an EEG to measure electrical impulses in the brain, and a blood and urine analysis. One of the things physicians were apparently looking for was an aneurysm—a burst blood vessel—in the brain, or a tumor, but nothing out of the ordinary was found. Apparently it was later, at the UCLA hospital, that Jason was actually diagnosed as having epilepsy.

Jason was released into his father's care later that day, after having been in observation for approximately eight hours.

The second and final visit Jason made to St. John's, according to these records, was on October 15, 1991, when he was transferred from Cedars-Sinai. According to the records, he was checked into their psychiatric ward for observation, further testing, and therapy, and there he remained for two weeks. Treatment consisted of individual and group psychotherapy in the East Psychiatric Unit. According to his psychotherapist's report, Jason's mental condition showed "marked improvement" while at the hospital, however, it also said that "the patient should be hospitalized for further evaluation of his depression and for further evaluation of the chemical dependency."

Among the issues the psychotherapist attempted to help Jason deal with was his mother and father's divorce. Few details were given, but it was clear that Jason blamed his father for the dissolution of the marriage, and that his father wouldn't address this issue with him. There was also the suggestion he harbored some hope the problems between his mother and father could somehow be resolved, though he didn't specify how this could be accomplished.

The difficulty Jason had in speaking about these issues was immediately apparent, for the records showed he sometimes lapsed into the third person when speaking about himself, as if this part of himself was somehow disconnected from important events in his life. Reading this report, I couldn't help but be reminded of a passage in O. J.'s "suicide" letter which Robert Kardashian had read during the slow-speed car chase: "Please think of the real O. J. and not *this lost person.*"

Another deep concern of Jason's stemmed from an incident in his early childhood when Aaren, his twenty-three-month-old sister, drowned in the Rockingham pool. Eight-year-old Jason rightfully or wrongfully blamed himself for her death. This issue was apparently dealt with at length during the therapy sessions, but no details were given about what had been said or discussed. This left me to wonder whether O. J. or Marguerite had blamed Jason for Aaren's death, just as O. J. had blamed Marguerite. No matter where the blame was put, however, the incident clearly left a deep emotional scar that Jason, thirteen years later, was still trying to deal with.

Other issues Jason wrestled with over the years were his negative feelings toward women, in particular, his stepmother, Nicole, and his girlfriend, DeeDee. Again, there were few details. However, two things were clear. He had a deep love for both Nicole and DeeDee. And he also couldn't stand anyone—especially the women he loved—lying to him. No examples were noted, but it was easy to speculate that at least one, if not all three of his suicide attempts, had been triggered by his belief that he had been lied to.

In what appeared to me to be an especially curious statement, Jason said he didn't remember any painful incidents when he had been mistreated by others. Jason didn't say he "didn't like" to remember such incidents, he said he "didn't remember." This, coupled with his frequent use of the third person when referring to himself, made me wonder whether or not he suffered from a split personality, and if, indeed, he had truly blocked out unpleasant incidents, such as his suicide attempts and his irrational behavior as a child and young adult. I couldn't help but wonder what more might have occurred in his past that he hadn't remembered or was unwilling to share.

I could glean little else from these documents, except that "stress" and "being lied to" could trigger serious emotional outbursts. Being lied to angered and enraged him. It also made him feel depressed. Feeling depressed, he would begin to drink and do drugs, and that, he admitted, resulted in "impulsive behavior." Could such behavior have resulted in the murders of Nicole Simpson and Ron Goldman?

Unfortunately, St. John's physicians and psychologists apparently didn't dwell on what that impulsive behavior entailed, though frequent mention was made of his previous suicide attempts. Nor did the St. John's physicians focus on Jason's use of Depakote. This, to me, was a curious omission, given the fact that Cedars-Sinai physicians clearly believed there to be some connection between his mental disorder and his impulsive behavior. I could only surmise, based on the documents, that the St. John's physicians either didn't believe there was a connection between his "epileptic" condition and his dysfunctional behavior, or they didn't know there *was* one. In fact, from what I could see, there was no evidence in these documents to indicate whether requests for reports had been made to Dr. Kittay, to the police, or to the two other known hospitals where Jason had been a patient. I couldn't see how it was possible to treat Jason without a more comprehensive history of the patient.

As for his mental state following his last suicide attempt, the documents indicated, "He was feeling trapped in his home . . . He feels that the only time [he] is not depressed is when he is playing with his little brother and sister. It is his impression that he did not want to die in taking the overdose, but that he wanted attention." Again, a cry for help.

The report also stated: "He feels he had a problem with alcohol in particular and somewhat with drugs. He knows that it is not good for him, that he should not be drinking with the anti-seizure medication, but he realizes he is not committed to sobriety."

About himself, Jason said: "I am concerned about my parents and how I hurt them. I'm losing a relationship that is important to me."

I could only read between the lines, but it didn't take a psychologist to see that Jason was headed for disaster. From the police reports it was clear he had continued using drugs and abusing alcohol. The Cedars-Sinai visits indicated he was taking Depakote in ever-increasing doses. The records revealed Jason found no emotional help at home in dealing with his problems and was becoming disconnected, much like a psychiatric patient with a split personality. Jason apparently couldn't control the "rages" that sometimes came over him and couldn't always remember what happened when they did.

It was early in the morning when I finally finished reading the last page. I put the pages back in the box and attached the lid. I put the box on the coffee table and leaned back on the couch. I could not believe what I had just read. This was exactly what I needed!

12

"GOING TO RAGE"

I **IMMEDIATELY RETURNED TO DALLAS.** I felt it was imperative to share my findings with Dr. Harvey Davisson, a clinical psychologist and former professor at Baylor University. In turn, he shared my investigative report with another psychologist, who told Dr. Davisson, "A man like Jason is a walking time bomb."

Psychiatrists have called "intermittent rage disorder"—now referred to as "intermittent explosive disorder"—the Jekyll and Hyde syndrome. Like most people, I knew what that meant from a layman's point of view, for Hollywood had created an entire industry loosely portraying such psychiatric disorders in horrific detail, from the knife-wielding Norman Bates in Hitchcock's *Psycho* to the homicidal seductress played by Glenn Close in *Fatal Attraction*. However, it wasn't until I returned from Los Angeles, interviewed physicians, and immersed myself in the literature of impulsivity and neuroleptic drugs that I truly came to appreciate and understand the clinical reality of how a seemingly normal and healthy individual could—in a matter of minutes—become a homicidal maniac.

To properly understand Jason's medical condition, and to truly convince myself that he was indeed capable of cutting the throat of his stepmother and slashing her would-be visitor to death, I had to first understand the complex biological and environmental factors that governed his behavior. The myriad of medical journals and books I consulted went a long way toward helping me. Ultimately, it was a team of prominent doctors who specialized in rage disorders—foremost among them Dr. Jan Ford-Mustin of Austin and Dr. Christine Adams of Houston—whose books I referred to.

Dr. Harvey Davisson and Dr. Charles Keller patiently guided me through books and other research works and fielded my questions that gave credibility to my research. None of these doctors, of course, could or would presume to diagnose Jason's particular case without personally evaluating him.

The most natural place for me to begin was with the condition that Jason himself and physicians at Cedars-Sinai and St. John's hospitals had indicated was the source of "organic" malfunctions in his brain: epilepsy. As I quickly learned—and contrary to popular belief—epilepsy is not a specific disease, but a group of symptoms related to a number of different mental and physiological conditions. The one thing all of these conditions have in common is an excessive and intermittent electrical activity of the neurons in the brain. This abnormal electrical activity results in brief electrical "overloads" or discharges that are followed by sudden, recurrent changes of mental functions or movements. These changes, or "seizures," commonly include loss of memory, muscle spasms, and other involuntary movements.

Perhaps most interesting to note in the larger picture of epileptic-related conditions is the profound effect that age, environment, stress, and other contributing factors such as alcohol and drug abuse, have on the type and regularity with which a person with epilepsy experiences seizures. Also interesting to note is the fact that epileptic conditions can be degenerative and that it is not uncommon—as I believe to be the case with Jason—that a patient who is diagnosed as suffering from one kind of epileptic condition as a child manifests another condition as an adult.

Despite eighty or more years of clinical research into the various manifestations of such conditions, psychologists have never fully understood what causes the excessive electrical brain activity that is at the root of the illness, or why and how that activity manifests itself in the way it does. In some patients, genetic inheritance appears to be the important factor, while in other cases a blow to the head at an early age creates a scar on the brain which becomes a source of electrical irregularity. Alcoholism on the part of the mother during pregnancy can also be a factor. Brain tumors and strokes are clearly another possible cause, though to a lesser degree.

I could only speculate about the origins of Jason's condition. By his own admission, there was a long history of alcoholism in his family, especially on his mother's side. I couldn't help but wonder whether his father's documented abusive behavior against Nicole couldn't also have contributed to Jason's condition. Perhaps O. J.—in an explosive rage—had struck his young son in the head, just as he was believed to have hit Nicole. Ron Shipp had said that O. J. beat Jason, so this possibility couldn't be dismissed. It could also explain why right up through the time of the murders, and perhaps including the night of the murders, O. J. consistently sought to bail his son out of trouble. Could it be that O. J. ultimately blamed himself?

Regardless of what may have caused Jason's condition, there was no question that he manifested many, if not all, the classic symptoms of epileptic seizures, and that both his parents, despite what appears to have been an early denial of his condition, accepted the fact that their son had epilepsy.

This did not mean, however, that Jason was given the long-term treatment he needed. Drugs such as Dilantin, Lithium, and Tegretol, as well as Depakote—the one Jason was prescribed—only mask or lessen the symptoms of the condition, but do not cure the underlying problem. To treat the illness in the most effective way, patients must make important lifestyle changes that include a regimented diet and a stable emotional environment. While the quality of Jason's diet is not certain, the emotional environment certainly did not show any signs of stability. It is also important that anyone with epilepsy refrain from the use of alcohol and mind-altering drugs, especially those such as cocaine and LSD, which attack the central nervous system and are known to trigger seizures. Jason, by his own admission, had been abusing such drugs since the age of fourteen, when he was first taken to St. John's Hospital.

In all likelihood, Jason had suffered from some form of seizure or epileptic condition since his very early childhood. Since his condition had gone undiagnosed until his teens, it is reasonable to believe that the type of seizures he may have suffered from were what is known as "petit mal," which is short in duration, lasting only a few seconds. Patients diagnosed as suffering from this condition are known to stare blankly out into space and momentarily lose conscious awareness of what is going on around them. The activity or behavior that is in progress when a seizure begins ceases during the attack and resumes immediately when the seizure is over.

Though Jason's medical information did not indicate he suffered from this type of seizure, I could well imagine this contributing to his poor academic performance and seeming inability to concentrate or sometimes do as he was told. He was not being disobedient, but rather literally didn't hear what was being asked of him. And the more stress and discomfort he experienced from his momentary lapses of consciousness, the more frequently he may have suffered from them.

Tonic-clonic, or "grand mal" seizures, which Jason was diagnosed as having as a teenager, result in a sudden and complete loss of consciousness. The patient falls down, his or her arms and legs stiffen and then begin a rhythmic jerking. Frequently, the patient bites down on his or her tongue and his or her bowels let loose. Again, the record of what may actually have occurred in Jason's case is not clear, but it is entirely conceivable that Jason's documented use of cocaine, which predated his visit to St. John's Hospital, may actually have triggered this second and more obvious manifestation of his illness.

Jason's continued use of cocaine, along with LSD and other psychedelic drugs that affect the central nervous system, clearly contributed to his experiencing, a few years later, yet another epileptic condition: temporal lobe seizures, which are most often associated with the various Jekyll and Hyde syndromes, among them, intermittent explosive disorder (IED) and impulsive control disorder (ICD).

IRD "attacks," as they are frequently described, vary widely in their intensity and manifestation. However, one of their most common features is that patients invariably realize that a seizure is coming on. Jason experienced something known in medical terms as an "aura," which may be anything from an unpleasant smell, an abdominal sensation, a distortion in perception, or an actual hallucination. These are accompanied by uncontrolled spasms or irrational behaviors that are grossly disproportionate to any provoking events and which the patient later regrets—if indeed he or she remembers them at all. Patients suffering this disorder can be cool, calm, and collected one moment, then suddenly irrational and prone to angry outbursts the next. After an attack, the patient is momentarily confused and cannot remember details of the episode.

Not all rage disorders appear to be organically based, but an astonishing number of epileptic patients suffer from them. The one characteristic all have in common is that impulsive aggression involves a hair-trigger response to provocation, with a loss of behavioral control. The important thing to note here is that the aggression is truly impulsive, there is no planning or premeditation involved, and invariably violence is directed at a family member or someone with whom there is an intimate or close relationship. An argument or stressful event frequently triggers the attack, but that argument or event doesn't warrant or explain the degree of violence shown.

The interesting point here is the seemingly contradictory aspects of these attacks. The individual is conscious and communicative on some level and, at the same time, unable to process information in a rational manner. For example, the victim of rage attack may be in the midst of an apology, but the perceived offender processes the apology in a way that only increases his or her state of anger and decreases the power to control impulsive behavior. Another characteristic of rage attacks is that the type of physical violence displayed is unusually primitive, and that once the violent activity begins, it becomes repetitive. As many patients report, "Once it gets started, I can't stop."

Even the experts are at a loss to understand exactly what is going on during such an attack, but the accepted explanation is that the neurons in the brain undergo a sudden and powerful discharge, almost like a micro-electrical storm, that creates a kind of "noise" that breaks down or confuses the normal brain filters. Patients suffering from such an attack are often unable to prioritize and sort perceptual and sensory stimuli. Physicians believe that the patient's aggressive or violent actions, whether directed toward the self or others, are a result of this inability to sort out stimuli, and represent a patient's efforts to alleviate internal distress and to organize the experience by focusing their attention on an outwardly directed action.

The challenges facing psychologists trying to diagnose and treat patients suffering from such a condition are phenomenal—not only because the patients themselves do not necessarily remember what they have done or how they have acted, but even when they *do* have partial recollection of their actions, the line between what is real and what is imagined becomes blurred. There is also the additional problem of diagnosis stemming from the fact that CAT scans and EEGs don't always reveal the brain dysfunction unless the psychologist is lucky enough to be testing the patient when such a rage is taking place. And since many patients will only suffer an attack once or twice a year, this is rarely the case.

It is also quite apparent in these attacks that there is clearly some higher-order process of mental association going on. The patient can and does communicate and, on some level, demonstrates many attributes of someone who is aware of what they are doing. Nor is the target of their abuse random. Invariably the victim of their outbursts is a spouse, a lover, friend or parent. As one study revealed, there is something specifically about intimate relationships that generates the violence. Clearly some high-order process of mental association between the meaning of the target person to the perpetrator and the context of the violence must direct and influence the act of violence.

It is not surprising that a great many people suffering from some form of this condition are drawn to a life in the military. And this, according to at least one psychiatrist, is frequently the best place for them. The structured, drug-free environment, stable living conditions, regular meals, regimented lifestyle, and opportunity to release violent tendencies acts like a soothing force upon them. This, as I knew, was certainly the case with Jason, whose life at the Army and Navy Academy in Carlsbad represented some of the happiest, if not *the* happiest years in his life.

Jason left the structured environment at Army and Navy to attend USC in Los Angeles, where drugs and a "free" and "open" environment were the norm. It is no wonder he fell to pieces, not only gaining a disproportionate amount of weight, but also suffering from severe depression, which ultimately resulted in his three suicide attempts.

There were many other parallels I could find between Jason and particular individuals and circumstances mentioned in the articles. In fact, examples of people suffering from IRD in the textbooks and articles I read were truly startling.

There was twenty-eight-year-old "Chuck" who was serving a prison sentence for assault with a knife. At the time of the incident, he claimed to have been intoxicated with alcohol and other drugs and had no apparent memory of what had happened. "I have a blackout about it, but the guy came at me, and I just sort of tried to throw a scare into him . . . I feel real bad about it."

Like Jason's incident with Paul Goldberg, the owner of the Revival Café, Chuck's story held a special relevance, for Chuck, like Jason, had had a previous history of suicide attempts, drug and alcohol abuse, automobile-related accidents and perhaps even an attention deficit disorder as a child.

Later questioned about his strong history of violence, Chuck replied, "Well, I've always had a bad temper." He described how, when he felt himself to be in a potentially threatening situation, he would just let himself go, "all or nothing, like a hair-trigger. I would just explode, I couldn't control it." Such a statement, I knew, could easily have been made by young Jason after his teenage rampage at Rockingham with the baseball bat.

Another example given was eighteen-year-old "Robert," who had been having epileptic seizures since the age of nine. They occurred approximately twice a week, when he would suddenly hear a strange and indecipherable voice—as did Jason—followed by a ringing in the ears before losing consciousness. Observers noted a stare, drooling, stiffening, and then jerking movements.

Robert's personal history was studied. Like Jason, he came from a broken home. Also like Jason, his moods would change unpredictably on a daily basis, and he tended to be irritable, frequently raising his voice in arguments and often hitting the wall in anger. He also suffered from insomnia. And during one particular seizure, he attacked his stepmother over a trifle. She slapped him, and it triggered a violent attack. Later in life, Robert reported hearing voices telling him to kill his family, and he had actually stalked various family members with a knife. And he too, like Jason, had been suicidal.

Yet another case was that of a young man, "Chris," who committed a particularly gruesome act of violence after attending his wife's office party. About thirty people were eating and drinking and chatting at the party, when Chris's wife disappeared. He went to look for her. After ten to fifteen minutes he found her and insisted they leave the party together. He was quite angry, though he didn't express that anger to her. He believed she had been cheating on him and had gone off into a car with a man, when in reality she had been standing out on a balcony with three or four coworkers. She didn't tell him this, nor did he tell her that he suspected she cheated on him. They drove home. She went to bed. He stayed up watching television.

Chris's next memory was of seeing his wife lying in a pool of blood on the floor of their bedroom. He called her relatives and the police and when asked what had happened he said, "I must have hit her." He pleaded guilty in court, saying only that, "I must have done it."

He truly did not know what had happened. I could well imagine that this had been the case with Jason when he had punched his hand through the window, or the time he had taken a pair of scissors and stabbed himself. He too appeared to have been in a state of "dissociative" rage with enormous physical arousal. And once he returned to his "normal state," he really could not remember what had happened. The memory never registered.

Chris's wife, however, remembered clearly. "I was asleep when he grabbed me. He pulled off the covers and then yanked me out of bed by the hair. The light was on in the bedroom and I could see his face. It was terrifying." His expression was grossly distorted: His mouth was pulled down at both corners. His teeth were clenched, his jaw protruded, his nostrils flared, and his eyes "were sort of blank." He started to punch her with a closed fist, first in her stomach and side, then in her face. "He was in a completely uncontrollable rage."

There was one other example that caught my attention—that of a construction engineer. He was known to be demanding and irritable, but had no major problems with the men he worked with. Then one day he went out with his wife and some friends, casually drinking. That was the last thing he remembered before waking in the middle of the night with the house trashed and his wife gone. He had a vague sense he had caused the problem, but could not remember anything. His wife later filled in the details. He had gotten upset about the dinner being cooked in a certain way, and he had screamed at her, pushed her, and began hitting her with a frying pan. There were three other occasions when "he became someone else" and exploded. The only constant he could recall was that he had been drinking.

That Jason suffered to some degree from these problems was obvious and everywhere apparent in these documents. Prior to what he admitted to as his "attacks," he had a shortness of breath, he sometimes heard voices and then lost memory of what he did or said. He too, like almost all others who were actually diagnosed, suffered depressive moods, excessive irritability, insomnia, fear and anxiety, not to mention drug and alcohol abuse. In short, Jason was a textbook example of intermittent explosive disorder.

Now, having read this material, I felt genuine sadness for Jason. In many respects I wished I hadn't studied this subject in as much depth and detail as I had, for one can't help but feel empathy and pain for someone whose mental illness is uncontrollable. Tracking down a man who has kidnapped a child, or someone who killed their wife for an insurance claim—which I have done many times—fills the investigator with a certain desire to right a wrong, to seek justice for the sake of justice. In studying rage disorder and the things that might have led Jason to commit the murders, I was filled with no sense of justice at all. Rather, I felt sickened at the range of human illness and at the same time, compassion for Jason and a desire that he should be helped, not hunted.

13

AIRTIGHT ALIBI?

THE MATERIAL I HAD received on Jason was more than I had ever expected to find, more than anyone could have imagined existed. And yet, if he was a walking time bomb—as at least one psychologist had indicated—a lot more people than just Jason might have their lives ruined if I didn't go forward.

Night after night I woke up haunted by these thoughts. I wondered to what length O. J. may have gone to protect his son and whether or not he blamed himself for what may have happened. I tried to put myself in O. J.'s place and asked myself, as a father, whether or not I would risk making myself the number one suspect in a double murder in order to try and ensure my son's freedom. I could only wonder what might have been going through O. J.'s mind had Jason called him on the evening of June 12, 1994. Over and over I kept hearing the phone ring, wondering what my response would have been had my son called to tell me he had his stepmother's blood on his hands.

I had never been an absentee father like O. J. I did not have a deeply troubled child, as did O. J. I considered myself a devoted father. Yet it wasn't difficult for me to imagine what life had been like for Jason and his father. I could picture O. J. doing his "thing," placing himself first and his wife and family second. He was doing what he knew how to do—play football, act in movies, golf, and sit on the boards of various multinational companies. I had to believe that if

Jason Simpson was guilty, then O. J. felt responsible for not having been there for him when he was needed. The documents I read over and over indicated to me that each time Jason attempted suicide or overdosed, it was his strong cry for help and attention. O. J. was not there. That did not mean, however, that O. J. did not love Jason. Quite the contrary.

If Jason was in fact guilty, O. J.'s decision to go to the crime scene after the murders made a great deal of sense. Not only would he have been concerned for Jason, but for Nicole, Justin, and Sydney. Imagine what it would have been like for O. J. if he had arrived at the scene after the murders, bent down over Nicole's crumpled body and discovered that she really had been killed—that her head had been nearly severed from her body, and then looking up, catching sight of Goldman's lifeless stare, and realizing that he too had been murdered. In one mind-blowing moment, O. J.'s world would begin to crumble. He would look up and see that the lights were not on in Justin and Sydney's rooms, that the front door to the house appeared to be closed, and that they were, for the time being, safe.

I could only wonder how O. J. might have reacted had Sydney and Justin actually been awake and crying that night. No doubt O. J. was pulled in two different directions: a desire to ensure that his and Nicole's children were safe, and an equally strong desire to protect his firstborn son. If Jason had indeed committed the murders on Bundy Drive in an act of uncontrollable rage, I wondered if it would have been possible for O. J. to sleep through the night not knowing who might be the next target of his son's rage. Were Sydney and Justin also at risk? I had to know what happened that night and was determined to keep coming back to Los Angeles until I was satisfied I had answered the important questions.

These thoughts still haunted me on February 22, 1997, when I left Dallas for Los Angeles accompanied by Chris Stewart, Herman King, Phil Smith and Don Pennington, Phil's assistant. Phil owns Phil Smith Productions, which is a documentary film company in Irving, Texas. He was my close friend and confidant and had agreed, at short notice, to film the crime scene and other important locations connected to the murders. The idea was to build a three-dimensional record for later use, should the time come to present our evidence to a jury.

I'm glad that we took this step, for construction had already begun on Nicole's residence on Bundy Drive. The property had been sold and the new owners, understandably, were trying to reconfigure the front entrance so it would not be easily recognizable. I suspected that the Rockingham house would also soon be changing hands, and that this location, too, had to be documented before the guesthouse, tennis courts, or even the main house itself underwent major changes. After filming the two residences we went on to document Mezzaluna Restaurant and Ron Goldman's apartment on Gorham Avenue.

The next day, February 23, while filming the alley behind Bundy Drive, we observed a woman who drove a station wagon bearing California plates going through the trash bins in the alleyway behind Nicole's. I learned her name was Emma Pearson. When the owners and renters in this alley put their trash out each week, Emma and another man would root through it looking for redeemable soda cans and other small treasures they might be able to sell.

Emma told me she did this so she could donate the proceeds to her church. "You'd be surprised at what you find in these trash bins!" she said. One time she found $2,000 rolled up in a shoe and another time an expensive watch. Emma said she wasn't there for herself, but to help others. I'm not sure about the other man's intentions, but I really believed Emma.

I asked her about June 12 and she said normally she would have gone down the alley that Sunday and Monday, but it was blocked off by the police. I asked her what she would have done had she found any clothes with blood on them.

"I wouldn't want to touch them," she said, "but I can assure you that if I had found them, knowing what had happened, I would have called the police!"

I truly believe she would have and that gave me an idea. After we completed filming, I went back to our hotel. I picked up the phone and called the *National Enquirer*. I disguised my voice. "I found the bloody clothes that the murderer of Nicole and Goldman had been wearing on the night of June 12. Are you interested?" The voice on the other end of the line asked me who I was.

"Never mind," I said. "Are you or are you not interested?"

"Are you sure these are the bloody clothes?" the response came.

"Yes."

"What do you want?"

"I want half a million dollars. Are you interested?"

"Yes, if they are in fact the clothes and you can prove it."

"Would you be willing to negotiate payment through a lawyer and keep my identity secret?"

"Yes. How can we get in touch with you?"

"I'll be in touch with you," was my response.

As I was putting the receiver down, I heard him say, "Don't hang up . . ."

The call actually served an important purpose, for it demonstrated to me that even three years after the murders, these bloody clothes, if I had them for real—not that I would ever have considered selling them—were worth half a million dollars. There was still that much interest in what had taken place on Bundy Drive. Plenty of people besides me were interested in closure and in solving the murders once and for all. They too wanted the truth.

Having just called the *National Enquirer*, I then pondered how much these bloody clothes would have been worth within weeks after the murders. As Dr. Lee, the renowned forensic expert stated, the person or persons who killed Nicole and Goldman would have been covered in blood.

O. J.'s Bronco had less than a thumbnail full of blood throughout the entire vehicle. There was not a single drop of blood on the brake or accelerator, despite the pints of blood that covered the Bundy Drive walkway.

No bloody clothes were found in the alley on Bundy Drive from any of the trash bins. The plumbing pipes in O. J.'s bathroom, laundry, and shower had been cut out and examined, and no blood was found.

It was hard, if not impossible, for me to believe that less than one hour before the murders, O. J. had returned to his residence with Kato, after a trip to McDonald's to buy a hamburger, and supposedly had taken a knife and gone to Nicole's residence to carry out a premeditated murder. There was no way for O. J. to know whether or not his children would be asleep or awake or if Nicole might or might not have company. But according to the police, he had designed a premeditated murder that had to occur within a twenty-minute time span.

I had investigated many murders in my day and I knew that anything is possible. However, the one thing of which I was still convinced was that O. J. was innocent of the killings. But if O. J. didn't do it, I had to be equally certain Jason could have. To that end, I returned to Jackson's Restaurant, to make absolutely sure he indeed had no convincing alibi.

That particular night I drove along with Chris Stewart and Herman King to the restaurant on Beverly Drive, where I had made reservations under the name of William Dear. Knowing that movie actors, producers, and directors eat there frequently, I thought that the hostess might recognize my name. There is a movie director by the name of William C. Dear, spelled the same way as mine.

The hostess seated us in a booth against the far wall, which gave me a clear and unobstructed view of chef Alan Ladd Jackson in the kitchen. This is the same view that, had I been seated there on Sunday, June 12, 1994, I would have had of Jason Lamar Simpson as the chef.

I told the hostess it had been a number of years, three in fact, since I had been to Los Angeles and first dined at their restaurant. I didn't tell her about my investigation, or that I had eaten there at least three times in the last two years.

"I used to come in on Sunday nights when there was hardly anybody here. The last time was the first Sunday in June of 1994," I told her. "It was virtually empty. Mr. Jackson wasn't cooking. It was someone else."

"Yes," she responded. "Mr. Jackson didn't cook on Sunday nights. There wasn't enough business to warrant his being here. We were lucky to have twenty to thirty people on a Sunday night. In fact, we closed altogether beginning in late July or early August on Sunday nights because of lack of business."

I looked over at Chris and Herman, for this was again confirmation of what I had suspected to be true. "I think the last time I was in here, there was a young man cooking by the name of Jason," I said.

"Yes," she replied. "He was our regular sous chef and would cook on Sunday nights when Alan was off."

I asked her why business was so heavy during the week, but so sparse on Sundays.

"This is a small restaurant, we only seat about eighty-five people and most of our customers come for lunch or dinner during the week. We're busy on Fridays and Saturdays too, but never on Sundays. That's why we finally decided to close Sunday nights."

As I had previously confirmed, and now reconfirmed, there could not have been 200 people on that night of June 12. The restaurant could not hold 200 people, even if it was crammed to the rafters. Had there been, the regular chef and owner, Alan Ladd Jackson, would have been there.

I had to know who had given Jason the airtight alibi. And why? As I engaged the hostess in general conversation, she mentioned that Alan had opened another restaurant called Jackson's Farms on Beverly Drive in Beverly Hills. I could feel the blood rush to my head, for I had assumed that he had only this one restaurant.

I had to resist the temptation to come right out and ask her if Jason had been here at Jackson's on the night of June 12, 1994, or if he had been the chef at Jackson's Farms. But I was still reluctant to tip my hand at this point. I had a gut feeling that I had to be extremely careful, for whoever had given Jason an alibi for the night of the murders had their reasons. I had come too far to risk having doors close on me before I had adequately explored what lay behind them.

As I contemplated these things while silently finishing my dessert, I realized I might have made a giant blunder by presuming that Jackson's Restaurant, not Jackson's Farms Restaurant, was where Jason had been cooking on the night of the murders. The mistake would be easy enough to make. Both restaurants had "Jackson's" in their name, and both were on a street prefixed with Beverly, one on Beverly Drive and the other on Beverly Boulevard. Perhaps Jackson's Farms was a restaurant that held 200 people and they had been open on June 12, 1994.

I paid my bill trying unsuccessfully to escape the sinking feeling that I had not properly checked all the facts before concluding that Jason's alibi had holes in it. After asking for the address for Jackson's Farms in Beverly Hills, we drove directly there.

No sooner had Chris parked the car than that sinking feeling turned into a knot in my stomach. Jackson's Farm, in the heart of the Beverly Hills shopping district, with its large, yellow awning and casual indoor and outdoor dining, was considerably larger than Jackson's Restaurant on Beverly Boulevard. I had only to stand out on the street and peer inside to see the difference between them. This restaurant was large enough to seat 200 people. It also had an open kitchen at the end of the room where patrons could watch their meals being prepared. I could see from the sign on the entrance door that Jackson's Farm was open for business on Sundays.

I sent Herman in. I watched through the window as he spoke to the hostess before crossing the room to the kitchen at the far end of the restaurant. I could see him speaking with one of the prep chefs. For an instant my hopes were raised when I saw the prep chef shake his head "No" at Herman. A few minutes later Herman was back outside, confirming my worst fears.

"I told them Jason was a friend of mine from USC," Herman said "and that I was looking for him."

"And?" I asked impatiently.

"He had been a chef here, though he left to be with his father during the trial. They say they haven't seen him since, but I don't believe them."

My head was now beginning to throb. The restaurant had been open on Sundays, could seat 200 or more people, and Jason had been a chef there. Jason's alibi on the night of the murders appeared to be as solid as other investigators I had spoken to said it would be. So far everything I had done appeared to be fruitless.

"I'm going for a walk," I told Chris and Herman. "Meet you back at the hotel."

Chris and Herman respected my need for time alone and didn't try to interfere. Nor did they try to inject any levity into what appeared to be one of the worst moments in my career. I could compose the headline myself: *Bill Dear, master investigator, spends thousands of dollars and countless hours pursuing an innocent suspect.* For the first time since I could remember, my instincts and intuition as an investigator seemed to be wrong. I had, apparently, blown it big-time.

I walked the two and a half miles back to my hotel where I put myself to bed only to spend the next eight hours tossing and turning. It was at sunrise, when I was still wide awake, that I decided to go back to square one and to check the facts as I should have checked them months and years earlier.

Over breakfast, I asked Herman to see what he could find out about Alan Jackson and his partners in the two restaurants and to see if he could come up with any leads on Jason. Chris was assigned to drive to Norwalk to see if he could get a copy of the tax records on the two restaurants and to see if Jason's name appeared on any recently incorporated Los Angeles County business records. In the meantime, I was going to the Beverly Hills City Hall, to the office of the city clerk, to find out what I could about Jackson's Farm.

I already knew that city hall was located on North Rexford Drive because I had passed it on my marathon walk the night before. I went to the permit office and asked to see records for Jackson's Farm Restaurant on Beverly Drive. It didn't take the clerk but a few minutes to pull the file and for me to then scan it, my heart pounding. Alan Jackson was the principal member of a syndicate of limited partners going by the name of Big Fish Enterprises. But before going to the trouble of copying down the list of partners, I needed to look at the date when the partnership had incorporated. This date, I knew, wouldn't tell me when a chef was hired, or on what days meals were served, but it would tell me when the process to open their restaurant had begun. According to the record, the partnership had formed on February 15, 1995, eight months after the murders.

"Yes! Yes! Yes!" I shouted, while people stared. *Never assume, always verify!* I knew that. I taught that. Jason couldn't have been a chef at Jackson's Farm on the night of the murders because the restaurant hadn't yet been opened!

City hall employees must have been wondering what kind of person would make a fool of himself over the contents of business records. It wasn't until I met up with Herman and Chris later that night at Jackson's Restaurant that I would begin to come down off my high.

Chris and Herman were as eager to tell me what they had discovered as I was to tell them my news. But dinner at Jackson's was not the place or the time to discuss such matters. However, Chris and Herman could tell by my disposition that what I had found out had put us back on track, and I could tell that they also had something important to share.

Alan Jackson was back cooking behind the grill that night, and our regular hostess, the one who had helped us the night before, was greeting customers. And as before, she was happy to stop by and chat with us.

I wanted to make this meal particularly memorable, something that Alan Jackson himself wouldn't soon forget and something that would also give me an opportunity to establish a rapport with him. By the time our meals had arrived, I knew what I was going to do. A small fly, buzzing in the window behind me, had provided the inspiration. When the hostess and our waiter were well out of sight, I caught the fly in my hand in one quick movement, shook it up so that it was dazed and flung it into my mashed potatoes. A direct hit. The fly, its wings caught in the potatoes, was on its back, its legs still kicking.

Chris, who sat across from me, looked incredulous. Herman looked equally baffled, but his shock dissolved into laughter. He knew I was always up to something. He called the waitress over to our table and pointed to the fly.

"Oh my God. Oh my God!" the waitress said repeatedly.

I smiled up at her. "I like your food but I don't like it raw."

"I just don't know how that fly could have gotten in there," she said.

"It's no big deal."

The fly's little legs were still pumping when our waitress took the plate to Alan Jackson. I saw him shake his head, obviously as upset as she was. Within minutes he was at our table, offering his apologies.

"I love your restaurant and I love your cooking," I told him, shaking his hand.

"I'm glad you do," he replied. "I don't know how something like this could have happened."

"Think nothing of it," I replied.

Once our conversation had gotten started, it was easy enough to ask him about himself and how he got into the restaurant business.

"I've always liked cooking," he told us. "I suppose it's got to be that way if you're going to survive in a business like this."

I asked him about the restaurant closing on Sundays. He couldn't remember exactly when that had begun, but thought it was around July or early August, due to lack of business.

However much I wanted to ask him about the alibi that he had provided Jason, I didn't press my questioning any further. Jackson finally returned to the open kitchen after a little more chitchat and after offering us dessert—crème brulée, my favorite—on the house. At least we had established a rapport. There was no question now that he would remember me. Who could forget the fly?

On leaving the restaurant, I wondered what Jackson's motive could have been if he was the one who supplied a false alibi for Jason. Chris and Herman helped me to possibly answer that question when they provided me with the details they had turned up while I had been at the Beverly Hills City Hall.

First, they discovered that Jason was indeed still in Los Angeles. Though he continued to move from one job to another and from one apartment to another, he apparently was picking up his mail at the Rockingham house. More important to me, Jason had also given a formal deposition in Los Angeles as part of the civil trial against his father.

The civil trial actually started in September 1996 after a continuance was filed on April 2, 1996, to allow further depositions—one of which was Jason's, which was taken on May 8, 1996. The civil verdict against O. J. was rendered on February 5, 1997.

I continued my investigation all through the civil trial. I learned that, in Jason's deposition, he had gone on record about his and his father's alleged activities on the night of the murders, but this wasn't the only thing I would learn.

Chris and Herman had also found out other important details about Alan Ladd Jackson and his two restaurants. They learned that Jackson had been deep in debt at the time of the Nicole Simpson and Ron Goldman murders. In 1994 and 1995 his home had been foreclosed, and the limited partnership that owned Jackson's Restaurant had an assortment of liens filed against it by major food and restaurant supply companies, along with two IRS tax liens. The total amount owed was in excess of $150,000. And yet, a year later, the 1995 tax liens and many of the other bills were gone. In fact, he and his partners even had the money to open yet another restaurant, Jackson's Farms. There was not a clue from the records as to where the money had come from to pay off the taxes and other debts at Jackson's Restaurant.

I couldn't help but now begin to wonder about this so-called airtight alibi for Jason Simpson that had come from Jackson's Restaurant for the night of June 12. Who at Jackson's Restaurant had given Jason that desperately needed alibi?

And why?

14

WEARING BLINDERS

A DEPOSITION IS TESTIMONY GIVEN under oath that is recorded for later use in a court proceeding. Though depositions are sometimes used in criminal court actions, they are primarily the domain of civil attorneys, who are legally permitted to interview witnesses in private, without a judge or jury being present, and to later use that testimony in court as part of the civil court proceedings. The testimony is taken by a certified court reporter and then typed up in a transcript. Depositions may also be videotaped, as they were during the civil case against O. J. Simpson brought by the heirs of Nicole Simpson and Ron Goldman.

Now that I knew Jason had provided such a deposition, as had Paula Barbieri, Al Cowlings, Robert Kardashian, Allan Park, Faye Resnick, Kato Kaelin and others, I was determined to find out what he had to say, and why he hadn't become a suspect in the LAPD investigation. This was the first and only time to my knowledge that he had been questioned under oath about the case. I didn't know what he had said because attorneys had not made the depositions public. I needed a copy of Jason's deposition.

I called a former client who, I knew, frequently did courier and copy work for major Los Angeles law firms.

"I'll get right on it," he told me, obviously pleased to have an opportunity to help me. "Can't promise you the videotapes, but I can certainly deliver the deposition."

In anticipation that he would be successful, I bided my time, engrossed in some of the many books that were now coming out about the Simpson trial. It seemed everyone who had been involved in the case had a book on the subject, including Christopher Darden, Marcia Clark, Detectives Vannatter and Lange, Johnnie Cochran and even Mark Fuhrman.

I hoped that some of the missing pieces of my investigative report would be contained in the pages of Jason's deposition. At the least, I would have new leads to explore.

The process was easy this time, compared to my earlier attempts to obtain Jason's medical information. My contact called me ten days after I made the request and asked that I meet him at a small take-out restaurant on Santa Monica Boulevard, just outside of Century City.

I arrived early, before the lunch crowd poured in from Century City. There was really not much to distinguish this restaurant from any of the thousand others on the boulevard, with the exception that this one served celebrity burgers. O. J.'s "Big Mac" was noticeably missing from the menu, so I had to content myself with a "Michael Douglas" on whole wheat. I hoped that I wouldn't have long to wait, but wait I did. I had just about given up when my contact arrived, complete with a trench coat and hat. I had to fight to keep from laughing. It was clear to me that he had watched too many detective movies. He nervously fidgeted with the plain wrapped package he carried under his arm.

All of a sudden he started to laugh, "Isn't this the way the P.I.s do it?"

He declined my offer to buy him a celebrity burger, just as he declined my offer to pay him for his trouble. I took the package from him and watched as he slipped out the door, glancing to his right and left, acting as if he thought he was being followed, smiling all the while.

I returned to my hotel room, showered, poured myself a tall glass of Evian water and propped myself up in bed. I broke the seal on the envelope and began to read Jason's deposition.

That night, and in the days ahead, I poured over each of the 275 pages, knowing—as I did—that this might be as close as I, or anyone else, would ever get to hearing about the case from Jason while he was under oath. This single interview, recorded nearly two years after the murders, long after evidence may have been tampered with, covered up or destroyed, represented the first and only time that Jason had been officially questioned about the deaths of Nicole Simpson and Ron Goldman.

The police hadn't even talked to Jason! Nor had anyone from the DA's office!

Jason's deposition was held on May 8, 1996, at the law offices of Mitchell, Silberberg & Knupp, in a 10th floor conference room on Olympic Boulevard. According to the index, it had lasted approximately six hours, running from 9:45 AM, with an hour off for lunch, until 4:48 PM. Daniel Petrocelli, who represented the Goldman family, did the questioning, with a few follow-up questions by Natasha Roit, one of the attorneys for the Brown family. Jason didn't have his own attorney present, but was represented by Daniel Leonard, his father's attorney.

Petrocelli began by covering some territory already familiar to me: Jason's previous arrest records and his overdose on Depakote. It was clear to me, reading this report, that Petrocelli had done some of his homework, and though he didn't seem to know the extent of Jason's medical history or police record, he knew enough to ask about at least one of the young man's three suicide attempts.

Jason admitted to the automobile accident, but didn't characterize it as a hit and run. He also denied being under the influence of alcohol when it occurred. He said that the victim in the traffic accident had dropped the charges against him, as he also later admitted that charges against him had been dropped by Paul Goldberg, Jason's previous employer at the Revival Café. It was interesting to note that, at first, Jason did not admit to the Goldberg arrest. Petrocelli had to pointedly ask him about the incident, at which point Jason said, "I totally forgot about that . . ."

I could only wonder about this response, for attacking someone with a kitchen knife was something someone could not easily forget, unless, of course, that assault had been committed by a mentally ill patient who literally blacked out all memory of the event. To Jason, in his rational state of mind, he was completely blameless.

At this point in the deposition, Petrocelli seemed adamant about introducing testimony concerning Jason's suicide attempt, most specifically his overdose on Depakote. I could only speculate that Petrocelli was hoping to blame the attempt on Jason's father, and that this testimony might highlight further alleged evidence of O. J.'s history of abuse. Dan Leonard objected to this line of questioning on the grounds that it wasn't relevant to the proceedings in this case, and he ultimately prevailed. Jason did, however, admit to being on Depakote, which he said was being taken for epilepsy. Nothing more was said on this subject.

Besides these few exchanges, there was little in the first twenty-five pages of testimony that appeared to be particularly relevant to my own investigation or that cleared up any great mysteries concerning the civil case against O. J. Petrocelli questioned Jason at length about whom he had talked to in preparation for giving the deposition and what, if anything, had been said during such meetings. Leonard objected to this line of questioning as he had earlier, only this time on the grounds of interfering with attorney-client privilege. Petrocelli's questions had to be confined to Jason, his father, and events directly concerning the murders.

"Have you ever asked your father whether he killed Nicole Brown Simpson?" Petrocelli asked.

"Absolutely not," Jason replied.

"Has he ever told you whether or not he killed Ron Goldman?"

"No, sir."

"Has he told you whether or not he killed Nicole?"

"No, sir."

"And any conversation with O. J. Simpson on the subject of whether he killed Nicole?"

"No."

Questioning continued on in this vein, with Petrocelli doing little more than establishing a few fundamental facts regarding Jason and his father after the murders. After repeated questioning, in which Jason claimed to have little memory of the events which transpired, he admitted to seeing and talking to his father on four separate occasions during the week following the murders, and of having learned about the murders while watching television.

Petrocelli then delved into the history of O. J.'s alleged physical abuse of Nicole and their stormy on-again, off-again relationship. Jason admitted hearing arguments between his father and Nicole, during which they would use much profanity. Nicole would routinely accuse O. J. of cheating on her.

"I knew there were other women," Jason said. "But I didn't know exactly who."

Jason claimed he never witnessed an argument in which his father had punched or hit Nicole, and that during the actual divorce, both his father and stepmother were civil with one another and with him. Each of them came to him individually and told him of their breakup. Jason characterized the separation and divorce as being quite amicable, in striking contrast to what I had personally come to believe about the relationships in question.

Asked to describe his relationship with Nicole, Jason said:

". . . like a good friend. She was like a real, real good friend, more like an older sister . . . I mean, mother doesn't really fit into the relationship, you know."

Petrocelli asked: "Do you believe she loved you?"

"Yeah," Jason said.

"And you loved her dearly?"

"Yes, sir."

"And was that true even after you moved out of Rockingham in 1988?"

"Yes, sir."

"Did you always remain close to Nicole?"

"Yes."

"All the way up until the end of her life?"

"Yes."

"And did that remain true even after Nicole and your father split up?"

"That—yes."

"You still remained close to Nicole?"

"Yeah."

"Did there ever come a period of time when you had a falling out with Nicole?"

"Lots of times."

Here, I would have liked Petrocelli to question Jason further about those times in which he and Nicole had "a falling out," but it was clear that Jason's attorney, Dan Leonard, was adamant the testimony be confined to a discussion of O. J.'s relationship with Nicole, not Jason's. However, in the ensuing pages, there were bits and pieces of testimony that did, in fact, address that issue. For instance, he mentioned that Nicole had given him a cookbook for Christmas. He also discussed going to Nicole's house on Gretna Green, where he said Nicole had "changed."

Jason said: "[Nicole] always was becoming a little bit more mature. You know what I'm saying? She was off on her own. I've never seen her alone before, you know, living in a house. I never really got to see what it would be like for her to have a place of her own . . ."

Jason would drop in to see her three or four times a week, first at Gretna Green, and then on Bundy Drive, and stay for anywhere from one to three hours each visit. During his later visits, he claimed to have parked right on Bundy Drive.

"I'd usually stop by because my bank's out there," Jason said. "It's on the way. I would go by my dad's, go by Nicole's, and go by my friends, whatever. It's just—I'd kinda sweep the whole area and say 'hi' to everybody. If she wasn't home, if I saw her car wasn't there I wouldn't stop in. If she was, I would go in. It was more like if she was home, I saw her. If she wasn't, I wouldn't. That kinda thing. I never usually called before I came by."

There were other points of interest in this part of the deposition. Jason said that he sometimes drove his father's Bronco, and that the keys were kept in a cup in the kitchen at Rockingham. He also admitted to going in and out of his father's closets, and that he

"This is why I admire Bill Dear greatly. If every case was spent like the time that he spent, this case would be solved a long time ago."
—Dr. Henry Lee

A record of a doctor's assessment on Jason at Cedars-Sinai when he ran out of Depakote, which he was taking to control his rage disorder.

Jason's Depakote prescription bottles found while combing through his discarded trash during 1998–2001.

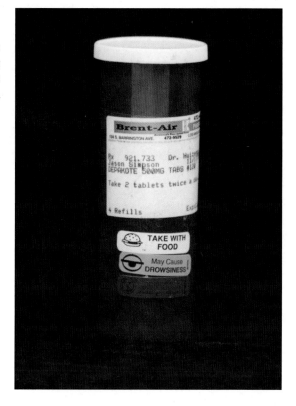

Front cover headline of the *National Enquirer* from October 4, 1994, featuring an article stating that Jason tried to kill his then girlfriend Jennifer Green. Reprinted with permission.

O. J. Simpson's mugshot from June 17, 1994, following his arrest for the murders of Nicole Brown Simpson and Ronald Goldman. ©*ImageCollect.com/ Globe Photos*

O. J. Simpson and Nicole
during the marriage.
©ImageCollect.com/Phil
Roach, Globe Photos, inc.

The author interviewing
Jason's former girlfriend
DeeDee Burnett along
with Bill's associate Joe Villanueva.

O.J., Nicole, Jason and girlfriend Jennifer, Justin, Sydney,
and friend at O.J.'s movie
premiere *The Naked Gun*.
©ImageCollect.com/Lisa Rose/
Globe Photos

Liquor bottles found while combing through Jason's discarded trash on Electra Street in Venice, California, which shows evidence of heavy drinking by Jason Simpson.

The 1993 Jeep that Jason was driving on the night of the murders on June 12, 1994.

Time clock in Jackson's Restaurant, where Jason was employed at the time of the murders. Although the time clock was functioning on the night of the murders, and Jason stated that he "punched out," his time was handwritten that night.

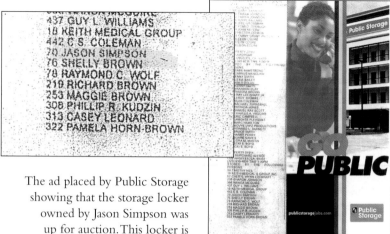

The ad placed by Public Storage showing that the storage locker owned by Jason Simpson was up for auction. This locker is where important personal items, including his knife and diaries, were found.

Photo of Bill and Brian Douglas showing Bill's purchase of Jason's storage contents on October 11, 2003.

Death certificate of Aaren Simpson found in Jason's storage locker. Jason had been supposed to be watching her when she fell into the pool and drowned at the age of twenty-three months.

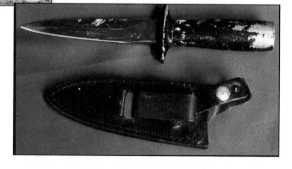

Jason's knife found alongside his diaries in his storage locker. Forensic experts believe this could be the murder weapon.

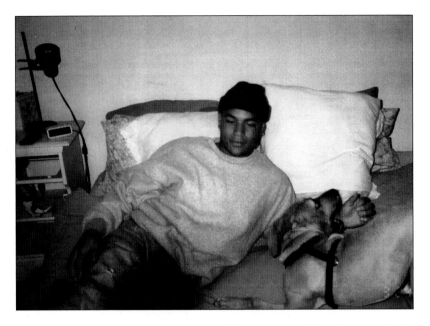

Jason wearing a dark-colored knit cap while playing with his dog on his bed. This knit cap is suspected to be the one found at the crime scene, which contained hairs from an African American male as well as hairs from a dog.

Jason Simpson now wearing a different knit cap, some months after the murders.

Johnny Cochran during the trial wearing a dark knit cap like the one found at the crime scene. ©*ImageCollect.com/Globe Photos*

O. J. Simpson during his trial, attempting to try on the bloody gloves that were found at the crime scenes. ©*ImageCollect.com/Globe Photos*

O. J. reacting to the verdict, along with Robert Kardashian, Johnnie Cochran, and Robert Shapiro. ©*ImageCollect.com/Globe Photos*

occasionally took things. "Snagging" was the term he used to describe the act of borrowing a shirt or a pair of sneakers. Reading this testimony I couldn't help but wonder if somewhere along the way Jason had "snagged" gloves and a pair of Bruno Magli shoes. As he himself mentioned in the deposition, Jason's feet were only a half size smaller than his father's, size 12.

Throughout his questioning Jason remained suspiciously vague about the last time he had spoken to Nicole. First questioned on the subject, he said they had last spoken in May, over Memorial Day weekend. However, upon later questioning, he admitted he had spoken to her on June 7, when he had seen her at Justin's graduation exercises. Then upon still further questioning, he admitted to speaking to Nicole on the day before the murders and then on the actual day.

To me, what Jason had said about his last communication with Nicole came as a significant revelation. He made, from my standpoint, perhaps the most important admission yet in the deposition, an admission that convinced me that he indeed may have been at Nicole's Bundy Drive residence on the night of the murders. Petrocelli may or may not have been surprised at what Jason had to say, for it was not clear in the deposition that Petrocelli fully grasped the implication of Jason's statements. Either that, or as I soon began to suspect, the "truth" of what happened that night was not something Petrocelli was interested in hearing. Like the LAPD and the DA's office, Petrocelli had one and only one suspect. Everything that didn't directly concern O. J. was irrelevant.

On the afternoon of June 11, the day before the murders, Nicole had allegedly called Jason to remind him that Sydney's dance recital would be the following day, and that she was hoping he would be able to attend. Jason said he couldn't make the recital because he was working that night at Jackson's Restaurant. However—according to Jason—he and Nicole had worked out a way for him still to be able to be with the family on that important day.

"They wanted to go to dinner [after the recital]," Jason told Petrocelli. "I had to work, so what better idea, [than] 'Why don't you come to my restaurant?'"

Petrocelli asked Jason to clarify what he had said. "[Do you mean]... that the family would go out to dinner after the recital?"

"Yes, sir."

"And you then suggested to her, 'Why not my restaurant?'"

"Yes."

Jason then explained his reasoning: "I had to work. That's why—it could kill two birds with one stone: I could see the kids—I could see Sydney . . . since I had to miss the recital, plus, you know, they were going to go out to eat, so why not just come in here."

At another point in the deposition he was asked to further clarify what he had previously said. "I think she wanted me to go, and I said I couldn't. I couldn't get out of it [working]. And I said, 'Why don't you guys come into the restaurant?' And she thought it was a great idea. So we were getting all excited about her coming to the restaurant, or the kids coming to the restaurant, the whole family coming to the restaurant. I was excited because I didn't want to have to miss another recital, and like I said, I felt like finally, you know, I'd be able to take care of everything."

Jason was planning to cook for Nicole and their combined families on the night of the murders! They were arranging to eat at Jackson's!

That this previous engagement had been overlooked by the countless detectives and attorneys who had studied this case, that no one to my knowledge had thought to question when or how the decision had been made to go to Mezzaluna's came as a shock, made all the more intense by Jason's obvious excitement at the prospect of showing off for his family.

They had watched him play football at the Rose Bowl; they had gathered to see him running track at the Army and Navy Academy; but they had never seen him perform in the one arena that truly mattered to Jason, the one area which he could truly call his own.

Jason, in essence, was saying, "Alan Jackson was not cooking on Sundays. I am finally going to be the chef! This was my chance to impress my dad, Nicole, my brother and sister and their friends! I'm going to be the star—like running down the football field with millions of people watching. This was my time of glory for a change!"

And according to Jason, Nicole had agreed to the proposition. She had said yes, that she and the family would come. Jason made reservations for 7 PM. He was ecstatic at the prospect of seeing them all at the restaurant.

"I wanted her to come," Jason told Petrocelli. "This was . . . she . . . finally was gonna come . . . [Emphasis added]. I wanted her to taste my food and taste all my stuff."

Nicole, according to Jason, then later had second thoughts. The next day, hours before the murders would take place, supposedly, she changed her mind. She reportedly told him: "We can't come. It's just a little bit too expensive, so we're just gonna go right up the street."

Petrocelli was having a difficult time pinning Jason down about whether he had called her or she had called him to impart this seemingly unimportant, but ultimately vital, piece of information. At first, he said she had called him. Later, however, he said that he had called her because he wanted to get an exact head count for the special meal he was going to prepare. He had already made reservations for them and was apparently ordering certain specialty items for the occasion.

Repeatedly, Petrocelli asked for specifics about the last call. Jason was vague, and had to be asked to speak up, and to answer the questions. Finally, he said, "I think I might have been at the apartment, at my house, at my apartment [when I made the call to Nicole]."

Even this response, however, was suspicious, because later in the deposition Jason specifically said he didn't have a telephone in his apartment. Petrocelli could obviously tell that Jason was getting caught up in his own lies. However, for reasons that wouldn't become clear to me until I had reached the end of the deposition, Petrocelli didn't seem willing to try and ferret out the truth. That truth, I believe, was quite a bit different from the story Jason was recounting. It was far more reasonable for me to believe that Nicole had never called him back to tell him she and O. J. were arguing again and that she and the children and her family would not be going to Jackson's for dinner. If, indeed, this were the case, it would have been better if Nicole had simply called Jason and told him they couldn't come. That would have shown him respect instead of leaving Jason to be embarrassed and humiliated in front of his coworkers. This was going to be the first time Nicole, O. J., and the other children were going to see Jason do the one thing he loved to do and did well: be a chef. This would have been enough to enrage anyone, much less a person suffering from intermittent explosive disorder, or irrational impulse. Now, in fact, I realized that here was a motive!

Jason was clearly getting rattled at this point in the deposition. He couldn't remember whether or not he had a telephone, nor could he remember exactly where Jackson's Restaurant was located. But before Petrocelli could ask the next logical question—about how Jason might have felt about being stood up, about being lied to—Jason's attorney, Dan Leonard, interrupted the proceedings and asked that they take a break.

I was mystified that Petrocelli would allow this portion of the deposition to abruptly come to an end. Then, I was very disappointed to see that when the recess was over, the entire topic had been dropped. Jason was now being asked about what he had done the year he left USC, where he had lived, and some of the places he had worked, not about the night of June 12, 1994!

Jason—clearly still rattled by the last series of questions about the night of the murders—apparently did his best to describe his checkered employment record, which began, he said, at the Atlas Bar and Grill. There he had been a busboy, before going to the Border Grill in Santa Monica, where he had begun working in the kitchens, then on to Bravo Cucina, also in Santa Monica, where he had continued his kitchen work, rising to the status of a prep chef, and finally on to Jackson's Restaurant. Throughout all of these exchanges he confused his dates of employment and then the chronology of the homes and people he had been living with. He couldn't seem to remember very clearly where he had been living the year before.

It is my opinion that Jason didn't purposefully try to confuse the names and dates. Rather, he truly was thrown by the earlier exchange and was trying desperately to keep his story straight. Asked if he had been supporting himself during this period of time, he said he had. "I'm a self-supported person," he said. "As a matter of fact, I pride myself on being self-supported." I knew, from reading the session logs from his short stay at St. John's Hospital that this certainly was not the case. His father had lent or given him a car to drive, and he also had help from his mother. Later in the deposition, Jason admitted to receiving $25,000 after the murders for his participation in a videotape that his father had put together to raise money for his criminal defense.

Jason was then asked whether or not he had given statements to the police or prosecutors regarding his activities before or after the murders. It was at this point he admitted that neither the LAPD nor the district attorney's office had questioned him. The only person, he said, who had questioned him was Johnnie Cochran, whom Jason had apparently told he was cooking on the night of the murders. If Jason was to be believed, the LAPD was so certain O. J. had committed the murders that they, and in turn the entire press corps, took the word of Johnnie Cochran! I was appalled!

It also became evident in the deposition that no one had subpoenaed Jason's personal financial and employment records, until, as it was revealed, the civil case when Petrocelli asked for but did not receive those records. Nor was there apparently a follow-up request for them. Jason first insisted he did not hand over the records because, as he said, "I don't have them." Later, however, it was revealed that he did indeed have them, or at least some of them.

"Have you read the subpoena [which requested that you give me the records]?" Petrocelli asked.

"I kinda quickly went over it. That was it. I didn't like sit down and
. . ."

"Why not?"

"I don't know. I just didn't."

Finally, Petrocelli came right out and asked for the telephone
records. "Do you have any . . . you have phone bills, don't you?"

"I think I might have last month's phone bill."

"Were your phone records subpoenaed in June of 1994?"

"Not that I recall, no."

"Did you have a cell phone at that time?"

"No."

"You had a phone at your apartment. Right?"

"I didn't . . ."

Again, Jason was waffling on whether or not he had a phone. The
only thing Jason admitted having that he said might have something
to do with Nicole or the issues under discussion were photographs. "I
got lots of photographs."

Jason was asked other questions. He discussed how easy it was to
come and go from Rockingham without being detected. He knew this
because of all the years he had lived at the house, occasionally sneaking
in and out. One gate was always left open or could be pushed open,
and besides this entrance and exit, there was a route behind the tennis
courts where someone could come and go without being seen from
Ashford or Rockingham. This piece of information was particularly
relevant because it suggested that Jason, like O. J., could actually have
come and gone without having to go through the neighbor's property
and hop the gate behind the guesthouse.

Jason was also asked if it was uncommon for his father to miss
family functions. He admitted his father was not in Los Angeles much
of the time, and O. J. was seldom present at important occasions.
Further, Jason admitted to having had, at times, a bad relationship
with his father. He characterized these difficult times as "fallings-out,"
much as he had described his on-again, off-again relationship with
Nicole.

One such incident he described took place when Jason was fourteen, when he wanted to have a party at Rockingham and his father refused to let his friends come over. That was the incident when Jason went around the property hitting things with a baseball bat, including the statue of his father. Jason said, however, that he only struck the statue of his father once, and that it was a tree he had hit repeatedly. Left unsaid, but everywhere apparent, was the fact that this was yet another example of a fit of rage that had come over the young man. Jason recounted another incident when he was sixteen and wanted to have his own car, which his father denied him. He again flew into a fit of rage. Yet another time he wanted a bedroom that was away from the main house.

"He won every time," Jason said of his dad.

In other words, his father always had the final say. It was either O. J.'s way or none at all.

Petrocelli asked if such "fallings-out" resulted in physical abuse.

"Did he ever beat you?" Petrocelli asked.

"No."

"Never?"

"Beat me? No."

"Did he ever hit you?"

"I've gotten a whipping on the butt before with his belt when I was a kid . . . [but] he's never struck me with his hands, though."

Pressed for more information on this subject, Jason finally admitted he had indeed been physically punished, though he couldn't remember the last time nor was he willing or able to describe any of those beatings.

Petrocelli then changed the topic back to his father's relationship with Nicole. It was Jason's belief that Nicole and his dad had reconciled before the murders. He recounted how he had seen his father nursing Nicole back to health after she had come down with pneumonia. Jason knew that his father and Nicole had been sleeping together since the separation, he said, because they were "lovey-dovey" with each other."

After more hours of testifying, in which he talked about his father's friends and about the men Nicole presumably had as lovers, Petrocelli again focused his questions on the night of the murders, and the conversation which took place between him and Nicole regarding the planned dinner at Jackson's Restaurant.

Jason said what he had said before, that he had called her to find out exactly how many people were coming to dinner that night at Jackson's. "... [Nicole] said she didn't think that they were gonna be swinging by Jackson's because it was just too expensive and the kids . . . they gonna be all restless . . . [And she said] 'We're just going to have dinner up the street.' I mean, she went to Mezzaluna all the time so it was just easier for her. I figured okay, fine, go. I was kinda hurt. I wish they would have come to the restaurant, but now I really wish they would have come to the restaurant [because of what later happened], but she wanted to go to Mezzaluna."

I wondered while reading this just how hurt Jason was to discover that Nicole and O. J. and the others were not going to show up. I wondered how he had reacted. Did he reach for a drink? Did he do a line of cocaine? Had his anger built up? Did he become short of breath, the first symptom of a rage attack? Did he blame Nicole, who was now yet another woman who had lied to him?

Petrocelli probed for more details, but was clearly only interested in what O. J. was up to that night. Jason was asked if he expected his dad to come to dinner and said that, "Yes, I would assume he would be there if he was in town."

Again, Petrocelli directed his line of questioning elsewhere, to the letter that O. J. had written to Nicole threatening to turn her over to the IRS for tax evasion. Jason claimed to know nothing about it until after the murders, nor had he any knowledge of the history of spousal abuse that Nicole recorded in her diaries.

It was not until well over 200 pages into the deposition that Petrocelli asked about Jason's alibi for that night. And here, to my mind, was the proverbial "smoking gun." Jason *had* no alibi on the night of the murders. He himself said that he had gotten off work within the time frame when the murders were believed to have been committed. Here is the exchange between Petrocelli and Jason as it appeared in the transcript:

Q: You were working on the night of June 12?

A: Yes.

Q: When did you leave work?

A: I think—I think it was around 10:00, 10:30.

Q: Did you punch out?

A: Yeah.

Q: Where did you go?

A: Home, to my apartment.

Q: What time did you get there?

A: I don't remember. It had to be around between 10:30 and 11:00.

Q: Your apartment on Sycamore?

A: Yes.

Q: How far was that from your job, which was at Jackson's at that time?

A: About three miles.

Q: Okay. And when you got to your apartment at Sycamore around 10:30 or so, did you call anyone?

A: I might have called my girlfriend.

Q: And who was that?

A: [Deleted]

Q: Do you know if you did?

A: I don't remember, no.

Q: Has she told you that you and she talked that evening?

A: No. No.

Q: Okay. What did you do at your house when you got there?"

A: Watched TV.

Q: Do you remember what you watched?

A: Not exactly.

Q: What time did you go to sleep?

A: Not till probably late, 3 AM

Q: So from 10:30 to 3:00 you watched television?

A: Yeah.

Q: Did you eat?

A: Probably.

Q: Did you drink anything?

A: Probably. I don't know.

Q: What did you drink?

A: Cranberry juice maybe.

Q: Did you drink any alcohol?

A: No.

Q: Did you take any drugs?

A: No.

Q: You think you spoke to (deleted)?

A: Maybe.

Q: Did you make any plans to do anything?

A: That night?

Q: Yes.

A: No.

A page or two later in the transcript, when Jason is questioned about the next morning, he contradicted himself yet again when he specifically said that he had first heard about the murders on television and that he didn't have a telephone. It was a curious statement because he truly might have seen a flash bulletin on one of the late-night or early morning news programs. Perhaps that was why he didn't wish to pick up the phone the next morning: someone was calling him about the murders.

Q: Did you then get a phone call sometime in the middle of the morning?

A: Yeah. Yes.

Q: From whom?

A: From first my sister, but I didn't answer the phone.

Q: Why not?

A: I didn't want to get up. I didn't know what it was. I didn't know what time it was.

Q: How do you know it was your sister?

A: I found out. In retrospect I knew it was my sister.

Q: Did you have an answering machine?

A: Yeah. It was— [Jason didn't finish his sentence.]

Q: Was the answering machine on?

A: The volume was turned down low.

Q: So you didn't hear the message being recorded?

A: No.

Q: You still have that answering machine message tape?

A: I think so.

Q: Can you bring it to the deposition at the next session, please?

A: Sure.

Q: With the machine so that we can hear the message?

A: Sure. Well, it's not—I don't have the message on the machine anymore.

Q: You don't?

A: No.

Q: You erased it?

A: I didn't erase it. I just rewinded it.

Q: You just rewinded it. I see. Okay. So you learned later on that you had that message.

A: Yeah. Can I tell you what the message—?

Q: Yes.

A: I mean, she just said, "Jason, call me back."

Q: That's all.

A: Yeah.

Q: Okay. What was the first thing that happened in the middle of the night or the next morning that you recall?

A: Well, then I got another phone call, and I decided to pick it up this time because I figured it must . . .

For the second time in this short exchange Jason didn't finish his sentence. I wondered, by filling in the words, if he had started to say, "I figured it must be about the murders . . ." That would have caught him up in his own lies, because he wouldn't have known anything about the murders at this point unless he had committed them.

Instead, Jason described getting a telephone call from his mother asking him to call Arnelle, his sister, which he eventually did, and learned that Nicole had been killed. According to Jason, his first assumption was that she had died of steroids. "I thought she was taking steroids because her body, every time I saw her, had changed. I thought—I don't know. I thought she had a heart attack or something. And Arnelle said, 'No. She was killed,' and that's it, and I hung up on the phone . . . and got in my car immediately."

I couldn't help but notice the awareness Jason seemed to have of Nicole's body. Did he have a crush on her? Was she more than a stepmother to him? Could Jason's attraction to her and her possible rejection have ultimately caused her death?

Instead of going directly to Rockingham, Jason first went to see his girlfriend, where he experienced what might be termed the first telltale signs of a seizure.

"I first went to my girlfriend's house on the way 'cause I couldn't drive. I couldn't breathe. I couldn't do anything. I told you before, I have epilepsy. I have to take my pills in the morning and at night. Sometimes—you know, when I'm scared—I didn't want to get too overly excited, and on the way I just had to pull over, and I was right by her house, so I went there and I banged on her door, kinda collapsed there for a second, and—no more than five minutes, and said, 'I gotta go get Arnelle.' So I went to the house, Rockingham."

"Without your girlfriend?" Petrocelli asked.

"No. By myself, I just said, 'I gotta leave.'"

Exactly why he had gone to her house, and then left without her, he didn't say and wasn't asked. Perhaps she didn't want to go. Perhaps he actually had a seizure and forgot why he had come. Or perhaps, as

I came to believe, he may have gone to her house that morning to establish some kind of alibi for the night before. Had he had a blackout? Maybe he didn't remember what had happened. Maybe he knew he had done something but couldn't remember what.

Instead of pressing Jason for clarification on this issue, Petrocelli did another about face and began asking him about the knives that his father was known to have had at the Rockingham house. Jason said the only ones he remembered were those Swiss Army knives that his father had been given as presents by the company he worked with. Far more significant to my mind were the knives that Jason himself said he had, and that O. J. may have had access to.

"Did you have a set of cooking knives?" Petrocelli asked.

"Yeah."

"And did you ever take those knives off of, you know, your work premises?"

"All the time."

"And where did you keep those chef's knives?"

"In a bag, chef's bag."

"In where?"

"What do you mean?"

"The bag."

"The bag, I'll take it home with me."

"Okay. On the evening of June 12 where was the bag with your chef's knives?"

"With me."

I could hardly contain myself when I came to this passage. Though I had known that Jason had a set of chef's knives, and that he had presumably kept them with him, almost as a badge of honor, here it was in sworn testimony.

Jason Lamar Simpson had left the restaurant, by his own admission, between 10:00 and 10:30 on the night of the murders. He was upset with Nicole for not showing up at Jackson's. Perhaps he had been drinking. But one thing was now certain. He was at large on the night of the murders with a set of razor-sharp knives, the kind that could have easily been used to stab Ron Goldman and slit Nicole Simpson's throat.

Petrocelli must have realized the implications of what had just been said. Here was a man with a known history of "rage" behavior that included assault with a deadly weapon, a man who disliked being lied to by women, and who had just been stood up by a woman he adored, who had every reason to be angry with her, and who had an intense desire to "set the record straight with her."

Dan Leonard didn't object to the questioning. I can only speculate that this came as much as a revelation to him as it did to everyone else in the room. Petrocelli then asked about Jason's movements on the night of the murders. His story was different again from the last one where he said he went home alone and watched television until 3 AM. This time he said he was with his girlfriend.

"When you left the restaurant on the evening of June 12, did you wait for your girlfriend there at the restaurant?

"Yeah. She had my car."

"So your girlfriend picked you up."

"In my car, yes."

"From the restaurant."

"Yes."

"And drove you where?"

"To her apartment."

"And what did you do there?"

"Dropped her off."

"And then went to your apartment?"

"Yes."

"Did you go into her apartment at all?"

"I don't think so. No, I didn't. I just kissed her in the car, and she went home."

By either account, Jason, who suffers from intermittent explosive disorder, who had the chef's knives with him that night, drove home alone on June 12, 1994, the night of the murders.

Why wasn't a deposition taken from Jennifer Green, Jason's girl-friend at the time of the murders?

For the third time in Jason's deposition, Petrocelli made a complete about face. Instead of following up with the natural question as to why Jason hadn't gone back to her apartment with her, and why he merely kissed her goodnight, only to return home and watch television until 3 AM, Petrocelli changed the subject. He asked about the slow-motion car chase and whether Jason believed his father had actually considered suicide.

"I didn't think about it," Jason said.

There was one other interesting exchange in Petrocelli's and Jason's discussion over the car chase and its aftermath. It concerned Jason's seemingly irrational decision to put himself in danger to see and presumably talk to his father upon the arrival of the Bronco at Rockingham that day. Most interesting to me was how Jason described himself in the third person, as if there truly were two different Jason Lamar Simpsons, the mentally ill Jason, and the normal healthy adult.

"This nut-head, me, just ran out after the car and jumped over two police cars, and they didn't want to let me go," he told Petrocelli. "I think it was pretty wise on their part."

Then, seemingly out of the blue, as if all that Jason had said had suddenly come into focus for Petrocelli, the attorney asked Jason about his previous attack on Paul Goldberg at the Revival Café.

"Did you attack the restaurant owner with a knife?" Dan Leonard objected, but before there could be any discussion over the issue, Jason answered, "No."

Again Leonard objected. "Are you going to pursue this with him?" Leonard asked. "I thought we wanted to get this thing over with."

Petrocelli considered the objection, and finally, after one more exchange, said, "I guess that's all I have for now."

I was stunned.

It was as if Petrocelli had come to realize what Leonard probably already knew, that Jason may have been the one who killed Nicole

Brown Simpson and Ron Goldman. To have pursued the questioning any further would have opened a door that no one—not O. J. Simpson, Leonard, Petrocelli or even the LAPD or the district attorney's office—could have closed. And to do so would have upset the bedrock foundation that each of their respective cases had been built upon. The truth was staring Petrocelli and the other attorneys in the face, and in deference to their clients and to their own careers, they couldn't acknowledge having seen it. Too many millions of dollars and man-hours had already been spent perpetuating the lie.

Did Petrocelli realize that Jason Lamar Simpson had been in a psychiatric ward just eighteen months prior to the murders of Nicole Simpson and Ron Goldman?

Did Petrocelli realize that Jason Lamar Simpson suffered from intermittent rage disorder?

Did Petrocelli realize that Jason Lamar Simpson was on probation for the assault on Paul Goldberg with a kitchen knife at the time of the murders of Nicole Simpson and Ron Goldman?

Did Petrocelli know that Jason had checked into a hospital only months before the murders because he was afraid he was about to rage?

Did Petrocelli know that O. J. had hired a criminal attorney, Carl Jones, for Jason, just one day after the murders had been committed?

It seemed entirely likely now, with what I had uncovered, that the next time Jason was questioned by authorities, it could be as a major suspect in the murders of Nicole Simpson and Ron Goldman.

A: Yes.

Q: And drove you where?

A: To her apartment.

Q: And what did you do there?

A: Dropped her off.

Q: And then went to your apartment?

A: Yes.

Q: Did you go into her apartment at all?

A: I don't think so. No, I didn't. I just kissed her in the car, and she went home.

A: Watched TV.

Q: Do you remember what you watched?

A: Not exactly.

Q: What time did you go to sleep?

A: Not till probably late, 3:00.

Q: So from 10:30 to 3:00 you watched television?

A: Yeah.

A: I was expecting whoever to show up.

Q: Including your father. Right?

A: Yeah.

Q: Including Sydney. Right?

A: Oh, absolutely.

Q: Including Justin. Right?

A: Yes.

Q: Including Nicole. Right?

A: Yeah.

Q: And Nicole's family. Right?

A: I didn't know -- parts of Nicole's family. I didn't know who was coming --

Q: You knew Lou and Judy were coming. Right?

A: Yeah, I knew those two were.

Q: When did you leave work?

A: I think -- I think it was around 10:00, 10:30.

Q: Did you punch out?

CAME BK. AFT M's

A: Yeah.

Q: Where did you go?

A: Home, to my apartment.

Q: What time did you get there?

A: I don't remember. It had to be around between 10:30 and 11:00.

Q: Your apartment on Sycamore?

A: Yes, sir.

Q: How far was that from your job, which was Jackson's at that time?

A: About three miles.

15

ENLISTING EXPERTISE

I DIDN'T WANT TO BE raked over the coals like Dennis Fung, or shown to be an outright liar like Mark Fuhrman. Nor did I want to be accused of the same tunnel vision that had caused the LAPD to lose their credibility in front of eighty million prime-time television viewers. Most importantly, I didn't want to step in front of a jury and have months—no years—of work go down the drain because I had merely assumed and not verified the facts of my investigation. That's why I began flipping through my Rolodex for the telephone numbers of experts who would give me their professional opinion of the evidence that I had gathered.

The first number I called belonged to retired Lieutenant James Cron. "Jim" had retired as commander from the crime scene unit of the Dallas County Sheriff's Department only a year or two earlier, after having been with them for thirty-plus years. During his career with the sheriff's department, and afterward, he had made a name for himself as an internationally recognized expert crime scene specialist. He had also appeared as a guest panelist and selected expert in my last homicide seminar. Among the other distinguished lecturers at my seminar had been Dr. Vincent DiMaio, Bexar County Medical Examiner in San Antonio, Texas, who wrote the "bible" on gunshot and knife wounds.

Another lecturer was Captain Larry Momchilov, one of the best homicide investigators I had ever met or worked with, who was with the Summit County Sheriff's Office in Akron, Ohio. Doug Jenney, another respected former homicide detective and former chief medical examiner investigator from Summit County, Ohio, was also considered one of the top experts in his field; his specialty was crime scene investigation. I considered all these men to be the experts in their fields. And, like the others, if Jim Cron agreed to look at my material, he would respond honestly as to his conclusions based on the evidence.

When I spoke to Jim on the phone he was surprised and shocked that I was working on the O. J. Simpson case. "Oh hell," he said, "Not you too?" I told him that what I had to show him and what I needed to talk to him about had to be done in private, so he agreed to meet me halfway, at the prestigious Northpark Shopping Center, just north of downtown Dallas.

Jim showed up right on time. I walked through Neiman Marcus, the famed Dallas department store, and as I strolled down the concourse of Northpark, I could see him seated in the outside portion of Café La Madeleine. The years had treated him well. He greeted me with a smile, despite the double-sized briefcase he saw me carrying.

"All right," he said. "What have you got?"

"Everyone's convinced O. J.'s guilty," I said. "They've written all the books in the world trying to make him into the fall guy and they've spent millions of taxpayer dollars trying him in court. But as far as I'm concerned, O. J. didn't commit the murders."

"Oh, hell," said Jim, shaking his head in exasperation. "You *know* he committed those murders!"

"You don't have to believe me," I told him. "Just listen to what I have to say, study the documents, and give me your opinion."

Exasperation was still clearly written on his face when he finally agreed to hear me out. "All right," he said. "You've worked hard at this kind of thing before, and you sometimes pull needles out of haystacks. I'll see what you've got—then I'll tell you again, O. J. Simpson is the killer."

Over lunch I explained my theory and showed him the various pieces of evidence which I hoped someday to turn over to a prosecutor. That evidence included police files, records, videotapes and, most of all, photographs. I also explained the tunnel vision that I believed led the LAPD to arrest O. J. Simpson in the first place.

By the time he'd heard my summary, Jim's look of exasperation had changed to interest. "I never thought I'd say this, but you might be right. It does appear to be tunnel vision on their part. They felt it was O. J. right from the beginning and didn't bother looking for any other suspects. After thirty-three years in the sheriff's office, I've seen this happen time and time again. Usually, they get the right man, but it sounds to me like they might have got the wrong one this time."

I handed the heavy briefcase to him. "Look at the rest of this, study it, and then call me. Let me know what you think."

"Sure, I'll do it."

Jim took the material and wished me good luck with a sheepish smile. And then, almost as an afterthought, he asked me who was footing the bill on this case. "You haven't joined the Dream Team, have you?"

I shook my head. "I'm footing the bill. I felt I couldn't get anyone else involved in this case if I was wrong."

"You never cease to amaze me, Bill."

Three days later, when we met again at Northpark, he was carrying an extra-large mailing envelope, which was sealed with a clasp.

"Here's the material you asked me to look at. Inside you've got my written report. Go ahead, read it!"

I opened the envelope and took out his letter. This is what it said:

> After reviewing your investigative work and research into the murders of Nicole Simpson and Ron Goldman, having detailed discussions with you and studying your findings, I can now give you my comments. Your opinion regarding this case is extremely plausible and believable, that being, O. J. Simpson did not commit the murders.
>
> The known facts combined with the results of your efforts present an intelligent and quite possible father and son theory,

which could bring closure to this crime. The compelling scenario you have put forth is worthy of your talents and deserves serious consideration.

Signed, Jim Cron

Naturally, I was elated. Here was someone I respected who has been involved in some of the most famous murder cases and crime scene investigations in the country. I thanked him profusely. And then I asked what I owed him.

"For what you're doing," he said, "I couldn't take any money. Good luck—you'll damn well need it!"

I had convinced Jim Cron, but I also wasn't going to stop seeking expert opinions about my investigation and the conclusions I had drawn.

The next number I searched for in my Rolodex was Dr. W. French Anderson, the professor of biochemistry and pediatrics and director of the Gene Therapy Laboratories at the University of Southern California School of Medicine. On his own, Dr. Anderson wrote the classic forensic analysis of an FBI firefight that occurred on April 11, 1986. This amazing investigation by Dr. Anderson has been highly acclaimed by everyone who has read it, including the FBI. He has made this detailed forensic analysis available to law enforcement officers all over the world at his own expense.

I first met Dr. Anderson when I wrote *The Dungeon Master: The Disappearance of James Dallas Egbert III*, over fifteen years ago. Like Dallas Egbert, Dr. Anderson was a prodigy. There was no man I respected more, or who, I believed, could sooner set me straight about my investigation. I called him at his home in San Marino, California. He told me to fly out as soon as I could and spend the night as his and his wife's guest.

I flew to Los Angeles, rented a car, and drove out to his house. After dinner, I sat down with him in his study and showed him all the evidence I had collected. Then I presented my theory.

Dr. Anderson was impressed, but not convinced. "Bill," he said, "I want to set the record straight. I like you. I think you're a great investigator. And your theory sounds intriguing. But I have to tell you right now, I think O. J. is guilty."

"Good," I replied. "Then my evidence will have to be pretty damn convincing, won't it? Take a look at it."

"I'll keep an open mind and I'll read it tonight."

"All I can say is there's a heck of a lot of material for you to look at."

"Don't worry, I'll read it all and give you my opinion in the morning."

I went to bed that night wondering how he could possibly digest such a vast amount of material in a single night. However, I knew him well enough to understand that if he said he was going to, he would read it all, in detail.

I awoke very early in the morning, not long after sunrise. Dr. Anderson was sitting by his swimming pool having breakfast while he waited for me.

"I've read every bit of your material," he said, "several times over as a matter of fact, and I think you're on the right track. Based on your investigation and the material I've seen here, it appears that O. J. may not have committed the murders. You've certainly put a question in my mind as to his guilt."

Again, I was elated. I had Jim Cron telling me I was on the right track, and now I had Dr. French Anderson saying the same thing. They were two experts whose opinions would be taken seriously in any courtroom in the country. However, there were still more experts to consult.

The next call I made was overseas, to a man who had no ties to any police department in the United States, who didn't have any fear of any repercussions to himself or his company, and who I knew would give me a fair and honest reading of the material. That man was Terry Merston, a private forensic investigator, from Complete Investigations, in Hertfordshire, England.

I reached him by phone in the UK and told him what I needed. It didn't come as any great surprise to him. "You always had a talent for getting the big cases," he said. "Bring it on!"

"I should mention that I'm on a very limited budget with this, Terry."

"Don't worry about the budget. Just send me everything you have, and my partner and I will take a look at it. You realize, I'm only going to tell it to you the way we see it—the facts will have to speak for themselves."

I told him I wouldn't want it any other way. "How long do you think it will take?" I added tentatively, not wanting to push but also not wanting to wait too long.

"It could take us a week; it could take us two months, depending on the evidence," he replied.

I hurriedly gathered my material and shipped it to Terry in England.

As it turned out, it did take them two months. And, for an impatient man like myself, that can be a lifetime. The time I spent waiting for Merston and his partner to finish their report was some of the hardest I spent on the case. I knew they were devoting their full attention to my investigation because of the frequency with which they called me—every two or three days—to request more information or another photo or more documents.

In the meantime, I visited the Ace Mart Restaurant Supply Company, which is one of the finest cooking and chef supplies stores in Texas. I asked the salesman, who was a former chef, to select for me a set of the finest chef's knives available.

"I want professional quality chef knives," I told him. "Nothing but the best."

"That's easy," he replied. "You want Forschner."

I asked him to select a typical set that a chef might carry with him.

He unrolled a black canvas bag on the counter, about the size of a pillowcase. Individual compartments inside contained six knives, from the smallest paring knife for dicing and cutting small vegetables, to a large carving knife for cutting substantial slabs of beef. They were exquisite knives, with polished rosewood handles, and so sharp that all a person had to do was rest the blade on the palm of your hand and it would cut the skin. I know that because I accidentally cut myself when I got the knives home and was demonstrating to a friend how razor-sharp they were.

Not only were they sharp, they also were expensive. All six, in the black bag, cost well over $200. However, I got more than I bargained for when I bought them. As the salesman was wrapping the knives up for me to take home, I started looking at the Forschner sales brochure, a glossy booklet showing the wide range and different sets of chef's knives. No sooner had I begun to page through the brochure than I noticed that Forschner was a division of Swiss Army Brands, Inc. which sold, among other things, watches and sunglasses in addition to the popular red pocketknives bearing the Swiss Army insignia.

Bingo! I had just won the Texas Lottery!

To anyone else that fact would have been insignificant. But to me, it was one of the most important pieces of the puzzle. As was shown during the trial, O. J. sat on the board of Swiss Army Brands Company. Also on the board, and the man most likely responsible for inviting O. J. to join the board, was M. Leo Hart, cochairman and chief executive, who was, in the early 1970s, a professional football player for the Buffalo Bills. At the Simpson trial, O. J. was described as once having returned home from a board meeting and handing out Swiss Army knives and watches and other goods which had been given to him on a business visit to the company. In other words, O. J. sat on the Board of Directors of the company that produced the chef's knives, made by Forschner, a division of Swiss Army Brands, that his son Jason may have been cooking with on the night of the murders. Unknowingly, O. J. could have given Jason the murder weapon!

I felt, based on my evidence at that time, that detectives Fuhrman, Vannatter, and Lange were wrong. It wasn't the four-inch Swiss Army knife that killed Nicole and Goldman, it was one, or possibly two, of the six knives contained in the chef's bag that Jason left Jackson's Restaurant with on the night of Sunday, June 12, 1994.

I sent this selection of knives to Terry Merston in England, which included a Swiss Army knife and stiletto, the latter two being identical to the ones known to have been owned by O. J.

I returned to London in January of 1998 to pick up Merston's report. It had been a long but worthwhile wait. Merston's company, Complete Investigations, had compiled not just a two- or three-page letter, but a twenty-four-page document of their scientific findings and analysis.

Merston and his partner Peter Harpur were both experienced crime scene examiners. They were retired British police officers with over fifty-eight years of combined investigative experience in the public and the private sectors, during which they had carried out in excess of 27,000 crime and major incident examinations, including burglary, armed robbery, murder, suicide, arson, rape, explosive and incendiary scenes, and rail and air crashes. Individually or jointly they were members of many prestigious professional organizations, which included The Fingerprint Society, The International Association for Identification, The Institute of Expert Witnesses, The Forensic Science Society and The Royal Photographic Society. No one in England, or anywhere else, could question their credentials.

Merston and Harpur had separated their study into three main areas: the Bundy Drive crime scene, the evidence discovered in the Bronco, and the evidence discovered at O. J.'s house on Rockingham Avenue.

They described to me the results of their investigation of the Bundy Drive crime scene first, based on the coroner's autopsy report. As I had fully anticipated, it was clear to Merston and Harpur that both Nicole Brown-Simpson and Ron Goldman had received fatal injuries inflicted with an extremely sharp and long-bladed knife. Also, as had been much discussed, Nicole had eight stab wounds to the head and neck, the most severe being to her neck, which caused her neck to be severed from side to side, cutting through both jugular veins. She also suffered multiple defense wounds to her hands. There was also a blunt force injury to the right side of the scalp, which measured one inch by one inch.

Merston and Harpur also acknowledged that Ron Goldman had received multiple stab wounds and one fatal wound to the left side of the neck, where the jugular was severed.

The weapon or weapons used had a single-edge smooth blade, with the opposite side of the blade being flat and squared off to a width of one thirty-second of an inch.

During the trial, the Dream Team had mercilessly hammered the LAPD as being inept and bungling their investigation of the crime scene. I was surprised to find these English examiners were not only critical, they attacked virtually every piece of evidence that had been used to prosecute Simpson. They went far beyond anything I had anticipated.

The photographs I had provided Merston and Harpur showed that Detective Fuhrman—not wearing any protective clothing, gloves, or overshoes—had actually walked through the river of blood at the crime scene. This resulted most assuredly in his becoming contaminated with the blood of Nicole Simpson and in all probability that of Ronald Goldman. As Merston's eventual report stated: "Due to the copious amounts of blood at the scene, there is no doubt that Detective Fuhrman will have blood on his shoes and probably his clothing."

Merston and Harpur pointed out that an unnamed detective, obviously not Fuhrman, was also standing in the blood.

There was one other disturbing thing they mentioned. In comparing two photographs, they observed that Nicole's body appeared to have been moved, presumably before the pathologist had actually made preparations to move the body off the premises.

The Merston and Harpur report also pointed out what had been made much of at the trial: the blanket—which had been taken out of the house—that was laid over Nicole's body. This blanket, of course, could and likely did contaminate the body and perhaps the entire crime scene. Equally important, the blanket should have been saved and studied as evidence.

There was no excuse for the slipshod practices, Merston and Harpur said. "From viewing the photographs and overview, it is obvious the actual murder scene is a small scene and as such would be extremely easy to seal, protect, contain, and manage. From the evidence supplied, it is quite obvious that this is not the case."

Merston and Harpur's appraisal gets even more intense: "... It can be seen that Detective Fuhrman has little or no regard to scene and evidence protection, or preventing contamination, being that he is beside the body of Nicole without any protection . . . He also commits the sin of attending other connected scenes during the investigation, therefore creating the real possibility of contaminating the other scenes."

In fact, as they further pointed out, all four of the main investigators visited North Rockingham, along with two other officers.

"Due to the fact that the four detectives have all been at the murder scene, where there is an abundance of blood and Detective Fuhrman is not wearing any protective footwear, it is entirely possible that he or any one of the other detectives has walked the blood onto the driveway at O. J. Simpson's house. Conversely, it is also possible that when returning to the murder scene from O. J. Simpson's house the detectives have inadvertently transferred the blood of O. J. Simpson from his house to the murder scene at Bundy Drive."

It was also obvious this was no "accident." Right in the police records, as Merston and Harpur point out, the officers say that they "might have an extension of the Bundy crime scene" at this new location. And this being the case, as Merston and Harpur said, "Why have supposedly experienced detectives gone from one scene to another suspected scene, therefore vastly increasing the possibility of contamination? These are basic mistakes that just should not have been made under any circumstances."

In a standard and thorough investigation, as Merston and Harpur pointed out, each body would have been assigned as a separate murder scene, with different officers dealing with different bodies.

"In the first instance [Bundy Drive] there was no evidence to suggest that the murders were not committed by more than one person, and to date the possibility still exists that there was more than one person involved in the murders. This can be borne out by the fact that to date there are still outstanding unidentified shoe prints found at the murder scene."

Further, they reported: "Due to the real possibility of cross contamination of the two bodies, any evidence to support the possibility of there being more than one offender has been lost forever."

Next, Merston and Harpur focus their attention onto O. J. Simpson's Ford Bronco, about which the investigators had this to say: "It is obvious from the carnage at the murder scene and other evidence that the murderer would have had to have been in close contact with both of the victims. Due to the severity of the injuries and the amount of wounds resulting in the severing of both jugular veins of Nicole Simpson and one jugular vein of Ronald Goldman, causing blood to gush from the victims, there is no doubt that the perpetrator of these vicious attacks would have been soaked in blood from head to foot. The distinct lack of blood in the Ford Bronco would therefore exclude it from being the murderer's 'get away' vehicle."

Further, regarding the Bronco: "If the murderer had traveled in this vehicle there is no doubt that there would have been a large amount of blood transferred by him/her from the scene to the vehicle. We would expect blood to have been found on the seats, the foot pedals, handbrake, the gear shift, the carpet, internal door covering and probably the interior mirror."

It was at this point that Merston and Harpur addressed the Rockingham glove. "From the evidence of the blood found in the vehicle it is probable that the glove was placed on the center console, and at some stage came into contact with the carpet of the vehicle."

Next, the criminologists turned to the possibility that O. J. discarded the bloody clothing. "If he discarded his clothing, why did he not also discard his socks which were found in his bedroom? Both socks had blood on them identified as belonging to Nicole Simpson and Ron Goldman. It is possible that the blood on his socks could be from brushing against vegetation at the scene or coming in contact with the body. Also if he has gone to the trouble to discard his clothing, why on earth would he retain the glove found at Rockingham Avenue, which contained so much incriminating evidence?"

Finally, before their summation, they turned to the evidence found at Rockingham. At the outset of presenting their evidence here, they pointed out that the detectives who had visited this crime scene had not found any visible evidence such as blood inside the premises on that initial visit. And that, apart from the blood on the driveway and in the foyer of O. J. Simpson's house, all of which has been identified as that of O. J. Simpson, no other blood—apart from the socks—was found in the house. They also pointed out they were aware of the fact that the shower drainage system was dismantled and forensically examined, with no blood being found. "There is no doubt that if the murderer had hurriedly taken a shower, that due to the enormous bloodshed, that there most certainly would have been traces of blood found in and around the shower and in the shower drainage system."

To them, this spelled only one thing. Just as I had concluded four years earlier: O. J. was at the crime scene, but he didn't commit the murders. Merston couldn't, or wouldn't, speculate as to why. "From the available evidence it appears that O. J. Simpson was in all probability at the murder scene, at some time after the events, for some reason best known to him."

There was still more to come: "Finally, another point about Rockingham, with such a distinct lack of blood at the house, it is extremely unlikely that this is the residence that the murderer returned to."

The investigators next turned to the murder weapons. The one constant they found in the postmortem reports is that the weapon used was a single-edged blade with a squared off end, the thickness of which is one thirty-second. This, as I knew, discounted both the stiletto and the Swiss Army knives, which were so much discussed in the books by Fuhrman, as well as Lange and Vannatter.

There was yet another factor to consider: the bruise on the top of Nicole Simpson's head. To Merston and Harpur, the bruise on the top of the head was most likely the result of Nicole being hit with the butt or the handle of the knife that was used to kill her. Neither the Swiss Army knife nor the stiletto fit the right dimensions.

Based on the various wound sizes, it appeared to them that not one, but two different knives may have been used to commit the murders. Only a chef, I believed, would likely have been carrying not one, but two knives.

"The most likely types of knives that would have been used to commit these murders are the boning knife and a chef's cutting knife," Merston said, as he took the two knives out of the chef's bag and showed them to me. I glanced at the rosewood handles.

In Dallas I had selected the same two knives as possibly the ones capable of killing Nicole Simpson and Ron Goldman, without Merston or Harpur knowing in advance.

With their detailed report in hand, I returned to Dallas.

The final call I made was to Dr. Harvey Davisson, one of the many psychologists who had helped me to understand intermittent rage disorder. A few years earlier, Harvey had helped me to solve the infamous "Black Widow" murders, a case in which an attractive young lady would seduce, marry, and then execute her victims in order to collect inheritance and insurance premiums. Harvey had helped me to profile murderers many times since then, and I knew I could count on his help again.

I called him up. "Harvey, I need you and at least two other psychology experts to study the documented evidence I've collected on Jason Simpson and give me your professional opinion as to his psychological profile and his potential as a suspect in the Bundy Drive murders."

"That's a tall order," he said. "But I'll see what I can do."

On the same day I spoke to Dr. Davisson, I delivered to his Dallas office a large catalogue case full of police documents and investigative records, in addition to several portfolio cases containing numerous pictures, charts, and diagrams. The only trial documents that I had available for the experts to examine at this time were the ones released to the general public after the trial. They were very limited.

Like Jim Cron, Dr. Anderson, and Terry Merston, Dr. Davisson went to work immediately. Less than a week later, he called me back, saying that he had enlisted the help of two internationally recognized psychologists in the field of criminal behavior, Dr. William Flynn and Dr. William Tedford, and that I could expect a full report shortly.

As promised, Dr. Davisson delivered a six-page report. This, in part, is what it said:

> The picture that developed was that of a young man who has suffered tremendous pain in his life, whose ability to control his impulses, especially his impulses of rage, has been significantly impaired by the physical condition of his seizures which had begun at age 14 with an overdose of cocaine. This seemed to be a significant turning point for a person who had already experienced tremendous frustration and disappointment in his life.
>
> The repeated suicide attempts which included the use of stabbing of self, his pattern of on-going violent interaction with women, his confused attitudes towards women, his conflict and violence including attacks with a knife against authority figures, his experience with the loss of impulse control due to his seizure problems and the history of a fear of loss of control, of rage if not fully controlled by his medication, his history of drug and alcohol abuse and a lack of impulse control during times of stress, all create a picture of a highly unstable young man who is predisposed to act in a violent way...

In summary, all three of us concurred that Jason is a man who is predisposed to act in violent ways both toward himself and other people, and the likelihood of that violence escalating in the future is very significant.

After reviewing all of the history of numerous suicide attempts and the history of failed relationships in which isolation and moods of violence and dependency were interwoven, it seems more and more likely that Jason psychologically could have been a very reasonable suspect in the murders.

Like Dr. Davisson, the two experts were in complete agreement. Even if Jason had not committed the murders, he was capable of the kind of violence that had resulted in the deaths of Nicole Simpson and Ron Goldman.

16

DISBELIEF

"**YOU'VE GOT TO MEET** with Dr. Kittay," Harvey told me after submitting his report. "He's the key to understanding this entire tragedy."

I knew Harvey was right. Dr. Burton Kittay's name popped up in my investigation at each new turn, first as the therapist whom Ron Shipp was seeing, then as the psychologist for O. J. and Nicole, and finally as the therapist for Jason and his former girlfriend DeeDee. In Kittay's fifteen-year relationship with the Simpson family and their friends, he must have seen it all: drugs, alcoholism, spousal abuse, suicide attempts, and then murder. Though I had considered approaching Kittay earlier in my investigation, I had not done so because I believed he would be the last person—except for perhaps O. J. himself—who would be willing to sit down and talk honestly with me about the evidence I had uncovered, and what precautions might need to be taken to protect Jason from himself and to protect others. Like me, Dr. Davisson did not hold out much hope that Dr. Kittay would speak to me.

"Even if he closes the door in your face, you'll have done the right thing by giving him a chance to speak his mind," Harvey explained. "I'm a licensed psychologist, and I know I'd want to be given that chance, especially if I had treated both father and son and one of the murder victims. If he opens up to you there's a good chance that this murder case can be put to rest without hurting a lot of innocent people. And if you're wrong about Jason, Dr. Kittay should tell you where you've gone astray and try to set you straight."

"But he could do more than just set us straight," I said. "Up until now, everything I've done has been behind the scenes. Jason, his father, and their friends don't know what I've been up to. Once Dr. Kittay knows how deeply I've gone into this, there's no telling what might happen or who he might tell."

Dr. Davisson, of course, knew I was right. O. J. was adept at bailing his son out of trouble, and I had no doubt he would continue trying to do so if he could. However, Dr. Davisson had followed my investigation, examined the evidence, and read the reports from the various medical and forensic experts I had consulted, and knew that the time had truly come for me to figuratively step from the frying pan and into the fire. I had gone about as far as I could without speaking directly to Jason, O. J., or Jason's girlfriends, DeeDee and Jennifer Green. Dr. Kittay was the logical first step. He could become our greatest friend or our worst enemy. There was only one way to find out.

I soon learned Dr. Kittay had closed his L.A. practice in 1994, just as Marcia Clark and Christopher Darden were handing out subpoenas in their case against O. J. He had literally closed shop and left town. A computer search eventually led me to my own backyard, in Corpus Christi, Texas, on the Gulf of Mexico, where Dr. Kittay had set up a small practice. I didn't know what had caused him to move to Corpus Christi at a time when a murder investigation was being conducted on one of his patients, Nicole, and at least two of his other patients— Jason and O. J.—who needed him more than perhaps at any other time in their lives, but I suspected the reason he had left was not for the sun and sea air. He had plenty of that right in Santa Monica.

Without letting Dr. Kittay know the reason for my wanting to see him, I called and made an hour-long appointment for Tuesday, July 27, 1999. Knowing how vitally important this interview might be, Dr. Harvey Davisson agreed to join me, thinking it might be better if

I was accompanied by a licensed psychologist. Just as lawyers feel most comfortable in the presence of other lawyers, I supposed the same would be true of psychologists. They speak the same language.

As it turned out, Dr. Davisson hardly said a word during our entire session. But that had nothing to do with the fact that they were both psychologists. Dr. Davisson was at a loss for words. Dr. Kittay wasn't like any psychologist Dr. Davisson had ever encountered, just as I, no doubt, wasn't like any of the patients who stepped into the doctor's office.

The fact that I actually was going to see Dr. Kittay as a patient, and not as a detective, was an important point, for the only safeguard I had in speaking to him rested in the confidentiality agreement that exists between a patient and his psychologist. That way, Dr. Kittay would be bound by law not to reveal to others what I had to tell him during my office visit. And as I discussed with Dr. Davisson, I planned on giving Dr. Kittay whatever information it would take for him to open up to me.

We arrived at his modest shoreline office at 2:45 PM, fifteen minutes before our 3:00 PM appointment. That gave me plenty of time to chat with his secretary, fill out the confidentiality and client's rights forms, and to hand her my $175 check for the hour-long session.

Dr. Kittay's secretary smiled at me when I handed her the check. "Thank you Mr. Dear," she said, "but I just started working for the doctor and I made a mistake when I quoted you his fee for an hour session. $175 is the rate we charge to insurance companies. Since you are paying for the visit yourself, it's only $120."

This was the first of many times throughout my short visit to the office that I was taken by surprise. I couldn't put much confidence in a psychologist who would charge one rate for patients paying for visits out of their own pocket and another rate for those whose insurance companies were footing the bill.

I didn't question the secretary on the matter, for Dr. Kittay himself—or at least the man I supposed was him—had walked up behind her at this point and was staring across the desk in my direction, trying to get a fix on why I had come to see him.

Dr. Kittay was a short, heavy-set, bespectacled man in his early fifties, clearly the kind of man who was more at ease in a leather armchair than he was standing on his feet. As we eyed one another, the secretary handed my $175 check back to me, and I gave her a credit card, which she promptly processed, for $120. I had hoped that the doctor would take the check, for this would be proof that I had indeed visited the office and, along with the signed confidentiality agreement which I now had in my hand, was further documentation of our patient and psychologist relationship. The credit card receipt would have to suffice.

"I assume you are Dr. Kittay," I said. "I'm Bill Dear. And this is Dr. Harvey Davisson, a psychologist from Dallas whom I've asked to join us."

Dr. Kittay eyed me warily, glanced at Dr. Davisson, then at my thick catalogue case which I had brought with me. Clearly, he thought it odd that a patient would be accompanied by another psychologist, but he didn't, at this point, stop and ask about Dr. Davisson or what I had brought with me in the case. He ushered us into his well-appointed office, showed us to a sofa, and then sat himself down in a large leather armchair.

"How can I help you?" he asked.

"I want to be completely honest with you, Dr. Kittay," I said. "I'm a private investigator and I want to talk to you about Jason Simpson and DeeDee."

Dr. Kittay noticeably tensed. "I can't discuss other patients' visits with you," he said. He looked pointedly at Harvey, "You should know that."

"Naturally I'm not asking that you reveal anything from your sessions," I replied quickly. "I'm a private investigator working on a murder case which I would like to discuss with you. Dr. Davisson has accompanied me here because, as a fellow psychologist, and as someone who has studied the evidence I've collected over the past six years, he may have important insights to contribute."

O. J. IS INNOCENT

Dr. Kittay obviously knew exactly what murder case I was talking about, which is why he had tensed up. I paused to give him a chance to collect his thoughts and then took out a brief résumé listing highlights of my work as an investigator, criminologist and expert witness. I reached out to hand it to him, but he didn't lean forward to take it.

"No, I don't want that," was all he said.

I put the résumé down on the table between us anyway, knowing full well that after what I had to tell him, he would have every reason to want to know exactly who I was and what cases I had solved. He would soon see that during my three decade long career I had earned an international reputation. He would also realize that I wasn't on a fishing trip. I had the facts of this case at my fingertips: names, dates, and relevant incidents leading up to the murders.

Thinking it best to ease slowly into my presentation, but mindful I had only an hour, I told him flat out that I didn't think O. J. had committed the murders.

"None of the facts of this case point to O. J. as the killer. He had no history of violence—at least not that of a man who would use a knife to kill his ex-wife. He couldn't have driven to the crime scene, committed the murders, and then gotten home without there being more blood evidence in the car or at the house on Rockingham, and he most assuredly wouldn't have acted in such an irrational manner as to premeditate a killing on a busy street like Bundy Drive while Sydney and Justin were only a few feet away."

Dr. Kittay cut me short. "O. J. didn't kill Nicole. He's innocent. I know that. I would even bet my life on it. In fact, I know that the very sight of all that blood would have made O. J. faint. He really is very squeamish about that sort of thing."

"Then that leaves the question of who did commit the murders."

Without mentioning Jason's name, I then went on to list potential suspects I had looked into during the early years of my investigation, and why I had ruled each of them out. Kittay seemed to agree with my reasoning at each step of the way, and added some of his own remarks. He advised that I take a long, hard look at Marcus Allen (the man

Nicole Simpson allegedly referred to as "Drinftwood.") and especially Ron Shipp.

"Marcus was always hitting on Nicole," Dr. Kittay said. "And Ron Shipp had both the motive and the opportunity. I should know because I treated Shipp for quite a while. He's the man I think you ought to be looking into."

I pondered his statement for a moment, wondering if he knew something about Shipp that I didn't. Dr. Kittay then began talking about drugs, and how he was certain they had figured prominently in the murders.

"Did you know that the waiters at the Mezzaluna Restaurant sold cocaine?" he asked.

I nodded.

"Then you must also know about Goldman. He wasn't just a waiter, he was a drug dealer, had been since high school, the way I heard it. He had also broken into his own father's house to steal money from him. When he died, Ron and his father hadn't spoken with one another in three years. He could have been the real target for the murderer, not Nicole. Before Mezzaluna, he worked at the Dragonfly, a nightclub run by Brett Cantor, who was also murdered with a knife, the same as Nicole and Ron. If you find out who killed Cantor, I think you'll know who was at Bundy Drive that night."

I stopped Dr. Kittay to explain to him the many reasons I was convinced that Goldman was not the target of the murderer. If a killer had been stalking Goldman, he would have attacked him back at his apartment, or when he parked on Dorothy Avenue or in the alley behind Nicole's condo. The killer would not have waited for him in front of Nicole's door. And besides, as I pointed out, the forensic evidence suggests that Nicole was hit in the head *before* Ron Goldman was attacked.

Even after I had said all this, Dr. Kittay still seemed to believe there was a drug connection and that I should investigate Ron Shipp. Listening to him speak, I wondered who his sources were. Had he heard these things in his therapy sessions, or had he become an adept student of the Bundy Drive murder case by reading about it in the papers? I couldn't help but notice that the longer he spoke, the further he steered our conversation away from the Simpson family. I wasn't about to let that happen.

"How about Jason?" I asked him.

Kittay smiled, looking genuinely surprised. "Jason had an airtight alibi. He was cooking in front of two hundred people at Jackson's Restaurant on the night of the murders."

"Have you been to Jackson's?" I asked.

He shook his head. "But I've tasted Jason's cooking. He's a fine chef. He's cooked at many of the parties I've been to at O. J.'s house."

"Well," I continued, "if you had been to Jackson's you would know the restaurant doesn't seat two hundred people. Eighty-seven at the most. That's not to say he wasn't cooking there on June 12, because I know in fact that he was the head chef that night. He was planning on cooking a special meal for Nicole, Sydney, and Justin and their family on the night of the murders. Only they didn't show up. No one did. Jason was stood up."

"I didn't know that," Dr. Kittay said.

"Then you must also not know that Jason left Jackson's Restaurant that night no later than 10 PM, carrying his chef's knives in a rolled up chef's bag."

Dr. Kittay responded: "I didn't know that."

"He may also have had a few drinks. Perhaps a line or two of cocaine. And that's dangerous business for someone in his condition. Drugs, alcohol, and stress can trigger a rage seizure."

Now I was looking directly at Kittay, and we were making eye contact. He looked genuinely surprised by what I was telling him, leading me to believe he was either a very good liar, or he truly believed Jason had an airtight alibi for the night of the murders. I also thought it strange that he hadn't stopped me to ask how I knew so much about Jason's activities, both before and after the murders. Nothing I had told him about Jason's activities on June 12, 1994, had ever appeared in the press or in any of the many books written about the murders.

However reluctant I was to share more of what I had learned, I knew I had to give a little in order to get a little.

"Did you know that Jason suffered from intermittent rage disorder, and that he had had several serious incidents of violent and aggressive behavior, and that at the time of the murders, he was on probation for assault with a deadly weapon?"

Again came the response, "I didn't know." Only this time, the doctor spoke these words with a poker face. I could read nothing into his body language or tone of voice.

"Did you know that Jason had attempted suicide on at least three different occasions, once with a pair of scissors, once with a jagged piece of glass from a broken window, and once with an overdose of Depakote, the drug he was taking to control his seizures?"

"I didn't know."

"Did you know that Jason was a patient at St. John's psychiatric ward?"

"I don't know anything about that, Mr. Dear."

"Did you know that Jason may have blamed himself for the death of his twenty-three-month-old little sister who drowned in the pool at Rockingham?"

"We never covered that."

"Don't you think it could have been important?" I asked him, now speaking more forcefully.

Dr. Kittay still didn't acknowledge knowing much, if anything, about Jason's medical history. I glanced at Dr. Davisson who provided me with mute confirmation of what I knew in my head and my heart: any therapist or psychologist worthy of hanging out a shingle had to know something about the root of their patient's problems. Gaining insights into the important incidents in a patient's past was what therapy was all about.

"Did you know Jason admitted he had frequently lied to you?" I asked Dr. Kittay.

As I said this, I rested my hand on the catalogue case I had brought with me, which not only contained a tape recorder, but also was stuffed to overflowing with documentation I had gathered on Jason.

The doctor had no way of knowing what was in that briefcase, but I wanted to let him know, if only in a subtle way, that I was prepared and willing to back up everything I had just told him.

"Jason admitted in therapy sessions that he told you exactly what you wanted to hear. Did you know that?"

Dr. Kittay shook his head.

I continued, even more emphatically, "Then why didn't you? Your name appears right here. You were his psychologist of record. You must have logged hundreds of hours with Jason."

He didn't say a word, just continued looking at me impassively. Finally, he stretched his arms and put his hands on his knees. I thought, at first, that this was a signal that our session had ended. We had already gone a few minutes over our one hour time limit. But Dr. Kittay was not through.

In a tone of voice not altogether confidential, but clearly familiar, he said that he honestly didn't know these things that I had brought to his attention.

"Jason is a very likeable and loving young man. He's had his problems, probably more than his fair share. And he's coped with them remarkably well. He loves his family. They've always been number one. Especially Sydney and Justin. I can't believe for an instant that he'd do anything to harm them."

"Jason has harmed himself and has threatened to hurt others," I said. "That's a fact. Didn't you know that?"

"I don't know that he ever tried to commit suicide. I also don't know that he didn't. But I do know that O. J. wouldn't have covered up for him. Not O. J. I know the man. He wouldn't have covered up for his son. And if, as you say, Jason was guilty, he would get off medically because of his mental problems. And besides, I don't think Jason is smart enough to have pulled off the murders and not gotten caught."

I found Dr. Kittay's responses curious to say the least. Being smart, or stupid, had nothing to do with it. I continued to play devil's advocate, trying to get something more substantial out of him than, "I don't know" and "Jason and O. J. aren't involved." This time I asked him what he thought would have happened if Nicole had been confronted by Jason on the night of the murders, "What might have been said?"

"Nicole could certainly hold her own," he said. "She was a German woman who can take care of herself. She's the kind of girl who can get in your face in no uncertain terms."

"Enough to push someone over the edge?"

"I don't know about that," he said defensively. "Jason loved Nicole very much. He had no reason to want to hurt her, unless, as you say, this was some kind of sudden rage that came over him."

"But you think it may be possible?"

"Anything is possible."

"Are you still treating Jason?"

"No," he said. "Haven't treated him since the murders. As you know, I moved to Texas. I hear he's doing fine. He's attending cooking school in Paris."

Jason, as Dr. Kittay had said, had indeed gone to Paris to cooking school. But I also knew from keeping tabs on various databases and from my repeated trips to Los Angeles that he was back in L.A. now and was a prep chef at a new restaurant that had opened in Santa Monica.

For the second time in the last hour, I couldn't make up my mind about Kittay. Either he was the most inept psychologist I had ever encountered, or he was one hell of a convincing liar.

"It's pretty hot here in Corpus Christi," I said. "What made you want to close down your practice and come out here?"

He smiled. "I never really thought of it until a friend of mine gave me and my wife plane tickets and said I'd absolutely fall in love with it. I did."

I wondered for a brief moment if the gentleman with the plane tickets was Robert Shapiro, O. J.'s attorney. That would explain a lot. But before I could ask that question, Kittay was already telling me what he didn't like about Santa Monica. "It's all the heat and water. Never did like too much sun or ocean."

"Right," I said. "All the sun and water. You move to Corpus Christi from Santa Monica to get away from the sun and ocean."

If the office windows had been open, I was sure I would be able to smell the ocean air blowing in from the Gulf. But the windows were closed because the air conditioner was on. Texas is hot, damn hot. And the ocean in Corpus Christi is anything *but* attractive. This made me wonder why the doctor had really left.

"Do you still have the records you had on Jason?" I asked.

"No," he said. "I shredded them in February of 1995, during O. J.'s trial."

"And DeeDee's records?"

"Yes, those are shredded too. I didn't think it was necessary to keep them."

I smiled. "I suppose that means that O. J.'s and Nicole's and Ron Shipp's records are also gone."

"Yes."

I stood up to stretch my legs. Then I looked at my watch. Our session had lasted forty-five minutes longer than the hour allotted me. "I've taken too much of your time," I said.

"Think nothing of it. I hope I've helped."

Dr. Kittay *had* helped, more than he had imagined. I now knew he had left a lucrative and established practice in Santa Monica to open a fledgling practice in Corpus Christi, just when his patients in California needed him the most. I knew that Kittay had once had medical records on O. J., Nicole, Jason, DeeDee, and Ron Shipp, and that he had shredded them because they contained facts he did not want prosecutors to have. It appeared to me from our conversation that Dr. Kittay was still good friends with O. J. and that, no doubt, they still talked. Finally, I learned he didn't know much about Jason, at least not what I felt a psychologist should have known about him, especially a psychologist who had been treating him for quite some time. Had Dr. Kittay done his job properly, he might have been able to prevent the murders of Nicole Simpson and Ron Goldman—if Jason was in fact the murderer. That was a lot to learn in one short therapy session. Usually it is the patient who does all the talking.

It was at this point that Dr. Davisson finally spoke up, saying he hoped we would be able to continue our conversation at a later time.

"I think Jason needs help," Harvey said. "He's like a time bomb waiting to go off. Between the three of us, I think we can find him the help he needs. That way no one will get hurt."

"I don't think that's necessary," Dr. Kittay responded. "I've told you everything I know."

He reached out and shook my hand, signaling an end to our session. Then he asked me if I had ever met O. J. "You would like him," Kittay said. "He's a real nice guy. He's a good family man and a good father."

"I'm sure he is," I replied, not knowing what purpose Dr. Kittay would have in telling me this, but imagining that I would soon be finding out.

After we had said goodbye, I couldn't wait to get back in the car and hear what Davisson had to say about the meeting. I couldn't tell for certain if Dr. Kittay was truly in the dark about Jason's private life, or whether he knew more and was not sharing it with us. Harvey didn't know for sure one way or the other, but he did observe that no other psychologist he'd ever met seemed to know so little about his or her patients, especially a psychologist who is savvy enough to make it in cities like Brentwood and Beverly Hills. "He's either the most cunning psychologist I've ever met, or the most inept."

I bet on the former. "I think he's cunning. I also bet he's on the phone right now to O. J."

Harvey agreed. He also guessed that the résumé I had left behind on the table, which Dr. Kittay refused to look at, would now be studied thoroughly, both in Corpus Christi and in Brentwood. "I think we'll hear from O. J. soon enough."

"Yes, I believe we will."

I didn't have long to wait. In fact, at 7:10 PM, just two and a half hours after we left Dr. Kittay's office and before Harvey and I had even arrived back in Dallas, I received a message on my voice mail.

17

ENCOURAGEMENT

"**B**ILL, THIS IS BURT Kittay," said the message on my voice mail. "It's important you call me as soon as you get in."

I fully anticipated what it was Kittay wished to tell me. He had, no doubt, called O. J. and discussed some of the things I had shared with him. O. J. and his inner circle were likely having brainstorming sessions to decide what, if anything, they were going to do about my investigation. Even if they realized at this point that I had already gathered most, if not all, the relevant police records and medical history documentation on Jason, and had enough circumstantial evidence to take to the Los Angeles district attorney, they may have believed that my investigation could somehow still be diverted. Either that or their intentions were to lure me back to Los Angeles where I could be intimidated into keeping my mouth shut or convinced to put my investigation on hold.

My flight had been delayed the day before, stranding me in Houston, Texas, where I'd had to spend the night. At 6 AM the next morning I flew back to Dallas. As I entered the office, I was given Dr. Kittay's message. Unknown to Kittay, within an hour I would be leaving on another flight, this time back to Los Angeles. Even though I was in a hurry, I called the phone number he had left at 7:15 PM the previous night. It turned out to be his residence. I was informed that the doctor had already left for the office, and that I could reach him there.

I reached over and pushed the record button on the tape recorder connected to my telephone as I dialed the office. The receptionist answered the phone.

"May I speak to Dr. Kittay please?" I asked.

"The doctor is in session," she replied. "May I ask who is calling?"

"My name is Bill Dear and I'm returning his call. Would you please tell the doctor that I called?"

There was a sudden pause. Then she said, "Just a moment, Mr. Dear. I've been instructed to put you through as soon as you called. Please hold on."

I knew then that Kittay was anxious to pass on some information to me. It was also nice to know I now had his home telephone number as well as his office number so that I could check phone records later, if need be, to prove that Dr. Kittay—after Dr. Davisson and I had left his office—had spoken long distance to O. J. Simpson.

Immediately, the doctor got on the phone.

"Dr. Kittay," I said. "This is Bill Dear. I'm sorry I couldn't return your call last night. I was stranded at the airport and didn't receive your message until this morning."

"You should have let me know," Dr. Kittay said. "You could have stayed with us."

"I appreciate the offer."

"Mr. Simpson has some documents and files that I think you'd like to see. No one outside of O. J. and his staff have ever read them before. If you're going to be in Los Angeles in the near future I can arrange for you to see them."

"As a matter of fact, I'm planning on being there today."

"Good," he said, obviously relieved. "Please call Cathy Randa or Bill Pavelic when you get into town. I'll give you their telephone numbers. They'll be expecting your call and will arrange a meeting."

Cathy Randa, who lived in North Hollywood, was O. J.'s longtime and deeply devoted secretary. Bill Pavelic, an ex-LAPD officer living in Glendale, was O. J.'s private investigator. They were not part of the inner circle; they were the inner circle, or at least what was left of it, along with A. C. Cowlings.

Dr. Kittay had apparently told O. J. everything we'd discussed, because a meeting with O. J.'s top brass could not have happened without O. J.'s permission. I was not surprised. In all honesty, I fully expected he would share the confidential details of our private session. No doubt O. J., and possibly Jason himself, would just "happen" to drop by while my meeting with Randa and Pavelic was taking place. I had no intention of meeting with Bill Pavelic, but I would meet with Cathy Randa. I was looking forward to it. She could fill in the gaps that I needed to complete my investigation, even though she might not realize the significance of what she might be telling me.

"I'll call Cathy Randa when I get to town," I told Kittay.

Before he hung up, he explained exactly what I was to do when I called. "Cathy Randa's phone will be answered by an answering machine. Wait for the beep, and then tell her who you are, and she will pick up the phone. Otherwise she will not take the call."

I had, in fact, already planned on making another trip to Los Angeles, where I intended to interview Ron Shipp and then track down Jennifer Green, Jason's girlfriend at the time of the murders. I just hadn't anticipated having to conduct the interviews so soon. Time was now of the essence because I had every reason to believe that O. J. and his inner circle would do everything within their power to keep me from making any more headway. I had one extremely good reason to believe this was already the case: since I had returned from Corpus Christi I found that my office and home were being watched.

I live on a cul-de-sac. It's hard to find me. As I pulled out of my driveway to go to the airport for my flight to Los Angeles, I spotted a late model Mercedes hidden at the end of the cul-de-sac, partially out of view. I knew it didn't belong there. As I continued to the stop sign and made my left turn, I checked my rearview mirror and saw that the Mercedes had started to move forward. There was no doubt that the two people in the car were following me. They were on my turf now. I made several more turns and then pulled into a familiar residential area. I knew exactly where I was going. I parked behind a friend's house, and then watched as the Mercedes slowly drove by. Then I picked up the microphone on my two-way radio and called Waylon Roberts, one of the investigators from my office, to tell him someone was following me.

"What's your ten-twenty?" I asked Waylon.

He told me he was on Belt Line Road and Highway 67, about three miles from where I was.

"That's perfect," I told him. "I'm going to pull out and let them catch up with me. You swing in behind them and get their tag number.

Within three minutes I saw Waylon swing in behind the Mercedes that was now three car lengths behind me. Like a professional, the driver was being careful to always keep at least two cars between us. He was good, but not that good.

Finally Waylon was back on the two-way radio telling me he had gotten the tag numbers on the Mercedes.

"Good work," I told him. "Now pass around him and pull in behind me."

The driver of the Mercedes had no idea the vehicle that just pulled in front of them, a blue 1997 Nissan pickup, belonged to one of my staff investigators.

I got back on the two-way radio with Waylon, instructing him to slow down. "Make it look like you're searching for the right street to make a turn on."

As Waylon made his maneuver, I sped up—not too noticeably, but enough so that I was able to make the intersection at Belt Line Road and Interstate 20 just as the traffic light turned red. There was no way they were going to follow me today.

"Good luck Bill," Waylon said. "I'll see you when you get back."

Before signing off, I told Waylon to have my secretary run the license tag on the Mercedes. "Pull up everything you have on the driver. I'll call you from Los Angeles."

As it turned out, that particular license number on the Mercedes, which had a Texas registration, showed not to be currently registered with the Department of Motor Vehicles in Austin. I was not surprised, because a good investigator should always anticipate that someone might get his tag number. The object is not to be identified.

It was just past 10 AM when I landed in Long Beach and picked up my rental car. Minutes later I was on the 405 Freeway traveling north to Santa Clarita, where I had made reservations at a Marriott Hotel. I had chosen to stay in Santa Clarita for two reasons. It was close to the home of Ron Shipp, whom I wished to interview first, and because no one would think to look for me there. If O. J. and his investigators actually had my Dallas offices under surveillance and were asking around Los Angeles for me, it wouldn't take them long to come looking for me at the Best Western on Santa Monica Boulevard, where I normally stayed. If that were the case, this would keep his people guessing.

Ron Shipp was not expecting to see me. I planned to drop in on him unannounced, preferring to take this more direct approach rather than contacting his attorney or sending him a letter. He could always tell me to leave, but at least this way I would have an opportunity to tell him how it was that I had come to be knocking on his door, and to appeal—as one former police officer to another—to his sense of justice and fair play. There wasn't a policeman or ex-policeman I had ever met who wouldn't stop and help someone if they could. And no doubt Shipp, of all people, who had openly been called a liar by O. J.'s family during their trial testimony, desired closure to this case as much as I did.

By noon, I had checked into my hotel and was driving up the winding road that led to Ron and Nina Shipp's two-story house. It was a lovely neighborhood of modest homes with well-kept lawns and families who clearly cared about their property and environment. It was also a community, I had been told, with more than its fair share of retired as well as active LAPD officers, who had come here to escape the problems of the inner city and see to it that those problems don't spread to their own neighborhoods.

Everything in Santa Clarita looked brand new. Construction was going on everywhere, including on the quiet tree-lined road where

Shipp's house sat on a hill overlooking what was identified by a sign as the Santa Clarita River, which was something of a misnomer, because it appeared to have been dry for years.

There was a blue Toyota parked in the driveway as I pulled up. This was a good sign that Shipp or his wife was home. I parked the car, walked up to the house, and rang the doorbell. After waiting a few moments, I knocked and then knocked again. There was still no answer. Finally, I called out in a voice loud enough for my words to carry through the front door and beyond, "Mr. Shipp, my name is Bill Dear. I'm a private investigator from Dallas. I'd like to talk to you."

I stood for a moment hoping for a response, but there was nothing except the sound of a dog scratching to get out and see who was standing on the porch. I was just about to turn and leave when I heard a man's gentle voice quiet the dog. He then asked, "Exactly what do you want?"

I introduced myself again, this time volunteering to show him my identification if he would open the door to look at it. He still did not open up.

"What do you want?" he asked again.

"I'm working on the Nicole Simpson and Ron Goldman murder case. I've been on the case for the past six years. I'm not working for O. J., and I'm not with the DA's office, and I'm not working for the Goldman or Brown families. I'm doing this entirely on my own. I would like to see closure brought to this case."

"I don't talk about the Simpson case anymore," he said. "It's caused me enough trouble. That's all behind me. No offense, but I'd like you to go away."

"I can respect that," I said. "And I will go away if that's what you want. But I think you'll see that I have collected some evidence in this case that no one else has seen before, and I think you'll want to talk to me. In fact, I've just come back from Corpus Christi where I interviewed Dr. Burton Kittay."

Now, from the other side of the door, I could hear the sound of a dead-bolt lock click open.

"Burt? You've talked to Burt Kittay?" he asked.

"That's right. He's said a few things about O. J. and Nicole and about you that you might like to hear."

"I wouldn't put much stock in anything Burt said. I could tell you things about that doctor that would make your head spin."

"That's what I'd like to know more about, Mr. Shipp, because, at this point, I don't put much stock in Dr. Kittay either. In fact, I wouldn't be a bit surprised if he was still working with O. J."

I thought for a moment that I might have caught Shipp's interest, but I discovered I was wrong. "I've stopped giving interviews," he said. "Please don't take offense. It's just that I've been there already and I can't keep talking about O. J. and Nicole or I won't have any time for anything else. It's hard enough making ends meet as it is."

"I can respect that," I said. "Your time is valuable."

"That's right. The last interview I gave was to a television network. I got $2,500 for it. I can get that much and more for my lectures and talks on domestic violence."

"Time is money," I said. "That's true for me as it is for you. And if that's what it will take for us to sit down and talk about this case and what I've learned, I don't mind paying for your time."

There was a long pause, as if Shipp hadn't expected me to be willing to go in that direction. I wasn't actually sure that I was, but it was a way of testing the water and, at the least, to have him open the door for a moment. That was all I would need.

"I would want a thousand dollars."

"That's a lot of money for a private investigator who's working on his own time and paying his own bills."

"It's a thousand dollars or nothing. Put the money in the mail and we can set something up."

For a brief moment, I considered his proposition. I had not paid a single person in my investigation for an interview, and I didn't wish to begin doing so now. However, I had paid people for their time. I also wanted to interview Shipp because he was the only person who had once been in O. J.'s inner circle who might be willing to speak frankly about the dynamics of O. J.'s relationship with Jason. Reading reports was one thing. I now wanted to hear what happened from someone who had actually been there, and I doubted very seriously that A. C. Cowlings, Jason's godfather, would talk to me. I also considered the fact that it would cost me well over $1,500 to make a return trip to Los Angeles, so paying the thousand was starting to look feasible.

"I hadn't planned on paying for an interview, but if that's what it will take for us to sit down together, then I'll consider doing it. Only it's got to be right here and right now. I don't want to have to come back to Los Angeles."

"I could do it now," Shipp said.

I had almost $1,000 in my billfold, but I wasn't about to give him all my cash, at least until I was certain he had something to contribute to my investigation. I suggested another proposition.

"As I said before, time is money. I can give you $500 in cash now, if that's what it will take for you and me to sit down and talk honestly about this case. And I'll send you another $500 when I get back to Dallas. You'll just have to trust me, as I'll trust you."

There was another long pause during which I could hear nothing except the dog scratching at the door. Then it opened and Ron Shipp stood in front of me. He was a black man of medium height and build, with short hair and freckles. He was dressed casually in jeans and a sport shirt, and looked as if he had been reading the paper and having his morning coffee when I knocked.

I showed Shipp my private investigator's license, then counted out five $100 bills.

"I'll still want something in writing," he said.

"I wouldn't have it any other way."

Shipp opened the door for me to come in. "You're lucky you caught me," he said. "I was just getting ready to leave."

As I stepped inside, I could see that Shipp's home was well kept, and decorated with family pictures and commendations from his fifteen or more years with the LAPD. None of the photographs included pictures of O. J. or Nicole. The focus was, understandably, on his family, especially one of his two sons, David, who was a high school track star. The family was clearly proud of him because across the living room wall was a banner celebrating David winning a silver medal at the junior Olympics that had been held in Omaha, Nebraska, only a few days earlier. Shipp was beaming as he showed me the medal. "He's worked very hard for this," he said.

I was shown into the dining room, where we took seats across from one another at a table cluttered with children's toys, papers, and an open Bible. Later, I would notice the pending foreclosure notice on his home, sitting underneath the Bible. Times were clearly hard for Ron Shipp.

Before discussing the case, we proceeded to draft and then to sign a short letter of agreement. I had him make me a copy.

"I'll want you to tell the truth," I said in no uncertain terms, "not what you think I might want to hear."

"I've got nothing to hide at this point," he replied, looking me straight in the eye. "I'll tell you the truth just as if I were on a witness stand."

"That's all I want, Ron, the truth."

I believed at this point that he would tell me the truth. I also believed that he had previously spoken the truth at the Simpson trial, though doing so had put him in the unfortunate position of losing friends on both sides of the case. The Simpson camp had disowned him for implicating O. J. in the murders and the LAPD and DA's office inherently distrusted him for having once been O. J.'s friend and confidant. It was one of those "no-win" situations.

I was also aware that journalist Neil Schulman had self-published a book on the Simpson murder case and was going on radio talk-shows promoting a theory which suggested that Shipp had killed Nicole Simpson and Ron Goldman in order to frame O. J. for murder. This was exactly the same theory Dr. Kittay had discussed at length with Dr. Davisson and me in Corpus Christi only a few days earlier. Having read the book and then meeting Dr. Kittay, I had every reason to believe the psychologist and Schulman had talked at length about the case, though the doctor's name didn't appear in the book.

"I put a stop to Schulman almost as soon as I heard what he was up to," Shipp explained. "I called up this one radio station when he was being interviewed and told him that if he kept telling people that I had killed Nicole and Goldman, I was going to sue him for every cent he had. And do you know what Schulman said? He said he didn't own anything so that there wasn't anything I could collect. I said, 'You're driving a car, aren't you? That's going to be mine if you keep maliciously spreading lies that you know not to be true.'"

I told Shipp I found it not a little coincidental that Dr. Kittay had told me some of the same things that had appeared in the Schulman book: that Shipp, as O. J.'s friend and confidant, had access to the Rockingham house, knew Nicole, and could have committed the murders and framed O. J. as a way of getting back at O. J. for ending their friendship.

"Mr. Dear," he said, "if the Los Angeles Police Department thought I was in any way guilty of the murders of Nicole or Goldman they would have polygraphed me. I have no problem being polygraphed by you or anyone else. I did not, nor am I responsible in any way for the murders of Nicole and Goldman. The LAPD knows it, and so does Schulman."

Now Shipp smiled. "I don't need friends that bad," he said. "It stretches the imagination that Schulman or Kittay or anyone else would think that I would commit double homicide, then risk driving over to Rockingham and sneaking around the house, while O. J. and Kato were home, to plant all the evidence. And all because O. J. supposedly didn't want to be my friend any longer. Hell, I was with O. J. right before the murders and right after he returned from Chicago. The only reason O. J. turned on me was because I wasn't willing to cover up for him."

I availed myself of the opportunity, while we were on the subject of Shipp's being a suspect in the murder case, to ask where he had been on the night of the murders.

Shipp laughed. "I was at home with my wife and children," he said. "The LAPD knew that. And so did O. J.'s defense team. They all knew it. That's why the only thing they could use to try and impeach me as a witness was to harp on my drinking problem and suggest that I also used drugs. I'm not squeaky clean. I did have alcohol problems. That's why I took early retirement from the force. But I never lied on that stand. Everything I said was the truth. That's why O. J. had it in for me."

I pointed out to him that Schulman, despite the fact that he himself acknowledged in the book that he had no money, took out a large and expensive newspaper ad promoting his theory. "Do you think O. J. is the one behind the book, and that Dr. Kittay is Schulman's secret source?" I asked.

"I don't think there's any question about that," he said. "O. J. wants to get me any way that he can. And he has friends who have money."

"Why would he want to frame you?"

"Because I know he's guilty and I'm the only one of his former friends who is willing to come right out and say so. There's just no other way to look at it. The facts speak for themselves."

Here was the opening I was looking for, a chance to steer our interview in the direction I wanted it to go. I had the facts. Now I was going to share them with Shipp.

"If I could prove to you that O. J. didn't commit the murder, would you be interested in what I have to say?" I asked.

Shipp shook his head no. "I wouldn't be interested because I know he killed Nicole and Ron Goldman as sure as I'm sitting here."

"But if, hypothetically, I could prove he didn't commit the murders, only that he was there at the crime scene after they happened, would you be interested?"

"I'd like to be able to tell you I would be interested but I just can't go there. I know he did it. I know he killed them."

I thanked him for his honesty but told him that before the day was over I hoped to convince him otherwise. And if I couldn't do that, I had wasted a thousand dollars.

He smirked, obviously thinking I had indeed wasted my money if I expected him to change his mind.

"Let's start with Dr. Kittay," I said. "If anyone was in a position to see what was going to happen or what may have happened, don't you think he would be the one? And yet, his name didn't appear anywhere in the criminal trial. From what I gather, no one asked him a single question."

Shipp agreed that Dr. Kittay certainly should have known what was happening. But according to Shipp, the doctor was "too stupid" to put it together or to be part of a conspiracy to protect O. J. "O. J. was using Dr. Kittay right from the start. He's still using him now."

According to Shipp, Kittay was the most "gullible" and "inept" psychologist he had ever met. Shipp had reached this conclusion early on in his own therapy sessions with the doctor, which was long before O. J., and then Nicole, began seeing him. The reason Shipp had started therapy was because of his drinking problem. It was either see Dr. Kittay or leave the LAPD. The doctor came recommended by other officers on the force because he was so personable and easy to get along with. Also, according to Shipp, Kittay's therapy sessions were done over the phone, so as not to interfere with Shipp's busy work schedule.

"It was kind of a joke around the precinct," he said. "I would be asked if I had had my weekly therapy session and I would say, 'Yes, I just got off the phone.'"

I laughed along with him, for "phone therapy" didn't exactly promote honest communication. For Shipp, it was merely a means of satisfying the terms of his agreement with the LAPD that he would seek counseling. Listening to him describe such sessions, I wondered if the same "telephone therapy" sessions had occurred between Jason and Dr. Kittay. That might explain how Jason's psychologist may truly *not* have known that his patient had slit his wrists with a shard of glass from a broken window or used a pair of scissors to stab himself in the stomach. Jason didn't volunteer the information, and Kittay didn't know enough to ask.

Phone therapy sessions were not the only thing about Dr. Kittay that eventually came to bother Ron Shipp. Kittay, according to Shipp, constantly talked about his own marital problems and the problems of other patients during therapy sessions. In one particularly notable incident, the doctor had told Shipp how angry and upset he was that another therapist had allegedly "stolen" Paul Newman's son from him as a patient. This was the son, I knew, who had later committed suicide in a Los Angeles hotel.

"I couldn't believe Kittay was telling me about another patient," Shipp said. "Later, he would talk with me about the sessions he had with O. J. and Nicole. There was this one particular day when he said to me, 'I can see why O. J. is having these problems because Nicole is always in his face.' I started telling myself, 'Hey, wait a minute, if Kittay is going to talk to me about sessions he has with O. J., then he's going to be telling O. J. about the sessions he has with me. I don't want O. J. knowing all this stuff about my life in the LAPD.'"

By this time, however, both O. J. and Nicole were having sessions with Dr. Kittay, along with the rest of the greater Simpson clan. According to Shipp, not only did Jason begin treatments with the doctor, but so did Arnelle, Cathy Randa, and members of Randa's family. "There's no telling how many people started with Dr. Kittay once O. J. had given his stamp of approval. Burt would tell me about Cathy Randa's drinking problem and that Nicole wanted Randa fired."

I couldn't help being disturbed that a doctor, especially a psychologist whom people opened up their lives to, had freely discussed what was told him in confidence. I now felt entirely justified in the conclusions I had previously reached about Dr. Kittay.

The attraction that O. J. had for the doctor, according to Shipp, was easy to explain. "O. J. did the talking, Kittay listened. Then he told O. J. exactly what he wanted to hear. In O. J.'s case, that mostly had to do with his treatment of Nicole. Shipp didn't deny that O. J. abused Nicole; he just said that the doctor appeared to be condoning O. J.'s behavior. Kittay suggested that Nicole kept pushing him to the edge by carrying on and making a "big deal" out of everything.

"There was this one day when Nicole called me up to complain about Kittay," Shipp said. "'Who is this guy?' she asked me. 'Where does he get off saying I'm the one to blame for what O. J.'s doing?'"

As Shipp explained to me, Nicole stopped seeing Dr. Kittay soon afterward. But this didn't stop the doctor from ingratiating himself further into the Simpson family. According to Shipp, Kittay would come to all the parties O. J. gave, and he, Dr. Kittay, would invite Cathy Randa and her family up to his vacation cabin.

"It was all one happy family," Shipp said. "But it was all based on lies. No one wanted to hear the truth."

From then on Shipp did his best to watch what he said to the therapist. One of the last conversations they had was on June 17, 1994, during O. J.'s slow-speed car chase, when Dr. Kittay called Shipp at his house in Santa Clarita. Shipp specifically remembered the call because it made him wonder about some of the things O. J. and Kittay must have talked about during their weekly sessions.

"Do you think he did it?" Shipp remembered Kittay asking him.

"Yes," Shipp had answered. "I think he did do it."

"Then if he really did kill Nicole, I'm not a very good psychologist, am I?"

Shipp was inclined to tell Dr. Kittay that, indeed, he wasn't a good psychologist, and that, yes, he was responsible, to one degree or another, for letting O. J. get away with as much as he did for as long as he did.

Dr. Kittay, according to Shipp, was genuinely surprised by the events that were taking place right after the murders. He then told him something important. The therapist told Shipp he had "nothing to worry about," that his secrets were safe. "Everything is going to be OK. Your records are destroyed. They're all gone."

The impression Shipp had, and that he had communicated to Nina, his wife, was that the doctor was busy shredding files, even as they were speaking on the phone. The doctor allegedly kept telling Shipp, "They are all gone. The records are gone. Not to worry."

Shipp wasn't worried about his own records. "Hell, I had my own copies," Shipp told me. "What Kittay was worried about was his own butt."

Everything Shipp was telling me made perfect sense. Dr. Kittay must have been running scared when it looked like O. J. Simpson, "fugitive from justice," was going to be arrested for killing his ex-wife and Ron Goldman. And that was probably when he shredded the records, not when the doctor decided to get away from all the "sea" and the "sun" and move to Corpus Christi. To me, this was proof that the doctor was lying to me when Dr. Davisson and I met with him in Corpus Christi. He told me he had shredded the records of these patients in February of 1995, but in actuality—based on what Shipp had just told me—he shredded them on June 17, 1994, the day of the slow-speed car chase.

The only question in my mind was whether Dr. Kittay was trying to escape being questioned about Jason as well as O. J. After hearing Shipp talk about Kittay, I suspected that the therapist was truly in the dark about the entire thing. Kittay didn't suspect Jason because his therapy sessions with him were as in-depth as the Shipp phone-in sessions at the LAPD. Dr. Kittay said as much to Dr. Davisson and me when he kept declaring: "I didn't know this . . . I didn't know this . . . I didn't know this . . ." It appeared the doctor merely told his patients what they wanted to hear.

I changed the subject by asking when Shipp first began to suspect that the Simpson family dynamics were not as healthy as they should or could have been. Shipp stepped back fifteen or more years, to the day when he first met O. J. He truly did adore O. J. at that time, and his infatuation with him only continued. Despite all the accusations that had been made about the drugs and alcohol, however, Shipp himself claimed never to have seen O. J. using drugs, and only once did he ever see him drunk.

"I knew there were problems," he said. "There are problems in every family. But I didn't begin to see the darker side of O. J. until I had a conversation one day with Nicole. She called me up on the phone and had me come over to Rockingham. I don't know where O. J. was, but Nicole and I were alone, seated in the sunken room off the kitchen where everyone watched television."

According to Shipp, Nicole said, "O. J. is not the person you think he is." Nicole allegedly went on to describe how O. J. physically abused her, as he was alleged to have previously abused Marguerite. "He'll listen to you," Shipp remembered Nicole telling him. "Talk to him. Make him stop."

Shipp said he tried talking to O. J. but that O. J. wouldn't listen. It just made him all the angrier that Nicole would confide in him and tell him the "family secrets."

He was absolutely convinced that O. J. did indeed beat her.

"I didn't see it for myself. But I believed her when Nicole told me. O. J. had this side to him that could be so cruel. The sad thing about it was that if you looked at Nicole and got to know her as I did, you could see that she really was a model wife. She loved and took care of Sydney and Justin as she loved and took care of Jason and Arnelle. But O. J. just kept fooling around. It would drive her nuts."

"Did Nicole try to get back at O. J. by sleeping with Marcus Allen?" I asked.

"I never saw her with Marcus so I really couldn't say. But she was certainly capable of it. You see, O. J. and Nicole really did have a love/hate relationship. Nicole couldn't stand O. J. fooling around, and he couldn't stand her seeing anyone else. Even when they were separated all they could talk about was each other. I would take O. J. aside and tell him that Nicole was her own person now and she had a right to sleep with anyone she chose. O. J. was certainly sleeping with anyone he wanted to go to bed with. But they just couldn't get each other out of their systems. Right up until the end, they were deeply in love."

Shipp remembered calling Nicole on her birthday, after she had come down with pneumonia. That was when O. J. had brought her the chicken soup. "Isn't that sweet of him?" Nicole told Shipp. "He's bringing me chicken soup. I really love that man."

Shipp was less concerned with her and O. J.'s love life than he was with the fact that Nicole, a young and healthy woman in the prime of life, had come down with pneumonia. "Don't you think you ought to slow down?" he asked her.

"Ron, I can't believe it. You, of all people, telling me to slow down!"

"OK, you've got me there," he'd said, referring to his own drinking binges. "I'm just worried for you."

I asked Shipp about Jason. "Did O. J. beat on him as he did Nicole?"

Shipp nodded. "Yeah, he beat Jason. I really felt sorry for that kid. O. J. was harder on him than he was on Arnelle or any of the other children. He rode him hard."

I pressed him further. "It's like this," he told me. "Jason was always embarrassing his dad. Like at USC, when Jason got kicked out, or whatever happened. It embarrassed O. J. O. J. didn't like being embarrassed. Jason just wasn't the athlete O. J. wanted, and he wasn't the smartest guy either, and O. J. knew it. Arnelle had her problems with her dad, but they weren't to the extreme that they were with Jason."

As I previously knew, and now reconfirmed, Shipp had been called by Rolf, O. J.'s Rockingham caretaker, on the night when Jason attacked the bronze statue of his father.

"I responded to the call. I sat down with Jason that night, and he opened up to me. I felt so bad about it. Jason just unloaded on me. 'Dad is always so hard on me,' he said. And he was saying all of this stuff about him and his dad and how they didn't get along and he made me promise I wouldn't tell O. J. I said, 'OK, I'm not going to tell him.' But that night I'm talking to O. J., and he wanted to know what happened, and I said everything is cool. Just let it go. And O. J. says, 'I want to know. I have to know what the problems are so I can deal with them.' And I told him a little about what happened. The next day Jason called me. He said, 'My dad beat me because of what you told him. You promised you wouldn't tell.' 'I know,' I told Jason, 'I was just trying to help, and I thought your dad was really concerned.' "

The irony was that what O. J. allegedly got the most upset about was that Jason had talked to Shipp, an outsider. "Yet it was an outsider whom O. J. called when Jason had trouble with cocaine and had a seizure," Shipp said. "I was called to come to the house and see what I could do."

I knew that story because I had read it in previous reports. I just didn't know that Jason's seizure had occurred at the Rockingham house. His father had been at the house and called Ron in to help deal with it or, at the very least, to help contain any bad press. This again confirmed to me that O. J. didn't like being embarrassed. He didn't want any bad publicity coming out of his house.

Shipp couldn't remember any other incidents involving Jason and drugs, but he suspected his troubles had just continued to get worse. "Jason and his father never did see eye to eye on things. Nicole took some of the pressure off, however. They both loved that woman."

I told Shipp I had heard much the same thing. Jason loved Nicole. I wondered, out loud, if he had physically loved her, like a man loves a woman, and whether or not Nicole might have toyed or flirted with Jason the way she did with other men just to get back at O. J.

I asked Shipp if Nicole could have tried to get back at O. J. by flirting with his son.

"I don't think so. At least I never saw her do something like that with him. But I will say that Jason loved her. It was hard not to. She was always so much fun. I remember how Nicole would always want to go out dancing, but O. J. would never want to go because he didn't like to dance. Jason, however, loved to dance. And it was Jason who would always accompany her out to the clubs. They would dance and have a great time together. Sometimes they would stand around in the kitchen and talk about cooking. I suppose, when the break-up occurred, it was really hard on Jason because he had lost a stepmother and a good friend."

"Do you remember whether or not Jason continued to see her after the divorce?" I asked.

"I'm sure he did. But it wasn't the same. She had changed."

I urged Shipp to tell me how Nicole had changed. This was of particular interest to me because I remembered that Jason, in his deposition, had also said so. He led me to believe that Nicole had not only emotionally changed, but also that she had physically undergone a change. He said she was more muscular. "Like a welterweight fighter," he seemed to be saying.

"Do you think Jason was affected by the changes?"

Shipp supposed he could have been. He also said it was possible that once his father was out of the picture, Jason might have entertained the notion of being with Nicole as so many other men had been. Jason could well have known about the other men. But there was one other thing . . ."

He stopped to compose his thoughts, as if he had suddenly remembered something he hadn't thought about for quite some time. "Here's something for you, Bill," he said. "I don't know if it means anything or not. But it is interesting and might shed some light on what was going on."

According to Shipp, Nicole had called him from Gretna Green, shortly before she moved to Bundy Drive. She called him because she was worried someone was spying on her. Shipp said he came over to the house, where they sat down on her sofa and shared a six-pack of Corona beer. Suddenly, in the middle of their conversation, Nicole jumped to her feet and ran to the window, as if she had seen someone outside. She stood there dumbfounded. Shipp said he looked through the window, then went outside to check but could see no one. He asked Nicole whom she had seen.

"I fully expected her to say that O. J. was out there, but instead she said, 'I don't think it was O. J., it looked like Jason.'"

This turned out to be extremely important to me. Jason wanted to know who Nicole was seeing. He was jealous, just like his Dad.

With this in mind, I asked Shipp to explain to me what convinced him beyond any shadow of doubt that O. J. had killed Nicole. "Couldn't he have been at the crime scene covering up for someone?"

"I don't think so," Shipp responded. "But as I said, I can't go there. After that night when O. J. had me up to his bedroom and started asking me all the questions, I no longer had any doubt that he was the killer."

The meeting which he was referring to allegedly took place when O. J. had returned from Chicago, but before the slow-speed car chase. As Shipp had testified in court, O. J. invited him over to the house, and then into his bedroom, where he asked him all kinds of questions about the LAPD and how they investigated murders.

Ron said he felt uncomfortable, as O. J. was standing there only in his underwear.

I interrupted Ron and asked whether or not he noticed any marks or bruises on O. J. that might indicate he had been in a scuffle or fight in the past couple of days.

Ron said, "No," he didn't see any bruises or unusual marks from where he was standing which was not that far away from O. J. Then O. J. allegedly asked how long it took for DNA and other forensic evidence to be processed. Shipp wanted to know why O. J. had refused to take a polygraph test when Vannatter and Lange asked him to do so. O. J. had said he couldn't bring himself to take the test because of the impure thoughts he had had about Nicole, and because he had dreamt about killing her. Shipp said O. J. felt that if he denied this during the polygraph test it would be perceived as lying and he would fail the test.

"I knew it right then," Shipp told me. "Anyone who won't take a polygraph test is afraid of being caught in a lie. I know because I've asked dozens of people to take a polygraph, and the ones who try and get around it, or come up with one excuse or another not to take it, are the guilty ones."

"Couldn't O. J. have been trying to get out of the polygraph test because he knew what happened on Bundy Drive, but wasn't the killer?"

"I suppose it's possible," Shipp said. "But as I said before, I can't go there. O. J. is guilty."

"Then why don't you let me try and take you there," I said.

Sensing that I had gotten about as much information as I could out of Shipp and feeling even more secure in my own theory of the murders, I proceeded to outline how I thought Nicole Simpson and Ron Goldman were killed. I told him about Jason's various medical disorders and his three suicide attempts. I told him that he had been on probation at the time of the murders for having attacked his boss with a deadly weapon at the Revival Café. I then told him about Jason's job at Jackson's Restaurant, his plans for cooking for Nicole that night, and Jason's supposed alibi.

"I think Jason went over that night to have it out with Nicole," I said. "He wanted to know why she stood him up at Jackson's, and why she had embarrassed him in front of his fellow employees."

Based on what Ron Shipp had told me earlier, O. J. didn't like being embarrassed. I was sure Jason felt the same way, and communicated this to Shipp. "I think Nicole just laid down the law with him. I think she told him to get the hell out of her life. That was enough to set him off."

For the first time since coming into Shipp's house, I think I had truly surprised and impressed him with the great detail I had gone into about Jason's medical problems, rages, temper, relationships with previous girlfriends, and arrests. These were things Ron Shipp had known nothing about.

"I didn't know all that stuff about Jason," he said. "If what you say is true, and I'm not saying it is, it's one hell of a story. Especially if you can get Jason's girlfriends to back you up. People are going to listen to what you have to say. And they'll believe it."

"Do you believe it, Mr. Shipp?" I asked.

"I honestly don't know what to believe at this point. I do know one thing. You better watch yourself, because dealing with the press is going to be the least of your problems."

I could only suppose that the problems Shipp was referring to were Jason and his father and the lengths they might go to to prevent the truth from becoming public—especially two people who were so concerned about being embarrassed. Shipp knew O. J. all too well. He was not about to let a story like this come out without a fight, not after all they had been through in the criminal and then the civil trial. Shipp also knew how important it was that I speak to Jason's girlfriend, Jennifer Green, and possibly his girlfriend before that, the so-called DeeDee.

"Ron," I asked, "Do you know DeeDee's last name?"

"No, I knew her only as DeeDee."

"Do you know where she works?"

"No, I don't."

I stopped at this point because I could see that Shipp was distracted. He was looking down at his Bible and appeared lost in thought. "What is it?" I asked.

"I'm thinking about what you said to me. You're making me begin to wonder. I can't help but think, based on what you've told me, if O. J. could have been covering for Jason after all."

I knew it was time for me to leave. I had what I wanted. Not only did I get the information I had sought, but also I had one of O. J.'s longtime friends, the single friend who had testified against him at the trial, now beginning to doubt O. J.'s guilt.

"I'll put your check in the mail on Tuesday, as soon as I return to Dallas."

"I trust you," he said and then fell silent again, lost in thought.

I stood up to leave. As I did so, he too stood up and walked me to the door. I turned to shake his hand, pleased that I had helped him—at least in some small way—toward making his mortgage payments, and thinking this might be the last time I would ever see Ron Shipp. But he surprised me by walking with me out to my car, which was parked in front of his house.

As I got in and started the engine, I glanced into my rearview mirror. Shipp was still standing on the curb in front of his driveway, his head down. It was obvious he was now considering the possibility that O. J. was innocent after all. Earlier, he had repeatedly said, "I can't go there .... I can't go there. I can't go there."

Now, it seemed that he had gone there.

18

DENIAL

FINDING JENNIFER GREEN, JASON'S girlfriend at the time of the murders, didn't pose much of a challenge. Neighbors at her and Jason's former residence on North Sycamore Avenue referred me to a hair salon on Beverly Drive where she once had worked as a receptionist. Then a hairdresser who knew her from that salon directed me to an upscale ladies clothing and accessories boutique on nearby La Brea Avenue where she was working as a salesgirl.

I did not have a plan in mind other than to approach her with complete honesty, as I had Ron Shipp, and then see what developed. Either she would give me the brush-off—as I fully expected would be the case—or she would share her side of the story. I didn't expect anything in-between for the sole reason that Jason and his family would surely have discussed with her the real possibility that reporters would eventually question her about them. Regardless of what she might have to say, however, I needed to hear her side of the story, if indeed she was willing to speak openly about the events surrounding the murders. And if I could engage her in a dialogue, I would at least have a chance to address the facts of the case as I knew them to be at this point in my investigation, and possibly uncover something I didn't know.

Since this was Jennifer's place of business and it was my desire to be as unobtrusive as possible, I made repeated visits to the boutique, biding my time until I would have an opportunity to find her alone. That came on a Thursday morning, when no customers were in the store.

Jennifer was, and is, a beautiful woman, just as she had been described to me by her former employer at the hair salon. The tall, former model and salon receptionist, now twenty eight years old, had sky blue eyes, black hair, and an olive complexion. There could be no mistaking her.

Before I entered the boutique I reached into my coat pocket. Inside, I had a special rollerball pen which had been modified to record fifty-eight minutes of conversation, for corroboration. This might be my one and only interview with Jennifer Green.

As I entered the boutique, I spotted her standing behind the counter in the middle of the room, idly flipping through the pages of a fashion magazine.

I didn't give her a chance to ask if she could help me, but stepped up to the counter. After confirming that she was indeed Jennifer Green, I shook her hand and introduced myself.

"I'm Bill Dear. I've flown in from Dallas. I'd like to talk to you."

Jennifer looked surprised and taken aback, as if someone had just slapped a subpoena in her hand. "You're not from the *National Enquirer*, are you? If that's where you're from, you can get out of here right this minute."

I smiled, showed her my credentials, and then handed her my business card. "No, I'm not from the *National Enquirer*. As I said before, my name is Bill Dear. I'm a private investigator from Dallas, Texas. I'm working on the Nicole Simpson and Ron Goldman murder case."

Jennifer's expression changed. She still looked tense and uncomfortable, but the anger had vanished from her blue eyes. "I'm sorry, Mr. Dear," she said, looking at my business card, "It's just that the *National Enquirer* ran this story about Jason and me and it wasn't true. I thought you might be with them."

I didn't know about the *Enquirer* story she was referring to, as our earlier research had not uncovered it, but I soon would be finding out.

"The story was all lies," Jennifer said. "They made it seem as if Jason was some kind of animal who uses his fist to make a point. Jason is not like that."

"He was never abusive with you? Not once?"

"No, absolutely not. He's a gentle, loving man. He wouldn't hurt anyone. Who are you working for Mr. Dear?"

"I'm working for myself. I've been a private investigator for over thirty-five years. Sometimes I'll take a case where I'm footing the bill because I like the challenge. I want to know what really did happen. I want to bring closure to this case. Nobody else has. I need your help."

"What do you need to know?"

"I've looked at everybody as a possible suspect," I said, then proceeded to tell her about some of my research. I concluded by saying, "In all honesty I have wanted to talk to you for quite some time. You dated Jason, O. J.'s son."

"Yes I did."

"If he was a gentle, loving man who wouldn't hurt anybody, why did you break up with him?"

"It was for personal reasons."

"But you broke up with him more than once."

"Mr. Dear, we're still the best of friends."

"Is Jason still friends with DeeDee?" I asked.

I instantly saw a change come over her face, the same wary look she had had when she thought I might be from the *Enquirer*.

"I know DeeDee," she said. "But why are you asking me these questions?"

I smiled again, trying unsuccessfully to get her to relax. "As I said, I'm a private investigator. I've been working on the Bundy Drive murder case for nearly six years. During that time I've uncovered a great deal of evidence that's never been made public. I don't believe O. J. is the murderer, and I think I can prove it."

"He didn't kill Nicole," Jennifer said.

"If he didn't, do you know who could have committed the murders?" I asked.

"If you want my opinion, it's the guy who killed Brett Cantor, the manager of the Dragonfly nightclub. You know, the guy who had his throat slit from ear to ear, just like Nicole and Goldman."

"I'm familiar with the Cantor murder."

"Did you know Ron Goldman worked for that guy?"

I nodded and told her I had indeed heard that.

"Then you must also know the police found $130,000 in the guy's safe. How come that stuff doesn't show up in the press? How come Ron Shipp isn't considered a suspect? You should look into his alibi for that night. I think he's involved."

I wanted to stop Jennifer at this point and tell her why I didn't believe the Brett Cantor murder was related to the ones on Bundy Drive. Cantor, I knew, was part of an FBI probe on narcotics trafficking. There was no reason to believe the same was true of Nicole Simpson or Ron Goldman. This, and the Ron Shipp conspiracy theory, seemed to be no more than a smoke screen thrown up by O. J. and his investigators, and possibly Dr. Kittay.

"I'm happy to talk about Cantor," I said. "But I'm really here to talk to you about Jason."

"Jason didn't have anything to do with the murders," she said.

"I just want to check the facts."

Jennifer was still looking at me, only now she was folding my business card I had given her in her hands. She would fold it in half, straighten it out, and then nervously fold it again.

"You've been a fashion model," I said, still trying to put her at ease.

"Yes, I've done a little modeling. But I'm much more interested in fashion from the design end of things. I'll soon be coming out with my own line of clothes."

"Like these," I said, looking at a rack of women's dresses. I couldn't see the price tags from where I was standing, but I couldn't imagine that anything on the rack cost less than $250.

"I'm told that I'm quite good. My father, who died recently, owned a furniture business. I'm going to use the proceeds from my inheritance to start my own line."

"I wish you a lot of luck. I'm sure you'll do very well."

"But that's not why you came, is it?"

"No," I said. "I want to talk about Jason. You weren't living with him at the time of the murders, but you had been living with him on Sycamore."

"That's right."

"When did you move out?"

"About a month or so before the murders. I got my own apartment. I don't see what this has to do with your investigation."

"As I said, I'm just trying to check some facts."

"The relationship between me and Jason is a private matter, and I don't see that it has anything to do with the murders."

"You're right. It may not. But I won't know unless I ask. I have to look at everyone in an attempt to solve this case. You dated Jason. You would know him best. How long had he been working at Jackson's Restaurant before the murders?"

"Two years," she replied.

I knew immediately this wasn't true. I had learned that Jason hadn't worked for Jackson's for more than a few months, certainly not two years as Jennifer was indicating. "Was Jason cooking on the night of the murders?"

"Yes, he was the chef that night. But he was almost always the chef because Alan Jackson, the owner, would be mingling with the customers; so Jason would have to do the cooking. You know, Jason is really a great cook."

"So I've heard. In fact he was set to cook a special meal for Nicole and her family after the dance recital."

"No," Jennifer said, forcefully. "You've got that wrong. Nicole had called him that day to talk about coming over to Jackson's but nothing was arranged. She told him it was going to cost too much, and she was just going to go up the street to Mezzaluna's."

"So he didn't plan on cooking a special meal for her that night? He hadn't ordered any special food nor had a table set for them?"

"No."

I took out a pad from my breast pocket, next to my pen, and made a note. Jennifer Green was telling a different story than Jason had told during his deposition in O. J.'s civil trial.

"Do you know what time Jason left Jackson's Restaurant that Sunday night of June 12?"

"Certainly I do."

"How do you know that?"

"Mr. Dear, I'm the one who picked him up." A smile now crept across her face, and her eyes seemed to twinkle. "He was with me when he left the restaurant."

"What time was that, Jennifer?"

"I had Jason's Jeep that night, and he told me to pick him up around nine-thirty because business is slow on Sunday nights."

"What time did you get to Jackson's?"

"I told you, nine-thirty."

"Is that when you picked him up?"

"I got to the restaurant at nine-thirty. Jason said he was running behind. We left the restaurant at 9:45 PM. We left together. You can check his time card. It says he checked out at nine-forty-five."

I couldn't help but remember that Jason had said in his deposition that he had left the restaurant sometime around 10:00 to 10:30 PM. If Marcia Clark felt that the time line she had prepared was so critical in establishing Nicole's and Goldman's death, it's too bad she never interviewed Jason. At most, it is only a fifteen-minute drive from the restaurant to Nicole's, and possibly even less on a Sunday night when there is not any traffic. That left forty-five minutes for Jason to have possibly killed Nicole and Goldman.

I was desperate to ask her what was really on my mind. Had Jason been drinking when he got into the Jeep with her? Was he angry and upset? Had he been using drugs? Did he have his chef's knives with him in his chef's bag? What was he like when they left the restaurant at 9:45 on Sunday night, June 12, 1994, just one hour before the murders?

I couldn't ask her these questions because I knew from past experience this would immediately end my interview. Jennifer Green was defending Jason, and I wanted to keep her talking. This was why I was going to have to be particularly careful in what I asked next.

"When you left the restaurant, did Jason have his chef's knives with him?"

"He brings his chef's knives home with him every night, so to answer your question—yes, he had them with him."

"So he had his knives when you picked him up at Jackson's Restaurant and he got into the Jeep."

"Yes."

"Were you and Jason alone in the Jeep?"

"Yes."

"Where did you go when you and Jason left the restaurant?"

"We went directly to my place. We parked the Jeep, and Jason and I went up to my apartment. He had an airtight alibi, Mr. Dear. Jason was with me in my apartment watching television until after eleven o'clock that night."

My hesitation in asking the previous questions paid off. Jennifer Green was lying. She was trying to give Jason an airtight alibi. The problem with it was that Jason in his civil deposition had said he left the restaurant between 10:00 and 10:30 PM and that Jennifer Green, his girlfriend, had his Jeep. She came to the restaurant to pick him up and he drove her directly to her apartment. He kissed her goodnight and she got out. Jason was specifically asked if he had gone into her apartment, and he said he had not. He dropped her off and went directly home, where he claimed to have watched television until 3 AM.

Listening to Jennifer, I wondered whether or not she knew Jason had provided Daniel Petrocelli a different account of his activities that night. It hardly mattered in the long run, because one or both of them was lying. Since Jason himself wouldn't knowingly implicate himself in the murders, if he indeed had a stronger or more credible alibi available to him, I could only assume that Jennifer had just concocted this new alibi to protect Jason. She obviously hadn't known what Jason had said in his deposition or that I had read it.

I continued on as I had begun, this time asking whether or not Jason had a phone at his apartment on Sycamore Avenue and whether or not he had called her that night or the next morning.

"Yes," she said, "Jason had a phone. But I didn't hear from him until Monday morning when he came over. He was upset after having spoken to Arnelle. He was in really bad shape. After that he went to Rockingham."

"Did he have a seizure when he arrived at your house that morning?"

"I wouldn't call it that. He was upset. You would be too, if your stepmother had just been murdered."

"Did you see him after that?"

"I saw him and his family. In fact, I attended Nicole's wake. It was a difficult time for everyone and I lent what support I could."

"Do you know if Jason was taking his seizure medication prior to the murders?"

"Listen, Mr. Dear, I don't know where you're trying to go with this, but if you're implying Jason had anything to do with the murders, you are wrong. I know he had nothing to do with it because he was with me that night. I've told you so."

"Is that what you told the police?"

"I didn't talk to the police, but that's what I would have told them had they interviewed me about an alibi for Jason."

"Are you telling me you were never interviewed by the Los Angeles Police Department?"

"Yes, that's what I'm telling you."

Jennifer was now looking at me again as if she wanted me to disappear off of the face of the earth. Our little chat was becoming more like a formal cross-examination. At this point I had nothing to lose by asking what was really on my mind. I was going to go for it.

"Did you know Jason had a drug problem?" I asked.

"He took drugs once in a while. But he never had a problem with them."

"Did you know that Jason has tried to commit suicide?"

"I don't know where you're getting your information, but Jason never tried to commit suicide. I was his girlfriend for several years, so I should know."

"The way I heard it, Jason didn't just try to kill himself once, but three times."

"I don't believe a *word* you're saying. He's a sweet, loving person and would never do anything to harm himself or anyone else."

"Did Jason ever strike you, abuse you, or threaten you during your several years as his girlfriend."

"Never. He wasn't that kind of person."

Jennifer's response made me wonder if she could explain her on-again, off-again relationship and her moves in and out of Jason's apartment on Sycamore Avenue. To me, she wasn't a convincing liar.

I was able to put two or three more questions to her before our interview was over. "Did you know Jason was committed to a psychiatric ward in 1991?"

"Jason was never in a psychiatric ward," she said indignantly.

"Did you know he used Depakote to control his intermittent rage disorder?"

"He uses Depakote because he is an epileptic. That's all."

"Did you know he was under a doctor's care?"

"He occasionally visited a therapist. That's all there was to it. You would see a therapist too if you had been through what he has."

"Did you know he was on probation at the time of the murders for attacking his boss with a deadly weapon?"

"You're talking about Paul Goldberg," she said, still indignant. "That simply isn't true. I was with him at the time. Jason came by the restaurant to see Paul because he owed him a lot of money for helping him to get his restaurant up and running. But Paul wouldn't pay him."

"Did this happen inside or outside the restaurant?"

"It happened outside, like I told you. Paul came out back of the restaurant and told Jason he wouldn't pay him. Jason said he would take him to court. That's when Paul called him a 'nigger.' Jason turned around and said, 'What did you call me?' Then Paul came at Jason and all Jason did was to give him a great big push and Paul landed on the ground. That's all that happened. There wasn't any knife. There never was."

"There's just one last thing," I said. "You yourself admitted that you moved in and out of his apartment. And I know from talking to other people that your relationship was on-again, off-again like Jason's relationship with DeeDee. That doesn't suggest to me that the two of you actually had a stable relationship. What was it about Jason you didn't like?"

"That's none of your business."

"Do you still see him?"

"Occasionally, but only as a friend. I'm still good friends with Arnelle."

"Jason has a new girlfriend, I understand. A waitress, Danielle Sapia."

"Yes, I know her. She's very nice."

There didn't seem to be any point to further questioning her. I thanked her for her time, then handed her a new business card. The one I had previously given her had now been folded and unfolded so many times the ink had begun to come off.

To break the tension, I asked her when she was going to be opening her shop.

"It won't be long now," she said. Then she added, "I've got to go. I have things to do."

I thanked her for her time. "Good luck with your new business," I said. "I'm sure it will be a success."

A minute later I was back in my car. In my mind I knew that in the time it took me to get back in my car, there would be a telephone ringing somewhere in Brentwood. "Hello, Arnelle . . . this is Jennifer . . ."

During my investigation, Jennifer Green had been lying to me. She was not about to tell me anything that might implicate Jason in the Bundy Drive murders. The proof, I suspected, might be found in the article in the *National Enquirer*. As Shakespeare once wrote in *Hamlet,* "the lady, she doth protest too much."

I had to travel all the way to the Long Beach Public Library in order to find a copy of the article. The trip, however, was more than worthwhile. However much pundits enjoyed attacking the *National Enquirer* for shoddy journalism, even their staunchest critics had to admit that when it came to the Nicole Simpson and Ron Goldman murders, the *Enquirer* had been the first to break many of the most sensational, and ultimately the most accurate, stories related to the case. This had been true in regards to the activities of O. J. Simpson, and now, I strongly suspected, it was true in regards to his son Jason.

I found that the story ran on October 4, 1994, and documented an incident that allegedly occurred two months before the murders. In bold headlines, the title read: "O. J.'s Son Tried to Kill His Own Girlfriend."

According to reporters David Duffy and David Wright, who interviewed eyewitnesses, Jason was in a drunken rage when he tried to kill Jennifer Green. This incident took place on April 21, 1994, at a Los Angeles nightclub where Jason was celebrating his twenty-fourth birthday. In the course of the evening, Jennifer, who had accompanied him to the club, noticed Jason had wandered off and was chatting with an old girlfriend. That was when the trouble began.

A friend of Jennifer's, who was there that night, was quoted as saying, "Jason was drinking heavily and he refused to leave the girl. Jennifer said, 'I'm going home.' She ran outside. He yelled after her, 'You can't leave—it's my birthday!' Then he chased after her into the parking lot, where their spat developed into a full-blown screaming match."

The situation allegedly kept escalating. Friends hustled the couple into a car and drove them home to their apartment, but the fight continued inside the car. As one of Jennifer's friends told reporters, "As the car pulled up outside the apartment, Jason leaped out in a drunken rage and started smashing large potted plants against the side of the building. Jennifer dashed past him into the apartment and he chased her into the bedroom. He picked up a heavy, wooden dressing table and threw it at her. One of the legs scraped the side of her chest and sent her staggering."

Then, according to the story, Jennifer fled the apartment and jumped into her gray Volkswagen Jetta parked outside. But Jason allegedly came roaring after her. Jennifer's friend reported: "Before she could start the car, Jason ripped open the door and knocked her into the passenger seat. She told me, 'My legs were hanging out of the car and I couldn't move. The next minute he was on top of me and his hands were around my throat. I couldn't breathe. I thought he was going to strangle me to death.'"

Jennifer, apparently, got lucky. A neighbor who had heard the noise ran over and dragged Jason off her.

Jason, according to this same article, was described as an "uncontrollable monster," and a man who was "insanely jealous" who would explode if his girlfriend "so much as looked at another guy." Jennifer was described as the battered woman who "continually went back to him even though she could have been killed." This was something, reporters pointed out, that was exactly the same situation as with Nicole and O. J., and it was Nicole, according to the article, who allegedly consoled Jennifer after the brutal attack, telling her that Jason is "just like his father."

According to the same article, Jennifer was growing increasingly afraid of Jason and his mood swings. She kept leaving him and then returning. "She was a fool when it came to Jason," Jennifer's friend was quoted as saying. "He'd explode, verbally abuse her and she'd move out. But within days she'd be back in his arms after he pleaded for another chance."

Here, in this one article, was a dramatic and apparently truthful representation of the exact kind of behavior that could be expected from someone with Jason's medical and psychological profile. This was a classic textbook case of intermittent rage disorder, and it had allegedly occurred less than two months before Nicole Simpson and Ron Goldman were murdered.

O. J. IS INNOCENT

Having now read the article, and having assured myself that Jennifer Green had lied to me, what I had to do next was all the more crucial. I had to find someone who would provide living testimony to what Jennifer denied and what reporters from the *National Enquirer* had printed as fact. I would have to find DeeDee.

Jennifer Green was strengthening my investigation against Jason Simpson as a major overlooked suspect by the Los Angeles Police Department.

19

DIVULGING THE DARK SIDE

I **HAD NEVER BEEN ABLE** to get the real first name or last name for DeeDee. In fact, I wasn't even sure I was spelling her nickname correctly. None of the books and articles written about O. J. and his family made reference to her, nor had her name appeared in the course of the criminal trial. Neither Dr. Kittay nor Ron Shipp could remember her full name. What I did have on her was an eight-year-old reference indicating that she, like Jennifer, had been a receptionist at an exclusive Beverly Hills beauty salon. Fortunately for me, I found the salon still open and doing business at the same location.

When I went in and introduced myself, the manager was polite, but my brief conversation with her was not encouraging. "Eight years ago is a long time in a business like ours. We must have had more than fifty different receptionists who have worked for us since then."

"But not that many named DeeDee," I pointed out.

The manager said she would ask the other hairdressers and see what she could come up with. The first name she came back with was that of an actress who had worked briefly at the salon around that time. No one knew much about her other than the fact that she had lived in New York and had dated Andrew Dice Clay, the comedian. The only other DeeDee anyone at the salon could remember was a former receptionist who had left to work as a waitress at the Cheesecake Factory, a popular Beverly Hills restaurant on Rodeo Drive.

I thanked the receptionist and went off in search of one or both of the DeeDees. I ruled the actress out almost immediately when I contacted her former talent agent and found out she was at least ten years older than the woman we were looking for. The other DeeDee seemed more promising. The bartender at the Cheesecake Factory in Beverly Hills remembered a DeeDee, and told me she had been transferred to the Cheesecake Factory in Irvine, California, but he was not sure if she had ever been employed at the salon.

After making a number of calls, I learned that the DeeDee who worked at the Cheesecake Factory in Irvine had taken yet another restaurant job, this time in Newport Beach, some eighty miles south of Los Angeles. This eventually led me to Flemmings, a posh steak house in the Fashion Island Shopping Center, where I made reservations for dinner. When I entered Flemmings Steakhouse, it didn't take me long to see that DeeDee, the manager, wasn't the woman I was looking for. This woman was older, had Irish red hair and a peaches and cream complexion. The DeeDee that Ron Shipp and others described to me was Hispanic, with an olive complexion like Jennifer's, and much shorter. But just to be sure, when she came over to my table, I confirmed with her that indeed she was not the DeeDee I was looking for. This DeeDee had, in fact, worked at the Cheesecake Factory at one time, but had never heard of Jason Simpson, nor had she ever worked at a Beverly Hills beauty salon. "DeeDee," I said. "I wish you were the woman I was looking for. You would have made my life a lot easier."

"Your story sounds interesting. Keep in touch, I'd like to see what happens."

I planned to come back. Even if she wasn't the right DeeDee. Now I was back to square one. Disappointed and discouraged, I drove back to Los Angeles. It was a long drive, made all the longer because I didn't know where I would find the woman I was so desperately seeking. She might not even be in California. For all I knew, she might not even be alive. I had no choice but to try my best to get a good night's sleep, then in the morning, drive to Beverly Hills and retrace my steps. The next day I returned to the hair salon. I began interviewing anyone and everyone about DeeDee, from the young woman who shampooed hair to the stylist who specialized in perms and coloring. Eventually I spoke to a handsome and gregarious stylist named Jessie, who had been there for over ten years. He appeared to be in charge of the salon. Jessie remembered yet another girl named DeeDee. "You must mean the DeeDee who went out with Jason Simpson," he said.

"Yes, that's the one," I responded, relieved to be finally on the right track.

Though Jessie couldn't remember DeeDee's last name, he did have quite a bit to say about her, as well as Jason, whom he had met on several different occasions. This DeeDee was Hispanic, perhaps from South America, although she spoke perfect English. She stood about five-foot-six, was strikingly beautiful, with delicate features, and had long brunette hair that had a natural curl to it. He guessed her now to be about twenty-eight years old. This had to be the DeeDee I was looking for. Jessie didn't hold out much hope of my finding her in Los Angeles. The last he knew of her was that she had moved to New York to get away from Jason.

"Did she have good reason to want to get away from him?" I asked.

"I damn well think so," Jessie said. "The guy is psycho. One minute he's the sweetest nicest guy you ever met and the next minute he's all angry and upset, a Dr. Jekyll and Mr. Hyde type. DeeDee often came into work with bruises on her face and arms from where he would hit and shove her around."

Jessie then related a story about how DeeDee arrived one morning in tears. "All her long beautiful hair had been chopped off," Jessie said. "It looked to me like someone had just grabbed her by the hair and started whacking away. When I asked her what had happened, she started to cry. She said Jason had attacked her. He had taken a chef's knife and cut off her hair."

"DeeDee told you he had used a chef's knife?" I asked.

"That's right. His chef's knife. He was a cook or worked at a restaurant."

I was stunned. Here indeed, finally, was direct knowledge of Jason Simpson's irrational behavior, not the kind and lovable Jason whom Jennifer Green had described. And for once, I had not described him as Dr. Jekyll and Mr. Hyde. Jessie had.

Jessie went on to describe how Jason would always be remorseful afterward. On the day in 1989, several hours after DeeDee had arrived at work with her hair chopped off, in walked Jason Simpson.

"I wouldn't let him come in," Jessie said. "I told him he had no business doing what he did to DeeDee, and that I wanted him to get out of my place of business and to leave her alone. 'But I want to apologize. I want to tell her I'm sorry,' he kept telling me. I said, 'I don't care *what* you have to say to her. You have no right doing what you did. Get out and stay out.'"

What Jason had done was typical of intermittent rage disorder. You hurt the one you love and then are sorry afterward. But in Nicole's case if he was guilty, it was now too late to say, I'm sorry.

Jessie went on to say this incident wasn't the first. "There were other places and times when Jason and DeeDee were together when I saw him go from being a nice guy one minute to flying into a jealous rage the next."

It wasn't long after the haircutting incident in 1989, Jessie said, that DeeDee left for New York. Unfortunately for me, he didn't know what became of her after that. He thought that Ralph, another veteran stylist, might know.

"Hey Ralph . . ." Jessie suddenly called out. "Who was the hairstylist who was with us when DeeDee was here back in 1989? DeeDee and she went to New York together."

"I don't know," Ralph replied. "Mary... do you know?"

Another stylist popped her head out from behind a curtain. "You must be talking about Terry. Her last name was Shaw."

"Yes," said Jessie. "That's the one, Terry Shaw. She was older than DeeDee. They both left together for New York. I know Terry is back in town because I saw her two years ago. Now let me think for a minute. I must know someone who knows Terry." Jessie then called out so loudly everyone in the salon could hear him. "Anyone know where Terry Shaw is working now?"

"Last time I heard, she was working at Bruno's," Ralph said.

"Yes," said Jessie. "That's it. Bruno's. It's right up the street. Ask for Karen."

I thanked Jessie for his time, and then asked him to step outside for a moment. We walked into the courtyard.

"Jessie," I said. "There's more to this than just DeeDee."

"I suspected there must be," he replied.

"I'm really interested in Jason Simpson. You've been a big help so far. But I need to know anything else you might know about him."

Jessie didn't mince his words. "Bill, I didn't like him. I certainly didn't trust him. In fact, I thought there was something wrong with him. It was the way he acted. That split personality of his. The last time I saw him was on television, the day the police arrested his father. I told the people around me that day, and I'll say it again. I never believed for an instant that O. J. committed those murders. I felt right from the start they arrested the wrong man. To me, Jason committed those murders. He had to be the one."

Up to this point in our conversation, I hadn't told Jessie anything at all about my investigation of Jason or that my search for DeeDee had anything to do with the murders. And yet, even without knowledge of police and medical history, Jessie had come to the same conclusion I had. Except he had reached it just days after the murders.

Perhaps I was reading more into Jessie's remark than was warranted, but as I looked into his eyes, I realized he was the kind of person who knew how to read people. In his line of work, he met and talked to people from early in the morning until late at night. Experience was the best teacher, and Jessie had a lot of experience. He had read Jason correctly right from the start, without the benefit of my investigation.

"I think you could be right, Jesse. Here's my card, if you think of anything else, please call me. It's important."

I left the salon, then turned north, and walked to Bruno's Hair Salon. My investigation was finally starting to come together.

Karen was pleasant and tried to be helpful but, like Jessie, hadn't seen or heard from Terry Shaw in years. She did, however, suggest that I talk to Jody, who also worked at the same salon and might know Terry's whereabouts. Jody wouldn't be coming in to work for another hour, so I bided my time walking around Rodeo Drive, thinking about how far I had come in the last six years, and how important it was that I find DeeDee.

Like Karen, Jody was happy to help out. Though she too couldn't give me DeeDee's last name, she said that Terry Shaw, with whom DeeDee had gone to New York, was now definitely back in Los Angeles.

"Do you have any idea where Terry might be living now?"

"The only thing I know is what I was told. She got married, her father died, and her mother sold her their old home." She thought that Shaw was living in the Los Feliz area of Los Angeles, just beneath the Griffith Park Observatory.

Our conversation was just about over when Jody suddenly remembered something else. "Terry was in a popular local play. A pretty big role. Just a few months ago, her picture appeared in the *Los Angeles Times* magazine supplement. I remember because I was surprised to see her photo."

"Do you remember which issue?"

"Yes, it was the one with Susan McDougal on the cover, the woman who got into so much trouble with President Clinton."

"Thanks, Jody. You've been a great help."

My tour of Los Angeles continued, this time taking me to the Beverly Hills Public Library. Sure enough, after an hour of searching through back issues, I found Terry Shaw in a photo spread in a maternity fashion layout. According to the caption, Terry Shaw was due in June, which meant that by now, the middle of August, she had already given birth.

My next stop was at the computer, where a librarian helped me to pull up the name Terry Shaw. There was a telephone number but no address. I took out my cell phone and dialed. Shaw's number had been disconnected, with no new listing in California.

After I got back into the car and pulled out of the library parking lot, I decided to call my new secretary Shannon Chasteen at home in Dallas. It was her day off.

"Shannon, I need you to go to the office immediately. I need you to look up on the computer, everything you can find on a Terry Shaw, from Los Angeles. That's all the information I have on her."

"What's up?"

"I've finally got a lead on DeeDee."

"I'll be there in about twenty minutes," she said.

Thirty minutes later my cell phone rang. It was Shannon. "I've got what you want on Terry Shaw. I have everything on her and her new husband. What do you need?"

Excitedly, I told her I needed an address.

"That I can give you."

My excitement turned to elation as I jotted down the new address. As I drove into her neighborhood, I suddenly realized she lived just two blocks away from a member of the Dream Team, Johnnie Cochran. What a coincidence. I had come full circle.

As I parked my car in front of Terry Shaw's home, two security cars pulled up at a distance and watched my every move. In my mind, I could picture Johnnie Cochran jogging past and my saying, "Mr. Cochran, you're right about the murders. O. J. is innocent. You have the right church, but the wrong pew." In other words, Cochran had the right family, but the wrong person.

The uniformed officers inside the two security cars continued to watch every movement I made as I walked up the steps and towards Terry Shaw's front door. I knocked.

At first, no one answered. Nor was there any evidence anyone was at home. There was no car in the driveway, and an express mail package sat on the doormat. I was sure, however, that this was the correct address, because the house was exactly as Jody had described it. Terry Shaw's house was in the shadow of the Griffith Park Observatory, which I recognized from the classic James Dean film *Rebel Without a Cause*. I also knew it was the right place because Shaw's married name was on the label on the package on the doormat.

I knocked a second and third time and was just about to leave and walk back to the car when the voice of a young woman called out, "What do you want?"

I looked up. There was Terry Shaw holding an infant on her hip, talking to me from an upstairs balcony. She had long, curly brunette hair, and that rosy pink complexion so becoming to new mothers. She looked exactly as she did in the picture in the *Los Angeles Times*, only considerably slimmer.

"My name is Bill Dear. I'm a private investigator from Dallas, Texas. I'm looking for DeeDee. I was hoping you could tell me her last name and whether or not she's back from New York."

Terry Shaw was noncommittal. "Why are you looking for her?"

"I'm doing my own investigation into the murders of Nicole Simpson and Ron Goldman. It's important I speak to DeeDee about Jason Simpson. She has information that might help me."

I was hesitant to say too much at this point because the two security guards, in separate cars, continued to watch me from two hundred feet away. For whatever reason, they were not letting me out of their sight. The security here was as tight as it was in Beverly Hills. I wondered if it was because of Johnnie Cochran living a few houses up the street.

I gave her the name of the hair salon where Karen and Jody worked and explained how it was that I came to be knocking on her door. I also told her about speaking to Jessie, and how I had been told that Jason could be violent and sometimes abuse DeeDee. "It's vital that I speak to her as soon as possible," I said.

Terry stood looking down at me for a few more moments, her small child cradled in her arms. I could tell she was debating whether or not she wanted to get involved in anything as sordid as the Bundy Drive murders and the family life of O. J.'s eldest son. I don't know what it was that made her decide to help me, but I got the impression something had suddenly crossed her mind, as if she had remembered something that might be important or might justify her talking with me. She told me to hold on for a moment while she came downstairs. Minutes later she opened the front door, looked at my identification, and before I knew it, I was busy describing to her some of the cases I had worked on over the years.

"Come inside so we can talk," she said.

A great relief came over me as I stepped inside and glanced back over my shoulder at the two security guards looking on in disbelief as I entered the home of Terry Shaw.

Terry's house was quite lovely, though it was arranged more for the benefit of her child than for adults. There were children's toys on the tables and chairs and a large bassinet and changing table just inside the entrance to the living room. She showed me to a seat and we launched into a discussion of Beverly Hills hair salons, how she had met DeeDee, and the so-called glamorous lifestyles of the rich and famous. As she reflected back on that period of her life, I didn't get a sense that she was at all nostalgic but rather happy to have moved on and grateful to now have a husband and child.

"The Beverly Hills lifestyle—especially at a hair salon—seems so inviting and exciting from the outside," Terry said. "But when you get up close you see how empty it all is. Just a parade of pretty faces."

"Is that why you and DeeDee went to New York together?"

"Yes, that's part of the reason," she replied. "It just seemed like the thing to do at the time. My acting career wasn't exactly taking off, and I needed a change. DeeDee needed one too."

"A change of boyfriends?"

"Yes," Terry said, without going into any details. "A change of boyfriends. Now it seems like a very long time ago. I was much older than DeeDee. I remember talking with her on a Friday about possibly going to New York, and then leaving on a plane just two weeks later. That's how free we were in those days. DeeDee and I had nothing to tie us down."

We chatted for a while about New York and how they had both found jobs. DeeDee was working as a waitress in a restaurant. Shaw was doing odd jobs and pursuing her acting career. They found an apartment in Greenwich Village on MacDougal Street. It was a basement apartment where, Terry said, they had problems with rats.

"I'm glad I lived there for a while, but it wasn't a place I would want to spend the rest of my life. Fun for a time, but it gets tiring."

I pressed Terry for more details about DeeDee's decision to move to New York, and she confirmed the move was motivated by a desire to get as far away from Jason as possible. "It was a very unhealthy relationship," she said. "I think DeeDee finally saw that and was willing to do something about it. But it wasn't all that easy. Jason was following her around and doing all kinds of crazy things."

"Like chopping off her hair?" I asked.

Terry paused, as if it pained her to have to dredge up old, unpleasant memories. "Yes, like chopping off her hair," she finally said. "I was with her right after it happened."

Terry described how DeeDee had called her on the telephone, pleading and crying for her to come over to the apartment that DeeDee and Jason shared on Alta Vista Drive. "I went upstairs. The door was open, and the entire apartment was a shambles. Everything was knocked over, and there was Chinese food all over the place. Giant heaps of it. DeeDee was sobbing. Her landlord was there, and he was upset too. Jason was in a rage. He stormed out of the room when I arrived. Then DeeDee told me how he had gotten mad at her over something and then began hitting her. Finally he dragged her into the bathroom, while she was kicking and screaming, and he cut off her hair with his chef's knife."

"Do you remember what they had been fighting over?"

"It was probably over DeeDee's old boyfriend, Greg. Jason was upset about Greg. He didn't want her seeing him. But I don't think there really was anything to it, at least with Greg. They were just friends. DeeDee wasn't fooling around. It was just that Jason had this short fuse and he couldn't deal with his tremendous jealousy."

"Were there other things that Jason did to her?"

"Plenty of other things. He was always following her around and doing these crazy things. There was a dark side of him. He could be a real psycho, a Dr. Jekyll and Mr. Hyde."

Once again, Jason was being described as a Jekyll and Hyde. How many times had I heard that? How many more times would I hear it?

"Terry, did Jason follow DeeDee to New York?"

"Yes. It took Jason a little while to find us. Once he did, Jason moved into an apartment that O. J. owned in Manhattan. He wouldn't leave DeeDee alone. He stalked her for six months."

"Is that when Jason tried to commit suicide?"

Terry didn't know for sure. "DeeDee told me a lot of things about her relationship with Jason, none of them good. As I said, it was years ago. And by the time Jason had shown up in New York, DeeDee and I were already heading in different directions. She couldn't hold down a job and was still living the life of a party girl. Doing drugs. Drinking. You know—the high life."

"Was Jason doing drugs in New York?"

"He and DeeDee were always doing drugs. I wasn't into all that. I was determined to make a career for myself. DeeDee eventually ditched Jason—at least for the time being—and went off to live with another boyfriend. Then DeeDee and I split. DeeDee went her way and I went mine."

"Did DeeDee stay in New York?"

"Yes. She lived there longer than I did. We both ended up returning to Los Angeles. From what DeeDee told me, Jason continued to stalk her once she came back. He would always find out where she was working. He was trying to get back together with her. DeeDee continued to change her telephone numbers and move to new apartments. She even went to South America at one point to get away from him. But I don't think he's bothered her since the murders."

"Is DeeDee still using drugs?"

"No. I'm proud of her. She finally cleaned up her act when she got back to LA. Has her own apartment. Opened her own business. She's really working hard. We're still good friends."

Terry said DeeDee was living in nearby Echo Park. She also said that she ran into Jason every now and again. "Last time was at a party in Silverlake, about a year or so ago. I didn't stick around to chat about old times."

"How did he seem to you? Had he changed?"

"No. If you are asking whether or not he was still using drugs, the answer is yes. He certainly was that night. He was hanging out with several guys, one of whom was the son of a famous actor."

"What kind of drugs was he using?"

"Psychedelics, I think, Ecstasy."

Ecstasy, I knew, was the latest rage in Los Angeles and elsewhere. It was a mood-enhancing chemical that worked on the nervous system— one of the most dangerous types of drugs for a person with epilepsy to take. Jason hadn't changed. This made my concern even greater.

Terry's baby started to cry. It was feeding time. It was also a signal to me that I had only a few minutes more to talk to her. I quickly told her about my investigation, the discoveries I had made, and my belief that Jason may have been at the Bundy Drive crime scene on the night of the murders. I also tried to impress upon Terry how imperative it was that I speak to DeeDee in person. Terry, however, was still reluctant to give me her telephone number or address.

"I don't know if she'll want to talk about any of this with you or not," she said. "DeeDee has straightened her life out. No drugs or drinking. She's happy now."

"Terry, please. This is important. Please call her and give her my telephone number. I'll only be in town for a couple more days. My son's expecting his first baby and I'd like to be there. Here's my cell phone number."

I reached over and handed her my card. "Please tell DeeDee I just want to talk, on her own terms. I think you know how important it is that I speak with her. I don't want anyone else getting hurt, and I know you don't either"

20

DR. JEKYLL/MR. HYDE

AS I LEFT THE foothills of Los Feliz, I had no way of knowing for sure if DeeDee would call me, or if she did, whether her response would be any different than Jennifer Green's had been. However, if she had suffered the kind of abuse that Terry, Jessie, and others had described, and was willing to speak to me about it, DeeDee would have something vital to add to my investigation. DeeDee had lived with Jason. She had experienced firsthand Jason's rage and his excessive use of alcohol and drugs. She had felt his wrath. No one truly knows someone else unless they live with them. DeeDee had. DeeDee's help could be all I would need to end my investigation.

I sat in the car and kept my cell phone in my lap for the next forty-five minutes. I wasn't taking any chances of missing her call. The wait paid off. I fumbled for the phone when it started to ring. The voice on the other end of the line sounded fragile and unsure. "This is DeeDee."

"DeeDee," I said. "This is Bill Dear. We need to talk. Can we meet?"

"All right," she said. "Meet me in an hour on the corner of Silverlake and Sunset, at a small Cuban restaurant, the Café Tropical. I'll be wearing a red scarf."

"I'll be wearing black cowboy boots and a beard," I replied.

She hung up before I had a chance to engage her in further conversation or even get a telephone number where I could reach her in the event I was delayed. I was left with the uneasy feeling that it had all been too easy to arrange. DeeDee hadn't asked me anything about my investigation or probed me to find out how much I knew about her or Jason. Terry would surely have filled her in on some of the details. Either she really had no intention of talking to me, or DeeDee had truly been waiting for just such an opportunity. Perhaps I was the first investigator to ask her to talk about Jason and the murders. That could well have been the case, since I knew her name had not appeared in the trial or in any of the books or hundreds of articles previously written about the case. Virtually no one who studied the case even knew she existed. Yet to me, DeeDee did exist. Potentially she could be the most important witness in this entire investigation.

At the agreed upon time I was standing on the corner of Silverlake and Sunset. This was not Los Feliz or Beverly Hills with their elegant homes, manicured lawns, and flower gardens, but a wide expanse of patched and broken asphalt and gray slabs of concrete with unsightly weeds growing up between the cracks. Drug dealers hovered around a pay phone across the street, apparently selling crack cocaine. A street vendor sold fruit and hard candy from a pushcart and recent immigrants crowded the bus stop. Dressed in my black suit and cowboy boots, I looked as out of place here as I had in Brentwood without a jogging suit.

After waiting ten minutes beyond the agreed upon time, I crossed the street, browsed for a few minutes at a pet store which sold tropical fish and rabbits, then returned to the same corner where I had been standing, much to the displeasure of a drug dealer across the street who, by now, was convinced I was law enforcement. Half an hour later I was sure DeeDee had stood me up.

I had left my cell phone in the car, so I retrieved it and then returned to the intersection where we had agreed to meet. Just as I arrived in front of the Cuban café, my phone rang. It was DeeDee.

"I'm sorry I'm running late. I'll be there in fifteen minutes."

No one will ever know how relieved I was to receive that call. In all honesty, however, I did have some second thoughts that perhaps I was being set up. An ambush would not have been difficult to arrange and made to look like a drive-by shooting, particularly in this part of Los Angeles. On one hand, I needed to talk to DeeDee; on the other hand, I didn't want to wind up a statistic.

Forty-five minutes after our agreed upon meeting time, a blue Honda sedan parked on Sunset, about a half block from where I was standing at the intersection. Ironically, the car pulled in and parked behind my car. A woman got out. She was not wearing the red scarf, but I had a gut feeling it was DeeDee. She walked to the intersection and stopped. As the light turned green, she started across the street toward me. I reached up to wave, and she waved back.

Finally, I was to meet DeeDee. I reached inside my pocket and touched the button on my rollerball pen recorder just as she crossed the street.

She was small, almost petite, and well proportioned in a compact but streamlined way. From a distance she was quite attractive, as I had come to expect from talking to Jessie and Terry, but as she walked closer to me, I could see that her hair had lost some of its luster, her complexion looked dull, and subtle lines were etched around her eyes. Perhaps it had been the drugs and alcohol, or the stress that comes along with a transient lifestyle. Perhaps both. But as she reached out to shake my hand and began to speak, I had the distinct impression that the drug and alcohol abuse were part of her past, not her present.

"You must be DeeDee," I said.

"And you're Bill Dear. I'm sorry I'm late. First I couldn't find my keys, and then I couldn't find my red scarf. I'm sorry I kept you waiting."

"I'm just glad to meet you after all."

DeeDee and I went into the Cuban café. She declined my offer to buy her something to eat, but accepted a mineral water. She seemed relaxed, almost eager to talk. As I quickly learned, she was now operating her own small company, a dog walking service. And as I later learned, an AA meeting was to be held in the back room of the café later that night. This was the reason, I suspected, that she chose Café Tropical as our meeting place.

"I want you to know this is the first time I've talked to anyone about this."

"About Jason?" I asked.

"Yes. At around the time of O. J.'s trial there was a television truck parked in front of my house. I don't know how they got my name or found out where I lived. But I didn't talk to them. I didn't talk to anyone except a few close friends."

"Why is that?"

"I don't know, exactly. I guess I just didn't feel right talking about Jason and his father, or Nicole, for that matter. Nicole especially, because I really liked her, and I think she liked me. I think that, if things had been different, we might have become good friends, because we had so much in common. I guess I didn't talk to the press because I figured everything would come out in the trial."

"But it didn't."

"You know it didn't. That's why you and I are here, isn't it?"

I said that this was exactly why I was here. I told her about how I had watched the trial from a hospital bed and that what I had seen only raised more questions for me than it answered. Then I talked about the dynamics of the relationship between Nicole and O. J., and how, after working on the case for six years, I had come to understand their love/hate relationship.

I think she began to understand what I was telling her, though I did get the distinct impression she was convinced, as was Ron Shipp, that O. J. had killed Nicole and Ron Goldman. Throughout our conversation she would make references to how boys pick up bad habits and ways of behavior from their fathers. DeeDee said such things as, "Jason must have gotten it from somewhere," and "He was just doing what his father had taught him to do." DeeDee wasn't trying to defend Jason as much as explain his behavior.

One of the first people we talked about was Jennifer, whom DeeDee said she had met a few times. "I would run into Jason every now and again, sometimes at Nicole's, when Jennifer would be there. I don't think she liked me very much. In fact, I know she didn't. I suppose it was just jealousy or something like that. I think Jason had her believing I was responsible for everything that had happened to him. I do know Jennifer covered up for Jason. Those things that were said in the *National Enquirer* article, about Jason beating Jennifer up, were true. I ought to know. I was there and saw him hit her. I was at the Luna Park nightclub on the night of Jason's twenty-fourth birthday, about two months before the murders. Jennifer saw Jason talking to me and made a snide remark. He told her to butt out. He didn't like Jennifer bad-mouthing me. Jennifer continued making snide remarks. Then Jason stepped in and started slapping her around. I told him to quit. But he wouldn't let it go. I saw him push Jennifer into a wall. Jennifer ran outside into the parking lot, followed by Jason. He had gone berserk. I went running out after them because I knew he was going to lose it."

"What do you mean by 'lose it'?"

"He was going to hurt her."

"And did he hit Jennifer?"

"Yes."

"You actually saw Jason hit her?"

"Yes, he hit her. And then his friends came rushing out and put them both into a car. I don't know what happened afterwards, but I'm sure it was like they said in the *Enquirer* article. That's Jason's style. That's what he does when he explodes."

"Did Jason hit you that way?"

"Many times."

DeeDee said this to me so matter-of-factly that I believed her. And like elsewhere in our conversation, she was willing to go into the kind of detail—names, dates, and locations—that I knew a jury would also find convincing.

DeeDee didn't deny they had had an extremely volatile relationship. It had been that way from the start, in early 1988, when they first met. At the time, DeeDee was working at the hair salon and living with a man named Greg, who was a fashion model. She knew Jason socially, and when he confided that he had a crush on her, they started having an affair. Greg found out and made her leave their apartment. That was how she and Jason came to live together on Orange Drive, in an apartment owned by Jason's mother, Marguerite.

"At the time, I didn't have anywhere else to go, so I moved in with Jason," DeeDee said. "But Marguerite didn't like that at all, and Arnelle, who lived in the same building, hated me. They both disliked me. They really made me feel uncomfortable."

At this point in our conversation, DeeDee stopped and explained to me the inner workings of Jason's family relationships.

"Arnelle was Daddy's pet," DeeDee said. "But in the beginning, it wasn't like that. She was overweight and not all that smart. Then, when she got older, she lost the weight and developed a good relationship with her father. O. J. didn't mind being seen with her now. Jason was considered the problem child. At first O. J. had all these big plans for him. But Jason just couldn't live up to his father's expectations. He didn't want to play football. I don't think he even enjoyed the game. All he wanted to do was be a chef. But his father never supported that. He eventually sent Arnelle to school and even hired a tutor to help her out. Not Jason. After he quit the football team at USC, his father practically disowned him. O. J. seemed to feel like Jason was an embarrassment. They got along sometimes but mostly they were fighting."

Just as Ron Shipp had said, and DeeDee now confirmed, Jason was an embarrassment to his dad, which was something O. J. did not tolerate.

I could see DeeDee becoming increasingly upset as she spoke. As she described it, there was a great deal of fighting between Jason and her. The problem in her mind was that Jason was a pathological liar, capable of lying about the smallest and seemingly most insignificant things. She referred to him as a "pathological liar" because he truly believed his lies.

"It was as if he sometimes had this split personality," DeeDee said. "He could say that someone else did something, when in fact it was him all along, only he truly believed that someone else wasn't him.

Here we go again, I thought. Dr. Jekyll and Mr. Hyde.

The fighting between Jason and DeeDee got so bad that Marguerite asked them to leave Orange Drive. They then moved to an apartment on Ogden. This was where DeeDee said she came to see the truly dark side of Jason, when he began beating and abusing her.

"He could be so sweet and loveable one minute, and then a madman the next," DeeDee said. "He could go crazy. I'm not saying I wasn't partially to blame, because I could get right in his face."

As DeeDee said this, I couldn't help but suspect that maybe Nicole had gotten in his face on the night of the murders. It had happened before, not only with DeeDee, but also with Jennifer Green.

DeeDee described how they would be arguing and then she would spit at him, or slap him, or make some remark, and then "something would just start coming over him." The times that were the worst were when he had been drinking or doing drugs. She said that his favorite drink was tequila, and that his preferred drug was "Ecstasy," the popular psychedelic or "designer" drug, which Terry had talked about. DeeDee was also aware he took Depakote, which he told her was for his epileptic condition.

As I had long suspected, Jason did indeed suffer various forms of seizures. These could range from a temporary loss of memory of what he had been doing minutes earlier to "grand mal" seizures, in which his body would become rigid and he would start to shake uncontrollably. During one such seizure, which DeeDee witnessed, Jason was lying in their bed. DeeDee got so worried that she called one of her neighbors to come and help her decide if they should call the paramedics. They ended up doing nothing because Jason came out of the seizure a minute or two later. He had no memory of what had happened and was furious with her for inviting someone into their bedroom without his permission. DeeDee wasn't aware of the condition known as "intermittent rage disorder" until I explained to her what it was. After I had done so, she recognized immediately what I was talking about.

"I know what you mean," she said. "You could see one of those fits coming on, especially if he wasn't on his Depakote and had been drinking or doing drugs. Something would just start coming over him. I could actually see it 'bubble up.' He would get this look in his eyes and he would start to shake and then he would go ballistic."

I asked her for examples.

"There was one time—I don't even remember what for—when he dragged me into the bathroom and picked me up and held me over his head and dropped me into the empty tub. It hurt so much I thought that Jason had broken my back."

DeeDee cowered slightly as the memories flooded back. She was struggling to fight back her tears as she went on.

The incident in the bathtub, and others, she said, convinced her that she had to get out of the relationship. But when she told Jason she was breaking up with him, he went ballistic again. It happened late one night at their apartment on Ogden. The police and fire department as well as their landlord got involved. Jason was out of control, breaking furniture, and slapping her around. She made a run for it, thinking he might try to kill her. As a police helicopter hovered overhead, she ran across the street to another building. She just managed to get inside the building and close the glass security door behind her when Jason arrived.

"I thought I was safe," DeeDee said. "But I wasn't. He ran right through this plate glass window to get to me. Then he grabbed one of the shards of glass and came at me. Only he didn't cut me, like I thought he would. He cut himself. He followed me up the stairs, slashing at his wrists, and saying, 'See what I'm going to do, I'm going to kill myself.' It was all so crazy. He was acting like a madman, somebody else, and somebody I didn't know."

This incident made it impossible for her and Jason to continue living at Ogden. They moved to an apartment on Alta Vista Drive. Though she wanted to leave him, he made it hard for her. Every time she suggested they spend some time apart, or he thought she was cheating on him, he would try and hurt her or threaten to kill himself. Then came the incident when he cut her hair off.

"I had been horseback riding that morning," DeeDee explained. "My hair was in braids. Once I arrived back in the apartment, an argument erupted. There was no reason for it. It was just his damn jealousy. I had brought home some Chinese food for us to share. He thought I had been with some other guy. He took the food and threw it at me. It went all over the apartment. I threw things back at him, trying to defend myself. He ripped pictures from the wall, glasses, dishes, whatever he could get his hands on. 'Jason, stop it!' I said. He started to come at me and I slapped him in the face. Then he started bubbling up. He went into the bedroom, still in a fit of rage. I ran to the bathroom to close the door. Before I could lock the door Jason was inside the bathroom with one of his chef's knives in his hands. He grabbed me and pinned me down on the bathroom floor. Then he grabbed for my braids. He started whacking off my hair with his chef's knife."

"Are you sure he used one of his chef's knives?"

"Yes. I think it might have been the one I had just bought for him. I had got it at Robinson's May Department Store. I wanted him to be happy, I wanted him to be a chef, and so I got him this expensive chef's knife. It was so sharp you could cut off the heel of your shoe with it."

Just the thought of what happened made DeeDee shudder. She was visibly upset, and I half expected her to burst into tears.

"DeeDee, did you buy Jason other chef's knives?"

"No, they were too expensive. I think his mother or sister bought him one, and his dad may have gotten him others."

As Terry had previously told me, and DeeDee now confirmed, it was at this point in DeeDee and Jason's relationship when she and Terry talked and they decided to go to New York.

"That was the only way to get away from Jason. There didn't seem to be any other option. I just had to get out of the relationship, and the only way I thought I could do it was to get on a plane and put as many miles between the two of us as I could. Only it wasn't far enough."

According to DeeDee, Jason found out where she was living and called her up on the phone. He said he had taken an overdose of his epilepsy medication, Depakote, and would be dead in a few hours.

"Mr. Dear, I believed him," DeeDee said. "This wasn't the first time he tried to commit suicide. I was with him the other two times. Maybe it was the tone of his voice that bothered me. Either way, I knew he was in trouble. His jealousy had gotten the best of him. He said, 'I can't stand living without you any longer. I'm really going to kill myself this time,' and then he abruptly hung up. That's when I called Marguerite and told her Jason had overdosed and she should check on him at his apartment."

DeeDee had no way of knowing I was aware of this incident, as well as the earlier suicide attempts. This made what she told me all the more credible, because the dates she gave me coincided perfectly. The only difference in the way she described this last incident was in who made the initial call. It was DeeDee who alerted Marguerite. Jason may also have called and left a message on Marguerite's machine, but the more likely scenario was the one DeeDee had provided. As I also knew, Jason was taken to the hospital and then later underwent therapy. However, according to DeeDee, no sooner had he finished his therapy than he left for New York to find her.

"He camped out in an apartment O. J. had in the city," DeeDee said. "And then went out looking for me. The whole thing just started up again. He would hit and abuse me and then get all sad and apologetic about it. Then I would take him back."

He was always sorry the next day: this was a classic behavior for someone suffering from intermittent rage disorder, according to the studies I had read.

"The thing was, I still loved the guy. I don't know why, but I did. I really think he cared about me and loved me. But there was this dark side to him that would just appear out of nowhere and I couldn't live with that."

Here was a typical example of a battered woman trapped in an abusive relationship, who continued to come back—just like Jennifer Green.

Though Jason had finally gotten the message that DeeDee wasn't going to go out with him anymore and moved back to Los Angeles, he still couldn't seem to get her out of his mind. When DeeDee returned to L.A. a year later, he kept calling her and showing up at the various restaurants where she was working as a waitress. But there were no more incidents of violence. She didn't allow it. She was not moving back in with him.

According to DeeDee, this was when Jason started going out with Jennifer Green. Jason and DeeDee established what could now be described as a more cordial and friendly relationship. It was at this point that DeeDee began seeing more of Nicole, whom she had gotten to know before moving to New York. Sometimes they would go out to nightclubs, other times just sit by her pool on Gretna Green. DeeDee specifically remembered one day when she and Nicole were sitting out by the pool and Nicole told her how "lucky" DeeDee was.

"Nicole said to me, 'You're so lucky you got out of this when you did. For me, it's too late.' I sort of knew what she was talking about at the time, but I didn't quite get it. Not like I do now. I thought that since Nicole had divorced O. J. that would be the end of it. I didn't realize the abuse continued."

DeeDee saw Jason twice in the two months before the murders. The first time was at his birthday party, when he attacked Jennifer Green. The second time was a few days later.

According to DeeDee, Jason came to a photography studio where she was working. He asked her to come back to see his apartment on Sycamore. Jennifer had just moved out, and he was now living alone. DeeDee accompanied him back to the apartment. Jason was his old loveable self: quiet, sensitive, kind and courteous. Only there was one significant difference. He was no longer taking his Depakote.

I asked DeeDee how she knew he wasn't taking his medication. DeeDee said, "I asked him when we were in the apartment. Jason said, 'No, that medication was fucking me up in the head. I'm not taking that shit anymore.' According to Jason, he wanted to perform at his best because of the new job he had as a chef at Jackson's Restaurant."

Later while in the apartment, he tried to make a pass at her. "I wasn't going to allow that to get started all over again," she said. "It had taken me too long to get out of this abusive relationship. Jason hadn't changed. Even though I loved him, I just wasn't willing to take all the rest that came with it."

Listening to DeeDee, I could well imagine what she meant by "all that went with it." For DeeDee, like myself, knew full well what could happen now that Jason had stopped taking his medication. He had regularly abused DeeDee. He had attacked his former boss, Paul Goldberg, with a cook's knife and might have killed him had kitchen workers not pulled him off. He had beaten up and abused Jennifer Green. He might have killed her too had neighbors not come to her rescue. Then there was Nicole, another woman in his life. In his mind, Nicole had lied to him. Nicole, like DeeDee, knew how to push a man's buttons. She knew how to rattle him and get into his face. She knew how to take Jason right to the edge.

DeeDee didn't see Jason again until after the murders. They remained on friendly terms, though there was one subject he wouldn't discuss with her. "No matter how many times I asked him to tell me about the murders," DeeDee said, "he refused to talk about it. I asked him repeatedly if his father had done it. He wouldn't say yes or no. In fact, he wouldn't say anything at all. I wanted to know. But Jason wouldn't tell me. I still want to know."

DeeDee noticed a marked change come over Jason after the murders. "I'm not exactly sure what it was," she said. "It just seemed to me as if the life had been drained out of him, as if that 'dark something' in his eyes had now taken over his entire body. That could be the drugs or the medication he's on. I don't know. But it scares me."

I told DeeDee that it scares me too. As I said this, a tear rolled down the side of her cheek, and she began to cry. I suddenly felt sad for her. She had been through such a great deal of pain, and though she had come through it, and could now express some of the things she had been unable to talk about earlier, the experience had left an indelible mark upon her, a weight she would have to carry for the rest of her life.

I looked into DeeDee's eyes and then I looked down at her hands. It was then that I noticed the tattoos on her forearms. They were old, and must have been there for a decade or longer, from about the time when she first met Jason, before all the trouble began. On her left arm was a coiled snake in the shape of an "S". I couldn't get a good look at the right arm, but it appeared to be a "J".

DeeDee had been indelibly scarred by her relationship with Jason, as, I believe, had Jennifer Green. Could Nicole and Ron Goldman have been his victims too? I was now certain of one thing: Jason Lamar Simpson was now my major suspect.

I couldn't do anything to change the past. I couldn't help Jennifer or DeeDee or Nicole. But I could try my best to stop Jason. In my mind, Jason—with his alleged Jekyll and Hyde personality disorder— was sick and needed help.

I couldn't help but wonder if all of Jason's problems didn't revert back to the day that twenty-three-month-old Aaren, Jason's sister, drowned in the swimming pool. Even though O. J. blamed Jason's mother, Marguerite, did Jason feel responsible for his sister's death?

21

TUNNEL VISION

TWELVE TIMES. FOR THE twelfth time since meeting with Dr. Kittay, I did as he suggested and called O. J. Simpson's personal secretary, Cathy Randa.

Each time an answering machine picked up and each time I left a message saying I was in Los Angeles and wanted to talk to her. According to Dr. Kittay, he had paved the way for me. All I had to do was leave my name and Randa would pick up the phone. There was no doubt in my mind that she understood the nature of my call.

Surely by now they knew I had interviewed Jennifer Green. The ball was in their court—they knew how to get in touch with me, they had my telephone number, and Jennifer Green had my business card. If she was as good a friend to Arnelle as she claimed to be, then O. J., Arnelle, Jason, Cathy Randa, and all the rest knew who I was and how to find me.

No one called my cell phone. I couldn't help but wonder if this had been a set up to catch me alone and vulnerable.

Like a chess player, I decided to make the next move. I called Sidney Kirkpatrick, a respected Los Angeles true-crime writer, with whom I had decided to share what I had discovered. I could trust Kirkpatrick, like I trusted Chris Stewart, to give me an honest assessment of the evidence I had collected and, at the same time, to tell me if I had been diligent, open-minded, and unbiased in how I handled this high-profile investigation. By telling Kirkpatrick, I felt confident the story would reach the press if circumstances made it impossible for me to tell it myself. Toward this end, I had instructed Stewart Bonnett, my attorney, that in the event of my death, he was to turn over to Kirkpatrick the master computer disk containing my investigative notes and backup material. I had come too far during the past six years to take any chances at this point.

"I'm in L.A.," I told Kirkpatrick. "Let's get together for dinner. My treat."

"I look forward to it," Sidney said, "but on one condition. You have to tell me what you've been up to."

"You can count on that," I replied.

I picked up my cell phone and made reservations at a new gourmet restaurant in Santa Monica. I was going to treat myself to a seven-course, five-star meal. After interviewing Jessie, Terry, and DeeDee on the same day, I felt the reward was justified.

I took a much-needed shower and was dressed in my favorite black suit when Kirkpatrick met me at my hotel. Minutes later we were driving down the Pacific Coast Highway. Along the way, I started to fill Sidney in on my six years of research into the Nicole Simpson and Ron Goldman murders.

"I believe O. J. is innocent," I told him right from the start.

He thought I was joking. "You can't be serious. O. J. is anything but innocent!"

I wasn't surprised by his response, like most other journalists and writers I knew, Kirkpatrick was skeptical that anyone besides O. J. Simpson could possibly be guilty of the Bundy Drive murders. He believed that the reason O. J. had not been convicted in the criminal trial was because of racial issues, police and prosecutorial bungling, and the profound lack of trust which many Angelinos feel toward the LAPD.

"And Mark Fuhrman didn't help matters any," Sidney added. "The Simpson case is only the most recent example of a long line of failures, including the Rodney King beating, the McMartin Preschool case and the Menendez Brothers murder trial."

O. J. IS INNOCENT

I knew where Sidney was coming from because I had once made the same assumptions, back in St. Louis when I had watched the slow-speed car chase. Now, six years later, it was my job to prove that O. J. was innocent and, in fact, covering up for his son, Jason.

I didn't argue with Kirkpatrick that Marcia Clark and Chris Darden could have done a better job. I just said they did remarkably well, considering my belief that the very foundation of their case—the assumption that O. J. was the one and only suspect—was inherently flawed.

"It's a matter of tunnel vision," I explained. "The LAPD, like the prosecutors and then the press, all believed there was one and only one suspect. In their one weapon and one killer scenario, they couldn't see the forest for the trees. Even Marcia Clark admitted as much in the pretrial hearing. Investigators didn't have to look beyond Rockingham because O. J. was the 'sole suspect.' But the truth has a way of rising to the surface, however unsettling or distasteful that truth may be."

Kirkpatrick had too much respect for my work to discount what I was telling him, but his natural skepticism for conspiracy theories and far-out explanations for events and phenomena that might otherwise be easily explained in simple, straightforward terms got the best of him. "The case against O. J. may not be airtight," he admitted. "But it's the best explanation that exists."

I knew I didn't have more than a few hours to present my case, so I decided to tackle the most volatile aspect of the murders first: O. J.'s supposed motive for having committed the crimes. To my mind, Marcia Clark said it best in her own book when she recounted what she had said when first informed of Nicole's murder and O. J.'s alleged history of spousal abuse. "That has-been football player is guilty!" she declared.

I asked Sidney to try and forget the imagined history of O. J.'s spousal abuse and to judge this case on the facts alone. "No one ever saw O. J. lay a hand on Nicole. No one ever saw him beat her, strike her, or even push her off the bed. I'm not saying he and Nicole didn't get into fights, because I know they did. Nicole didn't back down from an argument. She stood her ground. She could be as verbally and physically abusive as O. J. could be. But he certainly didn't use a knife. Nor was there a single shred of evidence to suggest that their fights had ever sent O. J. into an uncontrollable rage. In fact, the evidence suggests the opposite is true. If watching Nicole perform oral sex on Keith Zlomsowitch didn't set O. J. off, nothing would."

I then began to point out the many contradictions that existed between the physical evidence found at the crime scene and O. J.'s supposed motive for having committed the murders. "Sydney and Justin were at home in bed and had arranged to have a friend sleep over. O. J. knew that. How would he have known the plans had changed? How would he even know what time they would get home that night? How would he know they weren't still awake and watching television? It wasn't a school night. I can't believe for an instant that O. J. would kill the mother of his children just a few feet away from their bedrooms."

I then pointed out another reason why I didn't think he had committed the murders. "It is a well-documented fact that O. J. is actually squeamish at the sight of blood. His own therapist told me so. He doesn't even like to bait a fishhook. Yet the killer chose a knife, a weapon that was certain to draw blood and was sure to bring the killer in direct physical contact with the victims. I reminded him what Dr. Lee, PhD, had said at the trial. There would have been blood all over the assailant's hair, fingernails, shoes, and clothes. "Blood everywhere!" Dr. Lee proclaimed.

The enormous quantity of blood spilled at the crime scene, the lack of blood on O. J.'s clothes, the lack of blood in the Bronco, and the lack of blood at Rockingham were another important reasons why I believed he could not have been the killer.

"The general public has been led to believe that the Bronco was loaded with blood, when, in fact, there were no more than eleven tiny spots throughout the entire vehicle, barely enough to fit on a grown man's thumbnail. There was no blood found on the brake or the accelerator, even though an extensive bloody fight had resulted in Goldman's death. By Dr. Lee's own account, there should have been blood—saturated in sand and dirt acquired during the scuffle—on the bottom of the assailant's shoes, which would have been transferred to the floor board, accelerator, and brake pedal of the Bronco."

I continued as I had begun, now discussing the so-called trail of blood leading to O. J. Simpson's bedroom at Rockingham. "No blood was found on the white carpet on the stairway and only a drop or two of blood was on the socks supposedly found in front of O. J.'s bed. There were no bloody clothes in the hamper, no blood in the drain-pipes of the washer, dryer, and sink, and no other blood found in the house, just the two spots on the downstairs entrance leading into the foyer and several small drops of blood in the driveway leading to the front gate."

I could see that Sidney was growing visibly annoyed at what he perceived as my ignorance of other important evidence linking O. J. to the murders. "How about the bloody glove that was found behind the guesthouse?" he demanded. "How about the Bruno Magli shoes? I suppose you're going to tell me Mark Fuhrman planted all that evidence in order to frame O. J."

"No," I said. "I don't think the bloody glove was planted, and I have every reason to believe the Bruno Magli shoes belonged to O. J. In fact, I believe O. J. was actually at the crime scene. I just don't believe he committed the murders."

I had definitely caught Sidney off guard. He sat in rapt silence as I told him I believed that the killer knew O. J. and had called him on the phone and told him Nicole had been killed. This resulted in O. J. leaving Rockingham to find out what had actually happened. O. J. was desperate to know whether the children were safe. He knew the risk he was taking. But he was left with no choice. I then proceeded to paint a picture for Sidney of what I supposed might have happened that night. Though my scenario was imagined, and would not have held up in a court of law, it was based on the facts as I knew them up to this point in my investigation.

"Donning the black gloves, the ski cap and the Bruno Magli shoes, O. J. quickly leaves Rockingham, making a right turn onto Montana off of Bundy Drive, a left into the alley, and then parks next to several other cars that belonged to tenants living in adjacent apartment units. O. J. runs down the alley, cautiously entering the property from the rear, making his way to Nicole's front door. That's when he sees his ex-wife curled into a fetal position at the foot of the steps. Removing his cap to see better in the dense darkness, and one of his brown leather gloves, O. J. bends down to check Nicole's pulse, suddenly realizing that she is, in fact, dead and nearly decapitated. The sight of all that blood makes him sick. Then he looks up and sees the open eyes of Ron Goldman. Upset and suffering from shock, O. J. drops the glove and cap. He quickly makes his way out the back and into his waiting Bronco. He is careful to try not to step into the pools of blood, but he does, in fact, get a small quantity of blood on his shoes. It is this blood that first contaminates his Bronco and then his Rockingham home.

"He sees his limo driver parked on Rockingham, waiting to take him to the airport. With the other bloody glove in his hand he quickly parks the Bronco. Entering from the rear of the adjacent property, still in a state of shock, and with his bad knees, he jumps over the four-foot chain-link fence, loses his balance, and falls against the protruding air conditioner. He accidentally drops the remaining glove. It's too dark to find it, and there is too little time."

I explained how O. J. hurries across the driveway where Park, the limo driver, sees him. Knowing that the only evidence now placing him at the crime scene was the Bruno Magli shoes, O. J. takes them off, and after entering his residence, puts them in a knapsack which he sets on the floor just inside the door. O. J. then runs up the white carpeted staircase in his socks, changes his clothes, dresses, collects his garment bag, then comes back down the white carpeted stairway, picks up the knapsack containing the bloody shoes, then goes out the back door, where Kato Kaelin and Allan Park are waiting for him. O. J. gets into the limousine with two bags, one of which is the knapsack. The golf clubs and the garment bag are put into the trunk. As they leave Rockingham, rushing to the airport, O. J. complains of it being too hot in the back seat of the car. Park sees him rolling down the window.

"That's when O. J. disposes of the knapsack containing the Bruno Magli shoes. He tosses it out the window as they are driving through the downtown industrial section of Los Angeles, where O. J. is sure a trash collector or scavenger will soon pick it up. Now, what O. J. perceives as the most crucial piece of evidence placing him at the scene of the crime is eliminated. He sits back in the limousine, praying that he is safe. O. J. is friendly and cordial once he arrives at the airport. He signs autographs. O. J. is again "The Juice."

I also described how a witness who sat beside O. J. on the flight to Chicago said there was no cut on O. J.'s hand, and how no one who came into contact with O. J. during the flight became suspicious of his activities or behavior.

"I think O. J. intended on arriving in Chicago and being out on the golf course before the bodies of Nicole Simpson and Ron Goldman were found. With a drinking glass in his right hand, O. J. paced back and forth in his hotel room, praying for time to pass quickly. The call came at five o'clock in the morning. Instantly, O. J. knows that it must be the police, or someone calling about the murders. Frightened and upset, and without realizing it, he squeezes the glass he is clutching in his hand. It breaks. O. J.'s hand begins to bleed."

I pointed out that, later, Chicago detectives would in fact find this particular broken glass, with O. J. Simpson's blood on it, in the hotel room. I also pointed out that the Los Angeles detectives speculated that O. J. had put the bloody clothes in the garment bag and somehow disposed of them in Chicago, but in fact, the truth was that Kardashian, after picking O. J. up from the airport upon his arrival back from Chicago, tried to turn the garment bag over to a uniformed police officer standing guard at Rockingham. The officer refused to accept it, just as this same officer refused to permit Kardashian entrance into the Rockingham residence where O. J. was now being

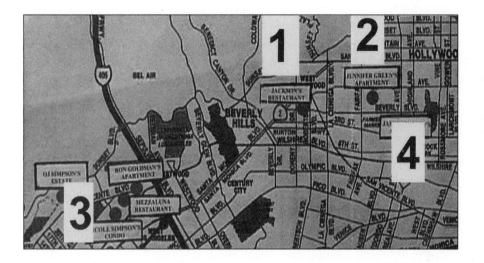

confronted by detectives Vannatter and Lange and other uniformed officers, one of whom had placed O. J.'s hands behind his back and handcuffed him.

I could see the wheels in Sidney's mind working overtime. Excited, he thought he knew where I was going, and attempted to second-guess me. "Bill, you've discovered a drug connection. Goldman was the target!"

I was sorry to disappoint him. "This was not a drug-related murder and Goldman was definitely not the target, it was Nicole."

I explained my reasoning. "If the killer intended on killing Goldman, he could have accosted him as he left the restaurant, or on his way home or as he came out of his apartment on Gorham Avenue and opened the door to the red Toyota. The killer could have ambushed him in the alleyway behind Bundy Drive, or as he parked on Dorothy Street, or as he walked through the alley toward Nicole's back gate."

Further, I pointed out that Nicole was being attacked as Goldman entered the crime scene from the alley, through the rear entrance to the condo. This was when the witness, Robert Heidstra, first heard the shouting, "Hey . . . Hey . . . Hey . . ." At this point Nicole was struck on the top of her head, presumably with the butt of the assailant's knife, rendering her unconscious, causing her to fall, her face striking the Spanish tiles, while the assailant confronted Goldman. After an extensive fight, Goldman was killed, and the assailant had no choice but to kill Nicole, pulling her head back, then with the razor-sharp knife nearly decapitating her.

"There's only one problem," Sidney said. "For your theory to be correct there would have to be a killer at large in Brentwood on the night of the murders, who not only personally knew Nicole, but whom O. J. would be willing to risk his life to protect. Not to mention the fact that this person would have to be carrying an unusually long knife and have some pathological reason for wanting to use it. Had there been such a person at large on Bundy Drive that night, I certainly think I would have heard about it by now."

"You will hear about it," I replied. "Tonight."

22

REFLECTION

ONCE WE ARRIVED AT the restaurant, I found it was considerably finer than I had imagined it would be, despite the fact that a film producer friend of mine, who had eaten there several nights earlier, had raved about it. I could see, from the moment Sidney and I came in, that no expense had been spared, from the imported wood paneling to the custom-designed china and the thick pile carpeting on the floor. Though the restaurant had been open only a few weeks, it was already crowded with customers who dressed and comforted themselves with as much style and care as the interior designer had lavished on the decor. For what I was going to spend, I hoped the menu and cooking reflected that same desire for perfection.

At my request, Sidney and I were seated in a booth directly across from a picture window, looking directly into the kitchen. This way, seated in the dining room, we could view the inner workings of the restaurant as our gourmet food was being prepared. Dining at a restaurant such as this, and savoring the atmosphere as well as the food, could well take an entire evening to fully appreciate, which is what I would need to tell the rest of the story.

I decided not to leave Sidney hanging, at least not for too long. After we had ordered a bottle of wine and began to look at the menu, I picked up where I had left off in the car. I reminded Sidney what I had said about tunnel vision. The police didn't look for another suspect because they believed they already knew who the killer was. They ignored evidence that was right in front of them. These were not premeditated murders by a professional killer. Marcia Clark ultimately reached this same conclusion when she said in her book that she thought the murders were the work of an "amateur," and that this was a "rage type" killing.

"According to my investigation, there was a person at large in Los Angeles on the night of the murders—not O. J. Simpson—who had a reason for being at Nicole's stated condo that evening and who had in his possession a bag containing a weapon identified as being the right shape, the right length, and the right width as the knife used to kill Nicole and Goldman," I told Sidney.

"The suspect I am talking about has a history of irrational and violent behavior toward women. He has been diagnosed as suffering from intermittent rage disorder and has been prescribed Depakote, a medication that has sometimes been used to treat mental patients who cannot control impulsive behavior. He has made numerous visits to hospitals because of his irrational acts, and was once committed to a psychiatric ward at a major Los Angeles hospital. At the time of the murders, he was known to have stopped taking his medication, for as he said, it was "fucking with my head."

I continued to build my case. "This same suspect had tried to commit suicide three times and has committed numerous acts of violence against his girlfriends and other women in his life over a period of ten years or more. That he knew and loved Nicole is beyond question. That Nicole would open her door to this man is also not in question. And Nicole herself once told former police officer and trusted friend Ron Shipp that this man, not O. J., may have been stalking her.

"This same man, at the time of the murders, was on probation for felony assault with a deadly weapon. Less than two months before the murders, this same suspect tried to strangle a woman with his bare hands. He might have actually killed her, if neighbors hadn't come to her rescue, according to the *National Enquirer* article. Like Nicole, this was a woman whom he was close to and once lived with.

"This same suspect is believed to have the same blood type and similar genetic characteristics as O. J. and to wear approximately the same size shoes. He is also known to have routinely borrowed personal items such as clothes, shoes and gloves from O. J.'s closet at Rockingham. He could come and go from Rockingham unnoticed, knew the way over the back gate, and also had the key code for the Rockingham alarm system. But that's not all.

"This same suspect is someone whom O. J. has bailed out of trouble in the past, and is perhaps the one person in the entire world he would risk his life and reputation to protect. He is also a man who was not questioned by the LAPD, or by anyone in the DA's office or the press. No one, to my knowledge, has ever investigated him until I came along."

Kirkpatrick was so engrossed in what I was saying that he couldn't concentrate on the menu. I went ahead and ordered for him.

"OK, you've piqued my interest," Sidney said after our waiter had gone. "I want to hear the rest. Who is this suspect you're talking about?"

"In their feeding frenzy to convict O. J.," I told Sidney, "they completely ignored his twenty-four-year-old son by his first marriage, Jason Lamar Simpson."

Sidney knew the name but had no idea what he looked like, did for a living, or where he figured in terms of the family dynamics. I quickly filled him in.

"Jason had wanted to be a chef since he was in high school, perhaps even earlier, but O. J. would have nothing to do with it. He wanted him to be a football player. I think it's interesting to note that O. J.'s own father, whom O. J. despised because of his sexual preference for men and who later died of AIDS, also had a great love and mastery of cooking and was known to have once worked as a cook. Perhaps that was the root of O. J.'s disdain for his son's desire to become a chef, or perhaps it was mere vanity on the part of an aging football player longing to have a son who would help keep his own legend alive. I don't honestly know. But I do know that Jason could never satisfy his father, and therein, perhaps, lay the root of many of Jason's psychological challenges. He alternately wanted to impress and then destroy his dad."

I wasn't cataloging Jason's insecurities with the intention of putting his father on the hot seat, but rather because I truly believed that O. J. ultimately felt responsible for Jason's behavior. He had attempted to make Jason into his clone and failed miserably at it. He also, on the other hand, hadn't really been there for him as a parent either. He tried. But it wasn't enough. O. J. was too busy making a career for himself, even after he had retired from football.

"This is not to say Jason didn't have physiological problems that compounded or exacerbated his existing psychological problems. Jason had epilepsy. He developed a wide range of conditions which, I believe, compounded by the use of drugs and alcohol, ultimately were manifested in a rage disorder."

I went on to chart, for Sidney's benefit, Jason's many incidents of irrational and violent behavior, beginning when he was fourteen years old and took the baseball bat to the prized statue of his father in the garden at Rockingham. I also described how alcohol and drugs were a surefire way to scramble already damaged neurotransmitters in the brain of anyone with epilepsy, and how Jason had started abusing both drugs and alcohol before he had even gone to high school.

"Instead of sending him to cooking school," I said, "O. J. put him in USC. The boy fell apart. He left or was kicked off the football team, dropped out of school, and then overdosed on drugs.

"He almost killed not one, but two of his now former girlfriends. The only thing keeping him from completely going off the deep end was his job as a prep chef, and his Depakote, which he was to take twice a day. Only, DeeDee—one of Jason's former girlfriends—said that Jason had told her he had stopped taking his Depakote two months before the murders. Jason was getting more out of control each day. First he had a fight with his former employer, Paul Goldberg, in which he pulled a knife on him. Then he tried to strangle his girlfriend, Jennifer. To me the handwriting was on the wall. Jason was crying out for help, but no one was listening."

I went on to explain the interest and affinity he had always felt for Nicole, and how Jason felt she had changed after her divorce from his dad. Jason may have believed that the opportunity was quickly approaching when he could love Nicole, not as a stepmother, but as a man loves a woman. But Nicole may not have been that easily had, especially by the son of the man she had just divorced. There were other men in her life. Nicole may have toyed with Jason just as she had with his father.

"Nicole had a way of turning on a man with a simple snap of her fingers," I told Kirkpatrick. "O. J. complained about that trait of Nicole's since even before they were married. She would keep him dangling, and then without so much as an explanation or apology, suddenly let go, change her mind and change her plans. I think that's what happened on the night of the murders. Jason was intending to impress the woman whom he had secretly admired and adored by cooking for her and her family on June 12, 1994. It was Jason's opportunity to show off. Jason wasn't running down the football field like his father. He was doing what he wanted to do, and what he did best. It was his time of glory—not carrying the football—but preparing food as a chef. That story didn't come out in the press.

"Jason was set to cook that night for Nicole and her family at Jackson's Restaurant, only she stood him up and went to the Mezzaluna Restaurant instead. I don't believe she ever told him she wasn't coming. His rage disorder set in. He began to 'bubble up,' as one of his girlfriends described it, and with alcohol and drugs, his rage took over. Jason then assumed the persona of what everyone has described as Dr. Jekyll and Mr. Hyde."

I had to stop at this point because our first course had arrived, along with the owner of the restaurant, who was also the chef. I told him I certainly was impressed with what I saw. He said this was his dream come true. "I've tried to make this the finest restaurant in the world. I hope that you will enjoy it."

I assured him we were pleased with the food and we resumed our conversation. "Didn't Jason have an alibi on the night of the murders?" Sidney asked.

"Jason had an alibi," I said. "Any number of them."

I discussed the first alibi, which appeared in various books that came out after the murder trial, including the one by Dream Team attorney Robert Shapiro. On the night of June 12, Jason was said to be cooking in front of two hundred people at Jackson's Restaurant on Beverly Boulevard.

"There is one major problem with that alibi. Jackson's Restaurant doesn't hold two hundred people. In fact, it couldn't hold more than eighty-seven people at any one time. On this particular Sunday night, they had less than twenty-five customers. The restaurant normally closes at 10:30, but business had been poor on Sunday night, and they undoubtedly shut the grill down early. Only two months later, Jackson's Restaurant shut down altogether on Sunday nights due to lack of business. That Sunday night, Jason was substituting for the owner as the head chef, not in his regular position as assistant chef. I've been able to prove that Jason left the restaurant at approximately 9:45 PM, one hour before Marcia Clark and Christopher Darden's time frame begins. When Jennifer, his girlfriend, picked him up, he left the restaurant with something and put it inside his Jeep. Would you care to know what it was?"

"You tell me," Sidney said.

"It was a chef's bag containing an assortment of chef's knives."

"Are you telling me that on the night of June 12, Jason Simpson left the restaurant with a bag full of chef's knives?"

"Yes, that's exactly what I'm telling you. Now here comes the important part: the second alibi. His girlfriend Jennifer Green, who supplied this alibi, said she had picked him up at Jackson's Restaurant at around 9:45 PM and they drove about three miles to her apartment. They parked his Jeep, and she and Jason entered her apartment where they watched television until after 11 PM."

"Bill, that's a perfect alibi," Sidney exclaimed. "Everyone knows the murders took place before 11 PM"

"That's true it's a perfect alibi. Only it doesn't hold up. I acquired a copy of Jason's civil deposition and that's not what he said. Jason stated that he dropped Jennifer off at her apartment, kissed her good-night and drove directly home. He was specifically asked if he had gone up to his girlfriend's apartment. His answer was no. According to Jason, when he arrived at his apartment he watched television until 3 AM, at which point he went to bed. Jason had no alibi for the night of June 12. Jennifer Green had lied to protect him."

"Why wasn't this brought out during the trial?" Sidney asked.

"Marcia Clark had made up her mind, as well as Vannatter and Lange. There could be only one killer, and that was O. J. They never looked beyond him. Jason, according to the doctors and experts I consulted, perfectly fits the profile of being the killer of Nicole Simpson and Ron Goldman."

"I'll be damned!" Sidney exclaimed. "That's why they never found the bloody clothes. O. J. had never worn them in the first place. His son had."

"Who is the one person you would protect no matter what, when you felt responsible for what might have happened?"

"I guess you're trying to tell me . . . his son."

"You're right. O. J. went to trial because he had made two mistakes. The first, that he was too embarrassed to get help for his son when he first needed it. The second was the night he went to Bundy Drive and found Nicole's body. Instead of reporting it, he gave the greatest gift he felt he could give to make up for his mistakes. That was to protect his son."

We were interrupted by our second course: lobster. After the waiter left, Sidney asked the question I knew would be coming. "Bill, where is Jason now?"

I took a bite of the lobster—it was soft and tender—and then motioned with my fork as I chewed. "See the tall, heavy-set young man in the kitchen there? The one with broad shoulders, oversized hands, large shaved head, and large round eyes . . . the man who is nearly as tall as his dad."

"You're kidding me."

"Would I kid you? Of course not! The man who cooked our dinner tonight, the man who is wielding those chef knives, that's Jason Lamar Simpson, O. J.'s son. He's the man who is my major suspect in the murders of Nicole Simpson and Ron Goldman."

As if our evening had been scripted in advance, Jason Simpson, dressed in a white chef's jacket and pants, turned and looked into the dining room. I continued to eat, while Kirkpatrick stared at him. Mesmerized.

"By the way, Jason is known to have been a pathological liar according to DeeDee, his former girlfriend. In fact, she says he believes his own lies, blacks out, and sometimes doesn't remember what he's done.

"Another thing, O. J. scored a minus twenty-two on a polygraph test he took privately—that means he failed every single question about the murders. You might say that's proof he did it, but I believe the real reason he failed that polygraph is simple—he knew about the murders, in fact, he was there at the crime scene and knew who killed Nicole and Goldman."

Even though we'd ordered the same dish, I have a feeling Sidney's meal wasn't nearly as delicious as mine. "There was also a letter signed 'peace and love, O. J.,' which O. J. had written after the murders," I continued, "which was analyzed by one of the district attorney's psychiatrists. The findings: 'He's guilty of something.' Oh, and also, according to Dr. Lee, there was definitely one shoe print in blood on the tiled walkway on Bundy which was not from the Bruno Magli shoes. There were also unidentified fingerprints found at the crime scene, along with traces of skin and blood found under Nicole's fingernails that didn't belong to her, O. J., or Ron Goldman."

Kirkpatrick was eager to hear my version of the events which I believed took place that night. But before sharing my thoughts with him, I pointed out the one important difference between the circumstantial case I had built against Jason and the one which prosecutors had brought against O. J.: No matter how hard Marcia Clark and

Christopher Darden had tried to convince a jury that O. J. had flown into an uncontrollable rage that left his ex-wife and Ron Goldman dead on the ground, their case was pure speculation. No one had ever seen O. J. lose his temper like that before. No one had ever seen him slashing about wildly with a knife. No one had ever seen O. J.'s hands and arms drenched in blood. To my mind, it didn't take the same leap of imagination to put Jason on Bundy Drive that night, engaged in a to-the-death struggle with Goldman, and cutting Nicole's throat. Jason had once gotten into a mad rage and used his chef's knife to slash and cut off the hair of his girlfriend, DeeDee. He had assaulted Paul Goldberg with what was believed to be a kitchen knife. And he had tried to squeeze the life out of Jennifer Green by choking her with his bare hands. He hadn't just punched and slapped her. He had gone for her throat.

"Imagination isn't necessary," I said. "These events have actually taken place. I can prove them. In addition, I have documentation that contains evidence of Jason's instability: his attempted suicides, his being under the care of a therapist and other mental health specialists, his confinement to a mental institution, and, in addition, his criminal records. This is not circumstantial. This is fact. I took my evidence to an internationally famous medical examiner who is the leading authority on knife wounds, as well as a retired judge, and several homicide investigators."

I went on to summarize their findings:

"Do I have enough circumstantial evidence to present to a district attorney? The unequivocal answer: Yes.

"Do I have enough circumstantial evidence to have a grand jury indict Jason Simpson? Yes.

"Do I have enough evidence for the district attorney to go to trial? Yes.

"Would the district attorney have sufficient circumstantial evidence for a conviction? Yes.

"I asked the experts what was missing. Only two things, they said: the bloody knife and Jason's confession."

O. J. IS INNOCENT

There was one other thing I wished to communicate to Sidney before painting a picture for him of what I believed had happened. As I had said previously, I reminded him that what I was to tell him was only a theory and though based on my investigation, contained suppositions which would be difficult to prove in a court of law. However, it was a theory I believed to be true after six years of investigation. And after those six years, it wasn't hard to paint such a picture because I had done so in my own mind countless times since the night I had first climbed over the back gate at Bundy Drive.

As we finished our main course, I began to describe how I believed Nicole Simpson and Ron Goldman had been murdered on Sunday, June 12, 1994.

"Jason was angry and upset," I explained. "He didn't like being made out to be a fool at the restaurant. Like his dad, he didn't like being embarrassed. And Jason had been made a fool in front of the waiters and waitresses and fellow kitchen staff at Jackson's, the very people he had told that he would be cooking for Nicole and her family and quite possibly his father.

"Before leaving the restaurant he may have been drinking, perhaps doing drugs, brooding about Nicole standing him up. The bar was readily accessible to him that night because he was the boss; he was the chef.

"He's still mad when Jennifer picks him up in his Jeep, then drops her off at her apartment. He was probably already bubbling with rage. His intention now was to confront Nicole about why she had stood him up. In all likelihood he had not gone over there to kill her.

"Jason parks in the back alley, probably right next to Nicole's Jeep Grand Cherokee. He has been to her home many times and knows how to get in. Jason is already in a state of rage when he knocks on her door and demands an explanation. Only Nicole doesn't want anything to do with him. From her point of view, she doesn't owe him an explanation. She's expecting someone else. She's expecting Ron Goldman, whom she intends to entertain in her hot tub. Jason is in the way. She's not about to let him spoil her evening.

"I can hear her saying: 'You've been drinking. Get the hell out of here. I can eat wherever I want to eat!'

"'I demand an answer,' he says. 'I worked hard to put that dinner together. You could have at least called me.'

"'I don't owe you explanations. I'm no longer your damn step-mother. I had to put up with you before. And I like you. But I don't have to account to you or O. J. for what I do and where I eat. Now get the hell out of here before you wake up Sydney and Justin. I'm not going to tell you again. This is my home. Not yours. Not your dad's.'

"As Dr. Kittay had said, 'This German girl knew how to get in your face.'

"Nicole makes one final statement; she slams the door. Now Jason was on the receiving end. Just as he had been with DeeDee, Paul Goldberg, and Jennifer Green. She had pushed him too far by slamming the door in his face. Dr. Jekyll and Mr. Hyde sets in.

"Jason, at this point, is beginning to lose it. He walks back to his Jeep, his persona now taking over. He remembers when DeeDee would spit in his face. Only now, this time, he wasn't going to just cut off DeeDee's hair or choke Jennifer Green with his bare hands or assault Paul Goldberg. He was going one step further. He was going to kill Nicole. Jason reaches down and pulls out his eight-inch boning knife from his chef's bag. This time his rage has gone too far. Jason has become Mr. Hyde.

"Hurrying back down the walkway with his chef's knife in his right hand, he bangs on Nicole's door again. She opens the door and steps out, partially closing the door behind her. 'I told you to get out of here.'

"'You're not telling me anything. My dad was right. Things could have been different if it hadn't been for you. You're the cause of all of our problems!'

"As he reaches up with the knife, Nicole puts up her hands, trying to protect herself, as the knife comes down. 'Oh my God . . . No . . . Jason . . . No . . . No.'

"At that same moment, Jason hears a voice call out, 'Hey . . . Hey . . . Hey' and the sound of someone running toward him down the walkway.

"Panicking, he strikes Nicole on the top of the head with the blunt end of the knife.

"Nicole falls to the ground, the side of her face hitting the Spanish tile, as Goldman approaches Jason.

"As Jason moves to the right, Goldman realizes he is confronting a man with a knife. Even though Goldman is a karate expert, he can't get out of the way. He puts his hands up to defend himself, but the razor-sharp blade cuts into his body time after time after time.

"Goldman, taking a karate defensive position, falls down onto his buttocks, kicking his feet out as he pivots around trying to protect himself from the blade of the knife. Bleeding heavily, Goldman kicks out, the blade striking the rubber soles of his shoes. Realizing he is fighting for his life, he struggles to get to his feet. But now it's too late. As this five-foot-eleven, 235-pound former football player comes at him again, slashing him through the throat, Goldman falls to the ground, dead.

"As Jason panics and turns, he realizes what he has done. There was no one to stop him this time. There is no turning back. Jason is now a murderer. He looks down, with blood dripping from his hands, face and clothes, as Nicole starts to stir. She is beginning to regain consciousness.

"Jason then puts his foot against Nicole's back, reaches down with his left hand and grabs her hair, pulling her head back, exposing her throat for the eight-inch boning knife to do its job. The razor-sharp knife touches the soft skin of Nicole Brown Simpson as the blade is raked across her throat from ear to ear nearly decapitating her.

"Jason looks up and sees no light coming on in the bedrooms. In panic, he rushes out the back, into his Jeep, quickly leaving the scene of the crime.

"I can picture Jason picking up his cell phone, assuming he had one; he dials his father. 'Dad . . . Dad . . . I didn't mean to do it. I didn't mean to kill her!'

"'What the hell are you talking about?'

"'Dad, I killed Nicole . . . I killed Nicole.'

"'Where are you?'

"'I'm in the Jeep.'

"'Are you sure she's dead? Are the kids OK?'

"'Yes, they're fine, but I don't know what to do.'

"'Get the hell out of there. Did anyone see you?'

"'I don't think so.'

"'Good. Now for once in your life listen to me! Go home. Clean up. Don't talk to anyone. No matter what happens, don't talk to anyone. If the police come, you are to call Carl Jones. I'll have it taken care of. But for God's sake, don't talk to anyone.'

"'Yes, Dad. Yes, Dad, I will. I'm sorry.'

"The phone goes dead. O. J. now visits the crime scene. But he quickly realizes there is nothing he can do.

"Only O. J. and Jason knew what happened that night, in my opinion. In his civil deposition Jason was so indecisive about having a phone at his apartment but adamant about not having a cell phone. It makes me believe that he may have had a cell phone but knew the records could incriminate him. If he didn't have a cell phone, within the time frame given, he could have easily gone to his apartment or back to Jackson's and made the call to O. J. while he cleaned up. Later, it was established Jason did have a key to the restaurant. Cowlings, Randa, Kittay were all kept in the dark, but I believe the one person who may have been told was pastor and former football great Rosey Greer. Being a man of the cloth, Greer couldn't or wouldn't break his trust.

"And remember one other thing, Sidney. Remember what O. J. keeps telling people. Over and over for the past six years.

"'I didn't do it . . . I didn't do it . . . I didn't do it . . . but it's all my fault.'"

Sidney looked at me with shock and amazement.

I would have continued with my version of the tragic events of that night but my attention was drawn back to the kitchen. Jason now stood at a sink behind the steam table. He was cleaning his knives. I could see him take each knife, one at a time, rinse it under the spigot and then wipe it clean. It was a ritual he must have performed hundreds of times before, only to me, and now Sidney, it held a far darker significance.

"Do you think one of those knives is the one he used on Bundy Drive?" Sidney asked, echoing my own thoughts.

"Possibly."

Sidney had more questions than there was time to answer, especially given the fact that we had to keep our voices down and stop talking altogether whenever a waiter was in the vicinity.

Perhaps I hadn't gotten all the details right. Even though there was the possibility of two knives, Terry Merston and Peter Harpur were now leaning toward my theory involving one particular knife, possibly the eight-inch chef's boning knife. At this point that's as far as I could go with the facts I had uncovered so far.

All I really believed, for certain now, was that Jason had become my major suspect in the murders. It was even possible that Nicole had called O. J. after Jason first knocked on her door confronting her as to why she failed to turn up at Jackson's Restaurant that night.

One thing I did know for sure, neither Nicole nor anyone else in L.A. would open their door to a stranger. Nicole had to know who it was. The same thing goes for the Akita dog named Kato. These are good watchdogs and would growl and bark unless they knew the person. If O. J. was not the killer, then there was no doubt in my mind that the person who killed Nicole and Goldman was no stranger to Nicole or to the dog.

If Nicole told O. J., "Jason was just here threatening me," O. J. could quickly have driven the five-minute drive to her condo and discovered the grim truth. He left Bundy Drive in a panic, completely unprepared for the gruesome sight that he had walked into.

By the time I had gotten to this point in my description of the events surrounding the murders, I noticed an unusual thing happen in the restaurant. Jason was again looking directly out the picture window, but this time he was looking at me. So were the owner and head chef, along with at least three of the waiters and assorted kitchen staff. Minutes prior to that, I had heard the phone in the kitchen ring. I glanced over in that direction and saw the owner-chef looking over at me while still on the phone.

At first I thought that Sidney or I had spoken too loudly and someone had overheard us. But on reflection, I was certain this was not the case. The owner-chef still held the receiver in his hands. As he watched our table, he spoke into it. I couldn't be sure, but I imagined that Arnelle had called for Jason after learning of my visit with Jennifer Green. Did Arnelle then call the restaurant to see if I was eating there that night? The reservation list was consulted and the discovery made that, indeed, William Dear and a companion were dining at the restaurant where Jason worked.

Dessert finally came. We had waited longer than we had anticipated. It probably had something to do with the telephone call, but it was worth waiting for. At the same time the waiter, whom I had asked earlier if I could keep the menu as a souvenir, reached down, picked it up off the seat beside me and walked away without explanation.

For the next twenty minutes, between the time I put my cheese knife down and our bill arrived, not a single waiter spoke to us or so much as smiled or made eye contact. Like Jason, who watched us from the kitchen, the staff was making sure we knew our presence at the restaurant was not welcome. It wasn't that I believed the owner-chef or the waiters, were part of a conspiracy, but rather that they had been told we were there to make trouble for Jason. No doubt the staff knew Jason as most people did: a warm and loveable individual who had the unfortunate fate of being the son of O. J. Simpson, the murderer. All they were trying to do was protect him, and for this, I couldn't blame them. They just didn't know what I knew.

As the room gradually began to empty out and no one had as much as spoken to us toward the end of our meal, Sidney asked me the same question which had been on my mind.

"Now what are you going to do about it?" he asked. "It isn't likely the LAPD will want to roll out the red carpet for you. They've already been humiliated once in this case. They're not about to let it happen again. Nor is the district attorney's office going to applaud your investigative work. It just makes them look bad and the DA relies on votes to keep his job."

I had no easy answer for Sidney, and as each new minute passed and we found ourselves the last two diners in the place. I seriously doubted that O. J. or his family were going to address the issues my investigation had raised.

I paid the bill. Then Sidney and I slowly got up and walked to the door. Just before leaving, I turned to the owner-chef and said, "That was a great meal."

His only reply was a curt, "Thank you, sir."

As Sidney and I walked outside, we turned to the left where the two valet parking attendants were standing. "Can I get your car, sir?"

"No, I parked it myself," I replied. I had had no intention of letting the valet attendants park my car that night. I had purposefully left it about a block away.

We turned left down the alley behind the restaurant. As Sidney and I walked about fifty feet, I heard someone call my name. I wheeled around to see the owner-chef now standing outside the back kitchen door.

"Have a nice trip back to Dallas, Mr. Dear," the restaurant owner said.

"Thanks, I will," I replied.

Standing beside him, now staring straight at me, was Jason Lamar Simpson. He looked at me and I looked at him.

"I'll be back," I said. "I'll be back."

23

ACCUMULATING EVIDENCE

AS I BOARDED THE plane the words *I'll be back, I'll be back* rang in my ears. Now, flying to Dallas to be with my son, I knew I would be back. I'd come too far to stop now. Observing Jason at the back of the restaurant, smoking a cigarette, talking to Joseph Citrin, the owner of Mélisse Restaurant, convinced me even more that I was approaching the end of the journey.

Once back in Dallas, I realized I couldn't go to the L.A. District Attorney's Office because Gil Garcetti was certainly not going to give me the time of day. Garcetti's reelection was coming up in six or eight months. If I was right, reopening this scandal could cost him the election. There were also rumbles in the Los Angeles Police Department that in a few months something was going to break within the department, dealing with corruption and possibly evidence tampering being used to falsify convictions.

I have great respect for law enforcement, and I know mistakes can be made. In this case I knew that a grave one *had* been made. To me, an innocent man had been convicted, rightfully or wrongfully; even though they found him innocent in the criminal trial, they found him guilty in the civil trial. I couldn't blame either the Los Angeles District Attorney's Office or the Los Angeles Police Department or even the jury in the civil trial for finding O. J. guilty of the murders of Nicole Simpson and Ron Goldman. O. J. had placed himself in a box, a box where there was no out. The evidence had to speak for itself. They'd had only the evidence available to them. They hadn't had the information and evidence that I had collected.

Sometimes at night when I closed my eyes, I could see O. J. looking into a mirror in the picture that accompanied an *Esquire* magazine article and hearing him saying over and over again, "*I didn't do it, I didn't do it, but it was all my fault.*" Everybody I knew was convinced that O. J. was guilty because there was no other choice for them. I had given myself another choice by uncovering new evidence.

I was determined to cover all my bases, and in an effort to do so, I put Jason under surveillance for the next four months. Either I or an associate would follow him back and forth from work and to and from parties and other engagements. We systematically searched his trash each Tuesday morning before the sanitation department trucks made their weekly collections. I was surprised, and then shocked, by what I found.

Each Tuesday morning, without fail, we would find bottles—bottles and more bottles—of tequila, liquor, and malt-liquor beer. There was very little indication of food, no indication of correspondence with his family or friends, but many empty bottles that had once contained what he was not supposed to consume: alcohol. Lifting fingerprints from these bottles was easy to do, and like everything else I fished from his trash, could be used in a court of law. In California, as elsewhere in the United States, the moment a person puts his trash out on the curb, it becomes the property of anyone who chooses to take it.

Also in the trash, on three different occasions, we found three empty prescription bottles filled at the Brent-Air Pharmacy in Los Angeles, for 500-milligram tablets of Depakote, prescribed by Dr. R. Huizenga. They were dated 10/18/99 with five refills left, 11/17/99 with four refills remaining and 1/24/2000 with only two refills left.

In a big red label on Jason's prescription bottles it directly states: Do Not Drink Alcoholic Beverages When Taking This Medication.

This was just the opposite of what Jason was doing, and was a crucial piece of information for it confirmed, in no uncertain terms, some of the things I had learned from my investigation.

Another piece of evidence I found during those months of gathering the trash was a photocopy of receipts for two particular prescriptions in 1999. Prescription number 921733, dated 4/10/99, was signed by Jason in the amount of $256.77. The other prescription, dated 6/8/99, was signed by Danielle Sapia, (Jason's girlfriend at the time), who had apparently picked up Jason's prescription for Depakote. At the bottom was a note from the Brent-Aire Pharmacy, stating that O. J. refused to pay and asking Jason to settle up. The amount was over $500.00. It said:

Please send a payment for this balance
O. J. refused to pay for these charges
Thanks _____
Julia
(310) 476-2211
Credit cards accepted

Jason Simpson was taking Depakote to control his rage disorder, but now his father had refused to pay for any further prescriptions. Taking the medication, Depakote, and mixing it with alcohol, would only cause him problems that would be even more severe than he had before, according to the doctors I had spoken with.

In the trash were past due bills for gas and electricity, and duns for previous bills Jason had failed to pay. I didn't know what he was doing with his money, and at this point in my investigation we were unable to determine exactly how much he was making. But, like pieces of a puzzle, everything soon became clear.

We found two paycheck stubs. The first was for the pay period 12/11/99 to 12/25/99 with the check dated on 12/30/99, in the amount of $1,333.33. The second paycheck stub was for pay period

12/26/99 to 1/10/2000 with the check being written on 1/14/2000, in the amount of $1,333.33. It appeared that the one dated 1/14/2000 might have been the next to last check he was to receive from the Mélisse Restaurant.

As my surveillance efforts soon confirmed, Jason had gotten into some kind of problem at the Mélisse Restaurant. He was no longer going to his workplace. I didn't know why, but I could imagine. Very seldom had he ever held a job for more than five or six months. Now Jason, who had finally attended cooking school in Paris and who had then worked at the Mélisse restaurant with Joseph Citrin—the former chef at Jackson's Restaurant—had lost his job again.

In the trash we found indications that Jason was no longer dating Danielle Sapia. There was something even more revealing in Jason's trash, a handwritten letter that would later confirm my worst suspicions and would help validate all my years of investigative research.

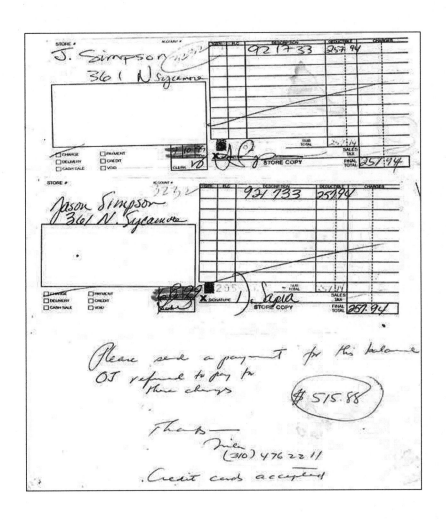

24

"DEAR JASON"

A **KNOTTED UP BALL OF** paper was found in Jason's trash. Written on a page torn from a three-ring binder, it appeared at first to be a letter or note to Jason from one of his girlfriends—a girl, it seemed, who was in the process of breaking up with him. The document had been hand printed from top to bottom, with circles and names in childish scribbles written all over it, making it difficult to read. The one thing legible at the top was the salutation, "Dear Jason."

I had just received this document by Federal Express.

Suddenly I got a gut feeling that this "Dear Jason" letter might have been written by Jason himself.

I took the note home, anxious to try to decipher as much as I could from the crumpled paper. I felt that this handwritten note, if written by Jason, might give me the insight I had been looking for into his true personality, beyond the Dr. Jekyll/Mr. Hyde analogy used by his friends and associates.

It took me three hours to decipher what I could, as shown:

Copy of Note

AAREN
JENNIFER
DANIELLE

DEAR JASON,
THERE ARE THREE OF US
HERE THAT I KNOW ABOUT
???
I WANT SOLICE
WORK WAS SOLICE
WAS A ???
NOW I AM A FAILURE
I CANNOT DO ANYTHING RIGHT
I CANNOT LEARN FROM IT ALL. I CANNOT
REMEMBER. ALCOHOL ALCOHOL IS THE
ROOT OF ALL MY SHORTCOMINGS
I KNOW I'M A GOOD GUY
SOMEWHERE BUT I CANNOT FIND HIM.
MY INNOCENCE IS LOST MY EAGER-
NESS IS GONE MOST OF ALL....???....AND
MOST...???... MY WILL AND INTGERITY
??? ABSENT. I DO NOT KNOW
WHAT TO DO. NO . . . I DO KNOW
WHAT TO DO, BUT I DON'T HAVE THE
WILL TO DO IT...IN SHORT I'M
FUCKED. I HAD SO MANY PLANS
BUT NOW WHAT. I CANNOT EXERCISE (?)
THE SIMPLEST DEEDS
SOBER. WALKING ON BROKEN GLASS

Was Jason the author? Was Jason all three of the people the note had referred to? Was the letter written *by* Jason *to* Jason?

I could make out the word "Aaren," the name of his little sister who was only twenty-three-months old when she drowned in the swimming pool at Rockingham, when Jason was eight—the sister that psychologist Dr. Burton Kittay said he knew nothing about. Even though I wasn't a psychologist, I believed in the back of my mind that Jason may have blamed himself for her death. All I do know is that, within a year, O. J. and Marguerite divorced and Jason's problems appeared to begin.

O. J. IS INNOCENT

From the day of the divorce until nearly his thirtieth birthday, Jason's rage and mental condition continued to worsen. The note began to speak for itself—showing Jason had a serious medical problem and has had it for a long, long time—long before I ever entered the picture.

25

ALIBI EXTINGUISHED

ONE PARTICULAR NIGHT IN my hotel room in Los Angeles, I was sitting talking to Herman King and suggested, "Let's go over to what used to be Jackson's Restaurant and have dinner."

For Herman and me it would bring back memories. Some people say I'm intuitive, I don't know.

All I do know is that on this particular night, *something was drawing me back to Jackson's.*

When Herman and I arrived at the restaurant, now known as Celestino's, I found it wasn't much different from its previous incarnation. Maybe a little more paint, but not much difference in the layout of the cooking area and the seating arrangements.

The hostess showed us to our table and I was seated with my back to the wall, looking forward. I had as clear and unobstructed a view of the entire space as I had had on my first trip with Herman years ago.

"How long has Celestino's been open?" I asked the hostess.

"Not very long."

"I used to eat here when it was Jackson's," I said. "Is anybody here who used to work for Jackson's?"

"Yes, your waiter tonight, Carlos. He's the only one left from the old staff."

In moments, Carlos Ramos introduced himself as our waiter for the evening. Small world, but my mind began to click. I wondered if he was working on the night of the murders.

O. J. IS INNOCENT

I looked over at Herman, who couldn't believe how fortunate we were. My intuition was paying off, as it had many times in the past.

According to Carlos Ramos, he had indeed worked as a waiter on Sunday, June 12, 1994, until the restaurant closed that night. Carlos had been employed by Alan Ladd Jackson from the time the restaurant originally opened, as Jackson's, until it closed its doors permanently.

After an excellent dinner, arrangements were made to meet with Carlos again. I told him I had a project for him in mind. I did, but more importantly, I needed to talk to him about the night of June 12, 1994, when Jason was the acting chef. Carlos might unwittingly hold the key to things I needed to know.

My mind was reeling with endless questions. Carlos Ramos could have the answers I needed to complete my investigation.

Two days later, on the corner of San Vicente Boulevard in Santa Monica, I sat at an outdoor table waiting for him to arrive. This was formerly the Revival Café, where Paul Goldberg had been attacked by Jason Simpson, back in 1992.

A horn honked. Startled, I turned to see Ramos in a new black Dodge pickup truck. With his passenger window down, he leaned over and said, "I'm going to park across the street and be right back."

I watched as he crossed the street wearing western clothes. He was a young man in his late twenties, very distinguished looking. You could tell that Carlos Ramos felt good about himself and had an air of confidence. I stood and shook his hand as he sat down.

According to Carlos, on the night of June 12 there were very few customers in the restaurant. Alan Ladd Jackson, the owner and chef, was definitely *not* working there on that Sunday. Jason, normally the sous chef, was the acting chef that night. Carlos said there were fewer than thirty to thirty-five diners at most in the restaurant all night, and the first thing they always did when business was slow was to shut down the grill. The restaurant normally closed at 10:30 to 11:00 PM. On that particular night, they closed early, as they had on previous Sundays, due to the lack of business. He said that the restaurant, at full capacity, could hold only 87 people, not 200.

Carlos also said that after the grill shut down, sometime between 9:15 and 9:30, Jason left.

Waiting for Jason was Jennifer Green, his girlfriend. Carlos said she was driving Jason's black 1993 Jeep, and was there to pick him up when he got off.

When Jason left, Carlos observed his chef's bag tucked under his arm. Jason had his own personal chef's knives and always took them home with him when he left.

Jason had been the only chef on duty that night.

Finally I was able to confirm my suspicions about Jason's airtight alibi.

The one thing Carlos knew nothing about was whether or not Nicole Simpson had planned on being at the restaurant that Sunday night. He just didn't remember.

I liked Carlos. He was a personable young man who, if I ever opened another restaurant, which I told him I might, would be the first one I would seek out as a manager. He had a pleasing personality when we met him as a waiter, and now was just as nice, honest, and forthright as I sat and talked to him on the corner in front of Paul Goldberg's former restaurant, the Revival Café.

When I asked him if he ever heard from Jason, he said, "No. It was real strange that right after the trial he came back and worked for one or two days and then totally disappeared." Alan Jackson had told him this, saying, "I don't know what ever happened to Jason; he just plain vanished."

"Last I ever heard," he said, "was that he was now working for Joseph Citrin, the former chef there at Jackson's, who had a new restaurant called Mélisse."

"Why didn't you go to work for Joseph Citrin?" I asked.

"I wouldn't work for him. He's arrogant, has a bad temper, and a tendency to degrade the employees. I don't work for people like that."

I could certainly relate to that.

I told him, "I just heard that Jason lost his job at Mélisse."

He appeared shocked, because Mélisse was the brightest of the new local restaurants.

Before Carlos and I got up, I said, "This used to be the Revival Café owned by Paul Goldberg. Did you know that?"

"No."

"This is where Jason was alleged to have attacked Goldberg with a knife and was arrested for assault with a deadly weapon and attempt to commit bodily harm. Did you know Jason was on probation at the time of the murders of Nicole and Goldman, for what he had done to Goldberg?"

"No, I had no idea."

We parted, Carlos getting back into his beautiful, brand-new, black pickup truck, which you could tell he was really proud of, and driving off. A young man I knew would go places.

I breathed a large sigh of relief. I now had a major piece of the puzzle in place.

Jason Simpson's *airtight alibi* for Sunday, June 12, 1994, had just gone out the window.

26

LOOSE ENDS

I **WAS IN LOS ANGELES** to work—not to enjoy myself. I was here to find out everything I possibly could to try to tie up all the loose ends.

Through an associate who had been given permission to examine and photograph the original documents, exhibits, photographs, and diagrams that had been used in the original O. J. Simpson trial, along with some that had never been introduced, I was allowed not only to examine these items for the first time but also to photograph them. These exhibits were now in a rental storage facility south of Los Angeles, where they have been stored since the trial.

I did not realize how important these trial documents, photographs, and diagrams would be in furthering my investigation. I only wished I had had all of these items originally to submit to Merston, Harpur, Cron, and the other experts at the onset, instead of the limited ones that I had—the same items which had been released to the general public after the trial.

Among the items I examined were several that helped me answer lingering questions—a lot of things that had been speculated about in the newspapers and magazines—which I could now determine for myself.

I could see the blood spatter patterns and the marks across Nicole's throat. I could see the wounds that poor Ron Goldman had sustained before he died. I had always felt that Nicole had been struck on the top of the head first, rendering her unconscious, while the assailant fought with Ron Goldman. All the evidence I was now viewing confirmed this. There in the autopsy photograph was the wound indicating the blow to the back of Nicole's head. It was obvious the assailant had struck her on the top of her head, rendering her unconscious, causing her to fall down and strike the Spanish tile. As Goldman fought for his life, Nicole laid unconscious, blood continuing to flow, which led to her bruising.

If Nicole had been killed first, with the way the wounds appeared, there would have been no blood flowing, and if no blood flowed through the body, there would have been no bruising. These autopsy pictures told me what I needed to know. Now it wasn't just speculation. It was all there, right in front of my eyes! Proof of the scenario I had long imagined.

One of the photographs showed the rear of Kato's bungalow and the chain-link fence. I could see sharp, exposed prongs along the top of the fence. Since the prongs pointed upwards, this would make it more difficult for somebody to climb over—especially at night and in a great hurry. Without gloves on, in all probability, the prongs would leave cuts on your hand.

Dr. Warner Spitz, the author of the definitive pathology textbook, *Medicolegal Investigation of Death: Guidelines for the Application of Pathology to Crime Investigation,* is considered one of the top forensic pathologists in the world. I had listened to Dr. Spitz's testimony in court regarding the marks on O. J.'s left hand, not the finger sliced by the glass in Chicago. He had pointed out that the jagged edges of three curved wounds on O. J. Simpson's hand were not caused by glass and not by a knife. Dr. Spitz explained that broken glass or a knife blade would produce smooth-edged cuts. Dr. Spitz said, "These are fingernail marks" that could have been inflicted by either Ron or Nicole during the struggle with the killer.

I have great admiration for Dr. Spitz and counseled with him during the Milo murder in Akron, Ohio. I could not dispute his testimony, even though it had given me some concern during the original criminal trial. But in this autopsy, I felt Dr. Spitz was wrong in his findings.

I had wondered whether these three jagged edges of curved wounds came not from Nicole or Ron but from O. J.'s climbing over the fence behind the bungalow where the bloody glove was found. Since I had been unable to see the on-scene photographs until March of 2000, after viewing them, I determined that if O. J. had climbed over this fence, the extended sharp, exposed prongs could have left the three marks on his left hand which Dr. Spitz referred to and not, as he had concluded, been inflicted by Nicole's fingernails or Ron during the struggle.

In addition, if O. J. Simpson had been wearing the gloves during the struggle, would those three jagged marks have been on O. J.'s hand in the first place?

Once you climbed over that four-foot chain-link fence, there appeared to be very little room to stand up. This would have made it easy for O. J. to have lost his balance, and, in his haste, to have stumbled against the rear of Kato's bungalow, dropping the glove and making the sounds Kato Kaelin described as "three thuds," on the night of June 12.

I was also able to view the photograph of the glove lying on the ground on top of the leaves, found behind Kato's bungalow, that matched the one left at the Bundy crime scene.

There was no blood found behind the bungalow. The only blood we could see in the on-scene photographs, which forensic experts had diagrammed, was a couple of spots in the driveway and a couple of spots in the foyer as you entered O. J.'s home.

There was no blood on the walkway or the staircase leading up to his bedroom, but there were the two socks lying there in plain sight in front of his bed.

If O. J. was as meticulous as they said he was, why would a man who had supposedly committed two premeditated murders leave telltale evidence of two socks lying on the light colored oriental rug for all to see? Why not just put them in your pocket? Could it have been that they came—not from O. J., but from someone else who needed to stage the crime scene?

There was no blood in the shower, no blood in the washer and dryer pipes. There was no blood in the toilet or washbasin. All of the pipes in O. J.'s bathroom and laundry room had been removed and examined for signs of blood. None was found.

Crime scene technician Dennis Fung found no trace of blood on any of O. J.'s dirty clothes in the laundry hamper.

Yet, in the on-scene photograph, two single socks remained, lying exposed on the carpet. It didn't make sense.

Originally, I never thought that the LAPD investigation was a cover-up. I never thought that Rockingham was the scene of a frame-up. But now I couldn't help but wonder about the two socks. It certainly left me with a lot of unanswered questions. Maybe the socks were, in fact, planted there. I didn't know.

I interviewed Rod Englert, the crime scene expert Marcia Clark had called while he was on vacation in Hawaii.

"You've got to return," she had told him. "There's blood all over O. J.'s vehicle, we need your help."

With that in mind, Englert said he immediately canceled his vacation and flew back to assist in the investigation.

According to Englert, when he arrived in L.A. he was shocked to find very little blood in the Bronco, not what he had anticipated based on his original conversation with Marcia Clark.

Englert said there was no blood on the brake, no blood on the accelerator, a speck of blood on the carpeted floor mats and a small smear on the rear of the Bronco's console. This was definitely not what he had expected from a man who supposedly had killed two people and had fought a to-the-death struggle with Ron Goldman.

I finally located Robert Heidstra, whom we had all assumed (and I hate that word assumed) had been in the alleyway behind Bundy when Nicole and Ron had been murdered.

As it turned out, during our conversation, when he showed us where he was standing that night—where he claimed he had heard the

"Hey . . . Hey . . . Hey . . ."—it was clear he was actually on the opposite side of Bundy Drive, in the opposite alley.

I then measured the distance as being 440 feet from the alley behind Nicole's residence to the alley behind the residence across the street from Bundy. I began to doubt Robert Heidstra's credibility. It further bothered me that Heidstra had waited for days, and then told his veterinarian what he had seen and heard, not the police.

Heidstra's story weighed heavily on my mind.

One evening I went for a walk on the Santa Monica pier to stretch my legs after a late dinner. The pier was virtually deserted. I stopped near the end and was looking out across the shoreline to Malibu, enjoying the cool night air, when four white males appeared out of the shadows and started walking toward me. As they got closer, I thought, if there was going to be trouble—if this was going to be a robbery attempt—I wanted to be ready to protect myself.

As the men approached, I turned to the right and took a defensive position. My instructor in karate had taught me that if anybody ever came at you with a knife and you had no way to defend yourself, you should take three steps forward and, with each step, you should holler, "Hey . . . Hey . . . Hey . . ." which provides a moment of surprise to throw the perpetrator off and to give you additional time to decide on what to do next.

The four men walked to within sixty feet of me, then veered off to the left. Perhaps my lack of fear had caused them to change their mind, if indeed they had viewed me as a target. But then I saw a police car had pulled up behind them, to my right. Maybe I was lucky, but during that brief moment when my adrenaline surged, preparing for confrontation, it occurred to me that "Hey . . . Hey . . . Hey . . ." may have been said by Goldman after the assailant heard the back gate open. The assailant then delivered the blow to the back of Nicole's head with the blunt end of the knife, rendering her unconscious, causing her to fall and hit her head on the Spanish tile.

The assailant, realizing he couldn't get away, then lay in wait for Ron Goldman. Goldman, finding Nicole crumpled on the walkway, was confronted by the killer. This left him trapped in a very short and narrow area near Nicole's front gate in which to defend himself. Goldman, reportedly proficient in karate and tae kwon do, goes into his defensive tactic, saying, "Hey . . . Hey . . . Hey . . . ."

Now, with the closer proximity to the front gate near Bundy Drive, it was possible that Robert Heidstra had heard "Hey . . . Hey . . . Hey . . ."

Those may have been Ron Goldman's last words, as he began the fight of his life against the assailant.

The repeated blows of the blade striking Goldman finally completed the deed, leaving him lying in a pool of blood with his eyes wide open, dead . . . his blood draining from some twenty-seven wounds, one right through the side of his neck, according to the autopsy photograph.

I talked to Charles England, a karate expert, in Dallas before we left for Los Angeles. He explained to me that, no matter how accomplished a karate expert you are, once you are cut, especially several times, you then forget a lot of things you've been taught and go automatically into survival mode, fighting for your life.

Upon returning to Dallas, with the colored photographs in hand, I met with England again and explained my new theory. Not only was he in agreement, he also pointed out something more.

"With these pictures," England said, "there is no doubt that Goldman had struck hard blows to the assailant, leaving his knuckles badly bruised and swollen."

England's observation concurred with what Dr. Henry Lee, the forensic expert, had testified. Dr. Lee said it appeared the assailant limped off after the attack, which meant to me that Ron Goldman had caused his attacker some injury. It was obvious Goldman had made contact with the face and/or body of the assailant because of his bruised and swollen knuckles shown in the autopsy photographs.

This information was crucial to establishing O. J.'s innocence, because within twenty-four hours of the murders or less, O. J. had been taken to the Los Angeles Police Department and had stripped, voluntarily, where they examined him from one end to the other, taking pictures and drawing blood. They found no marks or bruising on his body other than the cut on his left hand.

I also remembered that Ron Shipp, who had seen O. J. in his bedroom clad only in his boxer shorts the night after the murders, had said, "There were no marks or bruises on O. J. that would indicate he had been in any type of scuffle."

Even the jurors in O. J.'s criminal trial had concerns about Goldman having bruises on his knuckles. In the book *The Run of His Life*, on page 426, Jeffrey Toobin stated the jurors said, "If they [the bruises] were from fighting back, why didn't O. J. have any bruises on his body? . . . The jurors knew that Dave Aldana, the Hispanic man in seat four, was a martial arts expert. He got up and demonstrated how to defend in tae kwon do. He thought Goldman had put up a good fight."

I knew now that Goldman had definitely made numerous contacts with his assailant before he died. This was just another strong piece of evidence that proved to me O. J. was at the crime scene, but not until after the murders.

27

"BUBBLING UP"

ON FEBRUARY 17, 2000, I decided to spend the day watching Jason's residence on Electric Avenue in Venice, California.

Though I was hoping to be inconspicuous, I was driving a new white Ford Excursion that to me felt a little too much for the neighborhood. I pulled up and parked about a dozen car lengths south of Jason's residence. His black Jeep was parked in front. Three bungalows were laid out like a triangle. The one to the left was occupied by Edward Solby and his wife, and the one to the right by a young woman named Betty Phipps. Even when you stood in front of the gate it was difficult to see the small bungalow in the rear that was occupied by Jason.

Jason's windows were open as usual in his Jeep. You could tell the interior was wet, as it had rained earlier that morning.

At 11:50 AM Jason came out, opened the small gate and stood beside the little black mailbox attached to the chain-link fence. He was casually dressed. I watched as he opened the box and slammed it shut. He opened the gate, walked back through, opened and closed a secondary gate, then disappeared toward the rear bungalow.

Within an hour the postman arrived, put the mail in the box, and walked on. A few minutes later, Jason came out again, took out the mail and looked at each envelope. He suddenly appeared angry, hurling his mail into one of the three plastic trash containers in front of the bungalow complex. He reopened the little gate, walked back toward his bungalow, and again disappeared. He didn't once look in my direction.

Ten minutes later, Jason came out and got into his black 1993 Jeep, the same one we had now determined he had owned on the night of June 12, 1994. I followed carefully in pursuit as he pulled out and made a right-hand turn onto Westminster, a left turn on 6th Avenue, a right turn on Rose, a right turn onto Lincoln Boulevard, a right on Broadway, and a left on to 11th Street, now in the city limits of Santa Monica. All of a sudden I realized we were approaching Mélisse Restaurant. Jason turned right at 11th and Wilshire, and turned into the parking lot directly behind the rear employee entrance. He pulled in quickly, jumped out, and left the door on the driver's side flopping back and forth as he ran into the restaurant.

I now realized what Jason was there for—his last paycheck. He hadn't received it by mail and was angry. He was going to collect it in person.

I was prepared for the worst, thinking, Oh my God, don't tell me this is going to be a repetition of what happened when Jason went to get his final check from Paul Goldberg, which ended in Jason assaulting and attacking Goldberg with a kitchen knife.

I parked my vehicle and quickly ran up to where Jason had parked. I was determined that if I heard cries for help, I was going inside.

I felt some responsibility, to a degree, if something were to happen, because I had learned such a great deal about Jason and had not been able to share it because of the potential danger of giving it to the district attorney or the Los Angeles Police Department at this point in my investigation. Within four or five minutes, Jason, not noticing me standing there, came out, climbed back into his Jeep, and took off.

I ran to my car and followed him to the Santa Monica Bank parking lot. Jason parked, walked across the street, and put something into the bank deposit. He then returned to his Jeep and drove away. Traffic was heavy, but I was able to follow him all the way back to his bungalow in Venice, some fifteen miles away.

In one hair-raising hour of surveillance, I had been up one street, down another, pulled into driveways, run stop signs, run traffic lights—anything in an attempt not to lose sight of Jason and more determined than ever not to be seen.

I still felt, but couldn't prove, that Jason had been angry because he had not received his check from Mélisse and was determined to get it one way or the other.

Thank God no one was hurt, this time.

Once Jason had pulled up to his residence, he parked on the opposite side of the street, crossed over, and once again disappeared behind the chain link fence.

It was obvious that Jason, who needed to live in a structured environment, was doing anything but. Now he had no routine to fall back on. There was no more Danielle, no job, just plain loneliness and the bottles of booze he consumed daily as he watched the movies he rented from Blockbuster Video.

Two days before leaving Los Angeles, I had an opportunity to spend another few hours watching Jason on Electric Avenue. It had rained early that morning and some that afternoon. I saw him come out and once again roll up the windows on his Jeep only after it had stopped raining.

During the three weeks I was in Los Angeles it rained constantly on and off. Jason never seemed to roll up the windows until afterwards. It made me wonder why? Had he hoped, over the period of years, that the rain coming in would wash away any evidence that might be there? Why not roll your windows up first, before the rain?

Leaning into the Jeep, I noticed that somebody had cut through the vinyl covering on the console in between the two front seats, going about one inch deep into the foam rubber and leaving a three- to four-inch jagged oblong opening. The vinyl and foam had both been removed.

Someone had to have a good reason for intentionally carving this hole out of the console.

It was impossible for me to know how long ago it had happened, but I couldn't help wondering if there might have been blood there at one time, which could have been a constant reminder of what might have happened on the night of June 12.

While looking inside the Jeep, I also noticed that someone's head had struck the windshield from the inside, on the passenger's side, leaving a spiderweb of cracks. I speculated whether it might have been Danielle Sapia's head that hit the windshield.

Could it have been an altercation between Jason and Danielle, like the ones he'd had with DeeDee, Jennifer, and Paul Goldberg?

28

"HE'S SICK . . . HE'S SICK"

WHAT MIGHT JASON'S IMMEDIATE neighbors have witnessed about his recent behavior? I decided to interview Betty Phipps, who lived in the adjoining bungalow to Jason's. Edward Solby and his wife occupied the one to the left, but I was more concerned with Betty Phipps. While searching through the trash there on Electric Avenue, we found a great deal of Jason's garbage mixed in with hers. At first we thought they might have been dating, so I made a point to find out where she was working and paid a visit to her place of employment.

It turned out that Betty was a bartender at a plush restaurant about three miles from her house. One evening I walked in, sat down at the bar, and struck up a conversation. Betty was so easy to talk to that it didn't take me long to learn her life's history. In fact, she wouldn't even let me pay for my drink, Grey Goose vodka on the rocks with a twist.

I confirmed that she lived alone in one of the three bungalows adjacent to Jason's. It was mid-December and Betty was excited over the prospect of getting an engagement ring from her boyfriend for Christmas. It came as a surprise to me to learn that her parents lived in Dallas, Texas. What a small world.

I looked forward to seeing her again and even contemplated visiting with her parents in Dallas, explaining to them what I was doing and seeking their help for their daughter. I was concerned that Betty lived so close to my major suspect, innocent of any problems he might be having.

There were indications in the trash that Betty and Jason would visit from time to time; she sometimes helped out doing his laundry, and that worried me. I also felt that Betty could be a big help to me, but I remained chiefly concerned for her safety.

My next stop after meeting with Betty Phipps was at Paul Goldberg's residence in Manhattan Beach. As I had quickly learned, everybody—it seemed—was looking for Goldberg. It appeared he owed a great deal of money. The word on the streets was that he was no longer living in the United States, but his family still was.

As I pulled up to their small middle-class home in Manhattan Beach, the Goldberg's appeared to be doing better than I would have expected, given the number of creditors looking for Paul. A sprinkler system was being replaced and it was obvious the family was attempting to improve the landscape. It was a nice area of Manhattan Beach, not far from a middle school.

I parked my car, walked up to the door, and knocked. It was opened by Debbie, Paul Goldberg's wife. I apologized for coming on Sunday morning. She was very cordial and invited me in, explaining that her son had a sleepover and she was in the process of making breakfast.

We sat down over coffee at the kitchen table. I explained to her who I was and what I was doing. She told me Paul was out of the country, where he had been for quite some time and said she didn't know when he would be back.

At my request, Debbie gave me her impressions of Jason. She said he had helped her and her husband start the Revival Café. Debbie said Jason had even helped design the menus and the food. The one thing he couldn't do, according to Debbie, was work under pressure. She said Jason could be a really nice young man one moment and change completely the next.

Listening to Debbie, I sensed concern. I asked if it was possible for me to talk to Paul. Without hesitation she reached over, picked up the phone, and dialed his number. I could hear the phone ring and a male voice answer. Debbie talked to her husband for several minutes, then handed me the receiver. I was now to meet Paul Goldberg, if not in person, at least on the telephone.

It took only that short conversation for me to take an immediate dislike to him. He was arrogant, unfriendly, and uncooperative. It seemed obvious he was interested only in himself. I was able, however, to obtain from Paul the fact that Jason had assaulted him and had come at him with a knife while he was employed as chef at the Revival Café.

I asked Goldberg why the charges had been lowered to misdemeanors. He wouldn't discuss it. I preferred to talk to him in person, so I asked if he would be willing to meet with me.

"Paul, I understand you're out of the country. I'm willing to meet you there or anywhere in the United States."

"Why would you want to come all this way?"

"Because it's important to me. I'm trying to solve this case. I'm willing to pay you for your time."

"How much are you willing to pay?" he asked.

"How much do you want?"

"Well, I'd been offered $25,000 for an interview, right after it all happened, and I wouldn't take that."

I knew Paul needed money, but I wasn't willing to pay that kind of money for an interview with him or anyone else, unless the evidence would lead to information indicting the killer of Nicole Simpson and Ron Goldman. I already had most of the police documents, and most of the facts concerning the Goldberg incident. It would have been nice to sit down and talk to him one-on-one, but it wasn't going to make much difference now.

I had already established a pattern in Jason's life.

"Mr. Goldberg, I could use your help. But if you don't want to cooperate, that's your right."

"I guess that ends our conversation, doesn't it?" Goldberg said curtly.

"Yes sir, it does."

I handed the phone back to Debbie, who talked to her husband for a few moments more, then hung up. She turned to me and apologized for Paul's attitude.

I could sense there was some problem in the relationship. I could sense, too, that there was a daylight-to-dark difference between their personalities.

It was also clear that Debbie had constant contact with Goldberg. I admired the fact that she was working hard trying to raise her eleven-year-old son. It was obvious she cared. I could only wish the very best for her and her son. As a single parent, I realized how difficult her role could be.

I started to get up from the kitchen table when I turned to her and said, "Debbie, would you mind describing Jason for me one last time?"

She smiled sadly. "One minute Jason could be the nicest guy in the world and the next moment, entirely different. Mr. Dear, he's sick . . . he's sick."

On my notepad resting on the kitchen table I scribbled, "He's sick . . . he's sick."

I thanked Debbie for her help and apologized again for interrupting her Sunday morning. I walked out to my car, knowing that I had—at the least—made more progress. Paul Goldberg's statements to me now verified what was contained in the original police report—that Jason Simpson had indeed attacked and assaulted him with a knife.

This incident had occurred just eighteen months prior to the murders of Nicole Simpson and Ron Goldman.

Once I returned to Dallas, I was able to acquire, through a confidential source, the number Debbie had called in Thailand, from the date of the phone call made from Goldberg's permanent residence in Manhattan Beach. I now knew how to reach him if I had to. Paul Goldberg had told me what I needed to know, but more importantly, his wife had shared her feelings about Jason with me.

And Debbie's final words, "He's sick . . .he's sick," reconfirmed the possibility of Jason's mental instability on the night of June 12.

29

REITERATING CONCERNS

MEETING ME AT THE American Eagle gate was Dr. Harvey Davisson. This would be the second trip for both of us to see Dr. Burton Kittay. I hoped the meeting would prove even more fruitful than our first.

I wouldn't have been surprised if Dr. Kittay had refused to see me at all, because of the interviews he had supposedly set up for me with O. J. through Cathy Randa—interviews that never took place—and the real circumstances behind his motive. I didn't care; it was worth taking the chance.

Dr. Davisson and I piled onto the bus waiting to take us out to the small commuter airline for our trip to Corpus Christi, Texas.

As we sat down, I was startled when Dr. Davisson nudged me. He was looking significantly to my right. I followed his eyes, and suddenly my heart felt as if it had stopped. Seated right beside me was Dr. Burton Kittay, or at the very least, his twin. There was a woman across the aisle from Dr. Kittay, who appeared to be his wife. She kept looking from him to me and back again.

When we boarded the small plane, I found myself seated two seats in front of the couple we both thought at this point were the Kittays. It was a very intense hour-and-a-half flight to Corpus Christi. If I had, in fact, been sitting next to him on the bus, I knew we were in trouble because Kittay would surely have recognized me, as I had him.

Once we arrived at the airport I watched as the carousel circled, dispersing the luggage. The man I thought to be Dr. Kittay and his wife stood there waiting for their bags. Another couple joined them.

Dr. Davisson and I overheard the man we thought was Kittay being addressed as "Doctor." There was nothing we could do at this point but wait. Our so-called Dr. Kittay and wife retrieved their bags and walked off.

I had to take a chance. I walked directly up to the other couple, who were still waiting at the carousel and said, "Excuse me, was that Dr. Burton Kittay, the psychologist?"

"No, that was Dr. Hoffman."

Relieved, I didn't care what name they gave me, just as long as it wasn't Dr. Burton Kittay.

After Dr. Davisson and I gathered our bags, we headed to our hotel, which was right on the ocean. After what we had been through on the plane—and with the second interview ahead of us in the morning—we were anxious to relax and have a good dinner, so we asked the concierge to recommend a good place to eat. In we walked to what was described to us as Corpus Christi's finest seafood restaurant to finally enjoy a late-night dinner.

Fifteen minutes after being seated, waiting for our food with a good bottle of wine, talking, laughing, and just plain enjoying ourselves, I suddenly saw Dr. Davisson's face pale.

As I looked into the mirror across the room from me, I saw a party of seven come in. My face turned ashen, as I realized this time two of the seven people were definitely the Kittays.

They were being seated four tables behind us. Dr. Davisson had his back to them though I was in plain view facing them. I knew that the doctor would recognize me immediately. My heart began to hammer as I motioned for the waiter to come over, asking him to bend down, and whispering to him, "I'm sorry, but my wife just came into the restaurant with another man. It's important that she doesn't see me. I don't want any trouble. Could you show me how to leave without being noticed?"

The waiter motioned toward the emergency door, which had a sign that said, "If Door Opens Alarm Will Sound."

He said, "Give me a moment sir and let me shut off the alarm."

I watched as he walked toward the wall, hesitated, flipped a switch and then nodded to me it was okay to leave. Trying hard to be inconspicuous, I carefully stood up, as Dr. Davisson realized what I was about to do. With my back toward the Kittay party, I went out the side exit into the parking lot and to my car. I unlocked the door, sat down inside, and sighed.

Twice in one day was just too much! I needed a good night's sleep.

The next morning, I felt much better. I had opened the sliding door during the night, allowing the ocean breeze to blow into my room as I slept. Now, I felt rested and ready to meet the Simpson family therapist for the second time.

Dr. Davisson and I arrived at the doctor's office, and once again I told the receptionist I was there for my appointment.

"But we don't have you scheduled today, Mr. Dear," she said in a bewildered tone.

"You most certainly do," I said.

"No sir, we have an appointment for a William Eubanks."

"Damn it, we had a temp the other day who was supposed to make the appointment. She must have mistakenly made it under my associate's name: William Eubanks, instead of William Dear. This isn't the first time she's done something like this. I think, if you'll check, you'll see the phone number and address will be mine."

I handed her my card and she checked the numbers. "You're right, they are the same."

"I'm really sorry for the inconvenience."

"Those things happen, Mr. Dear. Dr. Kittay hasn't arrived yet. Please have a seat, I'll let you know when he does."

I went and sat down and Harvey sat opposite me. Several minutes passed. The receptionist's window slid open and she said, "Dr. Kittay called to say he was running late."

Twenty minutes later, he arrived and escorted us into his private office. "I don't mind paying for your time, because I feel it's important." I proceeded to share with Dr. Kittay some of the information I had uncovered and my concerns for Jason's safety and for the possible safety of others. He wasn't interested in hearing what I had to say.

"Jason is no longer my patient," he responded curtly. "I don't want to get involved." He told me he had called O. J. about getting him to okay a meeting for me with his secretary, Cathy Randa. He said neither O. J. nor Cathy Randa had ever called him back.

I very much doubted what the doctor was saying, especially after the voice mail message he had left me the night after our first meeting, followed up by a phone conversation between the two of us the next morning, in which he told me Cathy Randa was expecting my call and would share with me files and records that had never been seen before.

"You've never heard from them?" I said.

"No, not a word since the day I placed that phone call."

Evidently nothing I had told him about what I had uncovered affected him.

Again, Dr. Kittay said that he didn't know anything about the death of little Aaren, Jason's sister who had drowned in the pool, when Jason was eight years old.

Again, Dr. Kittay said repeatedly, "O. J. did not commit the murders. There is no doubt in my mind about it."

When I assured him that Jason had no airtight alibi and had become—in my mind—my major suspect in the murders of Nicole Simpson and Ron Goldman, he again replied, "Jason is too stupid to commit the murders."

Coming from a psychologist, that shocked me, but no more so than what I had learned in my first visit, when Dr. Kittay explained to me that, even had Jason been guilty, he would never be convicted because of his mental state.

I recalled that in 1991, Jason had been referred back to his psychologist, Dr. Kittay, for future follow-up after being released from Saint John's psychiatric ward.

I couldn't help but wonder yet again . . . if Dr. Kittay had been more interested in Jason as a patient, interested in Jason's well-being . . . if he had made more of an effort to identify the root of Jason's problems and acted accordingly, could he have prevented the murders of Nicole Simpson and Ron Goldman . . . if Jason Simpson was the murderer?

Dr. Davisson and I explained to Dr. Kittay that we were concerned that if Jason was guilty, we couldn't discount the possibility he could hurt somebody else as well as himself. From all the documentation we had uncovered plus his past history, we knew Jason was mentally unstable and a potential suicide.

Once again, he made it crystal clear: he wasn't interested in getting involved.

I paid the bill for his time and we left the office. Dr. Davisson and I caught the elevator to the 1st floor and went out to our car. "We got as much as we could, Bill," said Harvey.

I couldn't help remembering a copyrighted interview Dr. Kittay had given to the local Corpus Christi newspaper and the *Houston Chronicle*. The Tuesday afternoon after O. J. was found not guilty and was released from custody, Kittay was quoted as saying:

" . . . [his] relationship with Simpson was a complex one that sometimes crossed the line from client to confidant."

He stated that he had counseled O. J. since 1989 and never doubted that O. J. was innocent. From what I have been able to learn, it is unethical to counsel a patient and simultaneously be his confidant.

Dr. Davisson and I flew back to Dallas that day. I reviewed with him some of the facts I had uncovered in my investigation, like the fact that DeeDee had admitted, when we called her from Dallas (after my original interview), that there were many more problems during the relationship between her and Jason. And Jennifer Green had said that Jason was with her in her apartment until after 11:15, a statement contradicted by Jason's testimony in his civil deposition, and which was—I believed—a crucial point in my investigation, *destroying Jason's alibi.*

I understood now why detectives Lange and Vannatter never interrogated Jason. I wondered what Tom Lange would say now, after telling us in Los Angeles, *"Jason wasn't even considered as a suspect."*

I would now like to share with retired Detective Tom Lange the following:

- Jason left the restaurant early that night.
- He had no airtight alibi.
- There were not 200 people in the restaurant to witness his cooking.
- Around 9:15–9:30 PM, Jason carried out a chef's bag under his arm, which contained a set of razor-sharp chef's knives, one of which would have been capable of inflicting the wounds sustained by Nicole Simpson and Ron Goldman.
- Jason suffers from *intermittent rage disorder;* was under the care of a doctor and was prescribed medication, Depakote, by a doctor who was neither a psychologist nor a psychiatrist.
- Jason was on probation until the year 2000 for *assault with a deadly weapon* on a previous employer.
- He had been confined to a mental institution.
- He attempted suicide three times.
- He perpetrated violence against two of his former girlfriends, including one confirmed attack with a chef's knife.
- Nicole Simpson told Ron Shipp that she thought Jason Simpson was stalking her.
- He suffered from alcohol and drug abuse.
- He suffered from depression.
- He has been described as having a split personality— Dr. Jekyll and Mr. Hyde—with an uncontrollable temper.

- AND on the night of June 12, Nicole Simpson had made reservations for a dinner party of eleven at Jason's restaurant, and never showed up.

One thing I recalled learning in Los Angeles was that the unidentified fingerprints found at the Bundy Drive crime scene were compared with those of fifteen others. None of the fifteen had a match with those that were unidentified at the crime scene.

Jason Lamar Simpson's fingerprints were not among the fifteen compared to the unidentified prints found at the scene.

In other words, Detective Lange was right: the detective division of the LAPD never considered Jason as a suspect, so why should they compare his fingerprints to those that remained unidentified at the scene? I had eliminated all the other suspects.

I remember reading in the book *Raging Heart*, written by Sheila Weller, when O. J. arrived at the funeral home for Nicole's funeral, he was accompanied by Arnelle and Jason. O. J. had his arm around his oldest daughter, Arnelle; behind O. J. were Jason and Jason's girlfriend, Jennifer Green.

As O. J., Arnelle, Jason, and Jennifer approached the casket where Nicole Simpson lay at rest, Jason suddenly turned, bolted, ran out of the funeral home, and jumped into the front seat of the black hearse.

According to Weller's account, Judy Brown and O. J. ran to the car and tried to coax Jason out. He refused to view Nicole Simpson's body. O. J. had sat at the funeral home with Nicole's body for several hours the night before. O. J., Arnelle, and Jennifer were prepared to view Nicole's body for the last and final time.

Why wouldn't Jason?

30

HANDWRITING ON THE WALL

NOW, **BACK IN DALLAS,** I had the opportunity to follow up on what I considered a crucial part of my investigation. That was to determine whether or not the loose-leaf sheet of paper that started with "Dear Jason" *had* actually been written by him.

I picked up the phone and made arrangements to meet with Don Lehew at Owens on LBJ Freeway, just north of downtown Dallas. I knew he was one of the best as far as handwriting analysis went. His forensic expertise had been used in court successfully many times.

Over our meal, I reviewed for him what I had learned during my investigation into the murders.

Thirty minutes later, after I had given Don a summary of my findings, I handed him the sheet of notebook paper I had taken out of Jason's trash about a month earlier and told him I'd been able to decipher some of the writing in the document.

Don picked up the plastic sheet protector containing the handwritten note. Carefully he removed it.

"Maybe I can take it and enhance it enough to extract more words than what you've gotten so far," he said.

"Even though it starts off with 'Dear Jason,' I think that Jason wrote it to himself. I believe we're dealing with a mentally disturbed individual."

"Do you have anything else he's written that I can use for comparison?"

I handed Don what I had, which wasn't much. It included some of the records from Saint John's, Cedars-Sinai and some of the other bits and pieces on which Jason had signed his name. I knew it wasn't enough and Don agreed.

I had to have a sample of Jason's handwriting so Don could make some accurate determinations as to whether or not he had actually written this important piece of evidence. Don made some suggestions, but I had already covered all of those and came up empty-handed. I walked out of the restaurant concerned and frustrated, but I assured Don that somehow I would get what he needed.

The following week, my waiting paid off. In Jason's trash on Electric Avenue, we found a check drawn on his account at the Santa Monica Bank, ripped into little pieces at the bottom of the container. In addition to the liquor bottles there was another piece of paper listing all of the girlfriends—from the last one to the first—whom Jason had apparently ever dated.

We were within weeks of Jason's thirtieth birthday when we found these new items.

I understood how important it was for me to quickly try and determine whether or not Jason had written this note. The situation was volatile. Jason was unemployed and had been for months. He had lost his girlfriend, for whatever reason, and was now alone. During our surveillances there were no indications he had any visitors. From the trash it appeared he was continuing to drink heavily, which certainly was working against the prescriptions we had found for Depakote.

I couldn't help but worry. In a few weeks, on April 21, 2000, Jason would be thirty years old; he was alone, out of a job, had no money. Could he be contemplating a fourth and final attempt at suicide on his thirtieth birthday?

If Jason was the murderer, he was sick. If Jason wasn't the murderer, he was still mentally disturbed and in need of professional help. Either way, I was concerned. My investigation indicated that he had needed help since he was eight years old and had never received the proper medical treatment.

In my concern and worry about Jason, and my concern for the safety of those around him, I didn't know what to do. I wasn't his father. I wasn't a family member. And yet, I cared. I may have been a private investigator for over thirty-five years, but I was also a single parent and the father of a son who is just a year older than Jason. I was doing my best to try and think of what I could do.

I needed to determine for sure if the "Dear Jason" letter had been written by him. If so, that would answer even more questions.

As soon as overnight express brought the new material that had been found in the trash by one of my associates in L.A., my youngest son and I sat down and pieced together on a board the torn up check and the note containing the names of the young ladies Jason had dated so far in his life. Hopefully, when we were through we would have enough samples for Don Lehew to make a handwriting analysis.

The next afternoon when I again met with Don, I handed him the completely re-created check, along with the list. The only handwriting on the check was Jason's signature, otherwise, all the other information on the check had been printed. The other two sheets of information we had found in the trash were also handwritten.

However, Don was satisfied. "This is all I'll need. Give me seventy-two hours."

Seventy-two hours later, Don handed me a three-page report, using all the evidence I had given him. It was his final conclusion, beyond the shadow of a doubt, that Jason Lamar Simpson had written the "Dear Jason" letter to himself. It was Jason's handwriting. At the bottom of his report Don Lehew had stated:

"I have no hesitation in being able to appear in court and prove beyond a shadow of a doubt the authenticity of what I have been able to find in my analysis."

I now knew that Jason, who could write to himself as three different people, needed help more than ever.

In the meantime, Dr. Henry Lee, the famed forensic expert, was attending a seminar in London, England. My associate, Malcolm

Corwin, privately asked him, "Dr. Lee, if O. J. didn't commit the murders, who would you consider as suspects?"

Dr. Lee responded immediately. "A. C. Cowlings and Jason Simpson—O. J.'s older son."

Dr. Lee, I knew, had his own ideas about what happened that night. He had been put through a lot because he testified for the defense and not the prosecution. Dr. Henry Lee, to my mind, is the finest forensic expert in the world. He said there should have been a lot more blood in the Bronco than was found; the assailant should have had blood all over him. He said, "There's something wrong here."

He was right; there was something wrong.

I had put in a call to try and find Eugene Mercury Morris, a former football player in the NFL who had been close friends with O. J. Simpson for many years during the time he played football.

Back in January of 1996, Mercury Morris had been quoted in a *Globe* article presented in Joseph Bosco's book *A Problem with Evidence*, stating that in 1995 he had spoken to O. J. Simpson on the telephone, and O. J. had told him, "I was at the crime scene, but didn't commit the murders." I had to know for sure whether or not this was a true statement.

Mercury Morris called me back and we talked for nearly an hour. He said he gave the *Globe* just what they wanted. A friend of his had called and told him he had had a dream that O. J. was at the crime scene but didn't commit the murders, and Morris in turn told this to the *Globe*. Finally after three or four attempts, they insisted on the interview and paid him $35,000, so he gave them what they wanted. " . . . O. J. was at the crime scene, but didn't commit the murders."

I liked Mercury Morris right off. He was honest, straightforward, and told it like it was. He didn't mind admitting to me the problems he and O. J. had with drugs toward the end of their NFL careers.

"You know I've served time, which is a hard lesson, but maybe it helped me turn my life around. I think I have."

Mercury went on to tell me there was no doubt in his mind that O. J. had committed the murders. I felt at this point I had nothing to lose but to share with him what I had uncovered.

Near the end of our interview, he said, thoughtfully, "*Hmmm, hmmm, hmmm* . . . I never thought it would be coming out of my mouth, but you know with what you've told me, it makes me believe that maybe what my friend dreamed was true. Maybe O. J. was at the crime scene but didn't commit the murders . . . Maybe O. J. is covering for Jason."

After I hung up I thought, unlike *Globe* magazine, I hadn't had to pay Mercury Morris for my interview. He didn't have to talk to me, but he did. I felt he had told me what he believed to be the truth. The truth the way he knew it to be.

I could sense that both Ron Shipp and Mercury Morris now believed that maybe their former friend, "The Juice," who had turned on them for saying what they originally thought to be true, was possibly, in fact, "innocent."

Was it possible that O. J. was trying to protect his son, Jason, maybe blaming himself for not being there when Jason needed him the most, while he was growing up?

In attorney Daniel Petrocelli's book, *Triumph of Justice*, something that I had read stood out in my mind. On pages 273 and 274, Petrocelli wrote:

"I love the *Godfather* movies. If the Simpson family was the Corleones, Jason Simpson was Fredo . . .

"O. J. was attractive, sculpted, athletic, a leader. Jason was beefy, soft, not particularly good-looking, and anything but dynamic. He was the ugly duckling who didn't live up to his father's expectations . . .

Among the rumors that kept the fires of this case roaring was one that Jason had committed the killings or helped his dad clean up. My partner, Peter Gelblum, was particularly enamored of this theory. Jason didn't do it, his blood was not found anywhere in the crime scenes, and there wasn't a shred of evidence to indicate he was involved. Still, it became a running joke whenever we came to a stumbling block, I would say, 'Well, maybe Jason did it.'

Robin Greer, Nicole's friend, believed Jason knew what happened and would break if questioned . . ."

Petrocelli described Jason as *"guileless and seemed a sad person . . . I felt sorry for him almost immediately."*

Petrocelli may have been right in describing Jason during his deposition, in 1996, as "beefy, soft, not particularly good-looking and anything but dynamic." But in a yearbook photo, taken in 1988 when he attended the Army and Navy Academy, that is not the Jason Lamar Simpson I found. That Jason was tall, slender, and handsome, carrying himself with pride. For some reason, eight years later at the time of his civil deposition, appearing before Petrocelli was a very different Jason Lamar Simpson.

Petrocelli was quoted in his book as saying, "Jason's blood was not found anywhere in the crime scene. . . ."

But police records indicate Jason Simpson's fingerprints and blood were never compared to those found at the scene. I wonder if Petrocelli knew that, at the time of Jason's deposition, the unidentified prints were part of the Los Angeles Police Department Scientific Investigation Division Latent Print Section, under DR#94-0817431 and 32.

A lot of us can be Monday quarterbacks when the game is played on Sunday. All I knew was what I had found in my investigation.

I wasn't O. J.'s judge or his jury when it came to Jason, but it had hurt me from a parent's perspective when I saw the photocopy of the bill for the two Depakote prescriptions from the Brent-Air Pharmacy that O. J. refused to pay in 1999.

Could it be that O. J. felt he'd given Jason a new lease on life because of the trial but Jason had let his father down again, as he had so many times in the past with his continued drinking and use of drugs?

The day after I received Don Lehew's report, I picked up the phone and called Dr. Harvey Davisson again.

ACCURATE FORENSIC DOCUMENT LAB
3767 Forest Lane, No. 124-131
Dallas, Texas 75240
972/733-9630

April 02, 2000

William C. Dear
972/291-4604

On 30, March 2000, I personally received the documents listed below from William C. Dear, P.L., for the purpose of handwrting comparison.

EXAMINATION REQUEST

1. Accurate Forensic Docucment Lab was endaged to compare, contrast and evaluate the document in question with the comparison documents to determine whether or not they were written or penned by the same person.

2. We were futher asked to compare CD-1-6 to see whether or not they were written or penned by the same person.

DOCUMENT IN QUESTION

1. QD-1: is a single lined page that was written in pencil in a printed style and then obliterated with scrawls, scratch-outs, names and words written in every direction on top of the original words written on the lined sheet of paper. This sheet begins with "Dear Jason" and ends with "walking broken glass".

COMPARISON DOCUMENTS

1. CD-1: is a bank check #306, dated 3/24/00 in the amount of $23,98 payable to Ralphs.

2. CD-2: is a torn and pieced together small sheet of lined paper bearing the nine names beginning with Danielle and ending with Piper and a question mark. It is unsigned and undated.

3.   CD-3: is a small sheet of lined paper that begins with the numbers <u>547 9399</u> and ends with <u>1934</u>. It is unsigned and undated as well.

4.   CD-4: is a 8 1/2 x 11 sheet of paper beginning with the word "Westwood" and ending with the word "Central". There are also numbers 5 00, 4 40, 5 15 and 3 00. It is unsigned and undated.

5.   CD-5: is a partial sheet with printing on one side and the name Jason Luong and the mumer 310 399 6822. It is unsigned and undated.

6.   CD-6: is a crumpled sheet of blue lined paper dated 11/15 Monday to the top left and ending with three signatures that say Jason Simpson.

EXAMINATION CONDUCTED

The document(s) bearing both the comparison examples and writings in question have been scientifically examined with the aid of magnificaiton and illumination as well as various optical and measuring devises.

Documents were enlarged where special attention could be given to ink patterns, slant, size, puncuation, numbers, type styles, serifs, italics, brackets, parenthesis, and ellipses, abbreviations, acronyms and trademarks.

DOCUMENT EXAMINERS FINDINGS

After a complete examination, using accepted methods, where the known documents and writings were compared and contracted to the questioned documents and writings to determine distnctive individualistic characteristics; I find that there are enough similarities to be clearly convinced that the document in question was written by the affore mentioned Jason Simpson.

CONCLUSIONS

1. The document in question was written by Jason Simpson.
2. The are names written over the top of the first draft of the writing.
3. There are also other words written over the top of the first draft of the writing.
4. The writing is predomently all capital letters on both the QD-1 and CD-1-6.
5. The numbers on CD-1, 3, 4, 5 and 6 were all written by the same person.
6. CD-1-6 are written by the same person.

"Remember the 'Dear Jason' note I showed you?"

"How could I forget it? I'm sure the person who wrote it was mentally disturbed, maybe even suicidal. Did you get it analyzed?"

"Jason wrote the note, Harvey."

He wasn't surprised to hear it. "I thought he did from the moment I started reading it."

"I did too, Harvey."

After completing the call, I began reading again for the fourth time what I had been able to extract from the handwritten page that I now knew Jason had written.

AAREN
JENNIFER
DANIELLE

DEAR JASON,
THERE ARE THREE OF US
HERE THAT I KNOW ABOUT
???
I WANT SOLICE
WORK WAS SOLICE
WAS A ???
NOW I AM A FAILURE
I CANNOT DO ANYTHING RIGHT
I CANNOT LEARN FROM IT ALL. I CANNOT

O. J. IS INNOCENT

REMEMBER. ALCOHOL ALCOHOL IS THE
ROOT OF ALL MY SHORTCOMINGS
I KNOW I'M A GOOD GUY
SOMEWHERE BUT I CANNOT FIND HIM.
MY INNOCENCE IS LOST MY EAGER-
NESS IS GONE MOST OF ALL.....???.....AND
MOST...???.... MY WILL AND INTGERITY
??? ABSENT. I DO NOT KNOW
WHAT TO DO. NO . . . I DO KNOW
WHAT TO DO, BUT I DON'T HAVE THE
WILL TO DO IT...IN SHORT I'M
FUCKED. I HAD SO MANY PLANS
BUT NOW WHAT. I CANNOT EXERCISE (?)
THE SIMPLEST DEEDS
SOBER. WALKING ON BROKEN GLASS

31

OVERVIEW OF MAYHEM

DURING THE NEXT FOUR weeks Jason Simpson's trash no longer appeared. Either someone had tipped Jason off that we had been gathering his trash, or he himself had become suspicious. I realized that my investigation was grinding to a halt; a decision had to be made.

Events were spiraling:

In March 2000, headlines appear throughout the United States about a story copyrighted by the *Los Angeles Times*, "Rampart Division [of LAPD] Involved in Corruption and Framing People to Send Them to Prison."

Numerous indictments are made against a number of police officers and detectives of the Los Angeles Police Department, with more to come.

Gil Garcetti is having trouble with his own reelection.

The Los Angeles Police Department is suffering scandal that is appearing in articles all over the world.

F. Lee Bailey is fighting to keep his law license.

O. J. appears on the June 15, 2000, cover of the *National Enquirer*, the headline trumpets, "O. J. attacks lover. You'll die like Nicole."

On June 8, 2000, O. J. Simpson and Denise Brown exchange insults in a televised confrontation, Simpson's former sister-in-law calling him a pig.

O. J. IS INNOCENT

O. J. is claiming before cameras that he, too, was framed by the LAPD.

While searching through the police records we found no record of Nicole Simpson's phone bills being introduced into evidence in O. J.'s trial.

Why?

32

HE HAS A NEW JOB

IN THE LATTER PART of April 2000, after being out of work for months, Jason was hired by a local bistro located just a few blocks from his bungalow in Venice Beach. Before Jason was hired, the small bistro was supposed to be open for breakfast, lunch, and dinner, but the original chef was unreliable, so the owner, an Englishman, could only open for breakfast and lunch. In despair, he turned to a recommendation for "a chef who is out of work—his name is Jason Simpson." As a result, Jason was immediately hired.

According to the owner, "What an extraordinary piece of luck, to acquire somebody like Jason. He is going to go places in this business."

At the bottom of the bistro's business card and menu, it now read, "Executive Chef—Jason Simpson."

Jason, like his father, O. J., making a touchdown in front of millions of people, had finally achieved his goal. Like O. J., his day of glory was at hand. Jason was no longer a sous chef; he was now an executive chef. The restaurant was small, but that wasn't important to Jason. It was important to him that he finally made it to executive chef, accomplished by himself, alone, and without O. J.'s help.

In June of 2000, I made another trip to Los Angeles. My associate told me Jason's trash was still not being put out on the street into the trash bins. I thought he might be taking it to work with him, disposing of it there. He may have been warned to be careful, aware that a private investigator was now looking into him as a possible suspect in the Bundy Drive murders.

On June 13, I arrived at Jason's residence around 10:30 AM, knowing he would have to be leaving for his new job around 11 AM. Jason's Jeep was parked in front of his bungalow.

At 11:30 AM Jason still had not come out of his residence, so, on my cell phone, I called his place of employment at the bistro. I was told that Jason was running late, but was expected momentarily. No, he hadn't called in. By this time, the restaurant was already open for lunch. Where was Jason?

I got out of my parked car, wanting to see if Jason was still at home, knowing full well I couldn't see his hidden bungalow. It was 12:10 PM as I walked past his gate and looked toward the back entry. There was no sign of him. I walked about eight to ten steps north on the sidewalk when I heard the sound of a gate opening and closing behind me. Was it Jason? The only way I would know would be to turn around and look. I knew this would be a mistake, but I had to know. I had to look.

I turned to see Jason standing on the sidewalk in front of his gate, not more than twenty feet away, staring right at me. Jason looked at me as if he thought he might know me, but wasn't sure. You see, I had grown a beard since our last encounter, just prior to Christmas, at the Mélisse restaurant.

As we exchanged looks, Jason turned to his left and walked around the back of his Jeep. In his hand was his chef bag containing what I knew to be the tools of his trade, assorted razor-sharp chef knives. I watched as Jason got into the Jeep, and continued watching as he drove away and disappeared out of sight. Jason, now en route to his new job as executive chef at the local bistro was late again.

Suddenly it dawned on me: it had been six years and one day since the murders of Nicole Simpson and Ron Goldman. I couldn't help but think:

Will it only be a short time before his temper again snaps, and he bubbles up in a fit of rage?

Was he already having trouble at work? I knew for sure he was late. That was obvious.

Will it be another Paul Goldberg situation?

Will someone else get hurt?

Will we finally all know the truth?

In October, I again flew back to Los Angeles, this time to meet with a professor of law at Loyola Law School. The professor had been cordial in agreeing to meet me, not knowing fully what the meeting was about, other than it concerned O. J. Simpson and the murders of Nicole Simpson and Ron Goldman.

I wasn't so sure how he would feel after our meeting. It turned out, he couldn't have been nicer. I think he fully understood my concerns. I shared with him my complete investigation, up to this point, into the murders and told him who I now considered to be a major suspect. After a lengthy meeting, it was decided my best approach to reopening the murder investigation did not lie with either the LAPD or the district attorney's office, but through the California Attorney General's Office. The professor offered to help me set up a meeting with the attorney general, or a member of his staff. As it turned out though, he was unable to help, leaving me, once again, on my own, attempting to seek justice in the murders of Nicole Simpson and Ron Goldman.

I was left with no choice; Gil Garcetti wasn't interested, the LAPD wasn't interested, and neither was the attorney general. I needed more evidence. A book about my investigation would be my only answer.

After returning to Dallas I started on my investigative report. I titled it *O. J. is Guilty but Not of Murder*. At the end of November 2000, I completed the manuscript. In the interim I submitted it to major publishers. Everyone liked the manuscript but believed that no one cared about O. J. Simpson any longer. As a result no one wanted to publish my book.

I felt I had come too far to give up. If I had to print the book myself, I was going to do just that. I was proud of what I had accomplished so far but I wasn't through. Maybe with the book being published, the phone would ring and give me that final piece of evidence that might help me bring closure to this case.

In February 2001, as the book was being readied for release, I returned to Los Angeles and found that Jason Simpson had once again lost his job; he was no longer an executive chef at Angel's Bistro. At that point I decided to interview the owner, Ron Harper.

When I sat down and talked to Mr. Harper, he told me that Jason just didn't work out and was not eligible to be rehired. I could see by the look on his face that I didn't need to go any further. It didn't surprise me.

I realized Jason would never receive the solace he wanted so badly until he gets help. I felt I knew what was bothering him.

"Just after Jason left," Mr. Harper told me, "I think it was in the latter part of January, a car pulled up a little before lunch around ten thirty or so. A well-dressed man came into my restaurant. I saw him bend over and pick up a menu. I asked if I could help him. He said, 'I thought Jason Simpson was the chef?'

"'No sir, he is no longer with us.'

"'Do you know where he is?'

"'No sir, I have no idea.' The man threw down the menu, turned and walked out." Ron said, "I watched him as he got into his car and drove away."

"Did you recognize the man?"

"Oh yes, he was Gil Garcetti, the former district attorney."

Garcetti had lost his reelection, yet he was looking for Jason Simpson. Why? I could only wonder, as I got back into my car, had Gil Garcetti heard of my forthcoming book, and might he be concerned if asked if he had ever interviewed Jason? Maybe he wanted to be able to say, "Yes, I personally interviewed Jason and found nothing to it." Yet, now I knew the truth. Stopping by the little bistro had definitely paid off. Gil Garcetti was interested in Jason Simpson and to me that spoke for itself.

In 2001, after a major article on the front page of the *Los Angeles Observer*, showing me with a chef's knife in my hand as the possible murder weapon in the murders of Nicole Simpson and Ron Goldman, I realized it was time for me to confront Jason . . . I had nothing to lose.

I drove over to Venice Beach and pulled up in front of Jason's bungalow. As I parked the car, I realized it would be just him and me this time. I got out and slowly walked over to the chain-link gate. My heart began to race as I opened the gate and walked toward the back entrance. I hesitated, as just behind this gate I could see the outline of Jason's small bungalow. The gate swung open slowly, I walked about five paces and was now at Jason's front door. I wasn't sure what was going to happen at this point. I reached up with my right hand and knocked on the door. There was no response. Just as I started to knock a second time the door suddenly opened. It wasn't Jason. I had no idea who this man was. As I regained my composure, I said, "I'm looking for Jason Simpson."

The man said, "I'm just the painter. The previous tenant just moved out."

The painter stepped back, and I stepped inside. As I did, I couldn't help but realize, by quickly looking around, how much time Jason had spent alone inside this small bungalow since the murders of Nicole Simpson and Ron Goldman. I could also picture, in my mind, all those bottles of liquor he had consumed, which I had gathered out of the trash for the past several years.

According to Jason's neighbors, he moved out very quickly—overnight. One neighbor told me they thought it had been a quick decision on his part and understood that he had sold his Jeep and moved to Florida. As this neighbor spoke, I could not help but wonder if Jason had seen the front cover story in the *L.A. Observer*, and maybe that had caused him to make that abrupt decision to move out overnight, out of the jurisdiction of the Los Angeles Police Department.

It was time for me to sit down and write to District Attorney Steve Cooley one last time. Hoping, now, with all I had uncovered in nearly nine years, he would meet with me, and, in turn, ask for a formal grand jury hearing.

But this was not to happen. He was still not interested. His reply, "You have given me nothing I didn't already know."

That was not true and he knew it.

LOS ANGELES COUNTY DISTRICT ATTORNEY'S OFFICE

STEVE COOLEY • District Attorney
CURT LIVESAY • Chief Deputy District Attorney

PETER BOZANICH
Assistant District Attorney

April 10, 2003

Mr. William C. Dear
William Dear & Associates, Incorporated
3883 Turtle Creek Boulevard
Dallas, Texas 75219

Dear Mr. Dear:

In re *People v. Orenthal James Simpson*, Case No. BA097211

I am in receipt of your correspondence concerning the above referenced case. Because you fail to reveal new information, it does not appear that a meeting is warranted at this time. As you have indicated, you are free to discuss this matter with the California Attorney General, or any other party. If you wish to share additional information with this office, please direct your correspondence to me.

Very truly yours,

STEVE COOLEY
District Attorney

by

PETER BOZANICH
Assistant District Attorney

rd

18-201 Clara Shortridge Foltz Criminal Justice Center
210 West Temple Street
Los Angeles, CA 90012
(213) 974-5959

33

WAITING FOR THE PHONE TO RING

IN THE EARLY PART of 2001, my book had been out for just a short time. The reviews were favorable, from the *Washington Times* to the *Dallas Observer*. It appeared that everyone who read the book and took time out to answer the juror's ballot at the end, voted *O. J. Not Guilty*. Most importantly, they also felt I had uncovered a major suspect who had been overlooked.

I received a lot of calls, letters, and emails stating how they enjoyed my investigation, and how for the first time, it finally made sense. But I was hoping for more. I hoped someone who read my book would come forth with additional information that would help me accomplish my goal of bringing closure to this case.

This particular night while sitting at my desk in my home, it was late and I was about to prepare for bed, when suddenly my phone rang. The caller ID indicated it was from California, but did not show the caller's name. I reached over and picked it up.

The voice on the other end said, "Mr. Dear, I just finished your book, and I couldn't put it down. I was shocked, but not surprised. I had to call you because I think I have some information that you need. I'd like to meet you."

"May I ask what it is about, sir?"

"I'm Ross Harding. I live in Los Angeles. I have an important document that might help bring closure to this particular case."

I didn't hesitate for a second. "Tell me when and where."

O. J. IS INNOCENT

On April 20, 2001, I again flew to Los Angeles, rented a car and drove north on 405, then west on 101. I pulled into a large upscale shopping center and parked in front of the Starbucks coffee shop. It was similar to the one Nicole Simpson and Ron Goldman had frequented in Brentwood before they were murdered. I got out of the car, walked inside, and sat down, wondering just exactly what Mr. Harding could have for me that would be so important.

Ten minutes later, a very distinguished man in his late forties walked in directly toward me. "I recognized you immediately," he said.

When he sat down he started to explain. "I know Alan Ladd Jackson was not at the restaurant the night of the murders."

"How do you know that?"

"Because he was with me. I also know Jason Simpson was the acting chef that night at Jackson's Restaurant, replacing Alan. In fact, I'll even take it one step further. The next morning when I heard about the murders, I immediately said to myself, *O. J. did not commit the murders, Jason did.*"

"Why would you think that?"

"I knew Jason, not well, but well enough to know what type of person he was. After reading the headline stories during the week concerning the murders, I continued to wonder if it could have been Jason and not O. J.

"The following Monday, I picked up the newspaper again and most of the stories were devoted to O. J. and the murders. For some reason I couldn't get Jason Simpson out of my mind. I put down my newspaper and picked up the phone. I called Jackson's Restaurant to ask them to fax me Jason's time record for the night of June 12. You see, Mr. Dear, I was a silent partner in Jackson's Restaurant, so his time record was readily available to me. As a result, it was immediately faxed over to me at my residence. Mr. Dear, Jason did not leave the restaurant at 11:00 PM. His time card showed he clocked out at 10:20, twenty minutes before the murders. I was curious, so I drove the distance from the restaurant to Nicole's to see whether or not Jason could have made it in the time frame they indicated in the newspapers. I'm telling you, he could have made it. The only problem I have now is I know the time card said 10:20, but I've looked for my copy of his time card record and can't find it. I know I definitely didn't throw it away, I've just misplaced it. After all these years I had no reason to be looking for it. But because of your book I know how important it is to you, as it is to me. I agree with you, I don't think O. J. committed the murders."

"Ross, I need that time card."

"I promise you, I'll do everything I can to find it."

About twenty minutes later, Ross left me absorbing everything he had just told me. Though the lack of the time card was a setback, I still felt this trip to Los Angeles was worth it, knowing now that Jason could have committed the murders within the time frame Marcia Clark and Christopher Darden had established. And I wasn't the only one who thought so, Ross Harding did too.

After Ross drove off, I decided to drive back to Jackson's Restaurant myself. As I pulled up to park, I thought for a moment and then began to drive from Jackson's to Nicole's looking at the clock on the dash as I left the parking lot. Fourteen minutes later, I was parked on Bundy Drive directly in front of Nicole Simpson's condo. Ross and I were right; Jason did have enough time on Sunday, June 12, 1994, to have left Jackson's and committ the murders of Nicole Simpson and Ron Goldman in that twenty-minute time frame. Though I already knew that, it was nice to hear someone else back me up for a change. Especially since that someone had been connected with Jackson's Restaurant to some degree and had been in the position to know whether or not Alan Ladd Jackson had, in fact, been at Jackson's Restaurant on the night of June 12th.

If Alan Jackson had not been there, how could Jason have been given this so-called airtight alibi of cooking in front of 200 people? I knew it was not true then, and I knew, more than ever, that it was not true now. Ross had finally confirmed it. It was not just speculation on my part; it was now part of my facts. Carlos the waiter confirmed it earlier in my investigation, and now Ross, part owner of the restaurant, reconfirmed not only the fact that Alan Ladd Jackson was not at the restaurant that night, so he had no idea how many people were there, but also that he certainly had no idea what time Jason left work.

I suddenly recalled my interview with Jennifer Green, when she stated she picked Jason up at 9:45 PM. That would have given Jason fifty-five minutes prior to the murders, not twenty.

Now, what I needed most was Jason's time card.

34

CRUCIAL NEW EVIDENCE

ONCE I ARRIVED BACK in Dallas, waiting to hear from Ross Harding about the time card, I decided to find out, for sure, whether the LAPD had ever interviewed Jason Simpson. I realized the only way I could ever find out would be to file a formal request through the Freedom of Information Act with the LAPD. I filed the request, but months passed with no response. Still waiting to hear, the same as I had been waiting to hear from Ross Harding about the time card. Patience was not my best virtue.

On May 8, 2001, at 4:48 PM, I saw a blinking light on our incoming message line. Donna, my assistant, had left for the day, so I sat down, pushed the button and listened to the message. It wasn't from Ross Harding, but it was a message from the LAPD Detective Division, that stated, "Jason Lamar Simpson was never interviewed by the LAPD; he refused to cooperate, and was represented by legal counsel."

Yes! Yes! I knew it all along! Contrary to what they told the press originally, they had, in fact, never interviewed Jason Simpson and now I could prove it. A week after the call, I received a letter from Chief of Police Bernard C. Parks, dated May 1, 2001, confirming the phone call. The letter stated, "The department has conducted a search for records described in your request, and found no records responsive to your request." Yet, the earlier phone message had taken it even further.

It had been about three months since my meeting with Ross in Los Angeles, when my home fax line rang at around 11 PM. I quickly got up from my chair in my living room and hurriedly walked into my office. I heard the noise and saw a fax coming through. I picked it up and there, on the cover sheet, Ross had written, "Mr. Dear, I was right. Jason clocked out at 10:20 PM on the night of June 12, 1994. The second sheet will confirm it; it's a copy of his time card record, the one I had faxed over to me originally." The faxed note was signed *Ross*.

As I picked up the second sheet of the fax, I looked at the top of the time card record—Name: Simpson; underneath that: Jason; Pay Period Ending: 6-19-1994. At the bottom, on Sunday (SU), showed where Jason had "punched" IN at 2:57 PM, and OUT at 10:20 PM, for a total of 7 hours and 23 minutes. This was just what I needed. This was a crucial piece of information. I could now turn it over to the district attorney and, hopefully, get his attention.

I laid down the faxed copy of Jason Simpson's June 12 time card on my desk and retired for the night. I now realized that my printing of the first book was beginning to pay off.

At about 1:30 in the morning I suddenly woke up, sat up in bed, and said aloud, "Oh my God!" I jumped out of bed, ran down the hallway into my office and picked up the fax. I looked at it again. The last line was where he had "punched" IN on Sunday at 2:57 PM and OUT at 10:20 PM. I realized that was wrong! The Sunday he punched in at 2:57 PM was the pay period ending date of June 19, not Sunday, June 12. I started at the top and found that the time records began with a *handwritten* entry, had no day or date, IN at 2:30 PM, and OUT at *10:30* PM, with 8.0 DAILY HOURS, and the initials *JS* in the ACCUMULATED time column signifying Jason had made the entry himself. Beneath the handwritten times were Tuesday (TU), Wednesday (WE), Saturday (SA), and Sunday (SU) entries that were "punched" by the time clock. But I remembered in Jason's civil deposition, he said he had *"punched out"* on the night of the murders. Yet, now, looking at the faxed copy of his actual time card he did not "punch" the time card on the 12th. Jason had filled out the time card in his own handwriting. Ross had been right about the time card being punched on Sunday at 2:57 PM and 10:20 PM but that was on the 19th. Since Jason did not work on the Monday after the murders, the first handwritten entry had to be for Sunday, June 12.

I looked at my computer calendar to recheck the dates. Holding on to this time card, even though it was a faxed copy of Jason's time record, I knew it was a valuable piece of evidence.

I sat down in my chair for a few more moments, realizing now, here were the answers. If I was right and Jason Simpson had indeed committed the murders, he would have had blood all over him.

According to Dr. Henry Lee, the suspect would have blood in his hair, on his face, on his clothes, covered in blood.

"It would have had to have been a murder by an amateur." "A man in a fit of rage," according to Marcia Clark.

And, according to Ron Shipp, Nicole had said, "I don't think it was O. J., I think it was Jason that was outside stalking me."

Jason Simpson had been in a psychiatric hospital, suffered from rage disorder, and had quit taking his medication, Depakote, just two months prior to the murders. Here was a man who had been arrested during the trial for charges of hit and run, leaving the scene of an accident while driving under the influence, arrested for trying to assault his ex-employer, Paul Goldberg, with a kitchen knife, attacked his girlfriend, Jennifer Green, attacked his then-girlfriend, DeeDee, with a chef's knife, chopping off her hair, almost scalping her, and then stalking her after she moved away from him to New York, and had also stalked Nicole Simpson.

Jason left Jackson's Restaurant at 9:45 PM, according to his girlfriend Jennifer Green and associate Carlos Ramos. We now know he did not have an airtight alibi of cooking in front of 200 people; furthermore, he took fifty-five minutes to drop off his girlfriend at her apartment that was only five minutes away from Jackson's Restaurant; had been stood up by Nicole Simpson and embarrassed in front of his associates; may have gone over to confront Nicole to find out why she had failed to come to his restaurant without notifying him; carried a bag of razor-sharp chef's knives with him in his Jeep; was the acting chef at Jackson's Restaurant the night of June 12; and had access to the restaurant, even after hours.

Jason was also a man who could have gone back to Jackson's Restaurant, changed clothes, cleaned up the blood splatter, knowing the laundry would be picked up Monday morning and then realized he needed to remove his "punched" time card—the one piece of evidence that definitely could not be overlooked. A man who could have then picked up a blank time card and with no one there to witness, in his own pen, filled in his name: *Simpson – Jason*; Pay Period Ending: *6-19-1994*; writing time IN *P2:30* and OUT *P10:30*, giving him an airtight alibi for the night of June 12. The authorities would then determine from the time of 10:30 PM, there would be no way for Jason to arrive at the crime scene and commit the murders in ten minutes. A man who knew if he did not remove the old time card and replace it with a new one, in all likelihood he would become a major suspect.

My suspect realized they would find the bodies on Monday, and in doing so, Jason would not be expected to come to work on Monday, June 13, but instead be with his distraught father.

According to the time card, after the first handwritten entry, Jason clocked in on Tuesday the 14th at 3:03 PM and clocked out at 10:25 PM, Wednesday the 15th, in at 2:59 PM and clocked out at 11:00 PM. Then on Thursday the 16th and Friday the 17th, Jason was not at work. But Saturday the 18th he clocked in at 2:07 PM and clocked out at 11:42 PM. Then on Sunday, June 19th, *not* June 12th, Jason clocked in at 2:57 PM and out at 10:20 PM.

This is what the LAPD would have seen had they asked to obtain a copy of Jason Simpson's time card. This is what Ross saw when he received his faxed copy. Now, this is what I saw, and this is what I have: this crucial new piece of evidence.

There were a number of items on the time card that caused me concern. The important parts of the time card were handwritten, which was very unusual, especially the date signed in and out that night. It was handwritten in, yet we were able to verify that the time card was operational on Sunday, June 12, 1994. The date showing pay period ending 6/19/1994 caused me and others some concern.

I called Don Lehew, the handwriting expert who was familiar with Jason Simpson's handwriting. Don examined the handwriting on the time card and determined that all of the written items on the time card were, in fact, written by Jason Simpson. Now this began to make sense.

Now that I was able to prove that all the handwritten items including the time period ending was written by Jason, I realized that Jason, by destroying his time card, would have had to handwrite in the times and date that would provide him the alibi that he would need.

He chose not to state the day that the entry "IN: P2:30 – OUT: P10:30" was made on and then handwrite in "Pay Period Ending: 6-19/1994."

Once we knew Jason had written in the time himself, we knew why. He could not get the time clock to go back and cover Sunday for him and the entry could not ultimately be interpreted as Monday, June 13, 1994, because he did not work that day—the day right after the killings because he was with family. In addition, if it could be misconstrued as it being Monday because of the "Pay Period Ending: 6-19/1994" the problem he faced is if he worked on Monday, June 13, 1994, the time clock was working and he would have no reason to hand write his time. The only day he needed to hand write in his time was the night of the murders.

O. J. IS INNOCENT

SIMPSON

NAME JASON   N⁰

A   6-19-94

PAY PERIOD ENDING

DAY OR DATE	IN	OUT	DAILY HOURS	ACCUMULATED REG. HRS.	OVERTIME	SPECIAL
	P2:30	P10:30	8.0			
TU	P03:03	P10:25	7:22	7:22		
WE	P02:59	P11:00	8:01	15:22	0:01	
SA	P02:07	P11:42	9:35	23:22	1:36	
SU	P02:57	P10:20	7:23	30:45	1:36	

HUNTER EQUIPMENT COMPANY
(213) 936-7281   FORM 5030

342

O.J.'s family reacting to the not guilty verdict. The rest of the family seems exuberant while Jason wears a stoic or even somber expression. Photo by Myung J. Chun. *Copyright © 1995.* Los Angeles Times. *Reprinted with Permission.*

Jason Simpson preparing to read his father's statement to the news media following the not guilty verdict. ©*ImageCollect.com/Globe Photos*

The crime scene at Bundy Drive on June 12, 1994 (note the large amount of blood). ©ImageCollect.com/Globe Photos

Detective Vanatter, left, lead homicide detective was given 8cc of O.J. Simpson's blood drawn by RN Thano Peratis at the jail. Later in the day when Vannatter turned in the vial, it was missing 1.5cc of blood, which was enough to be placed on the back gate at Bundy and socks in the bedroom at Rockingham. The blood found in both locations contained EDTA, a blood preservative.

Blood drops mixed with EDTA found on the back gate at Bundy, three to four weeks after the murders.

The four-foot fence with sharp prongs on the top behind Kato Kaelin's bungalow at Rockingham where Kato heard the three bumps the night of June 12, 1994. These prongs could have cut O.J.'s finger while jumping over.

O.J. standing next to the air conditioning unit in the narrow walkway behind the bungalow where Kato heard three bumps and the bloody glove was found by Detective Furhman.

Detective Fuhrman at the crime scene pointing at the glove (notice Fuhrman without protective coverings on his shoes).

Close-up of Detective Fuhrman and the glove (notice also the dark-colored knit cap).

Nicole Simpson as she was found at the crime scene on June 12, 1994.

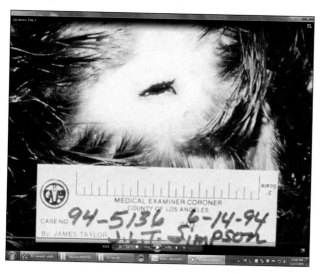

Autopsy photo of the laceration on Nicole Simpson's head, which forensic experts say could have been caused by the butt of the knife found in the suspect's storage locker.

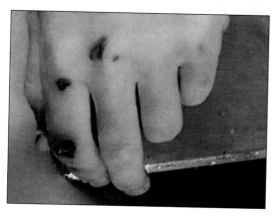

Defensive wounds sustained by Ron Goldman while fighting for his life on June 12, 1994.

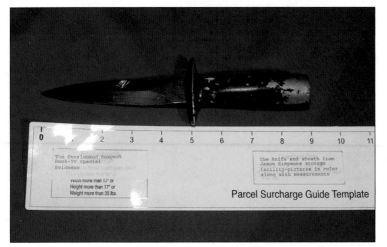

A double-bladed knife similar to the knife described by the Los Angeles medical examiner as the possible murder weapon. This particular knife was found in a storage locker abandoned by our suspect.

According to forensic experts, the butt of this knife matches the laceration on Nicole Simpson's head.

According to four experts, the initials of JS were etched into the sheath of the knife found in the suspect's storage locker.

Socks found at the foot of O.J.'s bed containing drops of blood, which later was determined to contain a mixture of blood and EDTA, a blood preservative.

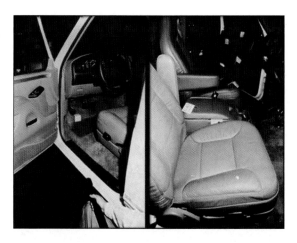

Only a very small amount of blood was actually found in O.J.'s Bronco, which Marsha Clark claimed was full of blood.

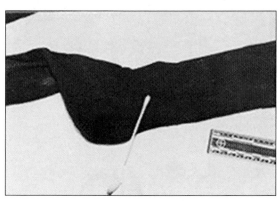

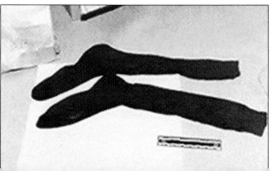

This sock was supposedly worn by O.J. at the crime scene, but the blood was found to have soaked through both sides, which meant that no foot was in the sock when it came in contact with blood.

The LAPD Homicide Convention in Las Vegas, Nevada, where famous crime memorabilia was being displayed in 2010.

According to district attorney Bill Hodgeman on August 7, 2009, he could not find the dark knit cap or the bloody gloves found at the murder scene, which we had requested under the FOIA. We found the missing evidence in Las Vegas at the LAPD Homicide Convention in 2010.

St. Martin of Tours Catholic church in Brentwood where Nicole's funeral was held. This is where Jason Simpson refused to view her body at the funeral, then ran out and locked himself in the limousine, according to Sheila Weller, author of *Raging Heart*. ©*ImageCollect. com/Globe Photos*

35

DISASTER AND DISAPPOINTMENT

THE TERRORIST ATTACKS OCCURRED on September 11, 2001. As a result of this awful tragedy I immediately pulled my book. I refused to promote it and hoped with time I would be given a second chance. I felt the devastation of September 11th was much more important than my book. No matter how many years or how much money I spent on this investigation and how much I wanted to bring closure to this case, it was not meant to be at this time.

On March 27, 2002, I had been invited by Reagan Williams to the campus of Southern Methodist University, to present my investigative report to the SMU Law School graduating class and their professors. I started off my lecture with, "Do you ladies and gentlemen believe O. J. Simpson is guilty in the murders of Nicole Simpson and Ron Goldman?" All hands immediately rose as to their belief that O. J. was guilty. As I looked out into the crowded auditorium, I noticed a group of women staring at me. It was obvious that they were definitely convinced O. J. was guilty. I made up my mind: if I could convince these graduating law students and their professors that O. J. Simpson was not guilty, then I could do the same before a special California grand jury. I felt this would be one of the most difficult tasks I would encounter.

I continued through my presentation. Two hours later, with the evidence presented, I asked, "Ladies and gentlemen, would you please raise your hands if you still believe that O. J. Simpson is guilty in the murders of Nicole Simpson and Ron Goldman, beyond a shadow of a doubt."

I held my breath as I looked each one of them in the eye. It was quiet as I looked around; there were no hands raised this time.

I hesitated . . . "Ladies and gentlemen, do you believe based on the evidence presented, O. J. Simpson is not guilty in the murders of Nicole Simpson and Ron Goldman?"

I looked over to where the four women sat. They all raised their hands in a vote of *Not Guilty*. Then, as I further looked around, I realized most of those in the room had also raised their hands, indicating I had convinced them. Based on the facts I had uncovered, O. J. Simpson was *Not Guilty* in the murders of Nicole Simpson and Ron Goldman. Encouraged by their response, I then asked, "Ladies and gentlemen, do you believe Jason Simpson should be considered a major suspect?"

Again, all hands rose immediately.

After my presentation and the voting session, the four ladies, along with two of the professors, walked over to me, put out their hands and shook mine.

One of them said, "I never thought you would ever convince me, in all probability, O. J. Simpson was not guilty, but Mr. Dear, you made a strong case. Strong enough for me to be convinced based on your investigation and presentation of the facts."

Another woman spoke up and said, "You should have been a lawyer. Thank you."

On April 10, 2003, I received another letter of reply from District Attorney Steven Cooley's office.

According to Assistant District Attorney Peter Bozanich, I had revealed no new evidence. As a result, they did not feel a meeting was warranted at this time. After reading this, I walked around in disbelief and frustration. Later, after I spoke with my friend, Phil Smith, about the letter, I realized that justice was again being hampered, only this time by politics: Cooley was up for reelection!

The tragedy of 9/11 and now the Iraq war . . . When would it end?

36

CONFERENCE AND JEEP

I WAS DETERMINED NOT TO give up; I was going back to Los Angeles. This time I was making arrangements to have a national press conference on Thursday, June 12, 2003, the nine-year anniversary date of the murders of Nicole Simpson and Ron Goldman. I wanted to have this press conference in the same place where it all started on Sunday, June 12, 1994: Jackson's Restaurant, now known as Celestino's.

Reservations were made at Celestino's for a private lunch to accommodate 100. Isaac, the owner and manager, only knew it was to be a press luncheon. He had no idea it was about the former sous chef, Jason Simpson. I decided it would give us time to film inside the restaurant and particularly get a picture of the time clock. I carefully prepared a two-page invitation to the press, starting and ending with "Did you know?" that I've included here:

1. Did you know that the LAPD issued a statement that this suspect had been investigated and was given an airtight alibi that he was cooking in front of 200 people at the time of the murders?
2. Did you know that this suspect was in fact never interviewed by the LAPD or the district attorney's office?
3. Did you know that this suspect was on probation until the year 2000 for assaulting his previous employer with a knife?

4. Did you know this suspect cut off the hair of his previous girlfriend with his chef's knife in a fit of rage?
5. Did you know that this suspect had assaulted and tried to choke to death another previous girlfriend in a fit of rage?
6. Did you know that this suspect had stalked previous girlfriends as well as Nicole Simpson?
7. Did you know that prior to the murders this suspect had been in an L.A. psychiatric hospital for three attempted suicides?
8. Did you know this suspect was taking Depakote to control his rage disorders and had been diagnosed with Intermittent Rage Disorder, also called Intermittent Explosive Disorder?
9. Did you know that this suspect has been described by former friends and associates as having a Dr. Jekyll/Mr. Hyde personality?
10. Did you know that under stress or pressure this suspect suffers from outbursts of rage against women?
11. Did you know that Nicole Simpson was supposed to eat after Sydney's recital, not at Mezzaluna Restaurant, but at Jackson's Restaurant?
12. Did you know this suspect was supposed to be preparing dinner at Jackson's Restaurant for Nicole, Sydney, Justin and Nicole's family, but she failed to show up on Sunday, June 12, 1994?
13. Did you know that this suspect left Jackson's Restaurant approximately fifty-five minutes prior to the murders and under his arm he carried a chef's bag containing an assortment of razor-sharp knives, one indicative of the type of knife used to kill Nicole Simpson and Ron Goldman?
14. Did you know that the day after the murders a prominent criminal attorney specializing in death-penalty murder cases was hired by O. J. Simpson to represent this suspect?

15. Did you know this suspect cut out the center console in his Jeep and left the windows open during rainstorms after the murders?

16. Did you know that several months prior to the murders this suspect checked into Cedars-Sinai Hospital emergency room saying he was out of his medication, Depakote, and felt he was about to rage?

17. Did you know that this suspect's own doctor stated if he committed these murders he would never be convicted because he was a mental case? Did you also know this suspect had been, for a number of years, under the care of this psychologist for his mental disorder?

18. Did you know this same suspect had altered his time card for the night of June 12, 1994, in attempt to give himself an airtight alibi?

19. Did you know that there is a note written by our suspect describing himself as three people?

Why was this suspect never interviewed by the LAPD or the district attorney's office?

Why was this suspect given an airtight alibi when upon our investigation we can prove he had no alibi at the time of the murders?

IT IS TIME FOR THE TRUTH TO BE KNOWN AND FOR JUSTICE TO PREVAIL.

I felt with all the information I put into the "Did you know?" document that anyone from news media would certainly have had their interest piqued. On top of that, they were being served free lunch, and very seldom do members of the media turn down a free lunch.

In the meantime, I made another decision. I wanted Jason Simpson's Jeep. Even though I had been told by several crime scene experts that with the passing of nine years and as much exposure to rain as Jason had let pour inside the Jeep, the possibility of finding blood evidence would nearly be impossible. But I wasn't going to let that deter me.

Joe Villanueva and I flew to Los Angeles on June 9 to prepare for the press conference and to obtain Jason's Jeep. After checking into our hotel, I told Joe of my determination to get Jason Simpson's Jeep. I wanted that Jeep! I was more determined now than ever. If I could buy the Jeep and find blood, then Steve Cooley could not possibly prevent me from receiving a special grand jury hearing. Maybe justice for Nicole Simpson and Ron Goldman could finally be achieved.

Joe, who has worked for me on and off for nearly thirty years, drove with me to see Rene Colorado, the new owner of the Jeep. We parked our rental car and with the help of another tenant, entered the locked gate at the apartment where Rene was living with his wife and family. I walked upstairs and knocked on the door of apartment 208. I knocked a second time, and then I saw the curtain being pulled back.

"Mr. Colorado, it's Bill Dear. We talked before and I need to talk to you again."

I heard the chain lock being removed from the door and out stepped Mr. Colorado. I began explaining to him the truth of my visit and why I had to be so careful.

After I shared with him what I had been doing for nine years, he said, "I'm glad you're being honest with me. Do you want to see the Jeep?"

"Yes sir, I do."

All three of us walked downstairs and, underneath the apartment complex, there was Jason's 1993 Jeep, still bearing California License 3DEW-520—the same tag that was on the Jeep the night of Sunday, June 12, 1994. The Jeep Jason had been driving when he left Jackson's Restaurant approximately one hour before the murders, carrying his rolled-up chef's bag containing razor-sharp chef's knives.

"Do you want to sit in it?" Rene asked.

I never replied. Instead I just climbed inside and sat where Jason had been sitting that night. Trying, in my mind, to sense what Jason might have been saying, over and over, to himself. I looked around after a few minutes and observed that the torn console which was so important to me had been removed.

"Rene, what happened to the console?"

"It was all ripped up, and gouges were in the foam, so I had to have it fixed."

"Have you changed anything else?"

"I taped up the steering wheel and put temporary covers on the torn seats. And, yeah, I put new tires all the way around, but that is all I did."

Two days later, on June 11, just one day before the nine-year anniversary of the murders, Joe and I met with Rene one last time. I had wire transferred money to Rene's bank account. As we pulled up, he was waiting for us on the curb in front of his apartment. We took some pictures together and I thanked him as he handed me the title and keys to the Jeep.

"I think, Mr. Dear, under the circumstances, I have done the right thing."

I knew, as we drove off, I had acquired a friend. He had not been aware of the Jeep's history when he first bought it, but he was now. I glanced in my rearview mirror and saw Rene watching us as we drove away. Now, I had one additional thing to share with the media at the press conference. An opportunity for the press to see the Jeep themselves, at the same place it was when Jason walked out of Jackson's Restaurant on that night of June 12, 1994, fifty-five minutes prior to the murders.

On Thursday, June 12, 2003, the following day, Joe and I arrived early at Celestino's, parked the Jeep in the back and waited. As the waiters were preparing the tables for lunch, I paced back and forth. The noon hour arrived and just the four of us were left sitting there waiting for the press . . . the press that never came. At 1 PM, I told the waiters and staff they may as well clear the tables, it was obvious that, just like the DA, the press didn't care either. As a friend later said, the press, like the DA, did not want to admit they could have been wrong.

I remembered when President Nixon lied to prevent the truth and how if he had just admitted he was wrong would have endeared him to the public. To me the same could have been possible for the press, now, nine years later.

Back in Texas, Phil Smith, my friend, pulled the Jeep into his facility where he normally films private events. This time he was going to film the Jeep while it was being tested for blood. In the meantime, I hired Dr. Max Courtney, one of the top forensic consultants in the country, because I knew we had to have the evidence documented by the numbers in the event Luminal testing showed indications of possible blood in the Jeep. On the evening of June 24, I picked up my two sons, Michael and Adam, along with my friends Jerry Jerrigan and Joe Jessing, and drove to Southlake, Texas, a suburb of Fort Worth, where the Jeep was being stored. Arrangements were made for several other people to witness the testing, to ensure every effort was being made to protect any evidence found. At 8:00 PM, Dr. Courtney pulled up with his associate, Michelle. The overhead doors were pulled closed; the bright lights illuminating the Jeep were turned off. Now in total darkness, the Luminal was sprayed throughout the entire Jeep. As Dr. Courtney and Michelle went about their business, Phil Smith filmed the entire procedure. I watched with great intensity, unaware there were any others in the room. As I stared at Jason's Jeep, all I could visualize, in my mind, was that Sunday, June 12, 1994, when the murders had occurred.

Suddenly I heard Dr. Courtney say, "Bill, I found the Luminal distinguished some hot spots on the driver's seat, beneath the bottom and back cushions."

I was excited, but not as excited as I should have been, since it had been nine years.

As the floorboard carpets were pulled back, I saw where the drain plugs on the driver's side and passenger's side had been removed to allow water to flow out. I remembered all the times I had watched Jason. His Jeep would be parked in front of his residence in the rain, with the canvas covers removed. Afterward, he would walk outside and proceed to close the canvas covers. Was it to wash away any evidence of the night of June 12? I couldn't help but think that was the case.

An hour and a half later, Dr. Courtney said he had found seven hot spots of possible blood indications with the Luminal process. The lights were turned on and the overhead door opened. All of us were wringing wet from the stifling Texas summer heat, after being enclosed in this metal storage room. As we opened the overhead door, we found Jeff Crilley, from Channel 4, an affiliate of Fox, with his crew, airing a live account of the Luminal testing process being performed on Jason's Jeep. I have a great deal of respect for Jeff Crilley and the way he presents his investigative stories. I just wished he, and other media representatives, had been present at Jackson's Restaurant on June 12, 2003, when I was prepared to lay out my investigative evidence, accompanied by facts and pictures.

"I'll test all of these hot spots that showed up during the Luminal testing in my laboratory on Wednesday," said Dr. Courtney, interrupting my thoughts.

"Phil and I will be there, Dr. Courtney."

Each sample had been cut out, removed, placed in individual evidence bags, and labeled, just like they do on CSI.

I was quiet after we left that night even though everyone else seemed excited over our possible findings. I felt I needed to reserve my excitement until I was sure of the results. Then, and only then, would I feel that my job was finally complete.

On Wednesday, Phil Smith and I arrived at Dr. Courtney's laboratory in Fort Worth. Again, Phil set up the cameras to film each of the seven samples being tested by Dr. Courtney. One by one, they each turned out negative. As the last piece was checked, Dr. Courtney turned to me and said, "Don't be discouraged. I told you the chances, after nine years, were just a half of one percent that the evidence would still be in the Jeep."

I knew it had been a long shot, but I had tried for so long to uncover the evidence and find closure in this case, and I was just drained, both mentally and financially.

I left Dr. Courtney's knowing full well my investigation was correct and factual. Jason Lamar Simpson was, and still is, my major suspect, should have been and now with all this evidence should still be considered by the LAPD, California DA and attorney general. Yet they weren't interested.

I arrived back at Phil Smith's warehouse at 11 PM, I wanted to be alone, and Phil had given me a key to the storage facility where the Jeep was stored.

I opened the main door, entered the interior door, and turned on the light. There in front of me was Jason's Jeep. I reached back over and turned off the light, walked over to the Jeep and climbed into the driver's seat. Then, I did what I had done best for more than forty years of working murder cases: put myself into the mind of the suspect

I could feel my mind drifting back through the nine years of the investigation. It was now Sunday, June 12, 1994. I was no longer Bill Dear, I was now Jason Simpson.

I could plainly see what had happened that night.

37

BRIAN DOUGLAS EVIDENCE

O**N SEPTEMBER 28, 2003,** I arrived at my office early. I sat down at
my desk and I looked out the window. I was so thankful that
because of my first book, *O. J. Is Guilty, But Not of Murder*, I had been
fortunate to hear from and then visit with Ross Harding, who had
furnished me Jason Simpson's time card for Sunday, June 12, 1994.
That is just what I had hoped to have happen because of the release of
the book.

I was alone that morning and could see from my window outside
toward my koi pond. There they were, all five of them swimming
around like they had no cares in the world. They were waiting for me
to feed them. First I was going to check my computer for any messages: I had seven. I scrolled down eliminating four until I reached
one that said, "Urgent. Please call me." I looked at the number. It was
from California. I looked at my watch: it was 7 AM here in Dallas,
which made it 5 AM in L.A. Hell, the person said *Urgent*. I picked up
the phone and called. A voice machine came on, "This is Brian
Douglas, please leave your name and number."

I started to leave my number when a groggy voice said, "Don't hang
up." Next he said, "Mr. Dear."

"Yes."

"My name is Brian Douglas. I am sure you know that by now."

"What can I do for you, Mr. Douglas?"

"Sir, it's not what you can do for me—it's what I can do for you. I have something that I think you need in your investigation into the murders of Nicole Simpson and Ron Goldman."

My heart stopped for a second. Could I be that lucky a second time? "What is it that is so important?"

"Let me tell you what I do for a living. First, my full-time job is in computer programming. My part-time job is collecting items belonging to important people like movie stars. I buy these collectibles, some I save and some I sell. I read the article in the L.A. paper about your investigation and went out and bought your book. Mr. Dear, Jason Simpson had put a box containing his personal possessions into the Public Storage Facility located on Burchard Avenue. When he failed to pay the storage unit fee his unit contents were put up for sale. I have those items. Are you interested?"

"How do I know they belong to Jason Simpson?"

"I have three of his diaries."

No way, I first thought, *I can't be that lucky.*

"One of the diaries says, 'I am tired of playing Dr. Jekyll/Mr. Hyde.' Another excerpt says, 'It is the year of the knife for me. It cuts away my problems.'"

That sounded like Jason. "What else do you have?" I asked.

"O. J.'s jacket from college, the jacket Jason was wearing when O. J. was found not guilty, and numerous color photographs of Jason, O. J., Nicole, Justin and Sydney plus friends. There might be sixty or seventy pictures. There is a card to Jason from his mother, Marguerite, saying 'I forgive you,' a box containing what I think might be Jason's dog's ashes, a menu showing Jason as a chef and a picture of Jason, O. J. and family with President Ford at the White House. There's also an envelope from the Superior Court of California addressed to Carl Jones and," he paused dramatically, "a knife, which is in a leather sheath."

What Brian was saying took my breath away. Everything that I had hoped for was being handed to me. I was right; this was going to be a great day.

"Please fax me a printout of the two excerpts from the diaries, the one saying 'I'm tired of playing Dr. Jekyll/Mr. Hyde' and the page saying 'It's the year of knife, it cuts away my problems.' I'll have my handwriting expert examine the two pages. If he determines they were written by Jason Simpson then I'm definitely interested."

"I'll send them in a few minutes."

With great anxiety I sat at the fax machine. Ten minutes later the two sheets arrived. I looked at them. It looked like Jason's penmanship to me, but my associate Don Lehew would know for sure. Don had examined the note I found in the trash in which Jason said he was three people.

I dialed Don's number. "Don—wake up."

"Why are you calling me this early?" he asked. I told him what I had received.

"All right, bring them over to my office."

"I'll be there in an hour."

An hour later, Don examined the two papers under a microscope. "These were written by Jason," he said.

I couldn't comprehend how fortunate I was. Now the most important thing was to call this Brian Douglas, and see what he wanted for the items, if in fact they were for sale. I called from Don's office. As I did, I recorded my conversation with Brian Douglas. It was legal to do so in Texas, but not in California.

"The items are for sale," Brian told me.

We arranged to meet at the Westin Hotel adjacent to the LAX airport at 12 noon in the lobby the following Saturday

"How will I recognize you?" I asked.

"I am black, tall, stocky and will probably be the only one carrying a box."

"You want to know what I look like?"

"Already do. I pulled you up on the Internet."

I told Brian I'd have someone with me, and when I put down the phone I immediately called Sidney Kirkpatrick and arranged for him to join us at the hotel on Saturday. I had no idea how much Brian

Douglas would want for all these items, but if they were what he had described, I would obtain the money somehow. I had come too far, had spent a lot of money, not counting my time, and wanted to bring this case to closure.

I arrived on Friday and checked into the Westin Hotel. I called Sidney and we met for dinner. We were excited to say the least and I continued to wish it was already Saturday. I went to bed but couldn't sleep. I had brought $5,000 in cash hoping that would be enough. The next morning, Saturday, Sidney and I met in the lobby at 11:00 AM and there both of us sat, not saying a word. When 12:10 came, no Brian Douglas. Then Sidney said, "I think that's him." I turned. There he was, carrying a box just like he said. Brian entered the lobby and walked directly over to me. "Mr. Dear, I'm Brian Douglas."

"It's nice to meet you. This is Sidney Kirkpatrick."

With Brian carrying the box, we took the elevator up to my floor, exited, and walked down the hallway. I put the card into the lock of my room and went inside.

"May I look at what you brought?" I asked him.

"Sure."

Brian sat the box down on the floor. I started going through it. It included:

1. A jacket belonging to O. J. from college
2. Sports coat worn by Jason when the verdict was read and Jason appeared on national TV
3. A box containing Jason's dog's ashes
4. A box containing numerous color photographs
   I started to flip through them and suddenly one of them caught my eye. It was Jason Simpson lying in his unmade bed with his dog beside him. What had caught my eye was that Jason Simpson was wearing the same type of dark knit cap or what is also called a navy watch cap, similar to the one found at the crime scene. The closer I looked, the more it appeared to be the same cap. The picture was dated March, 1993, a year

before the murders. Other pictures showed Jason wearing the same knit cap, but then in July, just after the murders, Jason started wearing a similar knit cap but now it was gray. I dropped the picture on the floor with the others. I continued looking at the other pictures. There were numerous ones of Jason, O. J., Nicole, Justin, and Sydney. Some with O. J. skiing. Yes, with a cap, but with a golfer's cap, not a watch cap.

5. A card addressed to Jason from his mother Marguerite saying, "Jason, I forgive you."

6. An envelope from the Superior Court of California addressed to Carl Jones. This was the attorney O. J. had hired the day after the murders to represent Jason. I opened the already opened envelope and took out the letter. It was a search warrant from District Attorney Christopher Darden for Jason Simpson's medical records. Why? Christopher Darden had always said that Jason had an airtight alibi that night and was cleared. I hoped to ask Christopher Darden one day as I placed the letter back into the envelope.

7. Suddenly, there at the bottom of the box, was a knife. I picked up the knife, which was in a black leather sheath and looked at it closely.

   There were initials scratched on to the leather sheath, JS. I pulled the knife out of the sheath and began to examine it, when Brian Douglas said, "My girlfriend was concerned that maybe this was the knife that killed Nicole and Mr. Goldman." I began to wonder the same thing. Sidney reached over and took the knife and sheath. The look in his eyes said it all. I went back to the box.

8. There were two menus showing Jason Simpson as the chef.

9. There was a Christmas gift to Jason from Nicole and O. J.: a book on cooking.

10. There were several other items in the box, but nothing like what I had seen so far. It was like striking gold. How much more could there be?

11. To my surprise there was one more important piece of evidence in the box, the death certificate of Aaren LaShone Simpson, Jason's 23-month-old sister who he was supposed to be watching at the time of her death, when she allegedly drowned in the swimming pool.

I asked Brian how much he wanted for all the items. Prior to my arrival, I had checked and found that Brian was behind on some bills. I began to negotiate and when Brian left my room, the contents of the box stayed with me. My work was just beginning. Over the next four years, the items played an important part in my continued investigation into the murders of Nicole Simpson and Ron Goldman.

Brian Douglas and I have stayed in touch ever since. I consider him a friend but will always wonder whether Brian has kept a crucial piece of evidence. What is that crucial piece of evidence? It is the fourth diary, the one for 1994?

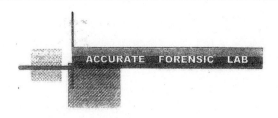

OCTOBER 08, 2003

MR. WILLIAM C. DEAR
3883 TURTLE CREEK BLVD. #2103
DALLAS, TX 75219

MR. DEAR:

IN LINE WITH YOUR REQUEST, I HAVE COMPARED AND CONTRASTED THE *DIARY SHEET* AKA QD-1 THAT BEGINS WITH "I DO NOT WANT TO PLAY JEKYL AND HYDE" TO THE KNOWN HANDWRITING OF JASON SIMPSON.

CONCLUSIONS:

1. THERE IS NO DOUBT THAT QD-1 MATCHES THE KNOWN HANDWRITING OF JASON SIMPSON.
2. JASON SIMPSON WROTE QD-1.

IF I CAN BE OF ANY FURTHER ASSISTANCE, PLEASE LET ME KNOW.

RESPECTFULLY,

Don Lehew

DON LEHEW

3767 FOREST LANE, #124-131 ♦ DALLAS, TX 75244
Phone / Fax (972) 733-9630 ♦ (800) 887-3788

ASSIGNMENT

I, the undersigned, Brian S. Douglas of 15507 Normandie Avenue #141, Gardena, California 90247, assign ownership of the documents and pictures and any other personal articles regarding Jason Simpson to William C. Dear of 3883 Turtle Creek Blvd., Suite 2103, Dallas, Texas 75219.

In consideration thereof, I acknowledge receipt of $ 1,500 United States Dollars paid by William C. Dear.

I warrant with regard to the property assigned herein that:

1: I am the legal owner;
2: I will defend the title against any and all claims and demands of all persons.
3: I will take all further steps necessary to effectively transfer ownership.
4: It is free from all liens and encumbrances.

I expressly disclaim all other warranties, whether expressed or implied, including but not limited to, any implied warranty of merchantability or fitness for a particular purpose. Further, I disclaim any warranty as to the condition of the property. William C. Dear has been given the opportunity to inspect the property or to have it inspected and has accepted the property in its condition.

I do assume, or authorize any other person to assume on my behalf, any liability in connection with the property. The disclaimer of warranties does not, in any way, affect the terms of any applicable warranties from the manufacturer of the property.

It is agreed that this assignment shall enure to the benefit of an be binding upon the parties to this assignment, their heirs, executors, administrators, successors and assigns, respectively.

This Agreement will be construed in accordance with and governed by the laws of the State of California.

In Witness whereof, the parties hereto have executed this Assignment on this 11 day of October, 2003.

_____
WITNESS

_____
WITNESS

_____
Brian S. Douglas

_____
William C. Dear

360

38

JASON SIMPSON DIARIES

WHEN WE MET BRIAN Douglas and acquired Jason Simpson's personal diaries for the years 1991 to 1993, along with the rest of the items that Jason had stored at Pacific Storage, I took the time to read them over and over. It was the voice of a young man crying out for help.

These were Jason's emotions and thoughts. It bothered me to read them but I had no choice. The diaries brought forth what I had uncovered years prior. I had determined that Jason was a Dr. Jekyll/Mr. Hyde type personality. In his diaries, he confirmed not only this—using those very same names, Dr. Jekyll and Mr. Hyde, to refer to himself—but my worst fears as well.

Jason describes his meetings with doctors and psychologists. His problems with his dad. Wanting so much to have his dad close. The demons inside his head. The jealousy over his girlfriends. His rage. His job. His use of alcohol and drugs. Even the part where Jason said, "It's the year of the knife for me, it cuts away my problems."

After reading these diaries multiple times, I could feel the danger of his emotions that came forth indicating his instability and his need for serious professional care before it was too late.

Maybe it was too late now. The last diary was written about a year before the murders of Nicole Brown Simpson and Ronald Goldman.

O. J. IS INNOCENT

Though it's not feasible, I wish I could print in this book all three of the diaries and let you decide for yourself about Jason Simpson and his possible involvement in the murders.

With all that I have read and reread in Jason Lamar Simpson's diaries, it concerns me greatly and strengthens my belief that the Los Angeles Police Department overlooked a major suspect.

Even some of Jason's former roommates at the Army and Navy Academy emailed me describing Jason as if they had already read these diaries, saying they felt that Jason—they called him J. J.—should have been considered a suspect. When you finish this book, I think you too will consider the fact that a major suspect has been overlooked.

39

THE POSSIBLE MURDER WEAPON:
THE KNIFE

I WAS SITTING IN MY office looking at the metal box containing the knife found in the bottom of the box that Jason Simpson had stored in the locker at Public Storage. It was 10 AM and I was due to leave for Los Angeles in about four hours. I wanted to take the knife with me and find someone other than the two men I had talked with at the Dallas Knife Show the previous Sunday. Both of the men had described the knife as a replica of a Gerber Mark I. Richard Eubanks and his brother Ron had said this was an older knife and had been purchased in the neighborhood of $40 to $50. I had taken the knife with me for them to look at, but I didn't tell them why, other than I was an investigator and was looking at this weapon as possibly being used in a double murder.

Ron Eubanks spoke up and said, "That is exactly what this weapon was originally designed for. Four short words can identify its primary purpose: To Cut and Kill."

"Would you mind looking at this knife closely? The cutting sides seem to be dull," I asked.

"Don't let that fool you," said Ron. "This knife has been made razor sharp on more than one occasion." He pointed down to each side of the knife. "This is a double-bladed knife.

"When you say double-bladed, Ron, if it was used to kill someone and was inserted into the flesh of an individual, could it leave you with the impression that the knife wounds might have been inflicted by more than one weapon?"

"Sure, this particular weapon, the way it was sharpened, would in fact leave two different marks upon entry. Remember, when the knife is sharpened there is no way each side would be identical."

I asked them to take a look at the top of the knife.

"Someone has removed the screw-on handle or cap and poured wax inside, leaving the jagged top open," said Richard. "It could have been removed for several reasons—so that he or she could use the knife from either the blade or use it to strike someone in a downward motion."

"That's what I'm interested in. Let me show you a picture of the scalp of the deceased." Without telling them who it was, I removed the color photograph and handed it to them to look at. "Could the top of this weapon have caused the abrasion or cutting of the scalp if it had been brought down on the top of the deceased's head?"

"Certainly," said Ron. "Just looking at your picture and not having the dimensions of the injury, it appears that the top of this knife may have inflicted the wound on the scalp of this woman. You might have to have whoever did the autopsy compare your knife to the wounds if you haven't already done so."

About this same time, two other men from another booth came over. "Mind if I look at the knife?" I handed the knife to a man about six foot three, stocky, with a beard. "I happened to look over and thought at first it was an older knife. A Gerber Mark I. Now, in looking at it closely, I'm sure it's a replica. The reason it caught my eye is that I know a Gerber rep who retired after thirty years and opened a business with his son in a suburb of Los Angeles—Irvine, California, I think."

"Do you by chance know his name?"

"Wait a minute, I think I've got his card." The man they called Steve left, entered his booth, took out a card, and came back over and said, "I'll bet Max Kragten could help you. He was the best in the business. He knows about every Gerber made."

THE POSSIBLE MURDER WEAPON: THE KNIFE

Next stop was Dallas–Ft. Worth airport and my trip to Los Angeles. I had added one more stop while there, Max Kragten.

I arrived in Los Angeles that afternoon and decided to stay in Irvine, which just happened to be only a mile from where Max Kragten and his son had their knife shop. I had made arrangements to again take the knife and its sheath back to Los Angeles. This time I was going to have a Gerber expert, hopefully, look at what I and others at this point considered to be a possible murder weapon.

I had only been checked into the Marriott Hotel for about an hour when I looked at my watch and found that it was only 4:10 PM. My next appointment wasn't until eight that night. More than enough time for me to see if I could make contact with Max Kragten.

I opened the door to my rental car, laid the metal case containing the knife on the passenger seat, and drove to the mall. I pulled up, parked the car, picked up the metal case, and started walking in the direction of the door leading into the mall. The marquee listed Mr. Kragten on the 2nd floor. I hoped that some security guard would not stop me from carrying the metal case. That's all I needed was to lose the knife.

The knife shop was just off the escalator. It was small but from the outside appeared to be well-stocked in all kinds of knives. I walked inside and saw no one. Then a voice with a German accent said, "May I help you?"

"Yes sir, my name is Bill Dear. I'm looking for Max Kragten."

"I am Max Kragten."

"Some friends of yours at a knife show in Dallas told me you might be able to help me. I have a knife I'd like you to look at." I laid the metal case on the counter, opened it up, removed the knife still inside its leather sheath, and handed it to him. Mr. Kragten removed the knife from the sheath, laid the sheath on the glass counter, and turned the knife over and over in his hand.

"What do you want to know?"

"Anything and everything."

"This is definitely not a Gerber. It's a replica of a Gerber Mark I. They don't make them anymore. It's an older version of the knife. Someone removed the metal cap and poured what I believe may be wax inside. This is a survival knife. It would have had a cap which made it hollow inside to store survival items.

"What is this knife designed for?"

"Simple; it's designed to cut and kill." I had heard the same words before and now from an expert.

"And is this a double-bladed knife?"

"Certainly sir, that's quite obvious. If you want to know something else, we couldn't sell this knife here in the store if we wanted to because it's outlawed in California. It's a double-bladed knife and it's a dangerous weapon in the wrong hands."

"Could this weapon have been made razor sharp on both sides?"

"Sure, in fact, it's obvious this particular weapon has been made razor sharp on more than one occasion, probably many times, even though it is dull right now."

"If this weapon was razor sharp and used to stab someone, would the wounds appear to be the same or would each side be different?"

"They would be different," he said. "Once you sharpen this or any double-bladed knife, the blades are no longer the same. Each side would have a different edge. If you had a medical examiner look at the wounds, it could appear the wound or wounds came from a different knife, but a good expert could tell you it was probably from a double-bladed knife."

I took out the same picture of Nicole Simpson I'd shown the guys at the Dallas knife show, and showed him the injury she had sustained to her scalp. "Look at the top of the knife, where the cap is missing, could this end of the knife have inflicted this wound?"

"Yes, I believe so, but to be exact, you need to have a medical expert examine the wound and this knife to be sure." He reached over and picked up the leather sheath, placing the knife into the sheath. "This is a boot knife. You could carry it on your belt like this, or in your boot. Like I said before, this weapon is designed to cut and kill and probably with this sheath, was carried in his or her boot or belt."

As Mr. Kragten handed me back the knife in the leather sheath, I recalled how Jason Simpson in his diaries described carrying a knife because he was a black man in Los Angeles. Suddenly, I remembered also in his diaries, "It's the year of the knife for me, it cuts away my problems."

Thanking Mr. Kragten, I found it strange he never asked me what case I was working on. I do know he said there were initials cut into the leather sheath: J. S.

Maybe Mr. Kragten knew, maybe he didn't, I thought, as I walked out of his store down the escalator, still carrying the metal case containing the knife, now back in its sheath. As I opened the door to the car I reached over and laid the metal case onto the passenger seat and drove back to my hotel.

As I looked over at the metal case, I thought, this is the possible murder weapon used to kill Nicole Simpson and Ron Goldman.

40

THE NONEXISTENT SUBPOENA

PROSECUTOR CHRISTOPHER DARDEN, ALONG with Marcia Clark, said that O. J. was their only suspect. They tried to make it appear that there was no rush to judgment and they looked at others. Now, seventeen years later, we know that is not true.

Christopher Darden appeared on several national television talk shows in December 2006 in response to the forthcoming O. J. special about O. J.'s book titled *If I Did It.* The last show on which Darden appeared made me mad. I had always had a great deal of respect for Christopher Darden, maybe not so much for Marcia Clark because I knew too much about her and her past. To me, Christopher Darden was different.

Now I feel totally different. As Christopher Darden talked about how disgraceful it was that O. J. was coming out with this so-called book confessing to the murders, knowing he could never be tried for the murders again, I could see and feel the disdain in his voice and face. As the show came to a conclusion, I heard Christopher Darden's last words, "If anyone believes O. J. Simpson did not commit the murders of Nicole Simpson and Ron Goldman, they are idiots." I took total offense to what Christopher Darden was saying. I wanted to say to Christopher Darden, face to face, Mr. Darden, "I am no idiot."

As I walked away from the television, I remembered something that very few, if any, knew. Christopher Darden had subpoenaed Jason

Simpson's medical records. Why would he have done this? And no one ever followed up with the question: Why?

When I purchased the contents of the box that Jason Simpson had placed into Public Storage, there was an envelope at the bottom of the box. On the outside of the envelope was stamped Superior Court of Los Angeles and it was dated January 10, 1995. I remember removing the contents of the envelope: a search warrant served on December 21, 1994, on Carl Jones, the attorney who had been hired by O. J. Simpson to represent his son, Jason Lamar Simpson. It had strengthened my investigation when I determined that O. J. had hired Carl Jones to represent Jason the day after the murders. Now six months later, the prosecutor, Christopher Darden, had issued a search warrant for Jason Simpson's medical records.

If Jason Simpson was not a suspect, then why would Christopher Darden issue a search warrant for Jason's medical records? What happened to the medical records obtained? Why had Jason Simpson never been interviewed by Christopher Darden, Marcia Clark or the Los Angeles Police Department investigators? With very little effort, they could have learned how critical Jason Simpson's medical records were to solving their case. The medical records showed that Jason Simpson had attempted suicide three times, had been in a mental institution, and was on probation for assault with a knife at the time of Nicole Simpson and Ron Goldman's murders. Most importantly, both Marcia Clark and Christopher Darden had said the assailant was suffering from rage. Who suffered from rage? Who checked into Cedars-Sinai Hospital just months prior to the murders, indicating to the doctors, "I am out of my Depakote medication and I'm about to rage." Didn't they say this was a rage killing by an amateur?

Their investigation should have indicated to Christopher Darden and Marcia Clark that they were overlooking a major suspect; a suspect who fit perfectly the criteria surrounding the murders of Nicole Simpson and Ron Goldman. Did they drop the ball or were they trying to cover up what they had uncovered. Someday I hope to ask Christopher Darden just that!

CRIMINAL DIVISION

The Superior Court

LOS ANGELES, CALIFORNIA 90012

CRIMINAL COURTS BUILDING
210 WEST TEMPLE STREET
(213) 974-1234

CHAMBERS OF
JOHN W. OUDERKIRK
JUDGE
(213) 974-5721

January 10, 1995

Jason Simpson
360 North Rockingham
Brentwood, CA 90049

RE: SEARCH WARRANT
      Served December 21, 1994, at 9735 Wilshire Boulevard, Suite 216, Beverly Hills

Dear Mr. Simpson:

On December 21, 1994, records relating to your medical treatment were seized pursuant to a search warrant. The records were removed from the office of Harvey D. Paley, M.D.

On January 17, 1995, at 8:30 a.m. in Department 109 of the Los Angeles Superior Court, Criminal Courts Building, 210 West Temple Street, Los Angeles, 90012, I will conduct a hearing to determine if there is any legal cause why the items should not be turned over to the Los Angeles District Attorney's Office.

If you wish to be heard, please appear at that time and place.

Very truly yours,

John W. Ouderkirk

JWO:vr

cc: Christopher Darden, Esq.
      Deputy District Attorney

      Carl Jones, Esq.

CRIMINAL DIVISION

The Superior Court
LOS ANGELES, CALIFORNIA 90012

CRIMINAL COURTS BUILDING
210 WEST TEMPLE STREET
(213) 974-1234

CHAMBERS OF
JOHN W. OUDERKIRK
JUDGE
(213) 974-5721

January 10, 1995

Carl Jones, Esq.
127 North Madison Avenue
Suite 303
Pasadena, CA 91101

RE: SEARCH WARRANT
     Served December 21, 1994, at 9735 Wilshire Boulevard, Suite 216, Beverly Hills

Dear Mr. Jones:

It is my understanding that you represent Mr. Jason Simpson. The enclosed letter relating to your client is provided for your information.

Very truly yours,

John W. Ouderkirk

JWO:vr

Enclosure

cc: Christopher Darden, Esq.
      Deputy District Attorney

      Jason Simpson

41

THE PHONE CALL

DONNA **ROLAND AND I** had left the office early on May 8, 2001. When I returned that night around 7 PM, I saw a message light blinking. I walked over and one new message appeared. I sat down in my office chair and pushed the play button.

"Hi, Ms. Roland, this is Detective Pietrantoni. I did, uhh, hand deliver the letter about the request for Jason Simpson, uhh, any records or statements regarding him, uhh, and I did hand deliver the letter. And then we did some research and Jason Simpson was never interviewed. He, well, refused to cooperate and was, uhh, represented by counsel. So he was never in fact interviewed. Umm, hopefully that will help you; if it doesn't, give me a call back. Bye."

The call had come in at 4:48 PM. Detective Vic Pietrantoni was a ranking detective for the Los Angeles Police Department. This was what I had been hoping for. Even though the Los Angeles Police Department, right after the murders of Nicole Simpson and Ron Goldman, had stated publicly on TV and in the press that Jason Simpson had been cleared by their investigation, which indicated that Jason had an airtight alibi: he was cooking in front of 200 people, Jason Simpson had never been interviewed. The Los Angeles Police Department and district attorney's office led you to believe they had in fact investigated Jason—even though I knew all along it could not be true. They were now confirming, "They never interviewed Jason Simpson."

On May, 1, 2001, I received a letter (see page 374) from the Los Angeles Police Department from Bernard C. Parks, chief of police.

How could the Los Angeles Police Department clear Jason without ever interviewing him? Overlooking Jason as a suspect was a major piece of the puzzle, lending importance to my investigation.

Jason Lamar Simpson

Transcript of a message left on office answering machine, Tuesday - May 8, 2001, 4:48PM, by Detective

Los Angeles Police Department - Detective Division

Hi Ms. Roland, this is Detective   did, ugh, hand deliver the letter about the request for Jason Simpson, ugh, any records or statements regarding him, ugh, and I did hand deliver the letter. And then we did some research and Jason Simpson was never interviewed he well, refused to cooperate and was, ugh, represented by council. So he was never in fact interviewed. Um, hopefully that will help ya, if it doesn't, give me a call back. Bye.

LOS ANGELES POLICE DEPARTMENT

BERNARD C. PARKS
Chief of Police

P. O. Box 30158
Los Angeles, Calif. 90030
Telephone: (213) 485-6473
Ref#:   2.1.1

RICHARD J. RIORDAN
Mayor

May 1, 2001

Ms. Donna M. Roland
William Dear & Associates Inc.
3883 Turtle Creek Blvd., Suite 2103
Dallas, Texas 75219

Re: **California Public Records Act Request**

Dear Ms. Roland:

This is in response to your letter dated March 21, 2001, requesting records from the Los Angeles Police Department (the "Department") pursuant to the California Public Records Act (the "Act"). Specifically, you requested information concerning the interview conducted with Jason Lamar Simpson relating to the Nicole Simpson and Ron Goldman murders.

The Department has conducted a search for records described in your request and found no records responsive to your request.

We greatly appreciate your patience and cooperation in this matter. If you have any questions regarding this matter please contact Management Analyst Wilfred F. Bernabe, Discovery Section at (213) 485-2150.

Very truly yours,

BERNARD C. PARKS
Chief of Police

C. L. CARTER, Captain
Commanding Officer
Risk Management Group

42

THE ROOMMATES

IT WAS 8:30 am on May 25, 2001, when I heard Donna Roland, my secretary, pull into the driveway of my residence. I peered out the window and saw Donna get out of her car and head toward the door that leads from my game room into our office. I was now working out of my residence more and more. The ambiance might not be what it was when I was in my downtown office, but here I felt more secure. I could think better. That is my job: think, think, think. See how a crime was planned and carried out—then solve it.

That is what I had been doing for the previous seven years on the O. J. case. It had taken over my life. I had come to the conclusion that even when the pressure was too great, by working here at my residence, I could just step outside and watch my Japanese koi fish swim back and forth under the small wooden bridge I had built just outside my office window. They seemed at peace, swimming gracefully in and out of the water lilies. Other times, I would swim twenty to thirty laps in my pool and walk back into my office refreshed. On many occasions, once relaxed, I could come up with new ideas on the murders of Nicole Simpson and Ron Goldman. But on this morning, like most mornings, I was tense and irritable. I couldn't really work. The maze of the puzzle, I knew, was right in front of me, but putting it all together seemed out of my reach. To lift my spirits I decided to get some fresh air while Donna opened the office. The sun was warm and I could see the water flowing over the waterfall in the pool. I reached for the doorknob, knowing my koi, waiting to be fed, would respond the minute I opened the door. Just as I turned the doorknob, I heard Donna's voice coming from the office that we shared. "Bill, Bill," her voice raised with a hint of excitement. I took my hand off the doorknob and headed back to the office, when I heard her say, "I think you'll want to read this." Sensing Donna's urgency, I hurried into the office. As I walked through the doorway, I could see Donna reading an email.

"What's it say?"

"Just read it, it'll make your day."

I reached for the email she had printed and sat down in my office chair. Our office used to be one of the master bedrooms that I had converted with wall-to-wall units containing specialized equipment which would have been envied by any police department, government agent, and especially, private investigator. As I leaned my elbows on my desk, I began to read. The email was from some former roommates of Jason Simpson when he had attended the Army and Navy Academy, just outside of Los Angeles, that O. J. had put him in with the hope that a structured environment might help him. I read the email three times, looked over at Donna, then read it a fourth time, but this time out loud.

I laid the email down on my desk, got up, walked through the doorway and out to the pond. It was time to indulge my fish. I sat down on the bench, pulled out the fish food, and fed the koi as I had so many times before, but this time, thinking, *even Jason Simpson's former roommates believed he should have been a major suspect.*

Subj: Jason Simpson
Date: 05/25/2001 2:58:42 PM Central Daylight Time
From: Justerik
To: Is He Guilty

Dear Sir:

I knew Jason Simpson back in his days at Army Navy.. A close friend of mine was in his class there, and I played football against Jason in the relatively small "Southern California prep-school league". I attended his graduation, partied with him, met O.J., a VERY pregnant Nicole, his mother, and the rest of the "clan".

At the time of the murders, I did not know what became of JJ. I too went on to play college football, but never heard his name mentioned in football circles again. I was surprised to hear that he had dropped out of SC, and was equally shocked to see how horrible he looked when I saw him on TV.

On the eve of his graduation from Army Navy, he had announced, much to his father's delight, that he would NOT be attending the University of Michigan as HE had planned, but rather would be following in his dad's footsteps at USC. Obviously, in hindsight, he should have gone to Michigan.

After reading your book, it seems I may have some information you were not aware of.

Upon hearing of the murders I (and everybody else I know, who knew him) immediately suspected JJ. That is not to say we didn't equally suspect OJ. OJ seemed to be the obvious suspect, because he is an egotistical SOB. But, who did Nicole know that was TRAINED in hand to hand combat, including knife fighting? Not OJ.... Jason.

Being an Angelino, and being familiar with the family on a personal level, I intently followed the local television coverage which was live almost 24 hours a day for that first week.

The day before the "slow speed chase" there were two aberrant news stories. I recall that they were reported on local KTLA Channel 5, but I believe other channels reported them as well. The first, was that police were looking for an Army style "entrenching tool" in connection with the murders. They went so far as to show an example of such a tool on the air. Immediately I started putting 2 and 2 together. Who except a person affiliated with the military or military school would own an "entrenching tool"?

Perhaps an hour later came an announcement that an unnamed member of Simpson's family, but not Simpson himself, was about to be arrested for the murders. To me that could only be one person, JJ.

The events of the next afternoon quickly cleared all of these reports out of the news, and out of peoples minds.

O. J. IS INNOCENT

I think you should see if you can find where these reports came from. Especially the talk of the "entrenching tool".

I think you should also look closer at Jason's days at Army/Navy Academy. You should question classmates about his behavior. I know there are SOME who MIGHT talk to you. From what I hear, he wasn't the model student you made him out to be, despite all of his successes there.

Having said this, in my opinion, the evidence still points to OJ being involved in at least ONE of the murders, not arriving after both were completed as you hypothesize.

Very truly yours,

Erik A. Hart, Esq.

43

ALIBI QUESTIONED

WHEN I FIRST BECAME involved in the investigation into the murders of Nicole Simpson and Ron Goldman, I had learned that O. J.'s oldest son, Jason Lamar Simpson, age twenty-four, had been given an airtight alibi—that he was cooking in front of 200 people on the night of the murders and, according to the Los Angeles Police Department, was cleared as a suspect.

After visiting Jackson's Restaurant personally and discovering it could not hold 200 people, learning that the restaurant had closed early that Sunday, and then receiving Jason's timecard from Ross Harding, one of the owners of Jackson's Restaurant, I became concerned how Jason could have been given this airtight alibi.

I discussed this with Ross Harding and told him I knew that Jason had been given this alibi by Alan Ladd Jackson, the operating partner at Jackson's. Mr. Harding informed me that Alan Jackson was with him and his wife that night and could not have been in a position to give Jason his alibi. And Ross Harding believed that Jason should have been a major suspect originally. I knew I needed to talk with Alan Jackson. He had refused over and over. Now Ross Harding took over and set up a phone interview between Alan Jackson and me.

On Saturday, April 21, 2001, I finally was able to talk to Mr. Jackson by phone. You could tell right from my hello that Mr. Jackson did not want to talk to me but was being pressured to do so. "Mr. Jackson, how would you describe Jason Simpson?"

"Very docile, nonaggressive and trustworthy," he replied.

This description was totally different than others had described Jason.

"How well did you know Jason Simpson?"

"I did not know Jason on a personal basis."

"Do you know how many people were at your restaurant on June 12, 1994?"

"No, not many from what I have been told."

"Isn't it true that Sundays were so slow that shortly after June 12 you closed altogether on Sunday nights?"

"Yes."

"Mr. Jackson, you gave Jason Simpson an alibi that night, but from what I have learned you weren't even there that night."

"No, but I did call in several times."

"When you called in did you ask for Jason personally to make sure he was there the whole night?"

"No."

"Isn't it true that the grill shuts down with the last customer before everyone else prepares to leave?"

"Yes."

"In fact, aren't you the usual chef and Jason just the prep chef?"

"Yes, but I let Jason be the chef on Sundays so I could take off occasionally."

"Did Jason have access to the restaurant premises?"

"Yes."

"Weren't you trying to protect Jason the next day when O. J. was suspected of killing Nicole Simpson and Ron Goldman?"

He didn't answer.

"Did you know that Jason Simpson left early the night of June 12, 1994?"

"I don't know."

"Sir, I do, your own employees have said Jason Simpson left early along with his girlfriend, Jennifer Green. If that is the case, then why did you give Jason Simpson his alibi that he was cooking in front of 200 people and did not leave the restaurant until after 10:30 PM?"

No answer.

Mr. Jackson said, "I've nothing more to say."

"Thank you for your time, Mr. Jackson." As the dial tone sounded in the phone, I knew Mr. Jackson had not even been at the restaurant on the night of June 12. Not being there, he could not have truthfully given Jason his much needed airtight alibi.

An interesting fact is that Alan Ladd Jackson was the grandson of the famous actor Alan Ladd. Mr. Jackson's father was Los Angeles talk-show host Michael Jackson.

Maybe Mr. Jackson, with good intentions, was trying to protect Jason because he knew how it felt to be the offspring of a famous father. Jason Simpson's alibi, verified by the Los Angeles Police Department, had not vanished. Why? Because there had been one, and only one, suspect: O. J. Simpson.

44

THE BLOODY SOCKS

DR. FREDERIC RIEDERS FOUNDED National Medical Services Lab in Willow Grove, Pennsylvania, in 1970, and, in 1994, he established the nonprofit Renaissance Foundation with the mission to cultivate and promote forensic science for future generations. Dr. Rieders held a master of science degree, and he and his foundation were used for lab work by the FBI and other law enforcement agencies around the world. Dr. Rieders, along with his son, Dr. Michael Rieders, trained and educated students majoring in forensic science.

I had first met Dr. Rieders's son, Dr. Michael Rieders, at the Markle Symposium headed up by Dr. Henry Lee, where I was a guest speaker on the topic of Nicole Simpson's and Ron Goldman's murders. When the symposium was over, I asked Dr. Michael Rieders if it was possible for me to meet with his father. He felt it would be.

On May 27, 2005, I flew to Pennsylvania and met with Dr. Rieders at his office and laboratory in Willow Grove.

Dr. Rieders was originally contacted by the prosecutors from the district attorney's office in Los Angeles to examine the two black socks found at the foot of O. J. Simpson's bed. Dr. Rieders said that, for whatever reason, they had changed their minds and turned the two socks over to the FBI. Dr. Rieders was asked to reexamine the two socks by the defense team and Dr. Henry Lee and Dr. Michael Baden, who were working on the case.

Dr. Rieders said he examined both socks and in turn testified at the trial. I took an immediate liking to Dr. Rieders; he was so professional and cared about his work and his reputation. He was held in the highest esteem by his peers. Dr. Rieders showed me upstairs and through his extensive laboratory where he works with his students and on cases submitted by agencies, including the FBI. After the tour, we sat down in his office. Dr. Rieders had donned his white lab jacket as we entered the lab. He still had it on as we sat down to talk. "Mr. Dear, I was anxious to meet you. I've been following your work on this case and my son told me you wanted to talk to me."

"Yes, sir, I need to hear from you just what you did concerning the two socks that were found at the foot of O. J.'s bed."

"Mr. Dear, I'm sure you have a number of questions but I can only address my answers to the two black socks."

"Yes, sir, that's fine."

"I did examine the two black socks. First, Mr. Dear, you must understand, I was originally contacted by the prosecution team, but for some reason they used the FBI instead. I understand. A number of times before the FBI had contacted me, but not in this case, to make the laboratory analysis."

"And what were your findings?"

"The blood found on the socks came from a vial of blood and not from contact with the crime scene or a bleeding person."

"So, Dr. Rieders, is it your expert conclusion that the blood on the two socks was placed on the socks by a person or persons unknown using a vial of blood?"

"Yes, sir, that's what I am saying." Dr. Rieders swung his desk chair around and toward me. He pulled up his pant leg showing me his dark socks. "You see, the blood on the socks went from side to side. As a result, there could not have been any feet inside the socks when the blood made contact with the two socks.

"In addition, the blood on the two socks I examined came from a vial of blood containing EDTA. EDTA is used when blood is drawn from an individual into a tube of blood, capped, and shaken. The EDTA mixes with the blood to preserve it for examination and analysis. In the case of the two socks, the blood found on the socks definitely had come from a vial of blood containing EDTA."

"Is it possible that the blood found on the two socks came from a vial of blood that had been drawn from O. J. Simpson at the Los Angeles jail at the request of Detective Vannatter, and mixed with the vial of blood taken during the autopsy of Nicole Simpson or blood found at the crime scene?"

"The one thing I can say as a scientist is that the blood on the socks came from a vial of blood that contained EDTA and not blood dripping from a person. I can also say that there were no feet in the two black socks found at the residence of O. J. Simpson when the blood was applied.

"These are the facts. I cannot testify to anything else since I was only involved in the examination and analysis of the two socks."

I had Phil Smith film the interview with Dr. Rieders. Fortunately for me I did so, as Dr. Rieders passed away shortly thereafter. His foundation, the Renaissance Foundation, run by his son, Dr. Michael Rieders, continues to this day.

45

O. J. FAILS POLYGRAPH TEST

ADAMANT THAT HE DID not commit the murders, O. J. asked Shapiro and his close friend and attorney Skip Taft if he could take a polygraph test. Shapiro agreed but only through a private company, so if the results were not favorable, no one would know the results. Shapiro called Edward Gelb's office and scheduled the test for the next day, Tuesday, June 14.

O. J.'s close friend Robert Kardashian, whom he had been staying with, took O. J. to Gelb's office on Wilshire Boulevard. When they arrived, Shapiro was told that Mr. Gelb was out of town but his associate, Dennis Nellany, would perform the test. Kardashian, Shapiro, and Skip Taft waited as the test was given. When the door opened and O. J. walked out, everyone knew the results were not good.

Shapiro asked Nellany, what were the results? O. J. failed with a minus 22. O. J. could not have gotten a worse score. "I want to take the test again. I didn't do it. I did not kill Nicole." As they all left, O. J. appeared to be shaken and depressed. "I don't know why I failed. I didn't do it." Kardashian drove O. J. back to his house. O. J. went up into the room he was staying in.

It was quite some time into my investigation when I learned of the test and O. J.'s score. I asked to meet with some of my friends who are considered the top in their field as polygraph examiners. Most of them agreed with the results. It doesn't surprise me that O. J. failed. If he was protecting someone, as I believe, and if O. J. feels responsible for the murders, then we can all see how he failed and received such a high score. Another factor: if O. J. was at the scene and saw the bodies, that too could be a factor. I also told them, from what I had learned, and O. J. had said to others, particularly in front of Jason, "I wish that bitch was dead." That, too, is a factor.

O. J. failing the polygraph test did not really concern me. It was not used in court, thankfully, and only a few people knew of the outcome. It was thirteen years later, I realized that O. J. did not commit the murders but failed the test because he had been at the scene and had withheld crucial evidence.

Only time will tell if I am right.

46

DR. HENRY LEE

WITH ALL OF THE new evidence, I wanted to meet with Dr. Henry Lee. I knew he was a man who just told it like it was. To me, he was an important player. Arrangements were made for me to meet with Dr. Lee during his stopover in Dallas on February 17, 2004. I had sent him a detailed PowerPoint presentation before his arrival. After our meeting at the Adam's Mark Hotel, I was to take Dr. Lee to DFW Airport to catch his return flight.

The following was transcribed in detail:

> Q: "Dr. Lee, you know who I am ("Sure.") so there is no need to go into that. I would like to ask you some questions concerning what part you played in the investigation into the murders of Nicole Simpson and Ron Goldman and the fact that you were on the defense's side, I guess at that particular time to present what you saw ("Sure."). When you went to the crime scene that particular day, was it a day or two after the murders? ("Yes.") and did you have firsthand visual, being there and walking the walkway and looking at all the area yourself?"
>
> A: "Yes, we got the permission from LAPD through Bob Shapiro, Robert Shapiro. Dr. Bob and I went there, of course

they still have the crime scene tape around it but we did get permission. But one condition, we have to finish, I forget exactly how many minutes, they give us time limitation. Also, second, we cannot use any chemical enhancements . . . which we agreed. So we did visit the scene, both Rockingham and Bundy scene."

Q: "Did you come in from the rear or from the front?"

A: "We came in through the rear. The rear gate was locked but we were able to climb over the fence to look at it."

Q: "OK, now once you were able to walk through the gate and re-create in your mind what may have occurred that day, and you approached the front door of Nicole Simpson's, in your mind, knowing Los Angeles in the way I am sure you do now, is there any doubt in your mind that Nicole Simpson would not have opened that door to a stranger?"

A: "Well, that is not just Los Angeles, that in other places like New York; we have locks on our apartment and do not open the door for anyone."

Q: "Even in Dallas ("Sure."). So if, when you read the reports, did it indicate that the front door of Nicole's was unlocked?"

A: "I do not remember exactly. As a forensic scientist, my focus is physical evidence. So basically the purpose of examining the crime scene is to look at the exact setting, to see any other additional physical evidence and try to find out what happened, how it happened, what the sequence was for future reconstruction. So, the investigative report I read some, but I did not pay much attention. Of course we, everyone has questions. And the first officer that gets there, what was his observation? That is the most important person. But what sticks in my mind is that the first officer says that he saw a dish of melting ice cream. That is an issue that was never resolved. The dish of melting ice cream. That should give us a lot of information but never, anybody can describe a dish or two dishes and how many spoons and . . . That can actually tell us the . . ."

Q: "Was there water in the bathtub?"

A: "Yea, apparently there was water in the bathtub and candles are on it, of course, the temperature of the water that also can tell us a lot about the scene. Look at the candle wax, that is additional information. So it is kind of interesting crime scene. It is a lesson for, I hope for all the law enforcement to learn how to investigate a case."

Q: "Did you find out whether or not if there was residue in the water in the bathtub indicating that someone may or may not have been in that bathtub?"

A: "We never see the bathtub. We never really had the opportunity because apparently it is all gone."

Q: "They never took any pictures of it?"

A: "No, no picture, no photograph, no detail description of it."

Q: "All right, now once you are outside and you are looking at the crime scene where Ron Goldman and Nicole Simpson's bodies were found, you have been described as saying that there was an enormous amount of blood ("Yes."). The blood that was found, would it have been very difficult not to have stepped in it in some way or fashion by the assailant or a second party?"

A: "Exactly, now this is a very small confined place. It is not like they show in the movies or the television screen and the walkway and this little cove area is pretty confined and you cannot avoid stepping in the blood."

Q: "All right, now you also have been described as saying in your professional opinion there were two sets of prints ("Yes."). Do you still feel this way today? This being where we are, in February of 2004, ten years, this June 12th, later?"

A: "Yes, I have documentation of the scene; in fact I have two sets of bloody print. Not only two sets prints, bloody prints ("Alright."). Of course, if that day we used chemical enhancement, this issue can be long gone. We would probably know exactly how the people walk. Often we use . . . to enhance the

389

bloody shoe print. Many cases solved, just recently we solve another case and the shoe print on the victim's body."

Q: "Let us go to Nicole Simpson's body that we described and discussed earlier. You showed me on the photographs of Nicole Simpson's body some marks, I believe on her arm ("arm, upper arm") and a mark indicated on the top of her back ("Yeah."). Do you know whether or not any prints were attempted to be taken from that?"

A: "On her arm, as clear as yours, three finger marks. And that finger mark can be enhanced, unfortunately they never collected that. On her back are seven vertical, low velocity blood drops, vertical drops."

Q: "That means someone was leaning over the body?"

A: "Yes, and they never collected no . . . being done. When the body was put in a body bag, probably already contaminated and smeared up and once got to the autopsy room they washed the whole body, never nobody pay attention on that."

Q: "You noticed, and I also saw when you testified, the mark on the top of her head. My understanding was that there was also bruising on the right side of her face, is that correct? ("Yes.") If that is correct then, Doctor, would it be possible that Nicole Simpson was the first victim, not killed, but struck on the top of the head rendering her unconscious, falling and her head hitting the Spanish tile, she is unconscious and blood begins to flow which would cause the bruising effect. Is that possible?"

A: "It is a possibility, she probably still had some consciousness because her, she had a defense posture if you look at her head clearly, she have some cut. Nicole, if I remember correctly, received seven different knife wounds. Her throat was cut, you cut someone's throat you have cut the artery, her artery, the blood go gushing out. Whoever commits the crime should be covered with blood. If you say the first . . . already cut the throat I mean you do not have additional cut on the arm and other part of the body. So that indicative, she was not killed right away."

Q: "All right, if that is the case then could it be also that there was only one assailant if she had been rendered unconscious. And let us say that Ron Goldman, who was being expected by her to bring over her glasses and came upon what was happening, and all of a sudden, she was struck, rendering her unconscious, then a fight began between the assailant and Ron Goldman, then could there also be the possibility that there was one assailant and one knife?"

A: "Well, this is a question we wish we could have the answer. It could be one assailant or it could be also two assailants because we did see two types of bloody shoe prints. Dr. Goldman, the first medical examiner, indicates it could be two types of weapons. This is an interesting observation and I think somebody should re-interview him, he never testified in the trial. ("I noticed that.") So whether or not one assailant and somebody were at the scene with another person or because his finger marks on her arm whether or not was someone hurting her or not, we do not know.

"Those are types of things this case; unfortunately, we did not get all the records to study that in detail. I only look at pieces of the information, the physical evidence, and the crime scene photo. Unfortunately this case no tape, no videotapes. Ordinarily this homicide, especially double homicide, you should tape it. That will give us a much clearer, three-dimensional projection of the case. Photographs are a two-dimensional representation so this case, because incomplete documentation of the scene and also select collection of the physical evidence, that makes the case much more difficult to find out exactly what had happened."

Q: "Did you actually get to visit and look at both of the bodies of Nicole Simpson and Ron Goldman at the morgue?"

A: "Dr. Bob did that and he gave me a description of it. I did not see the body directly but I do have a set of photographs that they provided me."

Q: "Would you describe this as a rage killing?"

A: "Yes, based on my experience, I consider this as a rage killing. Also I consider this a disorganized type of killing."

Q: "By a professional or an amateur?"

A: "By more likely an amateur. With knife and Ron Goldman twenty-seven stab wounds . . . defense all over the place, we find a fresh cut on his shoes and all those indicative of a fierce fight in that little area."

Q: "I notice that the knuckles on Ron Goldman were badly bruised so, in my mind, based on what you have seen both at the crime scene and the photographs, do you believe that the assailant should have had some marks or bruises on him?"

A: "Yea, more likely that we think the assailant should have some injuries or bruises or marks or scratches."

Q: "I am going to ask you a question, but I want to come right back to the crime scene. You had an occasion, within days, to visit with O. J. Simpson. ("Yes.") Did you have an occasion to examine the body of O. J. Simpson? ("Yes, I did.") Did you find any marks indicative of a fight or bruises that had been sustained from a fight on the body of O. J. Simpson?"

A: "I did not see anything except on his finger we noticed three small cuts. Initially prosecution said only one cut. We did document during the trial that was used as prosecution evidence."

Q: "The cut on his finger that the prosecution has made so much about, in your opinion was it by broken glass, a knife, what is your opinion on that?"

A: "My opinion is inconsistent with a knife."

Q: "So then if it is inconsistent with a knife and you found no other marks on O. J. Simpson, is it very difficult for you to say, if there were marks on Ron Goldman, bad bruises on him, a tremendous struggle fighting for his life, then there should have been more than ample marks?"

A: "Yes, you know in theory . . . logic you look at his case right away you see some problem. The theory says only one man, O. J. Simpson. First . . . Second, this fierce fight and struggle with a small knife because that is the weapon, if you have a gun, that is a different story. It is a small knife, hand-to-hand combat. Ron Goldman is a very strong young man and she also pretty strong, too. We can see a fierce fight and . . . has no injuries, that the one thing we question and we examined O. J. Simpson's body inch by inch, Dr. Bob and me. We document that, we examine his lip and usually, if you landed a punch on your mouth, you usually see bruises on soft tissue but we did not see any."

Q: "Ron Shipp said the same thing to me—that he had an occasion to be up in the room with him and he found no marks on him other than what you have just described on his left hand. Now if this was a rage killing by an amateur and now we found bruises on Nicole and we see all the defensive cuts on Ron Goldman, the mark on his tennis shoe. I also have seen where they described a stiletto or a Swiss Army knife. Let us first go with the Swiss Army knife and then the stiletto. Do you believe that either one of those were possible murder weapon?"

A: "The knife I examined, I made a conclusion, and it is not the knife. I did not find any blood on it. That is the knife . . . mystery envelope . . ."

Q: "The mark that is on Ron Goldman's tennis shoes and the words heard by so-called witness Robert Heidstra, of "Hey, Hey, Hey" is indicative of a posture of karate where you pivot, you do not have a weapon, and you advance forward to try to break the assailant's leg or knee or knock the weapon out of his possession. With the words of "Hey, Hey, Hey" that meant that Ron Goldman probably had no weapon to defend himself, is that correct? ("That is possible.") Now if he put up that kind of struggle, what kind of knife would you feel would be the type of knife that could have been used to have committed these murders or the attack?"

A: "Well, based on medical examiner's results it is a sharp knife and more likely a single blade but they cannot rule out that it could be a double blade. Because this question probably more suitable to ask . . . or Dr. Goldman directly examined the body have a firsthand knowledge."

Q: "It also could be a chef's knife, could it not?"

A: "It could be, we see a lot of, in my past, see some knife injury or a chef's knife that could be."

Q: "Chef's knives are razor sharp, used to cut meat, everything else?"

A: "Sure because the . . . is really nasty cut and deep and sharp, of course, we see a lot of other marking and laceration stabbings, so it is a combination type of injury."

Q: "It would be very difficult with a Swiss Army knife, wouldn't it?"

A: "A Swiss Army knife, we rule that out a long time ago. It is impossible to be a Swiss Army knife."

Q: "So we have ruled out the stiletto, we have ruled out the Swiss Army knife. Now let us go to the blood that was found at the crime scene where the fight was. The prosecution said that it was Bruno Magli shoes. Did you find any indication of a Bruno Magli type sole there at the crime scene in the photographs that you had occasion to look at?"

A: "Yes, also the actual scene we did see Bruno Magli kind of sole imprint."

Q: "Was it in the blood or could you determine because of the large amount of blood at the crime scene if that shoe was the shoe used in the scuffle between Ron Goldman and the assailant?"

A: "Uh, it is possible. We, of course the crime scene, by the time we visited, it is complete altered, movement of the body, the crime scene investigator assistants and us. During the trial those photographs were shown a body sheet, covered in blood so by the time you lift . . . body bag is rearranged so not much we can tell. But the original photograph we do see bloody, bloody Bruno Magli shoe print."

Q: "Did you also, is that correct, see other footprints? ("Yes.") So it just does not mean that Bruno Magli shoes and the thought that that could have been the assailant, it could have also been the other person?"

A: "Sure, it could be the assailant; it could be other individual at the scene."

Q: "Could it be possible that O. J. was at the scene after the murders, but did not commit the murders?"

A: "Well, that is a question . . . a hypothesis . . . scientist, open mind . . . instead of reaching one definite conclusion."

Q: "If the Bruno Magli shoes had been covered in blood, should not the assailant been covered in blood?"

A: "Well, first of all we have to assume that night O. J. was wearing the shoes . . . if anyone else wore those shoes . . . they should be covered in a tremendous amount of blood."

Q: "If that is the case, and O. J. was driving the Bronco, why was there not any blood on the brake or accelerator?"

A: "They found some blood . . . not enough blood . . . inconsistent with somebody who just killed two people . . . so bloody and sitting in a vehicle."

Q: "So if O. J. was the killer . . . then he did not drive the Bronco?"

A: "Well, either he did not drive the Bronco . . . prosecution theory . . . O. J. wear sweat suit . . . change clothes . . . get rid of clothes . . . then drive Bronco . . . too short of a time line and no time to change."

Q: "If O. J. had done this, he would have to plan this right down to the moment? ("Yes.") O. J. would have had to know the exact time the children came home after the recital or whether they came home at all? Were you told Sydney was having a sleepover with a friend?"

A: "I . . . witness statement . . . I did not know that fact."

Q: "It was brought out that Sydney's friend cancelled sleepover . . . O. J. at recital and would not have known that . . . Kato and O. J. having hamburger at McDonalds . . . difficult to time that, stay on schedule to commit murders?"

A: "That is the question . . . plan to kill two people . . . should not get hamburger . . . crime scene shows this was a disorganized killing."

Q: "Did you get to interview O. J.'s son, Jason?"

A: "I did not interview . . . met him . . . he is a very strong big man, not like a boy."

Q: "Did you know that he was trained in karate at the Army/Navy Academy? ("No.") The knit cap and gloves at the trial . . . did you ever see pictures of O. J. wearing the cap?"

A: "Not that I recall . . . I examined that cap . . . found foreign hairs . . . some of the hair was inconsistent with O. J. Simpson."

Q: "The fingernails . . . skin found under Nicole's nails—not O. J.'s?"

A: "I think it was inconsistent with O. J."

Q: "Skin under nails not O. J.'s . . . hair in knit cap not O. J.'s . . . Is it possible someone else was at the crime scene?"

A: "That is a possibility."

Q: "If this is a rage killing by an amateur . . . could O. J. been called at home, told what had happened, jumped in his Bronco, driven over, arrived in Bruno Magli shoes; he did not commit the murders but knows who did?"

A: "Well, anything is possible . . . have to keep my mind open, everything is possible."

Q: "So you have an open mind about what I have said? ("Yes.") If there were evidence that someone else had worn the cap, that would be of interest to you, would it not?"

A: "Of course, that is definitely something as an investigator that you should pursue."

Q: "Do you feel that this was a badly contaminated crime scene?"

A: "At the crime scene, some contamination took place, how badly, I really do not know. Uhh, Dr. Rieders . . . noticed EDTA . . . other experts agree with him . . . some others feel it is not EDTA . . . I am not a toxicologist and have to go by other people's results . . . if EDTA it came from a test tube."

Q: "The couple of drops found in the foyer of O. J.'s house, is it possible that it also contained EDTA?"

A: "I do not remember . . . cannot tell you on record."

Q: "Did you get to go upstairs to his bedroom? ("Yes.") If a man was covered in blood . . . how would you climb up a carpeted staircase without leaving blood in the foyer, the stairway or the carpet in the bedroom?"

A: "That is a good question. Police found three drops of blood in foyer . . . we found two drops . . . a total of five vertical drops . . . light carpet throughout house . . . cannot hide blood stain . . . covered inch by inch . . . impossible not to leave any blood trace."

Q: "The socks were found at the foot of the bed. O. J. is very meticulous. The blood found on the socks . . . was in an off position and not in the stretched position."

A: "Uhh, if I remember correctly . . . if you have a foot inside— how the blood got transferred from here to that side without leaving anything . . . it is kind of a very interesting issue and never resolved."

Q: "Did you find that an important part of your investigation?"

A: "Yes, that was an important part in regards to the socks . . . other issues involved in the case . . . that is why our conclusion from forensic evidence did not prove who is the killer."

Q: "Did the socks have EDTA in them?"

A: "I think some EDTA was detected."

Q: "Did you get to examine the vial of blood taken from O. J.? ("Yes.") "Did it contain EDTA in it? ("Yes."). Did you interview the jail nurse?"

A: "No, I did not interview him . . . do not interview anyone . . . just look at the scientific evidence."

Q: "Did you see the paperwork from the jail nurse regarding the blood drawn from O. J. and how much was placed in the vial?"

A: "Uh, there was conflict, he gave two statements . . . the first sheet stated that there was a full tube, about 8cc . . . only about 6.5cc accounted for."

Q: "If he took 8cc, and then there was only 6.5cc . . . we have 1.5 missing?"

A: "Yes, that is why later he gave a video interview apparently to prosecution saying now he remembers he only collect 6.5."

Q: "Suspicious a little bit. ("It is interesting.") I like the word interesting, I would probably go a little deeper than that . . . after ten years we still must consider this an unsolved murder. ("Yes.") I want the pendulum of justice to swing the right way . . . everyone has assumed O. J. is guilty. . . . Do you think O. J. is guilty?"

A: "Good question, I never make up my mind if someone is guilty or innocent. I only look at the physical evidence and present the scientific fact, let the jury make the decision . . . if I make a decision it makes it hard to be a forensic scientist . . . investigator deals with theories . . . as a forensic scientist I deal only in the facts of the evidence."

Q: "Did you find insufficient evidence to prove O. J. guilty?"

A: "Beyond a reasonable doubt, no."

Q: "If I told you that his personal psychologist, Dr. Kittay, said that he definitely did not commit this murder."

A: "Uh, that is beyond my area of expertise."

Q: "But if a large man with big hands raged and struck some-body, those marks would have inflicted a great deal of punish-ment on that individual?"

A: "Yes . . . and he himself should have some bruises or injury."

Q: "Is there anything else in this investigation . . . did you find some of the evidence I presented to you regarding who I feel is a major suspect interesting?"

A: "Well . . . you look at it from an investigative end and I look at it from a scientific end . . . you did really present a good case."

Q: "Do you think that particular suspect . . . should have been originally considered a suspect?"

A: "Yeah, what I tell . . . universal pool of suspects . . . use process of elimination . . . I never label the suspect, I just present the evidence."

Q: "Were you surprised by some of the evidence that I presented to you off camera today?"

A: "Yes."

47

DR. VINCENT J. M. DI MAIO

DR. VINCENT DIMAIO HAD been the Bexar County, San Antonio, Texas, medical examiner up until he retired in November 2006. Dr. DiMaio was known all over the world in the field of forensic science. His books *Forensic Pathology* and *Gunshot and Knife Wounds* were the bible in the medical pathology community.

I first became acquainted with Dr. DiMaio when I became part of the team selected to exhume the body of Lee Harvey Oswald, the alleged assassin of President John Kennedy. From that point on, if I had a concern in the field of pathology because of a murder case I was involved in, I would look to Dr. DiMaio for his professional opinion.

In the latter part of 2005, after spending over eleven years investigating the murders of Nicole Simpson and Ronald Goldman, I called Dr. DiMaio and asked if he would examine what we thought might be the murder weapon. He agreed. I called Phil Smith and had his team join us as I wanted the interview with Dr. DiMaio on film and for use in my book and documentary.

It was Friday afternoon when we arrived in San Antonio. As Phil and his crew unloaded the camera equipment, I walked through the glass doors leading into the Bexar County Forensic Building and showed my credentials. "Dr. DiMaio is expecting me." His secretary, Wanda, whom I have known for many years, opened the electric door and welcomed me inside.

"Dr. DiMaio is just finishing up an autopsy." Wanda took me down to the lab and I watched as Dr. DiMaio completed the autopsy.

In the meantime Phil and his crew set up in another autopsy room that had been cleared for us to use.

Ten minutes later, Dr. DiMaio joined us. I handed him the knife still in its sheath. "This knife with the metal clasp on the leather sheath can be hooked to your belt or in your boot," he said as he removed the knife from the sheath.

"Dr. DiMaio, I'm going to ask you a series of questions, just like you would respond to in a deposition. Phil Smith and Phil Thompson will be filming our entire interview. Before I start the questions, are you familiar with this type knife?"

"Yes."

"Dr. DiMaio, will you look at the leather sheath."

"Yes."

"What do you see?"

"There are two initials scratched into the leather sheath."

"What are they?"

"JS."

"Dr. DiMaio, you know I have been working on this murder case for many years."

"I do."

"I want you to know that the knife you are holding belonged to Jason Simpson, who was twenty-four at the time of the murders and is O. J. Simpson's oldest son. What I want to know is, could this weapon have been used to kill Nicole Simpson and Ronald Goldman?"

He examined the knife and turned it over and over. "Yes, this could be the murder weapon." He then picked up the autopsy pictures of Nicole Simpson, looked at the butt of the knife, then back to the wound on top of her scalp. Dr. DiMaio took out a ruler, measured the cut and put it down. "Bill, the cut on her scalp matches, from what I can determine, the butt of this knife. What you need to understand is that this particular weapon is designed for one purpose and one purpose only, that is to cut and kill."

401

I then handed Dr. DiMaio a set of chef's knives similar to the ones that Jason Simpson used as a prep chef and began my questions:

Q: "What about the chef's knife?"

A: "The problem you have with a knife like this is the blade is very flexible. If you violently cut tissue and hit bone there is a possibility the blade will bend or break. As blood got on handle, the hand would slide and would get deep cuts on the hand from handling this weapon. This is a cooking knife and that is what it is intended for."

Q: "During trial the prosecution brought forth the possibility of either a chef's or Swiss Army knife. I am now going to show you a Swiss Army knife."

A: "A Swiss Army knife or any folding knives are utility devices. Cutting cords, whittling. They are nice to have but not intended to inflict harm. You have the problem with the hand slipping up on the blade and getting severe cuts. With a knife like this the hand will tend to slide."

Q: "Ron Goldman sustained twenty-seven stab wounds. He was a karate expert and had no weapon. Could one of these knives have been used?"

A: "If you think about it, neither of these knives are not that sturdy, and plunging it in a number of times into an individual, it is not unexpected for a blade to bend or be damaged. This knife is not intended to stab people or cut people."

Q: "My major suspect is Jason. He was a chef, had a chef's bag, and had access to chef's knives. Since last time you and I visited we have uncovered this knife which was in the possession of our suspect. I would like for you to examine this knife further.

A: "This is a very interesting knife. It is illegal in many areas of the United States because it has only one purpose. And that purpose is to kill people! This knife is designed to stab and cut, not food, not cord, nor whittling, but to stab and cut people. Notice how the guard protects the hand from slipping. The blade is heavier. It is double edged so you can catch them both ways. It has a point so you can stab and you can also use the handle as a blunt object to hit somebody. So you can hit, cut, stab. And again, this knife has only one function and that is to kill people!"

Q: "Upon examining this knife, could you determine if it has previously been made razor sharp on both sides?"

A: "It's been sharpened; it is obvious it has been sharpened on both sides. You can see where part of the finish has been ground off. But that is how this knife has been designed. It is designed to have sharp edges on both sides. So it cuts cleanly when it goes into the body, when you stab into the body and you pull it out, drag it this way or the other way . . . It doesn't make any difference. You are still cutting through tissue. Again, this knife is designed to inflict serious harm . . . usually death in an individual. It is a fighting knife."

Q: "If they described two knives during autopsy, would this knife be different on one side compared to the other?"

A: "It can still be different. It is the way the knife is plunged into the body. If you plunge it straight in, then both edges should be sharp and cutting, but if you put it in at an angle so that the top goes in and you are cutting down, the side away from the cutting surface will be more blunt than the edge you are cutting down with. How far you plunge the knife depends on how sharp you have sharpened the knife."

Q: "Could it have cut the bottom of Goldman's shoe?"

A: "Sure."

Q: "You have seen some of the bodies and the autopsy photographs. Could this weapon be considered as the weapon which killed Ron Goldman and Nicole Simpson?"

A: "Oh, yes. This weapon could inflict all the cutting and stabbing wounds that are observed. Again, this is what this knife was designed for. This knife was designed to stab and cut people, that's its purpose. Look at the whole design. You don't need a kitchen knife to cut on both surfaces. You don't need a utility knife to carry around. You want a utility knife so it can fold. This you have to have a sheath to carry it in and it is designed to hurt and kill people. It is in fact illegal in many states including Texas where we are.

Q: "You said earlier the handle of this knife could be used as a blunt instrument. There was a mark and cut on top of Nicole Simpson's head which is similar to the butt of this knife. Could it cause her to fall unconscious on the Spanish tile?"

A: "If you strike somebody on the head with sufficient force to lacerate the scalp . . . a blunt force tears the scalp. You can render them stunned, semiconscious or even unconscious."

Q: "In Nicole Simpson there was bruising on the left side of face. But where her head was nearly decapitated, there was no bruising."

A: "That is correct. Essentially you do not get bruising once a person is dead, especially when you are talking about the side of the head."

Q: "If she had bruising, she could have been unconscious. She would have been killed last, correct?"

A: "Yes."

Q: "Notice on the sheath, the metal clip on back, what is it designed for?"

A: "A clip to hold the knife on a belt or boot."

Q: "If Jason Simpson was known to use the phrase, 'I am tired of being Dr. Jekyll/Mr. Hyde. I cut away problems with a knife.' If you were to read this in his personal diaries and knew the following: Jason Simpson was on probation for attacking his previous employer with a knife, confined to a mental institution, three attempted suicides, prior to murders attempted to kill his girlfriend, entered Cedars-Sinai Hospital ER stating, 'I am out of my medication Depakote and about to rage.' If you had been the medical examiner, knew all this, would you have considered Jason Simpson a major suspect?"

A: "If I knew these details, not as a medical examiner but as a police officer, I would investigate this individual and see if there was any way he was involved in the murders. Any person with violent tendencies and who knew the victims, and especially had problems with them, you are supposed to investigate suspects when you have a homicide."

Q: "The Los Angeles Police Department said they never interviewed Jason Simpson. He was represented by an attorney and refused to cooperate. Was this a rage killing?"

A: "Yes, this does not have the appearance of a planned cold-blooded murder. One gets the sense that this was a confrontation that went out of control. A person losing their temper. A rage type homicide. Where an innocent bystander walks into it and ends up being a victim of a rage. It has a feeling of a personal murder, a murder involving rage, confrontation, not planning, not cold-blooded."

Q: "If you knew that Jason Simpson was taking medication for a rage disorder, has serious problems with women, and considered himself a Dr. Jekyll/Mr. Hyde personality, using the phrase in his diaries, 'I cut away problems with a knife,' should this have concerned the LAPD?"

A: "Based on what you have told me . . . I am extremely surprised the police department did not do a better investigation of him. I think it warranted an investigation at that time. You know sometimes in homicide cases, one gets fixed on one individual and because of this does not look around to see if any other people can be the perpetrator or assailant. And this can lead to misjudgment and lead to innocent people being indicted and tried. You have to be objective and broadminded when one investigates a homicide and investigate any serious possible individual."

Q: "The skin under Nicole's fingernails did not match O. J.'s. If O. J.'s blood was found at the scene and he did not commit the murders, but his son did, would blood from the firstborn son have any DNA resemblance?"

A: "Yes, there would be some resemblance. They test for thirteen characteristics. There would be a match for a few of them. That is how you do a paternity test. There would be a certain number of matches because the father contributes 50 percent of the DNA."

Q: "In O. J.'s bedroom were two socks. Socks in an off position. The blood found on the socks contained EDTA. If socks contained EDTA, would that concern you as a medical examiner?"

A: "Yes, it would—why? The suggestion would be the blood was planted. I would like to be very careful not to make any allegations. Most people in crime labs are good people and do the best they can, but sometimes a person is a problem. Some people lose objectivity. Their job is to see that justice is served, not further a prejudice of their own. So I would hope there was a reasonable explanation for the detection of EDTA on the sock and that there was no planting of evidence because I have a great respect for people in crime labs."

Q: "Detective Vannatter had the jail nurse draw 8cc of blood from O. J. It was placed in a vial containing EDTA. The vial of blood was given to Vannatter. When it was turned over to the crime scene technicians it contained only 6.5cc. Would that cause you great concern?"

A: "I think it would be a very serious worry on my part, yes, it would."

Q: "What concerns you most about this case? What else can I do in my investigation after eleven years?"

A: "That is difficult to answer. The problem with the trial is it became a show. People were not interested in the truth. Some were interested in their own agendas. So, I do not know what you can do at this point. Go through the evidence; make sure that everything is as it should be."

Q: "The knife you hold in your hand belonged to Jason Lamar Simpson. Could it be the murder weapon?"

A: "Of course it can . . . Of course it can."

Q: "Please look at the hands of Ron Goldman in this picture. Would these marks be consistent with his striking the assailant?"

A: "Yes, if you have injuries like this. The individual would have struck someone with his fists."

Q: "Could he have struck his assailant and many times?"

A: "Yes, one is struck with the symmetry on the back of the fingers, running across the back of the hand and one thinks and expects someone punched a person. If a person is dragged or has fallen you would not expect this pattern of injuries."

Q: "Let me show you a crime scene photograph with Ron Goldman against the fence. He received twenty-seven stab wounds. Would the assailant not be covered in blood?"

A: "Yes. The assailant would be covered with blood. You are talking about wounds, arterial in nature, spurting blood. The person would be almost dripping blood in a fight like this with Mr. Goldman. The struggle with an adult male with multiple stab wounds like this, one would expect extensive transfer of blood from the victim to the assailant."

Q: "So there would have been blood on the shoes of the assailant. If I told you little blood was found in the Bronco and none on the brake or accelerator, would that surprise you?"

A: "If the vehicle was being driven by the assailant, I would be very surprised. This is a very bloody scene. There were multiple stab wounds. You can see there was some spurting of the blood. One would expect a lot of blood. If you are struggling with an individual and blood is dripping to the ground you would expect the soles of the shoes to be almost blood soaked and to step on carpet one would expect transfer . . . There should be a significant amount and one should be able to see it with the naked eye."

Q: "And if there was none?"

A: "I would find that very disturbing."

Q: "In the autopsy photo of Nicole Simpson lying on the gurney, her throat is cut and her head is nearly decapitated. There are several drops of blood on her back that were never checked. Could the assailant, after the fight with Goldman, have put his foot on her back and cut her throat, and in doing so several drops of his blood fell onto her back?"

A: "Oh, yes."

Q: "Describe the three slash marks on the concrete steps next to Nicole's body."

A: "I get the impression that something was placed there. Not the head. An instrument. It is so linear and sharp edged. It has a pattern to it. The head is irregular and amorphous. The only thing that would surprise me about this case. It is a spontaneous, unplanned case of rage that most times in cases like this . . . after rage has been expended one does not go and slit a person's throat as the last thing . . . it makes you think the rage has subsided and now there is a cold rage at the final moments."

Q: "Do you think he killed Nicole Simpson after he killed Ron Goldman?"

A: "Most people would just flee. Would not stay around. Not check the bodies. This has been contradictory with circumstances. To go to her and cut her throat would be cold rather than heat feelings."

Q: "Could the assailant have blamed her after he was forced to kill Goldman?"

A: "If it is a mixture of personal hatred and coldness that is . . . it is very difficult to kill or hurt someone that one loves. When you see crimes like slitting the throat it's more often an episode of rage."

Q: "Could the suspect have confronted Nicole without premeditation of murder, but things got out of control?"

A: "This scene, the nature of the killings has the appearance of an unplanned moment or moments of rage with attacking one individual, then an innocent bystander coming onto the scene and then attacking them. It is not something planned, it is not intentional. It is just sheer rage. An individual such as you are describing should be considered a major suspect, somebody who should be investigated thoroughly as to whether they were the perpetrator, somehow involved in the death of these individuals."

Q: "Let's go back to the picture of Ron Goldman's fists, what would this have done to the assailant?"

A: "To produce those marks on the hands one does not punch somebody in the chest or in the abdomen. It is soft padding and you would not expect the abrasions present. The marks you see on the hands are those you get where there is hard bone, such as the face. Skin over bone. One would expect bruising and some lacerations. Black and blue eye from being struck one or more times in the face."

Q: "Let me show you a picture of O. J. Notice there are no cuts or abrasions as you just described. Does this concern you?"

A: "If O. J. had been punched about the face those injuries would be present for a number of days following the occurrence. They would be quite obvious. You can cover your body but your face is visible to everybody."

Q: "The only injury to O. J. was a cut on one of his left knuckles. Could this be consistent with O. J. climbing over his chain-link fence and cutting it on one of the prongs?"

A: "Oh yes, definitely."

Q: "There was a glove and knit cap found at the Bundy Drive crime scene. There were hair follicles inside the knit cap that were not checked for DNA. Would that concern you?"

A: "Yes, the problem I have is that this was eleven years ago. Today, DNA has made greater advances.

Q: "Let me show you a photograph which contains a picture of two individuals. One is a picture of Johnnie Cochran wearing the dark knit cap found at the crime scene. The other individual is Jason Simpson also wearing a dark knit cap. The picture of Jason was taken months prior to the murders. Do you notice the similarity between the two caps?"

A: "Yes, but it is not just a knit cap, it is what we call a watch cap."

Q: "Being worn by O. J.'s son, Jason?"

A: "Yes."

Q: "Could DNA testing now be performed on this knife and the sheath that we know belonged to Jason Simpson?"

A: "Yes, but I do not think it would be very successful. I would not even try. It has been too long. You could open the sheath and examine the interior. You might uncover some DNA inside."

Q: "Could the wound on top of Nicole's head be consistent with the butt of this knife?"

A: "It is hard steel. If you hit someone on top of head with hard steel with enough force you can lacerate the scalp, so the answer is yes."

After we were through filming, I looked at Dr. DiMaio. "Based on all of my investigation which I have shared with you, would you consider Jason Lamar Simpson a major suspect in the murders of Nicole Simpson and Ronald Goldman?"

"Yes," Dr. DiMaio concluded. "The knife in the leather sheath could be the murder weapon. I will say again, this particular knife is designed for one purpose: to cut and kill."

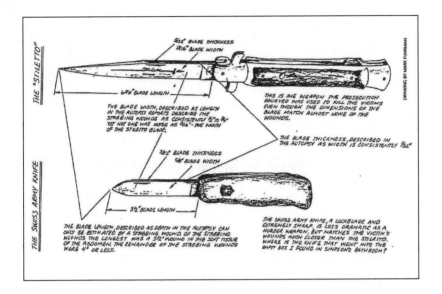

As Phil and I headed back to Dallas, I was now convinced we had the murder weapon used to murder Nicole Simpson and Ronald Goldman. It was also my professional opinion that this knife was in the hands of Jason Simpson on Sunday night, June 12, 1994.

48

MY PEERS/
THE MARKLE SYMPOSIUM

IHAD INTERVIEWED DR. HENRY Lee, whose reputation for his crime scene expertise was acclaimed nationwide. When we met in Dallas on February 17, 2004, after one of his speeches to a law enforcement gathering, I had no idea I would ever hear from him again.

Months passed. I had learned that Dr. Lee was discussing some of my findings in his speeches to other law enforcement agencies. Nearly a year had passed when the phone rang at my office. "Bill, there is a Jackie Koral on the phone. She says she works for Dr. Henry Lee at the Henry Lee Institute. You want to take the call?"

"Sure."

"Hello, Miss Koral."

"I've heard a great deal about you and your work on the murders of Nicole Simpson and Ron Goldman, Mr. Dear. Dr. Lee asked if you would accept his invitation to be a guest speaker at the Markle Symposium, which is to be held at the Foxwood Resort beginning March 28 and 29, 2005." Ms. Koral said there would be about 600 in attendance, most of whom would be district attorneys, prosecutors, crime scene experts, and students majoring in criminal justice. I said I would be more than honored to appear.

"We would like you to speak on Tuesday, March 29th. If you want to come up early, that is fine."

I asked her who else would be speaking.

"Dr. Henry Lee, Dr. Al Harper, Dr. Cyril Wecht, Dr. Michael Baden. Drs. Wecht and Baden are medical examiners." I had heard of them. "Also Catherine Crier, who has a show on Court TV and, by the way, is a former judge in Dallas."

"I remember Ms. Crier very well."

"Patricia Cornwell, the author, will be there to speak about Jack the Ripper and also FBI agent Charles Dorsey."

"Sounds like I'll be in great company."

"Actually, Mr. Dear, so far everyone I have talked with is looking forward to *your* presentation."

I arrived on Sunday, March 27, to find a member of the Connecticut State Police there at the airport to meet me. Dr. Cyril Wecht joined me and we drove from Hartford, Connecticut, to the Foxwood Resort. It was an interesting hour drive, and by the time we arrived at Foxwood, it was nearing 11 PM, so I retired for the night.

The next morning, I awoke early and went to the large meeting area where people were checking in at the Conference. The Markle Symposium is a yearly event with important figures in law enforcement attending. I spent the day listening to speeches and after it was over, I was asked by Dr. Al Harper and Dr. Henry Lee to join them for dinner. After dinner, I retired to my room to prepare for the following day.

I could not sleep. I kept waking up concerned about my presentation. As dawn broke, I showered, dressed, and went for a walk around this luxurious resort. At 9:10 AM, I walked into the conference area. Every seat was full. After the lunch break, it was my turn. I looked around and saw the large screens, the podium, and my adrenaline began to pump. These were my peers: law enforcement officers, district attorneys, criminal justice majors. I thought, *If I can show them what I have uncovered in the past eleven years, then I should be able to prove it to the Los Angeles Police Department, the district attorney and possibly the California attorney general.*

Lunch was over; I looked around and saw that the attendees had taken their seats—not one seat was unoccupied. I kept hearing people comment, "I want to hear what this man has to say." Suddenly, approaching me was Dr. Al Harper and Dr. Henry Lee's associate. "Bill, it's your turn. I will be introducing you."

"Fine."

We walked toward the podium—there was no turning back now. I felt I was prepared as well as I could be. After Dr. Harper introduced me, I walked up the steps, entered the stage, and approached the podium. I looked back and up on the two screens behind me was my picture. Everyone just appeared to be staring at me. Who was this man who was going to try and convince us that O. J. Simpson had not murdered Nicole Simpson and Ron Goldman?

"Ladies and gentlemen. How many of you in this room believe that O. J. Simpson is guilty beyond a shadow of a doubt?" As I looked out at more than 600 people, I saw that all of their hands were raised. "Thank you. I will be asking this same question when I am through." For the next ninety minutes, I noticed that not one person left to use the bathroom or to smoke. It was exciting that I had the attention of everyone in this room. I looked to my left; there was Dr. Henry Lee, Dr. Harper, Dr. Wecht, Dr. Baden, and FBI agent Dorsey. All of them were sitting there watching and listening to every word I had to say.

Finally my speech was coming to a close. I reached down and picked up the knife still in the leather sheath. I pulled it out and came down hard into a chunk of Styrofoam. With the blade still moving in the Styrofoam, I said, "According to experts this could be the murder weapon." I waited as the stunned crowd watched the knife and then said, "Now, please raise your hands. How many of you still believe O. J. Simpson is guilty of the murders of Nicole Simpson and Ron Goldman beyond a shadow of a doubt?" Only three hands rose. I had done it: I had convinced the experts that maybe my eleven-year investigation had started to pay off.

After questions and answers, especially by the three who had raised their hands, I turned from the podium to a loud ovation. As I exited the steps, crowds of people came forward to look more closely at the evidence and to speak to me. Dr. Harper said, "Bill, I think you convinced them. I know you did me."

I left the hotel, exhausted but pleased, and headed back to Dallas. Days later, I received a letter from Dr. Al Harper and Dr. Henry Lee that made all my work worthwhile. According to them, I had convinced my peers.

49

THE DRAWN BLOOD

I WAS IN LOS ANGELES to complete my new book and documentary—an accumulation of twelve years' work I had undertaken because of my strong belief that O. J. was at the crime scene but did not commit the murders of Nicole Simpson and Ron Goldman.

Joe Villanueva was with me to help, along with Phil Smith and the rest of the crew. Joe had been working for me for many years. He too was firmly convinced, based on my investigation, that O. J. did not commit the murders but was protecting someone: his son, Jason.

As Joe and I left the Marriott Courtyard Hotel, Joe was driving. We pulled out and entered Route 101 en route to visit Thano Peratis, the jail nurse who had drawn O. J.'s blood at the jail on Monday, June 13, 1994. I wasn't sure how we would be received but as my book and the filming of the documentary were nearing completion, I wanted to tie up any loose ends. This particular issue had become of great interest to me after visiting Dr. Frederic Rieders and hearing his conviction that the blood which had been on the two black socks had come from a vial of blood. There was only one person I knew of who had drawn blood from O. J. the day after the murders—Thano Peratis.

We approached 3500 Manchester in Inglewood, California, on a brisk Monday morning, November 6, 2004. As we pulled up and stopped at the gated entrance, the female guard on duty asked our business. "I'm here to visit with Thano Peratis."

"Is he expecting you?"

"No ma'am, but I think he will see me."

"Let me call him." We watched as she dialed the phone in the gatehouse. "Mr. Peratis wants to know what you want."

"Tell him my name is Bill Dear and I'm from Dallas working on the murders of Nicole Simpson and Ron Goldman."

Joe and I watched as she hung up, walked over to us, and said, "He will see you in about fifteen minutes. Do you know his unit number?"

"Yes ma'am." As the gate rose, we entered a well-manicured complex containing numerous condominiums or townhouses. Joe and I pulled into the area where Mr. Peratis's unit was. We sat in the car and looked around. Joe said, "I wouldn't mind retiring here if it wasn't a part of Los Angeles." We both got out and began our search for unit 464. As we turned the first corner of the building, there it was, unit 464, right in front of us.

I knocked. An elderly, well-dressed woman opened the door and invited us inside. "Thano will be right down," she said. "Won't you have a seat?" We walked into a well-furnished living room and sat down on the couch. "Would you like something to drink?"

We both said water would be fine.

The townhouse was immaculate. I wasn't sure what to expect. Thano was from all accounts a jail nurse. I didn't think it paid much, but he and his wife must have saved their money.

At that moment, a frail but well-dressed, elderly man entered the room and extended his hand to Joe and me. "Please, sit back down," he said. I introduced myself and gave him one of my business cards. Joe did the same.

"I've spent over ten years investigating the murders of Nicole Simpson and Ron Goldman, Mr. Peratis, and I need your help."

"How can I help you, sir?"

"It is my understanding you were the nurse on duty on Monday, June 13, 1994, when O. J. Simpson was brought into the jail by Vannatter and Lange of the Los Angeles Police Department, Detective Division."

"Yes sir, I was. The detective, Vannatter, asked that I examine Mr. Simpson and to take some blood. I did as requested."

"Mr. Peratis, what was your position on that date?"

"I was the registered nurse in charge of the medical unit of the Los Angeles Police Department jail. I was in charge when there was no doctor present. I guess you could also call me a doctor's assistant."

"How long had you been a registered nurse at the jail?"

"I'm retired now, but I spent over thirty-three years there. I have a serious heart condition and have had several heart attacks, so I felt it would be best to retire. I think it's nearly been two years since I retired."

I thought to myself, thirty-three years, a registered nurse, this is not what I thought on my drive out here. I was extremely glad though, as well as being surprised. He was not like most jailhouse nurses I was used to. Just in his conversation I could sense that this was a man who cared about his job and would have dealt compassionately with the prisoners for all those years.

Just then Mrs. Peratis entered carrying two glasses of water plus one for Thano. "It's time for your medicine." She didn't stay, but walked back out and into what appeared to be their kitchen.

"Mr. Peratis, I'm sure you remember the day O. J. Simpson was brought in."

"Yes sir, very well."

"How did Mr. Simpson appear?"

"Sir, he didn't seem to be worried or upset. He spoke to me and was friendly and cooperative. I did notice that there were no marks or bruises on him except for a cut on his left hand knuckle."

"How did you know that?"

"Vannatter had Mr. Simpson strip and pictures were taken of him as I examined him."

"Were there any indications that Mr. Simpson may have been in a fight or altercation?"

"No sir. I was very careful in examining Mr. Simpson."

"Were Detectives Vannatter and Lange present during the entire examination?"

"Yes sir, Vannatter took the pictures of Mr. Simpson nude."

"So from your professional observation Mr. Simpson did not appear to have been in a fight or scuffle?"

"No sir, just as I said. I looked and found nothing to indicate differently."

"When I was through, I asked Mr. Simpson if I could put a Band-Aid on his cut knuckle. He said yes. I did ask him how he cut his knuckle and he said on some broken glass. He was cooperative."

"When you examined the cut knuckle, could you determine if it was from broken glass?"

"No sir, I couldn't tell."

"Could it have come from climbing over a fence which had sharp pieces at the top?"

"It could have, I have no way of knowing."

"What did you do next?"

"Detective Vannatter asked me to draw blood from Mr. Simpson. I did."

"Describe to us just what you did."

"I picked up an empty vial with a purple cap. The purple cap indicates it contains EDTA inside."

"What does EDTA do?"

"Once I draw the blood into the vial, it mixes with the EDTA and preserves the blood."

"So on Monday June 13, 1994, you used a fresh vial, with a purple cap, one containing EDTA, and drew blood from Mr. Simpson directly into this vial?"

"Yes sir, that's just what I did."

"After you drew the blood, did Mr. Simpson object in any way?"

"No sir, just like I said, he was cooperative."

"Mr. Peratis?"

"Just call me Thano."

"Yes sir. Thano, what did you do next?"

"Once I drew the blood I shook the vial."

"Why?"

"I wanted to make sure the blood mixed with the preservative, EDTA. I checked and marked down on my medical sheet that I had withdrawn 8cc of Mr. Simpson's blood."

"Was this the same procedure you have done over and over?"

"Yes sir, for over thirty-three years, the same way."

"What happened to the vial of blood containing 8cc of O. J. Simpson's blood?"

"Detective Vannatter asked me for the vial of blood."

"Did you give it to him?"

"Yes sir, I did."

"What did he do with the vial of blood?"

"He put it in his pocket. Mr. Simpson and detectives Vannatter and Lange left."

"Left with the vial of blood?"

"Yes sir."

"Let me ask you this: When you testified in court it was indicated by the crime scene technicians that the vial only contained 6.5cc of blood, not 8cc. Are you sure you withdrew 8cc of Mr. Simpson's blood?"

"Yes sir."

"When you were on the stand during Mr. Simpson's trial and the discrepancy over the 8cc of blood and only 6.5cc when it was placed in the hands of the technicians, were you not asked by the district attorney whether it was possible you might have made a mistake in the amount withdrawn?"

"Yes sir."

"You said it was possible?"

"Mr. Dear, I was close to retiring and didn't want any problems. When it was said 'Isn't it possible,' I responded, 'Yes, it is possible.' I had already had several heart attacks."

I wanted to continue this with Thano, but I did not want to do anything to cause him any further heart attacks. Joe also noticed my concern. I would like to have had Phil Smith and the crews come over immediately and have Thano Peratis's testimony on film, but I decided not to. He didn't need any more stress.

As I shook his hand, I put my other hand on top of his and looked into his eyes, thinking *Why can't there be more people like Thano Peratis?* Thirty-three-plus years dealing with jailhouse inmates. I don't know how he did it.

Thano walked Joe and me to the door. We were quiet on our ride back to the Marriott Hotel.

I kept thinking about what Dr. Frederic Rieders had said and now what Thano Peratis had said. The missing 1.5cc of O. J.'s blood, which contained EDTA, was more than enough to have been placed on the two black socks at the foot of O. J.'s bed, all of which had played such a critical part of the investigation.

Maybe some people were right. Was this a cover-up because certain individuals felt O. J. was guilty and the evidence was lacking and needed to be strengthened?

Time will tell. Less than two years after my interview, Thano Peratis had a massive heart attack and passed away.

50

THE KNIT CAP/
THE BINDLE OF HAIRS

IN REVIEWING MY INVESTIGATION and the testimony of June 27, 1995, when Marcia Clark called to the stand Criminalist Susan Brockbank of the LAPD, I noted further oversights.

"Did you examine a bindle of evidence taken from the dark blue knit cap found at the Bundy crime scene?" asked Ms. Clark.

"Yes."

"How did you do that?"

"Well, at a later point I was asked to separate the darker pigmented hair from the lighter ones. There were some hairs that appeared to be blond in color, very light, and then there were some dark black to brown hairs.

Ms. Brockbank continued by saying, "I was asked to separate those from the animal hairs, so there became now three bindles instead of just the one. One had the dark colored hairs, one had the light colored hairs, and one had the animal hairs."

As Ms. Brockbank continued to testify, she indicated the dark brown to dark black hairs were human hairs found inside the cap. The other two bindles contained fabric hairs and the other animal hairs.

I had learned previously, from a source, the animal hairs taken from the cap belonged to a dog.

How would these animal hairs have found their way onto the knit cap? I looked down at the color photograph taken in Jason's bedroom with him wearing the dark knit, or watch, cap playing with his dog, prior to the murders. It seemed to me the animal hairs, which did belong to a dog, would have easily found their way onto the knit cap while the two of them played in bed.

Importantly, the knit cap Jason was wearing in the color photograph disappeared from photos the day after the murders of Nicole Simpson and Ron Goldman. The dark knit cap was now replaced by a grey knit cap.

There is no doubt that Marcia Clark wanted those four dark brown to black hairs, including the one with the fleshy root intact, to belong to O. J. Simpson. But Ms. Brockbank's testimony did not indicate to whom the hairs belonged.

Since the prosecutor's office had samples of O. J.'s hair and used DNA testing, they should have been able, without much trouble, to prove whether the hairs belonged to O. J. Simpson. They did not prove it.

It was the same with skin found underneath Nicole's fingernails. Again, no proof that it belonged to O. J. Simpson.

Two crucial pieces of evidence that could have played an important part in finding O. J. guilty could not be established as belonging to O. J. Simpson.

Since the LAPD never interviewed Jason Lamar Simpson, it remains unknown whether the unidentified prints found at the crime scene, the hair in the knit cap, and the skin found underneath Nicole Simpson's fingernails belonged to O. J.'s son Jason.

Why?

Because Jason Lamar Simpson was never interviewed by the LAPD. He was, however, represented by a top criminal lawyer, Carl Jones, who had been retained by O. J. Simpson the day after the murders, not to represent *him* but to represent *his son*, Jason. Jason refused to cooperate with the LAPD and as a result was never interviewed.

51

DR. WILLIAM FLYNN

DR. WILLIAM FLYNN IS considered an expert in criminal behavior and is also a criminal psychologist. Dr. Flynn normally testifies on behalf of the criminal defense.

When I first spoke with Dr. Flynn, he agreed to review Jason Simpson's medical and psychiatric records and talk to those who knew Jason, before rendering his psychological profile. Dr. Flynn said, "I will base my findings on all the evidence. My report may not come to the conclusion that you want, Mr. Dear, but that is the only way I am going to become involved."

I assured Dr. Flynn that was all I wanted.

"I would like to interview Jason and O. J. Simpson, so if you will fax me phone numbers and addresses along with the same for Jason's friends and associates, it would be helpful."

Two weeks later, Dr. Flynn called and said he had completed his findings and his report was complete even though he was unable to talk to Jason or his father, O. J.

I made an appointment to visit with Dr. William Flynn on April 20, 2006. I arrived around 3 PM.

Dr. Flynn handed me a copy of his report on Jason. He had another copy in his hand and began to read from it out loud: "Mr. Dear, you have asked me to give an expert opinion on the risk of violence, such as murder, from Jason Lamar Simpson. Because the best research on violence is able to predict violent acts following release from psychiatric hospitals, and recent research is also able to predict violence following convictions for violent crimes, I have reviewed Jason Simpson's hospital records from mental institutions, and I have reviewed Jason Simpson's criminal record.

"According to records from St. John's Hospital, Jason Simpson was admitted to the emergency room in 1984 (age fourteen) for grand mal seizures secondary to a cocaine overdose. In 1991, Jason was admitted to the mental health unit for Major Depression with a suicide attempt.

"According to legal and criminal records, Jason Simpson has been convicted of: Driving under the influence/drugs in vehicle (1990); Driving while license suspended (1992); Disturbing the peace (1993); Bargained down from assault with a deadly weapon; Hit and run with property damage; Driving with license suspended (1995). I have also reviewed excerpts from Jason's diary and reviewed his deposition taken in 1995.

"According to the risk factors that predict future violent offending following release from a mental health unit, one-fourth of these patients had committed a violent act within one year of release. The factors that best predicted which patient would offend violently included prior violence, criminality, and physical abuse by a parent. A diagnosis of a major mental disorder predicted an 18 percent likelihood of violence, a major mental disorder plus a diagnosis of substance abuse increased the likelihood of violence of 31 percent, and the addition of a personality disorder further increased the odds of future violence to 43 percent.

"According to records, Jason Simpson has most of these risk factors; he has been convicted of a prior violent offense (assault with a knife), he has persistent criminality, he has been physically abused by his father [in an interview with Ron Shipp, Jason said his father used to beat the hell out of him], he experienced parental fighting, he was diagnosed with a major mental disorder (Major Depression), he has been diagnosed with substance abuse, (alcohol, cocaine, LSD, psilocybin and designer drugs), and according to Dr. Lebas (3/25/1991), Jason has a personality disorder.

"The long-term (fifteen-year) prediction of violent re-offending is best predicted by the use of the Violence Risk Assessment Guide (VRAG). This risk instrument uses twelve risk factors to predict long-term violent re-offending. I have included an attachment of the VRAG and the scoring of the risk factors that apply to Jason Simpson.

"Jason's risk factors for violent re-offending include 1) that his parents divorced when he was ten years old, 2) that he had such severe discipline problems in elementary school that he was sent to military school, 3) He and his father both have a history of alcohol problems, 4) Jason failed/violated probation with a new offense, 5) He began his violence at a young age, 6) There was minimal victim injury resulting from his violent offense, 7) His violence was aggressive enough to target a male victim, and 8) He has been diagnosed with a personality disorder. Jason had enough risk factors for violent re-offending to be more dangerous than 95 percent of violent prisoners. According to research conducted with the VRAG, 55 percent of convicted felons in the high-risk group (Jason's group) committed a new violent offense within seven years of their last offense.

"In summary, according to medical and legal records, Jason Lamar Simpson has a high risk of violent re-offending behavior."

I was surprised by Dr. Flynn's findings, although not totally, because of my twelve years of investigating Jason. I felt from the very beginning that Jason was capable of killing again, but I had no idea he would rate so high on the chart in his potential of violent behavior. Dr. Flynn's report was just another piece of my investigation making Jason a major overlooked suspect in the murders of Nicole Simpson and Ron Goldman.

Dr. Flynn stood up and handed me three copies of his findings and I thanked him for his time. As I walked out of the office and approached the elevator, the elevator door opened. I stepped inside as the elevator door began to close. I could not help but wish, with Dr. Flynn's report in my right hand, it would be nice to be able to say, "Case closed."

DR. WILLIAM FLYNN, PHD, PSYCHOLOGIST
FORENSIC PSYCHOLOGY

April 20, 2006

Mr. Dear:

You have asked me to give an expert opinion on the risk of violence, such as murder, from Jason Lamar Simpson.

Because the best research on violence is able to predict violent acts following release from psychiatric hospitals and, recent research is also able to predict violence following convictions for violent crimes; I have reviewed Jason Simpson's' hospital records from mental institutions and, I have reviewed Jason Simpson's criminal record.

According to records from St. Johns' hospital, Jason Simpson was admitted to the emergency room in 1984 (age 14) for grand mal seizures secondary to a cocaine overdose. In 1991, Jason was admitted to the mental health unit for Major Depression with a suicide attempt.

According to legal and criminal records, Jason Simpson has been convicted of Driving under the influence/drugs in vehicle (1990).

Driving while license suspended (1992).

Disturbing the peace (1993). Bargained down from assault with a deadly weapon.

Hit and run with property damage; driving with license suspended (1995).

I have also reviewed excerpts from Jason's diary and reviewed his deposition taken in 1995.

Findings

According to the risk factors that predict future violent offending following release from a mental health unit, one-fourth of these patients had committed a violent act within one year of release. The factors that best predicted which patient would offend violently included prior violence, criminality, and physical abuse by a parent. A diagnosis of a major mental disorder predicted an 18% likelihood of violence; a major mental disorder plus a diagnosis of substance abuse increased the likelihood of violence to 31% and, the addition of a personality disorder further increased the odds of future violence to 43%.

According to records, Jason Simpson has most of these risk factors: he has been convicted of a prior violent offense (assault with a knife), he has persistent criminality, he has been physically abused by his father (in interview Ron Shipp says his Father used to beat the hell out of him), he experienced parental fighting, he was diagnosed with a major mental disorder (Major Depression), he has been diagnosed with substance abuse (alcohol, cocaine, LSD, psilocybin & designer drugs), and according to Dr. Lebas (3/25/1991), Jason has a personality disorder.

The long-term (15-year) prediction of violent re-offending is best predicted by the use of the Violence Risk Assessment Guide (VRAG). This risk instrument uses 12 risk factors to predict long-term violent re-offending. I have included an attachment of the VRAG and the scoring of the risk factors that apply to Jason Simpson.

Jason's risk factors for violent re-offending include 1) that his parents divorced when he was 10 years old, 2) that he had such severe discipline problems in elementary school that he was sent to military school, 3) he and his father both have a history of alcohol problems, 4) Jason failed/violated probation with a new offense, 5) he began his violence at a young age, 6) there was minimal victim injury resulting from his violent offense, 7) his violence was aggressive enough to target a male victim, and 8) he has been diagnosed with a personality disorder. Jason has enough risk factors for violent re-offending to be more dangerous than 95% of violent prisoners. According to research conducted with the VRAG, 55% of convicted felons in the high-risk group (Jason's group) committed a new violent offense within 7 years of their last offense.

Summary

According to medical and legal records, Jason Lamar Simpson has a high risk of violent re-offending behavior.

Sincerely,

William Flynn
Psychologist

52

WHAT DID THE LAPD EMAIL SAY?

THE SECOND WEEK OF November 2005, my producer, Phil Smith, Karl Newman, Phil Thompson, Chad Smith, and I were in Los Angeles to complete our filming for what I hoped would be a shocking documentary on the murders of Nicole Simpson and Ron Goldman. Phil and I wanted to meet with the Los Angeles Police Department Detective Division. I wanted again to try and share with them what I had uncovered in the past eleven years. We were told we would have to make a formal request through the media division of the Los Angeles Police Department and, in turn, they would set up the meeting. Several phone calls were made. We explained what we wanted and that it would only take a few minutes.

November 10, 2005, at 12:02 PM while all of us were in the hotel room, we received an email. The email was to Phil Smith, my producer, and this is exactly what it said:

Sent: Thursday, November 10, 2005 12:02 PM
Subject: Re: Documentary TV Interview
Mr. Smith,
OJ Simpson committed a double murder
Charges were filed on him
A jury decided that OJ was found not guilty
The case is closed

We have no further comments
Officer Harding
Media Relations Section

Subject: RE: lapd letter
Date: Friday, December 2, 2005 9:58 AM
From: Thompson
Reply-To:
To: 'Philip Smith'
Conversation: lapd letter


```
----- Original Message -----
From: "MEDIA RELATIONS PIO" <pio@lapd.lacity.org>
To: "Phil Smith"
Sent: Thursday, November 10, 2005 12:02 PM
Subject: Re: Documentaqry TV interview


> Mr. Smith,
>
> -OJ Simpson committed a double murder
> -Charges were filed on him
> -A jury decided that OJ was found not guilty
> -The case is closed
>
> We have no further comments
>
>
> Officer Harding
> Media Relations Section
> 213 485-3587
>
```

As Phil read the email out loud, I was shocked. When I had tried to obtain copies of the blood stains and unidentified fingerprints found at the crime scene, I was informed "Sorry, this is an ongoing open investigation."

Yet, now we were being told that, as far as the Los Angeles Police Department was concerned, O. J. Simpson committed a double murder and the case was closed.

I had spent at this point eleven years of my life trying to bring closure to this case and the proper suspect brought to justice. This is a country where we are supposed to have the ability and judgment to look at all the facts, old as well as new, in trying to pursue what our fathers and mothers had fought so hard for: Truth, Justice, and The American Way.

I could only say over and over, Why, Why, Why? All I wanted was the police department, district attorneys and the courts to grant me a special grand jury to look at and examine what I knew to be important new evidence in the murders of Nicole Simpson and Ron Goldman. This was being denied me.

No matter what Officer Harding of the Los Angeles Police Department had said to me, this case was not closed.

53

DENISE BROWN

DENISE BROWN, NICOLE'S SISTER, makes appearances and speaking engagements on behalf of the Nicole Brown Foundation. When I looked at the Sunday paper one morning in 2006, I saw an article announcing that Denise Brown would be appearing on March 25, at the Nokia Theater in Grand Prairie, Texas. Nokia is not what you might think; it is an auditorium where large events are held.

I wanted to hear what Denise Brown had to say. On March 25, I drove to Nokia, paid for my parking and my ticket, and entered the auditorium. I went right down to sit in front. The host walked to the stage and began to introduce Denise Brown. She entered and took her place behind the podium and began telling the story of her sister and the problems she had incurred with her marriage to O. J. Simpson. There were over 400 people in attendance, a lot less than I thought there would be.

As Denise Brown started into the close of her presentation, she said, "Some red flag warnings are a person who is overly jealous, a drinker, and a person having a Jekyll and Hyde-like demeanor. Ninety-five percent are abusive men."

I wanted to jump up and say, "Ms. Brown, you haven't described O. J. Simpson; you have described Jason Simpson, O. J.'s oldest son. In his own personal diary, Jason Simpson says, 'I am tired of playing

Dr. Jekyll and Mr. Hyde.' He goes on to describe his jealousy, his depression, his regrets, his abusing Jennifer Green and DeeDee Burnett.

I realized that there was no way Denise would recognize me and hear what I had to say. I left the theater and thought, *Ms. Brown, are you really wanting the truth as to who killed your sister and Ron Goldman? Or are you in this for your own personal reasons?*

Ms. Brown, you are in the right church, but, as my dad used to say, the wrong pew.

54

IF I DID IT

IN NOVEMBER 2006, JUDITH Regan, editor and president of Regan Books, announced they would be publishing a book titled *If I Did It*, by O. J. Simpson. Along with the book, which was to be released on November 30, there would be a Fox TV special and a book on CD with the same title. The book was to be ghostwritten by Pablo F. Fenjves.

You hate me and despise me, so why shouldn't I profit by it? This had to be what O. J. was thinking or in this case not thinking. To me, he was making a serious mistake. O. J. allowed himself to be easily manipulated. It was this same ease of manipulation that would have him serving nine to thirty-three years in a Nevada prison after his conviction in 2008.

But in this case, O. J. was pouring gasoline on smoldering ashes and the flames were beginning to grow.

Immediately, the story broke and every TV station, magazine, and newspaper took issue. At the same time, presale orders were beginning to flood in. Within days, the presale of *If I Did It* reached 100,000 and kept rising.

The book, TV special, and CD were the brainchild of Judith Regan. Ms. Regan was a very controversial editor—a woman to be reckoned with. She was despised by some who had to do business with her but admired by others for her success.

The publisher was absorbing a heavy dose of anger over this book, not only by newspapers and magazines but also by television power-houses like David Letterman, Jay Leno, and Larry King, just to mention a few.

For the next few weeks there was a steady hue and cry in the media. Many of the complaints were focused on News Corp, who also owned Regan Books, USA News, Fox Television and Harper Collins Publishing Company. The president of News Corp, the well-known Rupert Murdoch, was being blindsided no matter which way he turned.

The people running News Corp counted on the mountain of publicity making the sales skyrocket and the FOX TV special blowing the ratings off the charts, but they underestimated the powerful reaction of the general public.

Finally, due to the tremendous backlash, Rupert Murdoch bowed to the pressure, bit his tongue, and apologized to the families of Ron Goldman and Nicole Simpson for the pain this had caused. He cancelled the printing of *If I Did It* and the TV special and all copies that had been printed were to be destroyed with none to be released to the public.

Rupert Murdoch fired Judith Regan and shut down Regan Books. The once extremely vocal and outspoken Ms. Regan packed her bags and was shown the door of News Corp.

Copies of the book began to appear in limited quantities. I read portions of *If I Did It,* but it did not give me much insight into the murders. To me, it seemed more like a book of fiction. The 200-page book did not offer in any way what Judith Regan had promised in her original announcement concerning its contents.

In the meantime, the Goldman family had filed suit to stop the book from being printed. On July 30, 2007, the court awarded the rights to the book to the Goldman family to help toward the $33.5 million judgment they had obtained in 1997.

I felt the general public had been led to believe that the family had filed suit to stop O. J. from profiting from what they considered to be the murder of Ron Goldman. I was shocked when I read that the Goldmans were going ahead with publication of this same book but were changing the title to *If I Did It: Confessions of the Killer*.

Looking at the red lettering on the cover, I could see, in very tiny black print, the word "If" in the bold red "I" of the title *I Did It*. I turned to the inside cover of the book and read that only a portion of the proceeds were being donated to the Ron Goldman Foundation for Justice. I had hoped all proceeds would be going to the foundation.

Now the Goldmans were profiting, which really bothered me. I was invited to appear on the *Dr. Phil* show in 2008 along with the Goldman family. After giving it a great deal of thought, I made my decision: "No."

If the Goldmans knew what I had uncovered in my investigation, they might not be so adamant about O. J.'s guilt.

My goal, eighteen years after the murders, is for the evidence I have uncovered not only to be shared with you, the reader, but also with people who have the power to do something about it. Not only to bring closure, but also to shed light on the truth of what happened on June 12, 1994, and to bring justice to the murders of Nicole Brown Simpson and Ronald Goldman.

55

LAS VEGAS ARREST: THE SETUP

ON SEPTEMBER 13, 2007, O. J. left his Florida home located just south of Miami, Florida, to attend his friend's wedding in Las Vegas, where he was to be the best man.

Once arriving in McCarran Airport, O. J. walked through the elaborate terminal and took the elevator down to baggage claim. After claiming his luggage, he went out to the street level and hailed a taxi to take him directly to the Palms Hotel, an upscale hotel catering to young celebrities. As the taxi pulled underneath the overhang of the Palms and O. J. got out, a number of people turned his way. Without fanfare, O. J. entered the lobby of the hotel and walked directly to the check-in desk. Once he filled out the registration card, the young lady with a smile handed him two key cards for his room as people continued to look at "The Juice," the man whom they assumed had gotten away with murder, not the man they knew as the famous celebrity, as he headed toward the elevator.

The elevator door opened, O. J. entered along with four other people. Several of the people spoke to O. J., and he responded in his usual friendly manner as the elevator continued up. The doors opened several times and people exited, finally leaving O. J. alone in the elevator. As the elevator arrived at his floor, the doors opened and O. J. stepped into the hallway leading to his room. He put the key card in twice before the door showed the green light indicating that the room was unlocked.

He had been carrying two bags the entire way. He tossed the larger onto the bed, turned and opened the closet door where he hung up his garment bag. Closing the sliding door, he quickly exited the room walked back toward the elevator and pushed the down button.

O. J. appeared to be in a hurry as he exited the elevator on the ground floor. As he walked into the bar at the Palms he appeared to be looking for someone. It turned out to be Thomas J. Riccio, a.k.a. Tom Riccio. Riccio stuck out his hand and in turn shook O. J.'s and the two men sat together to have a drink.

I did not learn until later in my investigation that Riccio earlier had called O. J. at his home in Florida and informed him that Al Beardsley, a memorabilia dealer, had contacted him and wanted him to sell a number of items that belonged to O. J. Beardsley said he was in partnership with a man named Mike Gilbert, also a well-known memorabilia dealer.

O. J. became furious over the telephone when Riccio told him what type of items Beardsley and Gilbert had, which supposedly belonged to O. J. at one time. According to Riccio, O. J. went through the roof, "I've been looking for that stuff for years, Tom! I know that fucking weasel Mike Gilbert stole the stuff. He must have given it to that nut case Al to fence. You've got to help me get that stuff back, man. It's all my personal stuff, and this is not about the money. When I die, I want my kids to have these things!"

According to O. J., he had employed Mike Gilbert to store these items to prevent them from going toward the judgment Fred Goldman had won in the civil suit. I learned that O. J. had disputes with Gilbert and they had parted ways. Apparently, Mike Gilbert ran into some financial trouble and put up O. J.'s collection as collateral against a big loan that Gilbert had never paid back.

Who was Thomas Riccio? Riccio was a forty-four-year-old sports collectibles dealer. But that's not all he was. Thomas Riccio was an arsonist, prison escapee, and a dealer of stolen goods. He had spent a total of eight years in prison. The first conviction was a felony in 1984 on a federal charge of conspiracy out of New Jersey for receiving stolen goods. He was incarcerated at a federal prison in Danbury, Connecticut, where he escaped in October of 1984. Five months later, he was arrested in California. Riccio was convicted again. He spent four and a half years in prison both for the original charge and the escape. In 1994, Riccio was arrested and charged with arson and was sentenced to two and a half years in state court. While serving this two-and-a-half year sentence, he had another charge of theft of nearly $500,000 worth of rare gold and silver coins. He served this conviction concurrently with the arson charge.

Riccio spent thirty-seven months in prison and was released in October of 1997. In 1999 he was incarcerated again, this time for parole violation.

As O. J. sat at the bar drinking with Riccio, he had no knowledge that Riccio had another plan in mind. He offered to help O. J. get his memorabilia back from Beardsley and Gilbert. Riccio informed O. J., "I never do something for nothing. I expect to be compensated for setting up Beardsley and Gilbert. You promised you'd take care of me. I've got customers who need those books signed."

"Anything but the book," O. J. said.

"Why not put the inscription THIS IS NOT MY BOOK and then sign them?" Riccio suggested.

"That's a good idea," O. J. said. "OK, I'll do it."

According to Riccio, "We had a verbal agreement that I secretly captured on a digital recording to sign two hundred copies."

The above and future quotes came directly out of the book *Busted* that Thomas Riccio wrote and released by Phoenix Books in 2008.

Riccio and O. J. laid out a plan as to how to confront Beardsley and Gilbert. As the meeting broke up between O. J. and Riccio, O. J. went back up to his room while Riccio took a taxi back to his hotel, the Palace Station Hotel, a 2000-room hotel preferred by locals, that sits about a block off of the Strip.

O. J. IS INNOCENT

At around 4:30 PM, according to Riccio, O. J. called him and O. J. said, "Change of plans—I don't want those guys coming over to my room. Let's just do it at your place."

Riccio made arrangements to meet Beardsley and, at that time, Gilbert, at his room at the Palace Hotel.

What O. J. did not know was that Thomas Riccio had put a nine-hour recording system out of sight on top of the TV cabinet in his hotel room to catch all the conversation in the room without the knowledge of O. J., Beardsley, and Gilbert.

Riccio had walked around his entire room making sure that the recording device would pick up the entire conversation from all positions. He checked the machine several times and had it well hidden from view.

According to Riccio, Beardsley, who was six foot six and weighed about 300 pounds, called and said Mike Gilbert would not be coming but another man by the name of Bruce Fromong would. Riccio said, "Fromong had taken the collection as collateral from Mike (Gilbert) for an unpaid debt, and Bruce wanted to sell it all." Riccio and Beardsley met Fromong at the Palace Hotel parking lot, where he examined the items that Beardsley and Fromong wanted to sell.

After Riccio examined the items, he, Beardsley, and Fromong went back up to his room and waited for the so-called millionaire buyer that Riccio had set up to buy the O. J. memorabilia collection. O. J.'s stuff, along with other memorabilia, was laid out on Riccio's bed in his hotel room.

Riccio in his book *Busted* said, "I even got a chance to take some pictures with my new iPhone of weird Al [Beardsley] posing proudly with his collection of stolen O. J. crap."

Riccio received a call around 7:30 PM from O. J. stating he and his guys were in the lobby. After hanging up the phone, Riccio told Al and Fromong that he'd go down to the lobby and he'd bring the potential buyer back up to the room.

This man knew the system and how it works. Setting up O. J., Beardsley, and Fromong was like child's play for Thomas Riccio.

Once Riccio, O. J., and the rest of O. J.'s people arrived at the door, Riccio put in the card key and opened the door as all of them rushed in.

"O. J. was pissed and let them know it right away," Riccio said.

"You think you can steal my shit and get away with it," O. J. yelled.

"O. J. was yelling, and you know what? Everything was actually going as planned—everything was fine. Al and Bruce were completely cowed. They were happy to hand the stuff over to O. J. No problem," Riccio said.

As all this was going on, O. J., the people with him, Beardsley, and Fromong had no knowledge that Thomas J. Riccio, a convicted felon and a scam artist, had been recording the whole affair.

Keep in mind that recording conversations in the state of Nevada, as well as the phone conversation with O. J. in his Florida home while Riccio was in Los Angeles, is a criminal offense and is considered a felony in those states.

"Hours later," according to Riccio, in *Busted*, "I turned on the TV, and O. J. was not exaggerating. The early news reports were falsely accusing him of breaking into my room with a gun, but O. J. never broke into my room. I let him in and never saw him with a gun."

The day after the incident, Thomas J. Riccio began his quest to sell the tape recording of the incident in his hotel room in Vegas to the highest bidder. Riccio was asking $2 million dollars.

An excerpt from page 187 of the book *Busted* is as follows:

> I called TMZ and hinted that I had a recording of the now famous Las Vegas Caper. Harvey Levin called a special emergency meeting with us to negotiate a deal. My lawyer Stanley Lieber came with us to the meeting and made Levin sign a nondisclosure agreement promising not to talk about the digital recorder or its contents without an agreement in place. Once Harvey Levin signed our paperwork, we all sat down to listen to the recording, and I watched Harvey smile like a virgin in a whorehouse on a free night. Problem was this

wasn't a free night! So I stated my price and watched his reaction change."

"TWO MILLION DOLLARS! Wow! Please tell me that's a joke," Harvey begged.

Harvey made us a counteroffer as ridiculously low as mine was high. We went back and forth. They made a few "last offers," and we threatened to leave and take the recording elsewhere. Every classic dealing tactic was used by both sides, but in this case, we wanted to sell it. After they finally made a realistic counteroffer that we could live with, we took it. Done Deal! The digital recording would be heard by millions of people within hours.

The taped conversations aired immediately on *TMZ*. The Las Vegas police department contacted Riccio and his lawyer and arrangements were made to turn over the original tape. In doing so, Riccio's lawyer was able to get him immunity from prosecution for wiretapping and withholding evidence. Convicted felon Thomas J. Riccio had gotten away with another scam.

After O. J. Simpson was convicted for allegedly stealing his own items, Riccio continued to profit by publishing the book titled *Busted*, which was released in 2008.

O. J., on the other hand, at age sixty-one, was found guilty on all charges while Thomas Riccio was set free. On December 5, 2008, O. J. received the maximum sentence, nine to thirty-three years, all for trying to get back what belonged to him. As the clerk for Clark County District Court read out the sentence, O. J. slumped back in his seat as the guards approached the defense table to take him into custody.

I make no real attempt in this chapter to cover the trial and testimony. To me, this trial was a setup from the very beginning with Thomas Riccio and the Clark County Prosecutor's Office.

Was Thomas Riccio, from the very beginning, setting O. J. up for the money alone? Or was it that Riccio had agreed to help put O. J.

away, either as a bargaining tool, used by criminals so often, or in exchange for something he was threatened to be charged with if he didn't cooperate?

Either way, Thomas Riccio walked free. *Why?*

After setting up O. J., Thomas Riccio stands to make millions of dollars from the sale of the tape recording, his book, and now a movie.

Who says that a criminal cannot profit from a crime. Thomas Riccio did.

In a surprise ruling in August of 2009, a state district judge ruled that all of the items that belonged to O. J. that had been taken by O. J. from Riccio's room at the Palace Station Hotel were to be returned to O. J.

In other words, O. J. went to the Palace Hotel, met with Riccio, confronted Beardsley and Fromong, in Riccio's room, took *his* items that belonged to *him*, was later charged with kidnapping and burglary, only to have the same items *returned to him* by California Superior Court Judge Gerald Rosenberg on August 20, 2009.

Alfred Beardsley and Bruce Fromong were selling stolen merchandise. In Riccio's statement he admitted that Beardsley and Fromong knew full well that the items they were selling were stolen from O. J. Simpson and belonged to O. J. Like Riccio, Beardsley and Fromong also committed a felony taking stolen property across state lines, which is a state and federal offense titled Interstate Transportation of Stolen Goods. How did Beardsley, Fromong, as well as Riccio, commit a crime and have no charges filed against them and, at the same time, be complaining witnesses?

O. J. now sits in prison in Lovelock Correctional Facility in Nevada, serving nine to thirty-three years, while the original perpetrators walk free.

Is that justice? I don't think so.

Beardsley, one of the men robbed, admitted on the stand during the trial that he did not want O. J. prosecuted, but the district attorney forced him to. Strangely enough, I have learned that before the trial, the Clark County district attorney, who was prosecuting O. J., left Las Vegas and flew to Los Angeles and met with the county's district attorney. *Why?*

Did the jurors find O. J. guilty of this so-called robbery and kidnapping, or was it their way of punishing O. J. for not being found guilty in the murders of Nicole Simpson and Ron Goldman?

You be the judge.

I have been a private investigator for over forty-five years; I can't help but believe that this Las Vegas arrest and conviction was nothing more than a miscarriage of justice.

56

WHO REALLY IS CHRISTIE PRODY?

IN 1996, JURORS RETURNED a not guilty verdict for O. J. As soon as O. J. was released, he immediately wanted to go back to his home on Rockingham. When his vehicle arrived, the gates opened and the SUV entered. A guard stood just inside. Numerous bystanders, as well as many members of the press, had observed O. J. riding as a passenger through the gates.

What O. J. did not know, and very few others noticed, was that there was a striking blond woman with long hair, in her twenties, observing all this as it happened. Most interesting was the fact that this particular woman resembled Nicole Simpson.

This same woman appeared outside the gates, by the same driveway where O. J. entered, every day for the next two weeks. Evidently this woman had nothing more important to do than watching and hoping to meet O. J.

Finally, the guard realized she was not going to go away. They struck up a conversation. According to the guard, this young lady was not going to leave until she could meet O. J. and talk with him. The guard told O. J. that there was a woman who had been walking back and forth in front of the gate for several weeks who resembled Nicole. "What does she want?" O. J. asked. The guard told O. J. she wanted to meet him.

O. J. IS INNOCENT

O. J. watched her from upstairs for several days. He finally made up his mind that he wanted to meet this woman who looked so much like Nicole. He walked out of the house toward the guard at the front driveway gate and told him to open the gate just enough for him to slide out. The gate opened slightly and O. J. squeezed through. There, standing in the driveway, he first met Christie Michelle Prody.

That began a twelve-year relationship.

O. J. and Christie Prody, forty years his junior, began to appear together in articles and on television. The stories for the next twelve years were not flattering but Christie didn't seem to mind, just as long as she could appear with O. J.

When O. J. was arrested for the Las Vegas fiasco, Prody was in the Las Vegas courtroom. While O. J. was being arraigned and tried, Prody was filmed sitting in court. After October of 2008, when O. J. was found guilty and sentenced to nine to thirty-three years, Christie was no longer seen.

For whatever reason, Christie packed her bags and moved out of O. J.'s South Florida home and headed back to Minnesota. Christie wasted no time in starting a new life in Fergus Falls, Minnesota. On July 29, 2009, Christie Prody gave birth to a five-pound, eight-ounce little girl she named Madeline. The baby was not O. J.'s but was fathered by a man she took up with when she moved to Minnesota.

Before the baby was born, Christie claims she checked into a rehab facility for her addiction to alcohol. In looking at Christie's life, I found not only alcohol dependence but drug addiction as well.

She had been using drugs for quite some time. Not much was known about Christie Prody or her past; she just appeared on O. J. Simpson's doorstep out of nowhere.

I knew from the many articles written over the past twelve years that Christie and O. J. had a very explosive and volatile relationship. According to these articles, this was O. J.'s fault. Friends that I spoke to said that was not true, they said it was Christie's addiction to drugs and alcohol, a problem she had before she ever met O. J.

I wondered just why O. J. would continue this relationship for twelve years. I reached over and picked up a picture of Nicole and compared it with Christie Prody. Yes, there was some likeness between the two. Maybe having Christie around reminded him of Nicole. If I was right, and O. J. had not committed the murders, then his comfort with this resemblance would explain their relationship.

On September 15 and 16 of 2009, Christie appeared on the national TV show *Inside Edition*, in a two-part interview.

She was asked: "What went through your mind when you knew he [O. J.] was going to jail for a long time?"

Prody responded: "That it was now time for me to be free and start my life over."

She was asked: "Was he ever violent with you?"

Prody responded: "Yes."

"Did he hit you?"

Her response: "Yes."

She was then asked: "Did you honestly believe if you left, he would kill you?"

"Yeah, I did . . . . He called and said he would come over there and shoot me and shoot himself."

"Did he [O. J.] own a gun?"

Prody responded: "Yes, he did."

"Do you believe that O. J. Simpson killed Nicole and Ron?"

Prody said: "Yes."

Then she was asked: "Did he [O. J.] ever admit to you that he did it?"

Prody: "In so many words, he did."

She continued her appearance on other shows with similar questions and continued to blame O. J. for all her problems.

Then Christie Prody came out and said she had made a book deal for a tell-all that would be released in 2010.

Now, the whole story was coming out. Christie was coming out early to promote her upcoming book release. She admitted the book would contain details involving O. J., a twisted life on drugs and alcohol, as well as sex and violence. The kind of book a lot of people would run to order.

Christie was portraying herself as a victim. Was she really a victim or was this her way of being famous and living in the limelight as she had been when she lived with O. J.?

Who is Christie Prody?

She was born Christie Michelle Prody on April 21, 1975, in Fargo, North Dakota. Her social security card was issued between 1980 and 1981; she had a Minnesota driver's license that expired in 2000.

I decided to look into Christie Prody's life to see if she was another O. J. victim or if she herself might be hiding a criminal past. None of the numerous interviewers asked if she had a criminal record. Did she have a record and, if so, did it relate to drugs? I was interested in determining her truth and veracity. After all, this was the woman who stood outside the gate at Rockingham for weeks after O. J.'s trial, just to meet him. O. J. was not the stalker in this case. Prody was.

This was a woman who wanted to have her fifteen minutes of fame. Who is the victim in this strange situation? I don't think it's Christie Prody.

After viewing her criminal records, the one that stood out most was an arrest made on December 16, 2000, for Fraud–False Statement. Could she be making false statements about O. J.?

You will have to judge that for yourself.

Criminal Record: Christie Michelle Prody
DOB: 04/21/1975

State: Florida
County: Miami-Dade
Court Case #: B06050559
Offense: Drug Paraphernalia/Possession

State: Florida
County: Dade
Offense Date: 01/19/2002
Arrest Date: 06/11/2002
Court Case #: 132002MM0320110001XX
Court Level/Degree: First Degree Misdemeanor
Court Plea: Nolo Contendere

State: Florida
County: Dade
Offense Date: 12/16/2000
Arrest Date: 12/16/2000
Court Case #: M00070999
Arrest Statute: Fraud–False Statement
Arrest Level/Degree: Second Degree Misdemeanor
Court Disposition: Transfer to Traffic Court

State: Florida
County: Miami-Dade
Arrest Date: 03/28/2007
Offense: Bench Warrant

57

FILM FESTIVAL

ON FEBRUARY 10, 2008, we were invited to enter our documentary, *The Overlooked Suspect*, into the prestigious Backlot Film Festival in Culver City, California. I was surprised to receive the invitation as we had been turned down so many times before from film festivals all across the country, including my hometown, The Dallas Film Festival.

I called Phil Smith, John McCready, and all the members of our team to tell them the good news. They were so excited. Culver City is a suburb of Los Angeles, so hopefully the announcement and showing would reach the LAPD, the DA, and the attorney general's office. If so, my fourteen years investigating this case would not be in vain. Even though I thought the chances of winning were slim, I didn't care. Finally, someone else would view the film.

On April 2, 2008, Phil Smith, John McCready, Phil Thompson, and I arrived in L.A. for the three-day event. We rented a van and loaded the trunks inside. Instead of driving directly to the our hotel, we drove to the historic Veterans Memorial Building in Culver City, where the film festival was to take place. Inside, a huge auditorium had been decorated for the upcoming event. As we looked around the darkened auditorium, a man's voice called out, "Can I help you?"

I turned and said, "I'm Bill Dear."

A man could be seen walking up the darkened aisle. As he approached he said, "I'm Ross Hawkins, the director." As we shook hands, he added, "We all are certainly looking forward to the showing of your film. If I can help you in any way just let me or my staff know."

"I'd like to put up two easels with the announcement of our showing," I said, knowing that the poster board Phil Thompson had worked so hard on would draw a great deal of attention.

We followed Ross to the entrance so he could show us what he thought would be the best vantage point. Actually, when you first walked into the entrance doors, you couldn't miss it.

Of course, by this time we were all excited, ready for dinner and a good night's sleep. The film festival was to start the next day, Thursday, but our showing would not be until Friday, at 6 PM.

On Thursday, I drove over to the Memorial Building and sat through the next five hours of short films. You can always learn something from other people.

The time went by rapidly. As I left the auditorium, Ross came up and greeted me, "There is a lot of interest in your film."

As I left, my heart began to beat rapidly. Tomorrow would be my turn.

That night I had been invited to visit with a friend at his new home in Beverly Hills. We met originally after my O. J. book was published. He'd called my office and told my secretary, Donna, that it was the best book he had read so far on the murders of Nicole Simpson and Ron Goldman. Our first conversation was over the phone. Now, five years later, we had become good friends. I had visited with him a number of times and discussed my continuing investigation, which he always encouraged and urged me not to give up. I appreciated that and our friendship.

After I left his home, I went back to the hotel, parked the car, and took the elevator to the room. As I entered I saw the blinking light on my bedside phone: there were six messages wishing me good luck.

I sat down on the couch and reminisced about the past fourteen years. Why was my investigation into the murders of Nicole and Goldman not being taken seriously? But as my friend had said earlier that night, they just want this case to go away.

I laid my head back on the couch and dozed off. When I awoke, it was 7 AM and the phone was ringing.

"Bill, it's John." John had been my closest friend for the past twenty years. "Let's have breakfast."

"I'll meet you in the lobby. Give me thirty minutes."

John was seated by the booth inside the Marriott Hotel Coffee Shop.

"You know, John, I'm not the least bit hungry."

I told him I was going to head over to the festival and watch other documentaries.

Later that evening, I returned to find dozens of reporters and camera crews set up outside the front doors of the festival. John McCready and Phil Thompson were outside waiting for me. I greeted them. Ross Hawkins came over. "Did you see who just pulled up in that black limousine?" he asked.

Looking over toward the parking lot, I saw three men standing next to the limo.

One of the men waved as the reporters and camera crew rushed toward them. The man wasn't waving at them—he was waving at me. Casually dressed, he walked toward me. "Bill," he stuck out his hand and gave me hug, "glad we're not late." It was my friend, whom I'd had dinner with the night before, Charlie Sheen, accompanied by his friend, Michael Boatman (*Spin City*), and his chauffeur, Dylan Keane.

"What are you doing here?" I asked. "You've already seen the film several times."

"What are friends for?" he replied.

They walked inside and sat down near the front. Everyone there had come up and greeted Charlie as he entered the auditorium. Charlie was his usual self, taking time to shake hands and greet all of those who came up to him.

The theater darkened. As it did, Ross Hawkins came onto the stage and said, "The film you are about to see will make you wonder, *Have we overlooked a major suspect in the murders of Nicole Simpson and Ron*

Goldman? You judge for yourself." As Ross turned and exited, the film began.

I was seated by myself at the very back of the theater. I knew that if anyone in the audience got up at any time during the film to get a drink of water or use the bathroom, then my film was a failure. I could see Charlie, Michael, and his two other friends sitting there engrossed in the film. They had seen it before, but they still wanted to see it again.

Eighty-four minutes later the film was over. Ross entered the stage, approached the podium and introduced me for a Q and A session. I went onto the stage and was greeted with great applause from the audience. No one had left their seat during the eighty-four minutes it took to show the film. The film was good—not great. Improvements could be made; but it shocked those in attendance. That was evident from the many questions I answered for the next forty-five minutes.

I left the stage and Charlie and Michael said, "Bill, your fourteen years of investigating the murders speak for itself."

We all walked outside to the waiting reporters and cameras. I began to answer their questions. As I did, I saw Charlie and his friends walk toward his waiting limousine. Just as Charlie approached the car, he turned and stuck his thumb up, indicating it was a winner. I turned back to the reporters as my friend drove off. He had to be back on the set of *Two and Half Men*.

When I awoke the next morning, I realized it was Saturday. That night would be the main event honoring Carl Reiner, followed by the awards ceremony announcing the winners of this year's film festival.

I made arrangements for all of us to meet at the auditorium around 5:30 PM. There was to be a buffet for the guests. As I pulled up, the parking lot was full. I saw Carl Reiner and his son, Rob Reiner, get out of their car. Parked alongside was Lily Tomlin.

I met my group inside at the buffet. Looking around I saw Mary Tyler Moore, Dick Van Dyke, Steve Martin, Rose Marie, Henry Winkler, Mickey Rooney, Penny Marshall, and Stella Stevens. It was like a

Who's Who of Movies and Television. As the buffet came to a close, everyone departed for the auditorium.

This time my friends and I sat near the front. Rob Reiner was introduced and became the emcee for his father's tribute. As the tributes came to a close, Rob Reiner introduced his father, the honoree for the evening. For the next twenty minutes I listened as Carl Reiner spoke. I was so mesmerized I forgot that the award ceremony for the films would be next. As Carl Reiner left, to a standing ovation, Ross Harding approached the podium and introduced academy award winner Stella Stevens, who would announce the winners of this year's Backlot Film Festival.

Even though I am very much an optimist, I had convinced myself not to get my hopes up.

As Ms. Stevens announced the winners of the next two categories, I knew the nominees for best documentary came next.

Now I could feel what it was like at the Academy Awards. This was no comparison, but to me it was and I was sure it was to all of those there.

My heart began to pound so loudly inside my chest I thought everyone around me could hear it. Ms. Stevens was handed the envelope by Ross Harding—it seemed as if the whole event was happening in slow motion. She opened the envelope, pulled out the card and read, "The winner of the 2008 Backlot Film Festival goes to . . . *The Overlooked Suspect*, produced by William C. Dear."

This was not a dream or my imagination; she had read *my* name. I had won! It took me a few minutes, actually a few seconds, to stand up, walk toward the stage, up the stairs and to the podium where Ms. Stevens handed me the award.

"Ladies and gentlemen,"—as I began to speak, the struggles of my investigation passed through my mind. "I have spent fourteen years seeking the truth to the murders of Nicole Simpson and Ron Goldman. I will continue to do so in hopes that I will finally bring closure to the families of Nicole Simpson and Ron Goldman."

My journey toward closure was taking another step to fruition.

58

ATTORNEY GENERAL'S MEETING

O N JULY 5, 2008, John McCready sent a letter to the new California attorney general, Edmund G. Brown Jr., who had been previously governor of California. This was our last of many attempts to visit with the previous attorney generals and now possibly with Jerry Brown Jr.

This time we struck gold. A member of Attorney General Brown's Division of Law Enforcement called John McCready and from that conversation in August, a meeting for the first time in fourteen years was established. The agent who called was Special Agent Cavalieri from the Bureau of Investigation and Intelligence located in Commerce, California. John and Special Agent Cavalieri set the meeting for 1:30 PM on Friday, September 5, at the Department of Justice at 300 South Spring Street in Los Angeles.

We fully realized this meeting would be our only chance to present what we all considered facts and not theory. Because of this, we arranged to take with us only the most important facts and evidence related to our fourteen-year investigation.

The evidence to be presented included: the knife, the knife sheath, Jason's diaries, his prescription bottles for Depakote, his altered time card, photographs of Jason wearing the dark knit cap, Jason's deposition, criminal records showing that Jason was on probation at the time of the murders for assaulting his previous employer with a knife, the transcript of Lt. Pietroni of LAPD indicating they never interviewed Jason Simpson during their investigation, interviews with Jason's former coworkers stating he had left work early that night, and interviews with those close to Jason who stated Jason had an explosive temper and was considered to have a Dr. Jekyll and Mr. Hyde personality.

My main concern was that once the meeting occurred and the evidence was shown, all of this evidence could in turn be impounded by the attorney general's staff, including Jason's dog's ashes.

Reluctant as I was, I stood watching, several days before the meeting, as each of the items were placed in a huge trunk, locked, and sealed. When FedEx arrived that afternoon, I told John, "At least we can track its travel." For the next two days John carefully followed the truck until it arrived in L.A. at the destination we had selected. Once we arrived in L.A., the trunk would be picked up by Phil Smith and Phil Thompson.

On September 4, we all arrived at DFW airport in Dallas and boarded American Airlines flight 2401, which was scheduled to arrive in L.A. at 6:40 PM. Arriving on time, Phil Thompson checked and found that the trunk, with its important cargo, had arrived intact and was being held for us. So far, so good.

Phil Smith and Phil Thompson drove over and picked up the trunk while John and I set off for the Marriott Hotel adjacent to the L.A. airport. Smith and Thompson were scheduled to stay with Phil Thompson's parents, who lived in a nearby suburb.

After John and I arrived at the Marriott and checked into our rooms, I looked at my watch. It was 8:26 PM, just seventeen hours before our meeting.

I had brought with me a number of documents in my briefcase so I could prepare for the next day's crucial meeting. At 10:40 PM the bedside phone rang; it was Phil Smith.

He told me to pull the testimony of the crime scene expert who had been on the scene and gathered evidence at both Bundy and Rockingham.

"Let me call you right back." It took me about thirty minutes and from my laptop I found what Phil had called about. I called Phil back and said, "Yes, I have her testimony in front of me."

"Go to the section where she talks about the knit cap found at the crime scene."

"I have it."

"Now, read it out loud."

I did. "Found in the knit cap at the Bundy crime scene were human hairs, material fragments, and animal hairs," I read to Phil.

"Now, look at the picture of Jason in bed wearing the knit cap and playing with his dog."

Within minutes I found what I consider to be one of the most crucial pieces of evidence in the case. I hesitated for a minute, trying to catch my breath. "Phil, let me call you right back."

I immediately went to my address book and placed a call. A voice on the other end said, "Hello, who in the hell is this?"

"*****, it's me."

"Okay, now that I know who it is, what do you want at this hour, since I have to get up at 5 AM?"

"The animal hairs found in the knit cap—what kind of animal did the hairs come from?"

"Why do you want to know this?"

"*****, it's important."

"All right, a dog. Are you satisfied? Can I go back to sleep now?"

"Go back to sleep. I owe you."

"You bet you do." was his reply.

I quickly dialed Phil back. "Phil, the animal hair found in the knit cap was from a dog."

As I continued to talk to Phil, I looked again at the color picture with Jason in bed wearing what we all felt was the knit cap found at the Bundy crime scene, his dog there in bed with him.

Hanging up the phone, I was upset with myself for having overlooked the obvious. I was now convinced that the dog hair was from Jason Simpson's dog and the knit cap was the same cap found at the scene of the murders of Nicole and Goldman. With the unidentified human hair found in the knit cap not belonging to O. J., there was every possibility it belonged to his son, Jason.

The skin found underneath Nicole Simpson's fingernails was not proved to be from O. J., the hair found in the knit cap was not O. J.'s, and the animal hair found was from a dog.

Within minutes my phone rang again. It was *****.

"You've got me curious."

I then told him what we had uncovered.

"You're never going to give up on this case are you?"

"No. Hell, no."

"Just between me and you, I think you're on the right track. Good luck. Keep in mind you're fighting against heavy odds. They will stop you in every way possible. This is one case they do not want to come back and kick them in the ass. Please, Bill, just don't cost me my job."

"I won't. That's a promise."

He hung up.

The LAPD never compared Jason Simpson's fingerprints to those found unidentified at the crime scene and certainly hadn't compared his hair to the hair in the knit cap.

Why?

Because Jason was never considered a suspect and on top of that, he was never interviewed by the LAPD even though he was on probation for assault with a deadly weapon when the murders occurred.

There was nothing left for me to do but turn out the light and get some sleep. It would be a big day tomorrow. As I closed my eyes, I remembered what I had taught for so many years: *Never Assume, Always Verify.*

That was the rule the LAPD failed to follow.

I got up early the next morning, met John McCready and went downstairs then out front. Waiting for us was Phil Smith and Phil Thompson. Both smiled from inside the car.

John and I slid into the back seat and we set out for the Justice Building. We knew we were early but we wanted to take a look around and take a few shots of the front of the building.

The building was unimpressive. It was a tall, somewhat boxy structure with windows that were tinted to ensure you couldn't see inside

At 12:45 PM, we eased the car into a parking space, unloaded our trunk full of vital contents onto a borrowed dolly, and headed for the front door of the drab grey building.

I was proud of our investigation. There was no one opening doors for us during the past fourteen years. It was just pure determination.

With the trunk and file boxes in tow we approached the door as it was opened by a California state trooper. He was there to help us and give our boxes and trunk the VIP treatment. Everyone else went through a metal detector but we went right through, escorted by one of two troopers.

Once past the metal detectors, it wasn't five minutes before a man identifying himself as Special Agent Cary Cavalieri met us. We followed him and the evidence onto an elevator. The elevator doors opened and we shoved out the dolly and file boxes and headed down the hallway following Cavalieri, a man of few words. He showed us into a small conference room, no more than fifteen by twenty feet, where we were given time to unpack and lay out materials for our presentation.

It was less than fifteen minutes before the door opened and we were joined in the small, nondescript room by Special Agents Cavalieri, Diane Wigland, Supervisor Randall Hew, Danny Kim, and Agent in Charge Carlos Solano. Wigland, Hew, Kim, and Solano sat across from us at the conference table while Cavalieri sat by himself in a chair by the door.

We introduced ourselves and exchanged cards. I began passing out photocopies of Jason's diaries and other copied items of importance.

All four agents seated across from us were cordial and receptive. I presented our evidence, including the knife, the sheath, and photographs and at the end of our hour and a half with very few interruptions, I closed my presentation. John McCready said a few words, then all of the questions were turned over to the five agents. Solano and Wigland expressed concern for the evidence and wondered if it was being kept in a safe area. I assured them it was. It was in a bank vault.

Wigland said, "I hope the LAPD hasn't gotten rid of all their evidence."

"I hope not either," was my reply.

"I would hate to go over there [LAPD] and find the evidence missing," she said.

Four agents in particular, Hew, Solano, Wigland and Kim, seemed very interested in what we had uncovered in our long investigation. We were assured by Agent in Charge Solano that they would be back in touch with us within the next two weeks. As the meeting broke up, two agents headed to the men's bathroom. John McCready was already inside.

Hew, the supervising agent, said, "You know John, the LAPD and the DA have no intention of helping you."

"Yes, I know," said John.

"That's why we're involved. Do you know what the ramifications would be if this comes out? This information you have given us will have to go all the way to the top."

Hew went on to say he was a scientist and it became obvious not only from the meeting but from now, in conversation, that he was interested in Jason's dog's ashes. He wasn't sure if ashes could be used for DNA along with the animal hair found in the knit cap, but he was going to find out.

While John spoke with Hew, Phil Smith, Phil Thompson, and I loaded the file boxes and trunk under the watchful supervision of Cavalieri. Finally John joined us and we retraced our way back to the entrance of the Justice Building. Phil Smith hurried out first with his camera to snap pictures of us leaving so there would be no question as to whether we were there on September 5, 2008.

After loading the car, we headed out to eat and what I hoped would be an early bedtime for me. I was tired and more than that, I was exhausted. The next day Smith, Thompson and I headed back to Dallas with our evidence in hand while John left for Austin.

We would have to wait two weeks, as we had given our word to Solano not to do anything further until we heard from him.

Flying back to Dallas, I knew that our presentation had struck home. Was the evidence still with the LAPD or DA or had it been destroyed? Would politics now rear its ugly head again and strike us where it hurt the most?

Two weeks passed and O. J.'s trial was in full bloom. Still no word from Solano. We waited another week, and then contacted Solano. "No word yet," was the reply. Then five weeks, "Sorry, still no reply." O. J. was found guilty in Las Vegas and within a week we received a letter dated October 27, 2008, from Special Agent Carlos Solano. The last paragraph read: "The California Department of Justice considers this case closed and will not conduct any further investigation into this matter. In addition, the LAPD and the L.A. County District Attorney's Office have also stated to you they consider the investigation closed."

It took fifty-three days, not the two weeks that Solano had told us. They waited until the guilty verdict for O. J. in Vegas before notifying us: case closed.

I wonder, had O. J. been found innocent, would that have made a difference? In the meantime, we learned that Attorney General Jerry Brown Jr. was planning on running for governor again, possibly against Diane Feinstein. With the verdict going against O. J. and the general public glad O. J. was found guilty this time, were possible political ramifications the real reason they chose "not to conduct any further investigation"? Did the attorney general's office and possibly a future candidate for governor feel it was best to let sleeping dogs lie?

As I have said before . . . You be the judge.

O. J. IS INNOCENT

EDMUND G. BROWN JR.
Attorney General

State of California
DEPARTMENT OF JUSTICE

DIVISION OF LAW ENFORCEMENT
5700 SOUTH EASTERN AVENUE
LOS ANGELES, CA 90040
Public: (323) 869-3400
Facsimile: (323) 869-3444

October 27, 2008

John A. McCready, Chief Executive Officer
The Overlooked Suspect, Inc.
3883 Turtle Creek Blvd.
Dallas, TX 75219

Dear: Mr. McCready,

On Friday, September 8th 2008, you and your staff presented the results of your 14-year investigation regarding the murders of Nicole Simpson and Ron Goldman to members from the California Department of Justice, Bureau of Investigation and Intelligence.

After careful review of your suggested theory, we have concluded that due to the circumstantial nature and conjecture involved, the issues presented lack the proof that would be required in any court of law. Therefore, no further law enforcement investigation is warranted.

The California Department of Justice considers this case closed and will not conduct any further investigation into this matter. In addition, the Los Angeles Police Department and the Los Angeles County District Attorney's Office have also stated to you that they consider the investigation closed.

Sincerely,

Carlos Solano
Special Agent in Charge

For   Edmund G. Brown Jr.
       Attorney General

vs

cc: Administration File
       BII Headquarters
       Attorney General's Public Inquiry Unit, Reference #229820

59

FREEDOM OF INFORMATION ACT REQUESTS

ON A TELEVISION PROGRAM I watched recently, DNA evidence was used to exonerate an individual after eighteen years, As a result, the original case was reopened and this innocent man set free. If years and years later, evidence comes forth showing O. J. was in fact innocent, why not reopen the case to determine who actually is responsible for the crime?

Apparently, not in this case. No matter what evidence we've uncovered, the LAPD and DA's office is determined that O. J. is guilty. Period. How can such prominent law enforcement agencies have such closed-minded attitudes in determining, no matter what, they are right?

When Officer Harding stated the case was closed, I then felt there would be no reason why they would not allow us to look at the evidence.

Again I was wrong.

We had sent a Freedom of Information request in April of 2009 but were given the usual runaround. As a result, two new requests were made.

On July 15, 2009, I had Dwight Carmichael, my attorney again file a Freedom of Information Request to see the files and evidence in possession of the LAPD. On July 16, I filed the same request with the L.A. County District Attorney's Office. Both requests were sent certified mail with return receipt requested. LAPD signed their receipt on July 15 and the L.A. County District Attorney's Office on July 16.

On August 7, we received a response from the L.A. County District Attorney's Office by Chief Assistant DA William Hodgman, who had been involved originally in the O. J. trial.

Mr. Hodgman offered to make arrangements for us to look at the on-scene photographs taken by the LAPD.

With regard to the additional items in my request: the knit cap (watch cap) with hair, both dog and human; clothes of the victims; fingerprints, both identified and unidentified; and the DNA samples with the results, I was given the following response: "Please be advised, we are still attempting to locate them. If and when these are located, we will notify you in writing."

Suddenly, I remembered our meeting with the Bureau of Investigation and Intelligence in which Special Agent Diane Wigland had said after my presentation, "I hope the LAPD hasn't destroyed the files as it would make our job near impossible."

I couldn't help but think of that statement after reading, " . . . still attempting to locate them . . . "

August 24, I wrote another letter to Mr. Hodgman, which he signed for four days later. By November 1, I still had not received a response from my second letter to Mr. Hodgman.

On August 26, I did receive a response from the LAPD:

"I am denying this portion of your request," signed Raymond D. Crisp on behalf of William J. Braxton, Chief of Police, and the Los Angeles Police Department.

Most of the other portions of the request were directed to the DA's office, which had already responded to their letter.

It reminded me of a dog chasing its own tail. It was going nowhere.

You be the judge. The letters speak for themselves.

Oh, Just one last thing. Look at Hodgman's letter again. I guess they did establish the animal hair found on the knit cap was from a dog.

How surprising.

FREEDOM OF INFORMATION ACT REQUESTS

William Dear & Associates, INC
Internationally Acclaimed Private Investigator
TBOISA-C-00139

Texas Office
204 W. Highway 31
P.O. Box 32
Mt. Calm, TX. 76673
Office 254-993-1770
Fax   254-933-1171

William C. Dear,
President
Email: adearoo7@aol.com
Cell 972-679-5632**

Ranch
541/LCR131
P.O. Box 32
Mt. Calm, TX 76673
Office 254-993-1126
Fax   254-993-1241

June 18, 2009

Chief William J. Bratton
Los Angeles Police Department
150 N. Los Angeles Street
Los Angeles, California 90012

Subject: Public Records Request

Dear Chief Bratton:

    I am a Texas private investigator who has investigated and written a book regarding the Orenthal James Simpson case. This is an official request pursuant to the California Public Records Act or other law for production of the following things regarding People v. Orenthal James Simpson BA097211 (Nicole Simpson and Ronald Goldman murders):

        Knit watch cap with hair, dog and human;
        crime scene photographs;
        clothes of the victims;
        fingerprints, both identified and unidentified;
        DNA samples and results.

    Pursuant to Section 6250 et seq. of the Act, please notify me when the above-referenced information is available and of the time and place at which I may view it.

    I specifically do NOT request the following, described on your official website as being exempt:
        --Identifying juvenile information
        --Identifying victim information associated with crimes to Penal Code Section 261, 264, 264.1, 273a, 273d, 286, 288, or 289
        --Identifying confidential informant information
        --Criminal offender record information
        --Information that may endanger the safety of a witness or other person
        --Information that may jeopardize an investigation, related investigation or law enforcement proceeding

O. J. IS INNOCENT

--Any portion of the report that reflects analysis, recommendation, or conclusion of the investigating officer
--Information that may disclose investigative techniques
--Information that my deprive a person of a fair trial
--Preliminary drafts, notes, or memorandums which are not retained in the ordinary course of business
--Records pertaining to pending litigation to which the city is a party until the litigation is adjudicated or settled
--Personnel, medical or similar files

A check in the amount of $25.00 is enclosed for this request.

If the items are no longer in the possession of your department, please advise whether the items exist and if so where you believe them to be housed.

Thank you very much.

Sincerely,

William C. Dear

I declare under oath that this request is made for investigative purposes by a licensed professional investigator.

_____

Sworn before me by William C. Dear on _____, 2009.

_____
Notary public, State of Texas

Dear, Bill\records request California\5.27.09

LOS ANGELES POLICE DEPARTMENT

ANTONIO R. VILLARAIGOSA
Mayor

WILLIAM J. BRATTON
Chief of Police

P. O. Box 30158
Los Angeles, California 90030
Telephone: (213) 978-2100
TDD: (877) 275-5273
Reference Number: 14.4

August 24, 2009

Mr. William C. Dear
William Dear & Associates, Inc.
204 West Highway 31
Mt. Calm, Texas 76673

Dear Mr. Dear:

I have reviewed your request for materials related to *People vs. Orenthal James Simpson*, Case No. BA097211. Your request was forwarded to my office from the Los Angeles Police Department's (the Department) Office of the Chief of Police and was made pursuant to the California Public Records Act (the Act).

The Department recognizes that the statutory scheme was enacted in order to maximize citizen access to the workings of government. However, the Act does not mandate disclosure of all documents within the government's possession. Rather, by specific exemption and reference to other statutes, the Act recognizes that there are boundaries where the public's right to access must be balanced against such weighty considerations as the right to privacy, a right of constitutional dimension under California Constitution, Article 1, Section 1. The law also exempts from disclosure records that are privileged or confidential or otherwise exempt under either express provisions of the Act or pursuant to applicable federal or state law, per California Government Code Sections 6254(b); 6254(c); 6254(f); 6254(k); and 6255.

I am responding to your request as follows:

Item No. 1

Knit watch cap with hair, dog and human.

Please contact the Los Angeles County District Attorney's Office at 210 West Temple Street Los Angeles, California 90012, telephone number (213) 974-3512, for information on obtaining materials from court cases.

Mr. William Dear
Page 2
14.4

Item No. 2

Crime scene photographs.

In accordance with Section 6254(f), records of investigations conducted by, or investigatory files compiled by any local police agency for law enforcement purposes are exempt from disclosure. While Section 6254(f) and its subparts do set forth a list of specific information that must ordinarily be disclosed from law enforcement investigatory files, this information does not include the disclosure of the actual documents and need only be provided if it relates to contemporaneous law enforcement activity. (See *County of Los Angeles v. Superior Court (Kusar) (1993)* 18 Cal. App. 4th 588, 22 Cal Rptr. 2d 409.) Your request seeks documents or records that are either investigatory records themselves or properly part of an investigative file; therefore, I am denying this portion of your request.

Item No. 3

Clothes of the victims.

Please see the response to Item No. 1.

Item No. 4

Fingerprints, both identified and unidentified.

Item No. 5

DNA samples and results.

With respect to Item Nos. 4 and 5, please see the response to Item No. 2.

Any correspondence regarding this matter should include a copy of this letter and be directed to the Los Angeles Police Department, Discovery Section, 201 North Los Angeles Street, Space 301, Los Angeles, California 90012. If you have any questions regarding this correspondence, please contact Management Analyst Carol McDonough of the Discovery Section at (213) 978-2153.

Very truly yours,

WILLIAM J. BRATTON
Chief of Police

RAYMOND D. CRISP, Senior Management Analyst
Officer-in-Charge, Discovery Section
Legal Affairs Division

LOS ANGELES COUNTY DISTRICT ATTORNEY'S OFFICE
BUREAU OF SPECIALIZED PROSECUTIONS
TARGET CRIMES DIVISION

STEVE COOLEY • District Attorney
JOHN K. SPILLANE • Chief Deputy District Attorney
CURTIS A. HAZELL • Assistant District Attorney

RICHARD DOYLE • Director

August 7, 2009

Mr. William C. Dear
204 W. Highway 31
P.O. Box 32
Mt. Calm TX 76673

Dear Mr. Dear:

CALIFORNIA PUBLIC RECORDS ACT REQUEST

Pursuant to your request under the California Public Records Act received by our office on July 16, 2009, our office has reviewed archival materials regarding *People v. Orenthal James Simpson* (our case number BA097211). Pursuant to our search for the items specified in your letter, we have located crime scene photographs which we will produce for your review. Please contact me so that arrangements can be made for you to view these photographs.

With regard to the additional items specified in your request (knit watch cap with hair, dog and human; clothes of the victims; fingerprints, both identified and unidentified; and DNA samples and results), please be advised we are still attempting to locate them. If and when these items are located, we will notify you in writing.

Very truly yours,

STEVE COOLEY
District Attorney

By *William Hodgman*

WILLIAM HODGMAN
Head Deputy District Attorney

mp

780 Hall of Records
320 West Temple Street
Los Angeles, CA 90012
(213) 974-5986

O. J. IS INNOCENT

August 24, 2009

Mr. William Hodgman
Head Deputy District Attorney
Los Angeles County District Attorney's Office
780 Hall of Records
320 West Temple Street
Los Angeles, Ca 90012

Re: California Public Records Act Request

Dear Mr. Hodgman:

In regards to your letter dated August 7, 2009 regarding People vs. James Orenthal Simpson, your case #BA097211, we wish to thank you for responding to our letter dated July 16, 2009, under the California Public Records Act.

Within the next few weeks we would like to make arrangements with you to view the crime scene photographs which you have located and stated in our letter dated August 7, 2009.

In paragraph 2 of your letter dated August 7, 2009, concerning the crucial evidence in our request to examine or view the knit watch cap with hair, dog and human; clothes of the victims; fingerprints, identified and unidentified; and DNA samples and results, we are concerned why this evidence is not easily accessible to you. In your letter you stated that you were attempting to locate them. Are you insinuating that the evidence has been destroyed or misplaced? I do not understand how this crucial evidence considered to be one of the top cases of the twentieth century could be misplaced. Since O.J. Simpson was found not guilty, I consider this case to still be unsolved.

Mr. Hodgman, do you consider this case closed, and as a result, has the evidence that I have requested has been destroyed? If so, when and where and by whose authority?

At one time, a great deal of the evidence was stored in a public storage facility in section A-29. Have the items that have been stored in that storage rental facility been vacated, with the evidence involving the murders of Nicole Simpson and Ron Goldman?

In the last sentence of Paragraph 2, you stated if and when these items are located, we will notify you in writing. What time frame are you considering in this response you gave me on August 7, 2009?

Thank you for your assistance in this matter.

I remain respectfully yours,

William C. Dear

470

60

JUSTICE OR PUBLICITY

THE **HEADLINE READ** "**NOTORIOUS** LA County crime evidence on display in Las Vegas."

On March 1, 2010, my friend Jack Lockhart emailed me the above-titled information that he found on the Internet. Jack was a strong believer in what I have been trying to accomplish for the past seventeen years and knew that I had the credentials to back it up.

I had worked closely with law enforcement agencies all over the world helping to solve murders. I was inducted into the American Police Hall of Fame in 1988 as a private investigator.

I read the story that Jack had emailed me, describing the exhibit. As I finished the article, I couldn't tell if I was angry or truly disappointed in the Los Angeles Police Department.

I walked over and picked up a letter dated August 7, 2009, that I had received in reply to my Freedom of Information Act request of July 16, 2009, to view crucial evidence of the Simpson, Goldman murder case.

Now, seven months later, I reread, for the fifth time, the following letter from William Hodgman, Head Deputy District Attorney with the Los Angeles County District Attorney's Office.

CALIFORNIA PUBLIC RECORDS ACT REQUEST

Pursuant to your request under the California Public Records Act received by our office on July 16, 2009, our office has reviewed archival materials regarding People v. Orenthal James Simpson (our case number BA097211). Pursuant to our search for the items specified in your letter, we have located crime scene photographs which we will produce for your review. Please contact me so that arrangements can be made for you to view these photographs.

With regard to the additional items specified in your request (knit watch cap with hair, dog and human; clothes of the victims; fingerprints, both identified and unidentified; and DNA samples and results), please be advised we are still attempting to locate them. If and when these items are located, we will notify you in writing.

Very truly yours,
Steve Cooley
District Attorney

By William Hodgman
Head Deputy District Attorney

I laid the letter back down on my desk, put my elbows up, and rested my head on my folded hands, recalling how stunned I was when I received that letter in August 2009. Hodgman had made it very clear that they could not find the crucial evidence that I requested in my investigation. This was the same evidence that he and his staff had used in the trial of O. J. Simpson for the murders of Nicole Simpson and Ron Goldman.

Yet, here was an article stating that the infamous gloves and knit cap, along with objects from other grizzly murder cases, would be on display at the Palms Casino Resort in Las Vegas, hosted by the Los

Angeles Police Department during the 2010 California Homicide Investigators Association (CHIA) Convention, to be held in the first week of March 2010. After the exhibit was viewed by investigators, it would be open for public viewing, beginning on March 3.

The gloves and particularly the knit cap were crucial pieces of evidence in the murders of Nicole Simpson and Ron Goldman. The murders were and still are listed as "Unsolved," but instead of securing these items, the LAPD was putting them on public display for the entire world to see.

Hodgman in his letter dated August 7, 2009, had stated, "If and when these items are located, we will notify you in writing."

Obviously they did locate the items that I requested, but I was never notified. Why?

Why would the LAPD play games when it comes to an unsolved murder case?

Why keep this evidence away from someone like myself who has worked diligently in seeking the truth into the murders?

What was their motive behind the refusal to allow me and my experts to examine the evidence, but instead allow the evidence to be used as publicity, an "attention getter" at a convention?

Why did District Attorney William Hodgman not keep his word as stated in his letter of August 7?

Was he lying to me originally or was it a plain cover-up to prevent me from finding out the truth?

Are the Los Angeles Police Department and the district attorney's office more interested in publicity than justice?

Are the Los Angeles Police Department and the district attorney's office afraid we will find out the truth in the murders of Nicole Simpson and Ron Goldman?

Why wouldn't it be important for the district attorney to compare the human hairs found in the knit cap (which were identified as coming from an African American, but as experts testified during the trial, did not belong to O. J. Simpson) with human hair from our major overlooked suspect?

Did the animal hair come from our overlooked suspect's dog that used to sleep with him? We have pictures of the dog and our suspect as they both played on his bed while the suspect was wearing a knit cap similar to the one found at the murder scene.

We have in our possession the dog's ashes that belonged to our overlooked suspect from his dog which he had cremated after the murders of Nicole Simpson and Ron Goldman.

Was the knit cap our suspect is wearing in the photo, while playing with the dog, the same one found at the crime scene? To me, the only way that this could be determined is by comparing the human and dog hairs with our overlooked suspect's.

I recalled a meeting John McCready and I had on Friday, September 5, 2008, with five agents of the State of California Investigative and Intelligence Division, who I understood were to report directly back to the attorney general, Jerry Brown. In this meeting, as I handed Special Agent Supervisor Randall Hew our suspect's dog's ashes he responded, "On Monday when our lab opens we will check with them to see if we can pull DNA from the dog's ashes."

That's why my original request was so important. Instead, the LAPD and district attorney's office chose to put the so-called missing items on public display.

This also caused me to recall that during a break, at that same meeting, Special Agent Randall Hew said to John McCready, in the bathroom,

"I am a science guy and I believe this is how this case will eventually be solved." He went on to say, "Do you realize that the LAPD and the district attorney's office do not want to have anything to do with you guys and that is why we are involved!"

The knit cap that was to be on display on March 3 for viewing by the general public was a crucial piece of evidence for me and the experts in my investigation. The knit cap and gloves should have been stored in a secured evidence facility and not put on public display where it could be contaminated, damaged, or lost.

As it turned out, many of the items on display caused a great deal of controversy.

The clothing Robert Kennedy wore when he was murdered was in the exhibit, much to the horror of his family. His son, Maxwell Taylor Kennedy, who had made a previous attempt to have these items returned to the Kennedy family, made these remarks, "As the child of a crime victim, I am guaranteed by the state constitution that my family and I will be treated with respect and dignity . . . I was horrified to learn that the LAPD had included the shirt, tie, and jacket my father was wearing when he was assassinated in an exhibit at the CHIA conference in Las Vegas."

In the *Los Angeles Times*, Maxwell Kennedy called the display "a cheap bid for attention" and went on to deride the LAPD: "The chief of police and the district attorney took my father's blood-soaked clothing and displayed it as part of a macabre publicity stunt. It is almost incomprehensible to imagine what circumstances would have led to a decision to transport these items across state lines to be gawked at by gamblers and tourists. It is demeaning to my family, but just as important, it is demeaning to the trust that the citizens place in their law enforcement officers."

Robert Kennedy's bloodstained clothing was removed from the exhibit and a public apology was issued to the Kennedy family.

Ropes and other items from the Tate murders were also on display. Debra Tate, the victim's sister said, "From my perspective, it's very disturbing."

On March 3, I hired RC, a professional cinematographer, to attend the opening of this homicide display viewing at The Palms. As RC pulled into the parking lot, he saw, on the hotel's marquee in large letters, that it advertised the homicide convention and the public viewing. It listed not only items of O. J., but items of Marilyn Monroe, Sharon Tate, and the assassination of Robert Kennedy.

As RC entered the hotel, he had no trouble finding where the homicide exhibition was. There were uniformed armed guards at the entrance. He began his filming as he started into the exhibition room, weaving his way around the crowd looking at the murder exhibits on display.

RC casually made his way to the display that contained items from the murders of Nicole Simpson and Ron Goldman. Within the display was a large see-through case that held the knit cap found at the murder scene! According to William Hodgman, Head Deputy District Attorney, the knit cap could not be located. To the left of the knit cap was a large brown clasp envelope titled EVIDENCE. Above this were the words "District Attorney's Office Los Angeles County" . . . At the bottom of the display case, below the knit cap, were the two bloody gloves found at the crime scene.

RC continued to film close-ups and distance shots of the entire exhibit involving the murders of Nicole Simpson and Ron Goldman.

To the left of the exhibit there was a uniformed LAPD sergeant, badge number 14184. As RC turned to face the officer, the camera continuing to roll, he asked the sergeant, "Is this case still open?"

"No," the officer replied as he shook his head.

I was shocked but not surprised the LAPD said this case is closed—but this case is not closed! There is no statute of limitations on murder. No one has been arrested and convicted in the murders of Nicole Brown Simpson and Ronald Goldman.

Is that justice for the families of Nicole and Ron?

My answer to that question is NO!

It is now January 1, 2012, and I still have not been able to view the evidence that I was promised by Head Deputy District Attorney William Hodgman.

Is that justice? NO!

Author's Closing Statement

YOU HAVE NOW COMPLETED my book *O. J. Is Innocent and I Can Prove It!* Before you continue with the following pages, I feel it is important for you, the reader, to understand that I am not a prosecutor nor am I attempting to play the part of a prosecutor. I consider myself a homicide investigator, a damned good one. What I have tried to bring forth are the facts that I have uncovered in my eighteen-year investigation into the murders of Nicole Simpson and Ron Goldman.

On Sunday, November 12, 2000, CBS aired a two-part miniseries about the behind-the-scenes activity in the O. J. Simpson trial. In its presentation, CBS made sure the viewer heard more than once the statement at the beginning of each of the miniseries that O. J. Simpson had filed a lawsuit to prevent the program from being aired, but his request had been denied. The show went even further by saying it was a story O. J. doesn't want you to see.

I viewed both parts of the program eagerly, hoping new facts would be discovered, but instead, all I saw was O. J.'s continuing denial: "I didn't do it," "I'm not guilty," and "I want to testify." Instead, the constant ethical and personality conflicts presented of the so-called Dream Team were featured. The inner turmoil certainly did not speak well of the judicial system. Only F. Lee Bailey throughout the show continued to state to the other attorneys that O. J. was innocent. He still does to this very day. There was no new evidence presented to refute what I had uncovered in my unbiased investigation into the murders.

O. J. IS INNOCENT

Seventeen years later, as O. J. sits in a Nevada prison, he continues to make the news, no longer on the cover but inside the pages of tabloids. He is still being accused of the murders of Nicole Simpson and Ron Goldman. His Las Vegas arrest and trial proved that.

After reading my book, you can see for yourself that the Los Angeles Police Department and Los Angeles County District Attorney's Office were determined to find O. J. guilty no matter what. If they couldn't get him one way, they made every effort to get him another, and with the Las Vegas arrest, trial, and conviction, *they did.*

You can also see for yourself how they were more than determined to prevent me from examining the crucial pieces of evidence that could bring closure to this case by determining that O. J. Simpson was not guilty of the murders, but may be guilty of protecting the overlooked suspect.

The facts along with the hypothesis are not an accusation of O. J.'s or our suspect's guilt or innocence. I am not on a vendetta or a political advocacy campaign. I may be wrong in my hypothesis, but I assure you, I have made every effort in attempting to seek the truth. I hope justice can be served by an arrest and conviction of the person or persons who committed the murders of Nicole Simpson and Ron Goldman.

In closing, I ask you to review the red flags, as they point to major issues at the heart of my investigation. These red flags should not be taken lightly and should cause you great concern, as they have me, regarding the guilt or innocence of O. J. Simpson.

After you have reached your conclusions, I ask that you take time to fill out the ballot on our website: www.ojisinnocentandicanproveit. com.

Even after eighteen years I feel that justice should prevail and closure should be brought to the brutal murders of Nicole Simpson and Ronald Goldman.

It is with your help that I hope a just conclusion will finally be met.

—William C. Dear
2012

IMPORTANT

*DO NOT READ THE
FOLLOWING PAGES UNTIL
YOU HAVE READ THE
INVESTIGATIVE REPORT
IN ITS ENTIRETY*

RED FLAGS

HOW MANY RED FLAGS do you need before you hoist a white flag? (This statement is directed toward all levels of the judicial system in the state of California who have to date never interviewed our suspect and want the case closed).

The following are the "red flags" we have uncovered that point to our suspect:

1. Phone rings repeatedly at suspect's residence beginning in the early hours of the morning of the murders with urgent recorded messages from his mother, grandmother and sister (he had a working answering machine), but suspect refused to pick up or call back until around 6:00 PM.

2. Girlfriend (Jennifer Green) and suspect leave Jackson's restaurant around 9:45 PM and suspect drops Jennifer off at her apartment and does not go up to her apartment.

3. Suspect's girlfriend (Jennifer Green) said that suspect came up to her apartment after they left the restaurant and they watched movies but separately and under oath (suspect's civil trial depositions) suspect said he kissed her and went home to his apartment and watched TV from 10:30 PM–3:00 AM.

4. Suspect says he was watching TV from 10:30 PM–3:00 AM night of murders. TV channels following midnight began to cut in announcing the reported killing of O. J.'s ex and someone else.

5. *L.A. Observer* weekend magazine featured our investigative report. After its publication, suspect suddenly sold his vehicle (Jeep—which we currently own and have in possession); leaves Los Angeles and heads to Florida where O. J. lives.

6. Suspect under oath (civil trial deposition) revealed that the recital dinner held at Mezzaluna restaurant was supposed to be held at Jackson's restaurant where our suspect was the sous chef the night of the murders, but Nicole failed to show up which upset our suspect and hurt him.

7. Discovered suspect's time card for the night of the murders. The suspect's official time card had been destroyed and replaced with an unofficial time card and the suspect hand wrote in his name and time for the day of the murders even though the time clock was working.

8. Discovered a picture of the suspect sitting on a bed with his dog wearing a dark seaman's/watch cap on his head, the same type of cap that was found at the crime scene. The picture shows a date prior to the murders. All other pictures of the suspect dated after the murders shows suspect wearing the same type of cap but never the same color.

9. The dark seaman cap found at the crime scene contained African American hair fibers that did not match O. J. and it also contained animal hair.

10. Our suspect sustained injuries (cuts) to his hand that were observed shortly after the murders.

11. Discovered and have in our possession the suspect's knife, which internationally acclaimed experts believe is the murder weapon. It is known as a boot knife and it has a cutting edge on

both sides of the blade along with a hand protector. This knife was designed for one purpose and one purpose only—to kill.

12. After examination of the knife by a world-renown forensic scientist, the butt of the knife appears to match the blow/injury Nicole Simpson suffered on the top of her head.

13. All experts who examined the crime scene and killings agree that it was a rage killing done by an amateur. Our suspect was diagnosed with a rage disorder known as intermittent rage disorder and just prior to the killings stopped taking his prescription, a drug known as Depakote, which was prescribed to control his rage and seizures.

14. The unknown set of footprints at the crime scene discovered by Dr. Henry Lee matches the size of our suspect's foot size (11½).

15. Discovered within suspect's personal possessions that he placed within a public storage facility was a death certificate of Aaren La Shone Simpson. Aaren drowned on August 26, 1979, at the age of twenty-three months, under our suspect's watch. Our suspect at the time of Aaren's death was nine and a half years old (born April 21, 1970).

16. In addition to the picture we have of our suspect with his dog, we also have the dog's ashes and evidence that the cap contained animal hair.

17. A short time prior to the killings of Nicole Simpson and Ron Goldman our suspect attacked a restaurant owner with a knife.

18. Following the murders (June 13, 1994) O. J. hired Carl Jones, a top criminal attorney in the L.A. area, not for himself but instead for our suspect. This was prior to O. J.'s arrest for murder.

19. On October 3, 1995 when the verdict was announced that O. J. Simpson was "not guilty" there were pictures that were taken within the courtroom which show all of O. J.'s family celebrating except for our suspect who was stone-faced, showing no emotion and no movement.

20. Our suspect has never been interviewed by the LAPD, or Any judicial agency in the state of California. Our suspect's fingerprints and DNA has never been tested and examined against the evidence found at the crime scene.
21. Our suspect has no alibi that can be supported by anyone else as to where he was while the killings occurred.
22. Discovered and have within our possession a number of our suspect's diaries where he describes himself as "Jekyll and Hyde" and the monster within.
23. Prior to the killings of Nicole Simpson and Ron Goldman our suspect nearly killed a girlfriend and almost seriously injured another girlfriend.

JASON LAMAR SIMPSON: WHY HE SHOULD BE CONSIDERED A MAJOR SUSPECT

1. **ANTISOCIAL BEHAVIOR IN SCHOOL:** As an adolescent, Jason performed poorly in school and demonstrated many antisocial behaviors.

2. **PUBLICLY CONSIDERED A "PROBLEM CHILD" IN MEDIA:** Considered a "problem child" at an early age, documented in articles of interviews given by O. J.

3. **OVERDOSED ON DRUGS AND ALCOHOL AT A PARTY, AT AGE 14:** Jason overdosed on drugs and alcohol at age 14 and was rushed to the hospital.

4. **MOTHER UNABLE TO KEEP HIM UNDER CONTROL:** Jason reportedly had difficulty communicating with his mother and at an early age moved in with O. J. and Nicole because Marguerite could not control him.

5. **DURING FIT OF RAGE—ATTACKED FATHER'S STATUE WITH BAT:** As a teenager, Jason flew into a fit of rage and attacked a statue of his father with a baseball bat.

6. **STOLE FATHER'S CAR:** Jason stole his father's car and was turned in by Nicole.

7. **PHYSICALLY ABUSED AT A YOUNG AGE:** Ronald Shipp stated Jason began being physically abused by his father at a young age.

8. **DESCRIBED AS HAVING PSYCHOLOGICAL PROB-LEMS AND ABUSING DRUGS AND ALCOHOL:** Ronald G. Shipp—retired Los Angeles Police Officer and former close friend of O. J. Simpson—described Jason Simpson as having psychological problems, along with abusing drugs and alcohol.

9. **UCLA DIAGNOSED WITH "INTERMITTENT RAGE DISORDER":** Jason was treated at the UCLA Neuropsychiatric Institute for a mental condition, later being diagnosed as "Intermittent Rage Disorder" accompanied by seizures. He was prescribed Depakote, a drug frequently prescribed to individuals suffering from *rage*.

10. **DROPPED OUT OF USC WITH BAD GRADES:** Jason dropped out or flunked out of USC.

11. **JASON STALKED NICOLE:** According to Shipp, Jason had possibly stalked Nicole Simpson while she lived on Gretna Green.

12. **JASON AND NICOLE PARTY TOGETHER:** According to Shipp, Jason and Nicole would go out dancing and partying together.

13. **HEAVILY IN DEBT:** At the time of the murders, Jason was heavily in debt.

14. **JASON ARRESTED AND TAKEN TO HOSPITAL FOR CUTS ON WRIST:** Had an argument with his girlfriend. Jason drank a lot of tequila, attempted suicide by punching his hand through his girlfriend's glass door, cutting his wrist with broken glass. (03/90)

15. **JASON ARRESTED FOR DUI with .12 BLOOD ALCOHOL LEVEL:** Jason was arrested for driving under the influence and having drugs and alcohol in the car with him at the time of the arrest. A blood alcohol test registered a .12, meaning he was legally blind drunk. He was placed on forty-eight months of probation, plus fines. He was also ordered to Alcohol Education and required to participate in a

ninety-day program with a psychiatrist for treatment or counseling. His driver's license was revoked and he was restricted
to driving to and from work and to and from the required
programs for a year. (07/90)

16. **UNABLE TO DEAL WITH AUTHORITATIVE FIG-
URES:** On more than one occasion Jason left or was fired
from his job as a prep chef. Indications were he was unable to
get along with people of authority.

17. **DURING ARGUMENT WITH GIRLFRIEND, JASON
ATTEMPED SUICIDE BY STABBING HIMSELF:** Jason
attempted suicide by *stabbing himself twice* in the stomach
with a pair of scissors. (03/91)

18. **IN FIT OF RAGE, THREW GIRLFRIEND INTO EMPTY
BATHTUB:** Jason, in a fit of rage, assaulted his girlfriend
DeeDee wherein he nearly breaks her back by throwing her
into an empty bathtub.

19. **ATTACKED GIRLFRIEND WITH A CHEF'S KNIFE:**
Jason attacked his girlfriend DeeDee with a chef's knife and
cut off her hair, almost scalping her.

20. **SECOND RECORDED SUICIDE ATTEMPT:** Jason
attempted suicide a second time by *overdosing on Depakote.*
He was committed to the psychiatric ward at Saint John's
Hospital by his family. (10/91)

21. **JASON CONTINUED TO USE DRUGS AND
ALCOHOL THOUGH WARNED OF THE CONSE-
QUENCES:** Jason had repeatedly been warned not to use
drugs or alcohol while taking the medication Depakote,
because it could further complicate his existing neurological
condition, but continued to do so.

22. **ARRESTED FOR DRIVING WITH SUSPENDED
LICENSE AND NO REGISTRATION:** Jason was arrested
at the time of a routine traffic violation because he violated his
probation by driving while his license was suspended and he
also did not have the registration in his vehicle. (7/92)

23. **ON PROBATION FOR ASSAULTING HIS FORMER EMPLOYER WITH A DEADLY WEAPON:** Jason was arrested for assaulting his former employer, Paul Goldberg, with a kitchen knife. At the time of the murders, Jason was still on twenty-four months of probation for this assault with a deadly weapon. (Incident 12/92 - 01/93 complaint filed)

24. **JASON STATED HE FELT HE WAS "GOING TO RAGE":** Prior to the murders, Jason felt he was "going to rage," and went to Cedars-Sinai Hospital emergency room. Previously, when he was about to rage, he claimed to hallucinate by hearing voices of people who weren't there.

25. **JASON ATTACKED GIRLFRIEND IN BLIND RAGE AT HIS BIRTHDAY PARTY:** Two months prior to the murders, Jason, in a blind rage, assaulted his girlfriend, Jennifer Green, at his birthday party. Later that night, according to an article and witnesses, he tried to strangle her. (04/94)

26. **JASON NOT TAKING HIS DEPAKOTE PRESCRIPTION:** Two months prior to the murders, Jason was known to have stopped taking his Depakote because, as he was reported to have said to an ex-girlfriend, "It's fucking with my head."

27. **NICOLE MADE PLANS WITH JASON FOR DINNER AT JACKSON'S AFTER SYDNEY'S RECITAL:** On the night before the murders, Nicole had arranged to eat at Jackson's Restaurant, where Jason was the acting chef, but she failed to show up. This is per Jason Simpson's civil deposition.

28. **NICOLE PROBABLY CHANGED PLANS WITHOUT NOTIFYING JASON:** At 7:00 PM on the night of the murders, Nicole and her family went to Mezzaluna Restaurant to eat instead of dining at Jackson's Restaurant, where Jason was the acting chef.

29. **UPSET WITH NICOLE FOR NOT SHOWING UP AT JACKSON'S:** Jason was allegedly upset that Nicole and her party did not come to Jackson's after Sydney's recital as planned, on the night of June 12, 1994.

30. **COWORKER AND GIRLFRIEND CONFIRMED JASON LEFT WORK AROUND 9:45 PM:** According to Jennifer Green and a waiter from Jackson's, Jason left the restaurant where he worked around 9:45 PM, approximately forty-five minutes to an hour prior to the murders.

31. **JASON'S GIRLFRIEND'S LIE:** During an interview, Jennifer Green claimed that Jason was with her until after 11 PM on the night of the murders.

32. **JASON'S GIRLFRIEND CAUGHT IN LIES:** Jennifer Green, Jason's girlfriend at the time of the murders, was caught up in her own lies while trying to produce an alibi for Jason.

33. **JASON DROPPED GIRLFRIEND OFF IMMEDIATELY AFTER WORK, PER HIS CIVIL DEPOSITION:** Jason's civil deposition indicated he did not spend the evening with Jennifer Green as she indicated, but went directly home after he dropped Jennifer off at her apartment. Jennifer lived only five minutes from Jackson's Restaurant.

34. **JASON BY HIMSELF AFTER APPROXIMATELY 9:50 PM:** Jason had no alibi after approximately 9:50 PM, once he dropped off his girlfriend Jennifer Green, other than the claim in his civil deposition that he was alone at his apartment watching television until after 3 AM.

35. **AIRTIGHT ALIBI:** Supposedly Jason had an airtight alibi, according to the police, that he was cooking in front of 200 people at Jackson's restaurant. On that particular night there were less than 40 patrons at the restaurant the entire night. Jason closed the restaurant early because of lack of business. This was not unusual for Sunday nights.

36. **DNA WITH SIMILAR GENETIC CHARACTERISTICS:** Jason's blood chemistry has very similar genetic characteristics as O. J.'s.

37. **SHOE SIZE APPROXIMATELY SAME AS O. J.'S:** O. J. and Jason have approximately the same size feet. Jason wears

an 11½ while O. J. wears a size 12. Jason also had access to O. J.'s clothes closet and was known to take items of clothing from his dad's closet at will.

38. **CRIME SCENE EXPERT FELT JASON SHOULD HAVE BEEN CONSIDERED A SUSPECT:** James G. Cron, crime scene expert, studied the investigative material and determined that Jason Simpson should have been considered a major suspect in the murders of Nicole Simpson and Ron Goldman.

39. **ENGLAND CRIME SCENE EXPERTS FELT JASON SHOULD HAVE BEEN CONSIDERED A SUSPECT:** England crime scene experts Terry Merston and his partner, Peter Harpur, stated O. J. is not the killer of Nicole Simpson and Ron Goldman, but in all probability was at the crime scene after the murders. They both felt that Jason Simpson should have been considered a major suspect.

40. **PSYCHOLOGICALLY DISTURBED PER EXPERTS:** Dr. Harvey Davisson, Dr. William Flynn, Dr. William Tedford, and Dr. Charles Keller reviewed Jason's records and felt, based on my investigative material, that Jason Simpson is psychologically disturbed and in need of help.

41. **WALKING TIME BOMB:** A prominent physician in Massachusetts described Jason Lamar Simpson as "a walking time bomb."

42. **ALLEGED AIRTIGHT ALIBI:** Robert Shapiro, O. J.'s attorney, indicated that Jason was his first suspect, except for his airtight alibi on the night of June 12, 1994.

43. **NEVER INTERVIEWED:** In his civil deposition Jason said he was never interviewed by either the Los Angeles police law enforcement agencies or the prosecutor's office. Nor was he asked to furnish an alibi for the evening of Sunday, June 12, 1994, in connection with the murders of Nicole Simpson and Ron Goldman.

44. **JASON'S FINGERPRINTS AND FOOTPRINTS NEVER COMPARED WITH THE UNIDENTIFIED PRINTS:** According to the LAPD, no records were found of Jason's fin-

gerprints or footprints being examined in comparison to the unidentified prints found at the crime scene.

45. **PSYCHIATRIST CONFIRMS JASON'S MENTAL CONDITION:** Jason's psychiatrist stated that if Jason was guilty he could never be convicted because of his mental condition.

46. **PSYCHOLOGICAL RECORDS DESTROYED:** Jason's psychiatrist, Dr. Kittay, shredded all of Jason's medical records immediately after the murders.

47. **CRIMINAL LAWYER HIRED BY O. J.:** On the very day after the murders, June 13, 1994, O. J. hired a well-known criminal attorney to represent Jason. This was prior to O. J.'s arrest for the murders.

48. **JASON DASHED FOR O. J. IN THE BRONCO AFTER THE SLOW-SPEED CHASE:** Jason breaks through the police line to reach his father at the conclusion of the slow-speed car chase.

49. **AVOIDS TALKING ABOUT MURDERS:** Jason wouldn't give DeeDee, his ex-girlfriend, any straight answers about the murders when she questioned him.

50. **RAGE KILLING BY AMATEUR:** Marcia Clark and the Los Angeles District Attorney's Office considered this to be a "rage killing by an amateur."

51. **JASON BOLTED FROM NICOLE'S FUNERAL:** Jason bolted from the funeral home, visibly upset, at the time of Nicole Simpson's funeral, not wanting to view Nicole's body.

52. **ALCOHOL AND DEPAKOTE: A DANGEROUS MIX:** Jason continued, in the year 2000, drinking alcoholic beverages mixed with his Depakote medication, even though it states clearly on all of the prescription bottles "Do Not Consume Alcohol."

53. **ARRESTED FOR HIT AND RUN:** Jason was arrested for hit and run during O. J.'s trial. He left the scene of the crime

and was an unlicensed driver, driving while his license was suspended.

54. **ANOTHER SHORT-TERM EMPLOYMENT:** In January of 2000 Jason was terminated as the sous chef from Mélisse Restaurant, a prestigious restaurant, in less than six months.

55. **PROBLEM WITH WOMEN LYING:** Jason was said to have a serious problem when women lied to him. Though he himself was known to lie all the time.

56. **PATHOLOGICAL LIAR:** Per former girlfriends he was proven to be a pathological liar—the kind that truly believes his own lies.

57. **DR. JEKYLL/MR. HYDE PERSONALITY CON-FIRMED:** Former girlfriends and associates of Jason describe him as having a "Dr. Jekyll and Mr. Hyde" personality with uncontrollable rage.

58. **NOTE WRITTEN BY JASON:** Found in Jason's trash in February of 2000, a piece of notebook paper with layers of handwritten notes written on top of each other, which appears to be scribbling at first sight, stating "Dear Jason" and describing the writer as "three people . . . I do know what to do, but I haven't got the will to do it . . . in short I'm fucked. I cannot exercise the simplest deeds. Sober. Walking on broken glass . . . ." It also has the following names scribbled on top of the note: Aaren (his deceased sister), Jennifer, and Danielle (ex-girlfriends).

59. **HANDWRITING OF NOTE CONFIRMED BY EXPERTS:** The "Dear Jason" note that was found in Jason's trash, describing the writer as being three persons, was identified by handwriting experts as being written by Jason Lamar Simpson. Don Lehew, a forensic handwriting analyst, used cancelled checks and other handwriting samples that belonged to Jason. A shocking but revealing piece of evidence of his own perception of his true personality.

60. **OTHER ITEMS FOUND IN TRASH:** Throughout the investigation many tequila bottles, cancelled checks, a note from the pharmacy stating O. J. refused to pay for Jason's Depakote prescription and other short handwritten notes were found in Jason's trash.

61. **ANOTHER SHORT-TERM EMPLOYMENT:** Jason was hired as executive chef at Angel's Bistro and terminated in less than a year. Owner stated he was not eligible for rehire.

62. **GIL GARCETTI LOOKING FOR JASON AT ANGEL'S BISTRO:** The owner of Angel's Bistro stated Gil Garcetti, former district attorney of Los Angeles County, came looking for Jason. When told he no longer worked there by Mr. Harper, Garcetti left in an irritated manner.

63. **JASON SOLD HIS JEEP AND ABRUPTLY LEFT LOS ANGELES AFTER MY INVESTIGATIVE REPORT WAS PUBLISHED:** Neighbors stated Jason moved out of his apartment abruptly and was reported to have moved to Florida. This was immediately after an article was published in the *L.A. Observer* about the Investigative Report *O. J. Is Guilty But Not Of Murder* by William C. Dear. It was later discovered he sold his Jeep at this time, too.

64. **NO AIRTIGHT ALIBI—CONFIRMED BY SILENT PARTNER OF JACKSON'S RESTAURANT:** The silent partner of Jackson's Restaurant, Ross Harding, confirmed Alan Ladd Jackson was with him on the night of the murders and that he did not go to Jackson's Restaurant that night. Therefore, Jackson did not know how many people were in the restaurant that night, nor did he have any way of knowing when Jason closed the restaurant and left work.

65. **NEVER BEEN INTERVIEWED—CONFIRMED BY PHONE CALL:** A phone call was received from Detective Pietratoni of the LAPD stating "Jason Lamar Simpson was never interviewed by the LAPD; he refused to cooperate and was represented by legal counsel."

66. **NEVER BEEN INTERVIEWED—FURTHER CON-FIRMED IN WRITING:** A letter received from the Los Angeles Chief of Police stating "The department has conducted a search for records described in your request, and found no records responsive to your request."

67. **EMAIL RECEIVED FROM JASON'S EX-CLASSMATE AT THE ARMY AND NAVY ACADEMY:** Ex-classmate stated Jason was trained in hand to hand combat as well as field knife training while attending the Army and Navy Academy.

68. **TIME CARD RECEIVED—ENTRY HANDWRITTEN ON DAY OF MURDERS:** In Jason's deposition he stated he punched out on the day of the murders. A copy of his time card was obtained from Ross Harding, the silent partner of Jackson's Restaurant. Jason's times on the night of the murders were handwritten, yet all other nights he worked after the murders were punched by the time clock.

69. **JASON HAD ACCESS TO JACKSON'S RESTAURANT AFTER HOURS:** As the acting chef, with Alan Ladd Jackson absent from work, Jason would have a key to lock up after closing the restaurant. This would give him access to the restaurant after hours and give him a place to go to clean up after the murders, plus the ability to change his time card, without witnesses around, giving him an alibi.

70. **JEEP OBTAINED FOR EXAMINATION:** Jason's Jeep was purchased from the present owner. The car was tested with Luminal, by Dr. Max Courtney, a leading forensic expert, for blood evidence. Some hot spots were found.

71. **JASON'S POSSESSIONS OBTAINED FROM ABANDONED STORAGE SALE:** Several items of interest were recovered from the storage unit when Jason quit paying the rent. A hunting knife, over 300 pictures, a jacket that looks like the one Jason wore at O. J.'s acquittal, a warrant from the L.A. Superior Court trying to obtain Jason's medical

records in 1995, and three handwritten diaries were retrieved.

72. **A PICTURE OF JASON IN A DARK COLORED KNIT CAP:** In reviewing the 300 pictures found in Jason's storage, one was found that pictured Jason lying on his bed wearing a knit cap identical to the one found at the Bundy crime scene. This was a photograph stamped with the date 03/24/93. Several pictures of Jason wearing knit caps were found, giving evidence that Jason wore knit caps quite often.

73. **JASON IS VERY SELF-REVEALING IN HIS DIARIES:** Jason is very self-critical and describes himself as having a "Jekyll and Hyde" personality. His writing reflects his state of mind, which is desperate, somewhat resigned, and careless. He seemed to write at night, trying to make peace with himself so he could rest. His 1993 diary suggests he is highly self-critical, depressed, and reckless in how he was living. Alcohol, ecstasy, and cocaine are the drugs of his choice that he writes about craving. He chastises himself for being insecure, codependent, and obsessing over his girlfriends in an uncontrollable manner. He also is very jealous of their past boyfriends. When actual events happen to him (i.e., arrests) he writes about them as a dream, as though he's watching through someone else's eyes.

74. **EXCERPTS FROM JASON'S DIARIES:** These diaries are from 1991 to December 1993. They describe the following:
    Knowledge of His Split Personality: Jason's awareness of the dangers and frustrations of his split personality is revealed when writing about his thoughts of the Dr. Jekyll and Mr. Hyde story. He wonders why a man, if induced with a chemical and knowing the outcome of becoming a mad man, still does it?
    His Knowledge of Being a Pathological Liar: He goes on to state that he is a liar, an alcoholic, and that he does act to protect the characters that he creates.

About the Shame of Past Incidents: He says, "This is the Year of the Knife for me. For me to start cutting." "Compulsive, Compulsive," are the two words he uses over and over in his diaries. He says he feels everything in the extreme: "Love, Sex, intoxication, heartache, sadness, melancholy, hurt, denial, fever, compassion"

Wanting to Commit Suicide: He describes how he often wants to kill himself. I found in my investigation that he had made three attempts: one with a knife, the next with an overdose, and the third with broken glass.

Knowing he Needs Help: He goes on and describe that he needs help.

Stating Killing Thoughts: In his diaries, he goes on to describe that he would kill anyone who hurt someone he dearly cared about.

Fear of Himself: He describes how he is so alone and frightened. In addition, he finds himself in a prison of his own making.

His Feeling of Inadequacy: He compares himself to O.J; he contrasts himself as a drunken chef whose life is in disarray with his father as a "business God."

Reoccurring Dreams: In his diaries, he finds himself having a reoccurring dream where he is transformed into his competitor with the finish line quickly approaching. But he comes from behind to win. He describes his victory as bitter. He says he's not an animal and that he should be more human. He describes the fact that dogs represent parts of his life. That a dog's life is intriguing, that "animals live their lives without the knowledge of death," but "humans live their lives in fear or perplexed by death." He goes on to say that he has been acting like an animal.

Note Prior to Overdosing on Depakote: In his diaries, he questions why he should go on living. He says everything is deceit and begins saying goodbye to his family, whom he loves. He says his "definition of love sucks" and expresses sadness at the idea that he doesn't know the last time his dad called him just to see how he was doing. In closing, he portends his intent saying that his father won't have to worry about him anymore.

Coming to the Realization while in St. John's: In his diaries he comes to the realization that he tried to kill himself, that he is scared of himself, and doesn't know what to do. Jason states, "I survived 21 years, two suicide attempts, countless drug-filled nights . . ."

Knowledge of His Failings after Rehabilitation: Jason describes how his attempts at functional, moderate drinking lead to a spiral into "crack, cocaine, ecstasy, [and] more to drink." He identifies that he is dysfunctional in beliefs and actions and that he craves drugs and alcohol to numb himself.

Infatuation and Control over His Girlfriends: He becomes infatuated with everyone that he is attracted to and that he wants to feel needed by someone.

Knowledge of His Limitations: It was obvious from his statements that he does not like to work in the morning. His description of lack of sleep concerns him because he believes it is not safe and puts his health at risk. He hates when the "jolts" visit him while he's working.

Continuous Fighting and Highs and Lows: In his diary, he notes up and down mood swings and fights with his girlfriend Jennifer, being late for work, and his explosive arguments with Jennifer toward the end of 1993.

Fear and Anger: "Fear Begets Fear? Anger Begets Fear? Fear Begets Anger, Yes! . . . If I fear straying, it's my actions that perpetuate it. (That is to say if I am unbalanced mentally. If I'm balanced; my mind state sound, sound it will remain . . . I am what I am, I be Jason, Me hurt, Me happy, Me sad, Me confused . . . ME"

Insecurity Controlling His Life: Jason describes his insecurity and that the fact that he lets it out of control has led to the "demise of this character." He says he seeks to understand the reasons for his actions because they are the downfalls of his character.

75. **JASON'S DRUGS OF CHOICE INCLUDE ECSTASY:** The National Institute on Drug Abuse found if ecstasy is used for a long period of time it can have many long-term side effects. The pertinent side effects that show true in Jason's diaries and documented reports is aggressiveness, impulsiveness, depression, a state of confusion, and memory loss.

76. **HAIR IN THE DARK KNIT CAP FOUND AT THE CRIME SCENE:** The hair found in the knit cap did not match O. J.'s. Was this hair tested for DNA or compared to Jason's?

77. **INTERVIEW WITH DR. HENRY LEE:** During a filmed interview between Dr. Henry Lee and William C. Dear, in February 2004, Dr. Lee stated, "Yes," he was surprised with the evidence presented to him prior to the interview. Dr. Lee then stated, "This is why I admire you greatly. If every case was spent like the time that you spent, this case would be solved a long time ago." Dr. Lee also said " . . . you look at it from investigative end; I look at from scientific end. Whether or not these two can meet is a subject for discussion."

78. **COLOR PHOTOGRAPH SHOWING JASON WEARING CAP WHILE PLAYING WITH DOG:** Photograph shows Jason wearing knit cap while playing with his dog.

79. **WEAPON FOUND IN JASON'S STORAGE UNIT CONSISTENT WITH MURDER WEAPON:** After Jason's storage unit payment became delinquent, among his personal items was found a knife consistent with the weapon used in the murders. The knife had Jason's initials crudely cut into the sheath.

O. J. SIMPSON IS INNOCENT

BUT LIKELY AT THE CRIME SCENE
AFTER THE MURDERS

1. **NO RAGE BEHAVIOR:** Marcia Clark: "These were rage type murders." O. J. does not have a history of rage behavior.
2. **ABUSE HISTORY DOESN'T FIT PATTERN—PER EXPERT:** O. J.'s alleged history of abuse reviewed by spousal abuse expert Dr. Lenore Walker; by her standards, O. J. doesn't fit a pattern that would culminate in murder.
3. **THERE IS NO EVIDENCE OF O. J. EVER USING WEAPONS DURING DISPUTES:** Despite all the allegations of spousal abuse, there is no evidence of O. J. using a weapon to solve domestic disputes.
4. **NICOLE AND O. J. RECONCILED ON AND OFF EVEN IN MAY 1994:** Nicole and O. J. were known to have reconciled as recently as May 10, 1994, and O. J. had every reason to believe that they would be back together again.
5. **O. J. HATES SIGHT OF BLOOD:** O. J. is known to hate the sight of blood, yet allegedly selected a knife to commit the murders. This is entirely inconsistent with accepted scientific research on the subject.
6. **SMART MAN BUT LAME ALIBI:** O. J. is smart enough to sit on the board of several multinational corporations, yet the only alibi he could come up with for a premeditated murder was that he was "chipping golf balls."

7. **O. J. KNEW HIS CHILDREN WERE THERE AND POSSIBLY SYDNEY'S FRIEND:** O. J. may have hated Nicole enough to say that he wanted to kill her, but he always went out of his way to protect and love his children. A loving father is not likely to have killed the mother of his children while those children were a few yards away—especially when those children could have been up watching television on a summer night. O. J. was aware that his daughter Sydney was to have a friend over for a sleepover on that night.

8. **FAMOUS MAN WOULD LOOK FOR SECLUSION TO MURDER:** A premeditated murderer does not select a busy street like Bundy Drive to ambush his ex-wife—especially someone as recognizable as O. J.

9. **O. J.'S KNIVES NOT THE MURDER WEAPONS— CONCLUSIVE:** O. J. Simpson's Swiss Army knife and his stiletto were conclusively shown not to have been the murder weapon used at Bundy Drive.

10. **SECOND PAIR OF FOOTPRINTS AT CRIME SCENE:** Other unidentified shoe prints found at the crime scene, which were not from Bruno Magli shoes.

11. **BLOOD AND SKIN UNDER NICOLE'S NAILS DID NOT MATCH O. J.'S:** Investigators found blood and skin under Nicole's fingernails—suggesting that she had fought or clawed at her attacker—along with blood drops on her back that didn't match those of O. J. Simpson.

12. **FINGERPRINTS FOUND AT THE CRIME SCENE DID NOT MATCH O. J.'S:** Though the Los Angeles Police Department found fifteen separate unidentified fingerprints at the crime scene, none belonged to O. J.

13. **DNA WAS NOT EXACT MATCH TO O. J.'S:** According to the book *Killing Time* by Donald Freed and Raymond P. Briggs, PhD, the DNA experts interviewed for this study explained that any blood drops at Bundy, left by any of the four children (Jason, Arnelle, Sydney, Justin), would have

been virtually indistinguishable from the blood of their father, O. J.

14. **GLOVE TOO TIGHT TO JUST FALL OFF:** A glove cannot "fall" off a hand unless it is loose fitting. O. J. had large hands and the glove was a tight fit as shown at his trial.

15. **NO BLOODY CLOTHES FOUND AND TIME WAS LIMITED:** O. J. should have been covered in blood, yet no bloody clothes were found.

16. **VERY LITTLE BLOOD IN BRONCO AND AT HOME:** Only a small amount of blood was found in the Bronco and only a few drops at the Rockingham residence. This is evidence that suggests he was at the crime scene, but did not commit the murders.

17. **NO BLOOD ON BRONCO BRAKE OR ACCELERATOR:** No blood was found on the brake pedal or the accelerator of O. J.'s Bronco.

18. **O. J. ACTS AS IF HE IS RESPONSIBLE FOR SOME UNKNOWN REASON:** O. J. has consistently said that he did not commit the murders, yet acts as if he is somehow responsible for what happened.

19. **POLYGRAPH FAILURE MAY JUST MEAN HE KNOWS WHO COMMITTED THE MURDERS:** O. J. failed his private polygraph test. This does not necessarily mean he committed the murders, only that he may have known who did, and was covering up for that person.

20. **NO BRUISES OR SEVERE CUTS ON O. J.:** Based on pictures of Ron Goldman at the crime scene, showing his badly bruised knuckles, there should have been cuts and bruises on the assailant. According to Ron Shipp and the Los Angeles Police Department Detective Division there were no bruises or cuts on O. J. except for the cut on his left hand.

21. **O. J.'S FRIENDS THINK O. J. COULD POSSIBLY BE COVERING FOR JASON:** Based on the investigation information, Mercury Morris and Ron Shipp now believe there is

a possibility that O. J. is innocent and possibly was protecting his son, Jason.

22. **O. J.'S REASONS FOR CUT ON HIS KNUCKLE:** According to the BBC Documentary: "Simpson has given various answers about the cut—from a broken glass in his hotel room in Chicago, to *wrestling with his son.*"

23. **O. J. HIRED CRIMINAL ATTORNEY FOR JASON THE DAY AFTER THE MURDERS:** O. J. hired Carl Jones, a criminal attorney, to represent his son, Jason, the day after the murders, prior to O. J.'s arrest in the murder case. Why?

Juror's Ballot

1. Based on the evidence you have been presented, is O. J. Simpson guilty of the murders of Nicole Simpson and Ron Goldman?
   Answer: _____ Yes _____ No

2. Based on the preponderance of the evidence presented, do you believe that someone other than O. J. Simpson is guilty of the murders of Nicole Simpson and Ron Goldman?
   Answer: _____ Yes _____ No

3. Based on the evidence presented, do you believe that O. J. Simpson is not guilty but knows who committed the murders of Nicole Simpson and Ron Goldman?
   Answer: _____ Yes _____ No

4. Based on the evidence submitted, do you believe that O. J. Simpson went to the crime scene after the murder and left his cap and left-hand glove by the bodies of Nicole Simpson and Ron Goldman?
   Answer: _____ Yes _____ No

5. Based on the evidence submitted, do you believe Jason Lamar Simpson should be a major suspect in the murders of Nicole Simpson and Ron Goldman?

   Answer: _____ Yes _____No

6. Based on the evidence presented, do you believe the Governor of the State of California and the Attorney General should request a special grand jury to review this new evidence concerning the murders of Nicole Simpson and Ron Goldman?

   Answer: _____ Yes _____No

7. Were you surprised to learn that neither the Los Angeles Police Department nor the district attorney's office ever interviewed Jason Lamar Simpson as a possible suspect in the murders of Nicole Simpson and Ron Goldman?

   Answer: _____ Yes _____No

8. Based on the investigative report *O. J. Is Innocent And I Can Prove It!*, do you believe the Los Angeles Police Department and the district attorney's office considered O. J. as the one and only suspect, once arriving at Bundy Drive and then at Rockingham, for the murders of Nicole Simpson and Ron Goldman?

   Answer: _____ Yes _____No

Submit answers and/or comments via email at Bill@BillDear.com

ACKNOWLEDGMENTS

O. J. Is Innocent and I Can Prove It has taken a great deal out of my life for the past seventeen years, but I truly believed in what I was doing, and still do.

There are so many I owe so much to, both mentally and financially. They were all there for me when I needed them.

Dr. Vincent DiMaio, Dr. Henry Lee, Dr. Harvey Davisson, Ret. Captain James Cron, Ret. Chief Rick White, Ret. Captain Larry Momchilov (Joan Rice), Don Lehew, Ret. Sheriff Dick Wagman, Terry Mertson, Phil Smith, the late Chris Stewart, Joe Villanueva, Capt. Rich Munsey, Dep. Bill Madding, Donna Roland, Sidney Kirkpatrick.

A special thanks to Dr. Al and Janet Harper and Dan Rather.

Dr. Charles Keller, Dr. James Garriott, Dr. William Flynn, Dr. William Tedford, Dr. Jim Knox, Jim Fowler PhD, Dr. Max Courtney, and Judge B. McGregor.

Charlie Sheen, the late Farrah Fawcett, Karen Severyn.

Dan McBride, Joyce Meret, E. J. Whitenhafer, Aubrey and Judith Golden, Tommy Fallin, Dr. C. Miller-Ballem, Waylon Roberts, Mike and Nancy Furlich, Dr. Joe and Barbara Phipps, JoAnn McKee, and Jack and Cynthia Lockhart.

Richard and Diane Eubanks and Family, Ron and Diane Eubanks and Family, Bo Razzano and Family, Brenda and Alan Burnette and

Family, Jo Ann Bortz and Family, Don Roush, Susan Hallford and Family, Judge Eugene and Paulette Fulton, Jo Hammons, Roger and Cindy Mann, Randy and Sharon Barton, Fran Hicks, Trisha Murray, Linda Howerton, Tom Cowart, Harry Wasoff, J. L. Jackson, Todd and Christie Ritchie and Family, Norm Lassiter, Kyle Tucker, Dwight Carmichael, Barbara Wong, Jody Wilson, Dave Salyers, Jake and Evelyn Clifton, Marianne Courson, The Cockerhams, Kathy James, John and JoAnn Ritchie, Doug and Cinda Jenney, Tom and Vanna Hawkins, Marla Messersmith, Gil Hudson, Connie McGuire, Theresa Whitaker, Brenda Cauthen, Rey Orozco, Mrs. Eli Momchilov, Bob Adams, Dean and Cindy Savell, Tony Villanueva, Wyatt Carr and Family, Carl Lily, Billy and Glenda Reynolds, Jose Garcia, Bill and Gayle Waller, Kim Waller, Greg Zacharias, Dr. Andrew Clavenna and Lupe Couch, Cynthia Studenko, Chuck Wyatt, Ralph Merlino, Stan and Sherri Moore, Garrett Chambers, Lyle and Andrea Odelein, Mike and Joanie Watson, Wes and Lily Munselle, Wyatt Wilson, Kay and Herb Kuykendall, Dixie Roberts, Charles Beseda, Jarrett and Kristi Pendley, and Lisa Moore.

If I have forgotten someone, I truly apologize.

About the Author

William C. Dear
Private Investigator

DURING THE LAST FIVE decades, William C. Dear has worked all over the world, including the continental United States, Canada, the United Kingdom, Western Europe, the Orient, Asia, and the Caribbean, predominately on homicide investigations. He began his career as a police officer in Miami, Florida. In 1961, he opened his own investigation agency, William C. Dear & Associates Inc., in Dallas, Texas. He developed a private i-nvestigation video and text course that is nationally certified for continuing education credit. He has also produced a video homicide course and holds continuing education seminars on his ranch in Mt. Calm, Texas, where he has a complete and modern CSI room. Dear is a renowned and entertaining speaker at conventions, training seminars, workshops, and banquets. As a certified instructor in the field of homicide, Dear lectures and teaches law enforcement around the world.

William Dear was inducted into the American Police Hall of Fame on April 14 1988, as a private investigator receiving the Archangel Award for the Milo murder case. He was also appointed by the court to the Exhumation of Lee Harvey Oswald in 1981.

Dear has received national and international acclaim on cases that made worldwide news coverage. Most notably, the Dean Milo murder in Akron, Ohio, which resulted in eleven arrests and convictions (the most ever in U.S. history for a single murder case).

Other homicide cases:

Wax Museum
Dan Beckton
Patsy Wright
Jerry Sternadel
Amber Crum
Casey Roberts and Robbie Biggars
Charles Whitenhafer
Donna Benevides
Allen Rehrig
Olive Dry
Christy Meeks
The Black Widow
Leon Laureles
Mary Leonard
Glen Courson
Ricky Beard
The Missing Link

Kidnapping and disappearances:

Dungeons and Dragons case (Michigan State University)
Cherie Ann Kennedy
Gwen Burke
Nigel Newton

William Dear is a respected author who has penned:

The Dungeon Master—The Disappearance of James Dallas Egbert III, (Winner of the American Library Award in 1984).
Please Don't Kill Me (An account of the Milo murder)
Private Investigator (Semi-autobiography)
O. J. Is Guilty But Not Of Murder (A nonfiction book)

The *London Times*, the *Dallas Times Herald* and the *Toronto Star* have all referred to William Dear as "the real James Bond" and he has been featured in national and international media productions including:

A&E channel: *Watching the Detectives*
City Confidential: Akron: Brother Against Brother
Good Morning America
Unsolved Mysteries
Inside Edition
Inside Story
Entertainment Tonight
P.M. Magazine
Live With Regis and Kathy Lee
Pat Sajak Show
Current Affair
BBC Special: *O. J. The Untold Story*
Cold Case File with Bill Curtis

And featured in national magazines:

Time
Newsweek
Playboy ("Outstanding Men of Dallas")
Parade

William Dear produced a documentary, *The Overlooked Suspect*, winner of the 2008 Backlot Film Festival. The documentary was awarded first place for "Best Investigative Documentary" in the 2011 DocMiami International Film Festival in Miami, Florida.

WORKS CITED

AP/Wide World Photos.

Baker, Terri.
  I Want To Tell You. Ballantine, 1997
Barbieri, Paula.
  The Other Woman. Little Brown, 1997
Bess, Carrie, Armanda Cooley, and Marsha Rubin-Jackson.
  Madam Foreman, Dove Books, 1996
Bosco, Joseph.
  A Problem of Evidence. Morrow, 1996
Briggs, Raymond P., and Donald Freed.
  Killing Time. MacMillan, 1996
Bugliosi, Vincent.
  Outrage. Norton, 1996
Clark, Marcia.
  Without a Doubt. Penguin, 1997
Cochran Jr., Johnnie.
  Journey to Justice. Ballantine, 1996
Darden, Christopher with Jess Walter.
  In Contempt. Harper Collins, 1996
Dershowitz, Alan M.
  Reasonable Doubts. Simon & Schuster, 1996

Dimitrius, Jo-Ellan and Mark Mazzarella.
    Reading People. Random House, 1998
Eliot, Marc.
    Kato Kaelin, The Whole Truth. Harper, 1995
Fuhrman, Mark.
    Murder in Brentwood. Regnery, 1997
Gilbert, Mike.
    How I Helped O. J. Get Away With Murder. Regnery, 2008
Goldman - Hoffer.
    His Name Is Ron. Morrow, 1997
Lange, Det., and Det. Vannatter.
    Evidence Dismissed. Pocket Book, 1997
Linedecker, Clifford.
    A to Z OJ. St. Martins Griffin, 1995
Medical Economics Company.
    Physicians' Desk Reference, PDR, 54th Edition, 2000
Petrocelli, Daniel.
    Triumph of Justice, Random House, 1998
Ratey, Dr. John J., and C. Johnson.
    Shadow Syndromes. Bantam, 1998
Resnick, Faye.
    Nicole Brown Simpson. Dove Books, 1994
Riccio, Thomas J.
    Busted. Phoenix Books, 2008
Schiller, Lawrence.
    American Tragedy.
Schulman, J. Neil
    The Frame of The Century? Pulpless.com, Inc., 1999
Shapiro, Robert.
    The Search for Justice. Wagner, 1996
Simpson, O. J.
    I Want To Tell You. Little Brown, 1995
Spence, Gerry.
    OJ the Last Word. St. Martin's Press, 1997

Stowers, Carlton.
> *Marcus.* St. Martin's Press, 1997
Toobin, Jeffrey.
> *The Run of His Life.* Random House, 1996
Webster, C., and M. Jackson.
> *Impulsivity.* Gilford, 1997
Wecht, Cyril H., Greg Saitz, and Mark Curriden.
> *Mortal Evidence: The Forensics Behind Nine Shocking Cases.*
> Prometheus Books, 2003
Weller, Sheila.
> *Raging Heart.* Pocket Book, 1995
Williams, Virginia, and Redford Williams.
> *Anger Kills.* Harper Paperbacks, 1993

INDEX

A

ABC, 4
Adam (Dear's son), 118
Adams, Christine, 125
Adell, Traci, 57
Aldana, Dave, 325
Allen, Marcus, 43, 48–50
  affair with Nicole, 48
  All-Pro MVP, 49
  NFL Rookie of the Year, 49
  Super Bowl MVP, 49
Anderson, W. French, 172
  Gene Therapy Laboratories, 172
ARCO Tower, 6
Army and Navy Academy, 112

B

Backlot Film Festival, 450, 454, 508
Baden, Michael, 86, 382, 413–14
bag containing chef's knives, 270
Bailey, F. Lee, 81, 85, 325, 477
Baker, Terry, 49
Barbieri, Paula, 145
Baur, Rolf, 73, 212
Beardsley, Al, 438–41, 443
Big Fish Enterprises, 142
black gloves, 260
Boatman, Michael, 452
Bonnett, Stewart, 257
Bosco, Joseph, xxiii, 76
  Problem of Evidence, A, 21, 76
Bozanich, Peter, 344
Braxton, William J., 464
Brent-Air Pharmacy, 282–83, 320
Brockbank, Susan, 422
Bronco, 4–8 15–18, 27, 29–30, 43, 66,
  69, 83–84, 137, 165, 176, 179,
  259–61, 296, 318

Ford Motors, 17
Brown, Denise, 46, 80, 325, 432–33
Brown, Edmund G. Jr., 455
Brown, Jerry, 455, 461, 474
Brown, Juditha, 23, 82
Brown, Judy, 314
Brown, Lou, 23
Brown-Simpson and Goldman murder,
  42, 60, 89
Brown-Simpson, Nicole, 176. *See also*
  Simpson, Nicole
Bruno Magli shoes, 16, 29, 52, 83, 151,
  260–61, 272
Bubba Scott, 74
Bundy Drive, 4, 8, 13–14, 16, 25–28,
  30–31, 40, 45, 81, 136–37, 188,
  273–74, 298
Bundy Drive crime scene, 4–5, 12, 18,
  63, 66, 97, 176, 242, 314
Bundy Drive murders, 45–46, 58, 62,
  64–65, 67, 75–76, 86, 88, 100, 189,
  220, 227, 238, 257, 328
Burnett, DeeDee, 433. *See also* DeeDee
  (Jason's girlfriend)
Bushey, Keith, 88
Busted (Riccio), 439–42

C

California DA, 352
California Homicide Investigators
  Association (CHIA) Convention,
  473
Cantor, Brett, 62–63, 189, 221
  The Dragonfly, 62
car chase, 4–5, 9, 43. *See also* slow-speed
  car chase
Carmichael, Dwight, 463
Cavalieri, Cary, 455, 459–60

CBS News, xxiv
CBS, xxv, 4, 477
Cedars-Sinai Medical Center, 102–03, 112
Cellmark tests, 84
Chasteen, Shannon, 237
Chris (suffering from "going to rage"), 131
Chuck (suffering from "going to rage"), 130
Citrin, Joseph, 281, 284, 291
Clark, Marcia, 77–82, 85, 87–88, 146, 185, 223, 258, 266, 270–72, 296, 335, 339, 368–69, 422–23
   Without a Doubt, 88
   rage-type killing, 266
CNN, 4
Cochran, Johnnie Jr., 77, 79–82, 85, 88, 146, 155, 237–38
Colorado, Rene, 348
Cooley, Steven, 331, 344, 348
Corwin, Malcom, 317
Couric, Katie, 72
Courson, Glen, 10
Courtney, Max, 350–51
Cowlings, A. C., 4–6, 8, 43–50, 52–54, 62, 64, 66, 69–71, 145, 198, 203, 277, 318
   Buffalo Bills, 44
   drug connections, 46
   FBI arrest, 47
   hooked on cocaine, 45
   played a trick on O. J., 45
   romance with singer Dionne Warwick, 45
   San Francisco 49ers, 45
   San Francisco City College, 44
   traded to Houston, 45
   University of Southern California, 44
Crilley, Jeff, 351
crime scene investigation, xx–xxi
crime scene, 30–31, 34–35, 40, 53
   acts of violence directed at Nicole, 53
   diagrams, 35
   personal inspection, 35

photographs, 55
crimes, 36
   DNA scanners, 36
Criminal Courts Building, 94, 96–97
Cron, James "Jim," 169–70,172–73, 182, 293
custody arrangement, 98

D
DA, 280, 349, 450, 460–61
DA's office, 147, 151, 201, 204, 267, 463–64
Dallas Film Festival, 450
Dallas Observer, 333
Darden, Christopher, 77–79, 85, 87, 146, 185, 258, 270, 273, 335, 357, 368–69
Davisson, Harvey, 124–25, 181–87, 191, 194–95, 197, 204, 210, 308–10, 312, 320
Dean Milo murder case, 31
Dear Jason letter, 286, 317
Dear, Adam, 108, 350
Dear, Bill, xviii–xxii, xxiv, 11, 64–65, 77, 89, 172, 188, 198–00, 203–04, 220, 331, 355, 424, 441, 464, 489. *See also* Dear, William C.
   back and neck surgery, 11, 64, 77
   being followed on the way to the airport, 198
   car accident, 11
   death of father, 89
   Dungeon Master, The: The Disappearance of James Dallas Egbert III, 172
   guest panelist on a nationally syndicated TV talk show, 74
   losing his stalkers, 210
   lousy patient, 77
   meeting with a professor of law at Loyola Law School, 341
   modern-day Sherlock Holmes, 14
   O. J. Is Innocent and I Can Prove It!, 477
   OJ Is Guilty, but Not of Murder, 329, 353

paying Ron Shipp for interview, 203
private investigator from Dallas, 204
requested by Dr. Lee as guest speaker at
the Markle Symposium, 412
solved notorious missing persons case,
65
Dear, Michael, 362
Dear, William C., 138, 279, 310, 454
winner of the 2008 Backlot Film
Festival, 454
Overlooked Suspect, The, 454
DeeDee (Jason's girlfriend), 74, 113–14,
117, 122, 220, 227, 230, 232,
248–55, 268, 273, 312, 339
battered woman, 253
break up with Jason, 117
calling Marguerite to check on Jason's
another suicide attempt, 252
cutting her hair, 251
dated Andrew Dice Clay, 231
disliked by Marguerite and Arnelle,
248
incident in the bathtub, 250
Jason calling her on the phone while
overdosing on Depakote, 252
Jason's violence, 253
scarred with her relationship with
Jason, 255
tattoos on her forearms, 255
wanted to know if O. J. killed Nicole
and Ron, 254
Deedrick, Doug, 84
Department of Motor Vehicles in Austin,
200
depositions, 144–45
detective, 3
homicide detectives, 3
DiMaio, Vincent, 169, 400, 410
Forensic Pathology, 400
Gunshot and Knife Wounds, 400
divorce, 288
DMV records, 75, 93
DNA analysis, 84
DNA evidence, 78, 82, 463
used to exonerate an individual, 463

DNA samples, 464,
knit cap with hair of dog and human,
464, 472, 474
DNA test results, 79
DNA testing, 423
DNA, 215, 460, 474
Douglas, Brian, 353, 355–58, 361
acquired Jason Simpson's personal
diaries, 361
carrying the box of Jason's possessions,
356
Dr. Phil show, 436
drug use (Denise, Nicole, A. C., and O.
J.), 46
drugs, 126
Depakote, 126
Dilantin, 126
Lithium, 126
Tegretol, 126
Duffy, David, 228
*Dungeon Master, The: The Disappearance of
James Dallas Egbert III* (Dear), 172
dysfunctional behavior in young people,
102
drug and alcohol abuse, 102

E

Ecstasy (drug), 242, 249
EDTA (blood preservative), xxi, 383–84,
419–21
e-mail, 362
from former roommates of Jason
Simpson from Army and Navy
Academy, 362
England, Charles (karate expert), 298
Englert, Rod, 296
English, Charles, 97
Esquire magazine, 28
Eubanks, Richard, 363
Eubanks, Ron, 363
evidence, xvii, xix–xxi, xxv, 27, 476
dried blood, 27
knit cap, 476
gloves, 476

F

FBI, 46–47, 221, 382–83
  investigations, 77
Feinstein, Diane, 461
Fiato, Larry, 88
Fiato, Tony, 46, 88
  The Animal, 46, 88
Fingerprint Society, 176
Fischman, Cora, 59
Flynn, William, 182, 424, 426
  findings of Jason Simpson, 426
Ford-Mustin, Jan, 125
Forensic Pathology (DiMaio), 400
Forensic Science Society, 176
Forschner knives, 174–75
  division of Swiss Army Brands, Inc.,
  175
Francesca (Resnick's daughter), 60
Freedom of Information Act, 95, 103,
  337
Freedom of Information Act request, 471
Fromong, Bruce, 440–41, 443
Fuhrman, Mark, 17, 53–54, 79, 81, 146,
  169, 175, 177–78, 181, 260,
  blatant racism, 81
Fung, Dennis, 82–83, 169, 296

G

Garcetti, Gil, 281, 325, 329–30
Gelb, Edward, 385
Gelblum, Peter, 319
Gigi (housekeeper), 15
Gilbert, Mike, 438–40
Globe magazine, 319
Goldberg, Debbie, 305
Goldberg, Hank, 82
Goldberg, Paul, 98, 100, 130, 147, 292,
  306–07, 339
Goldman, Fred, 438
Goldman, Ron, xviii–xix, 5, 21, 23–24,
  32, 39, 48, 59, 62, 83–84, 164,
  177, 180–81, 261, 274, 297–99. *See
  also* Goldman, Ronald
  eyes opened, 261
  fashion model, 24

waiter, 24–25
Goldman, Ronald, xv, xxii, 3, 76, 177,
  179, 361, 400, 411, 436
good investigator, xx
  "never assumes, always verifies," xx
Green, Jennifer, 74, 165, 218–25, 230,
  254, 270, 291, 312, 314, 339
  former model, 219, 221
  had Jason's Jeep (first instance), 223–24
  National Enquirer story, 219
  scarred with her relationship with
  Jason, 255
  waiting for Jason, 291
Greer, Robin, 320
Greer, Rosey, 277
Gunshot and Knife Wounds (DiMaio), 400

H

Harding (Officer), 431, 463
Harding, Ross, 333, 335, 337, 353, 379,
  454
Harper, Al, 413
Harper, Ron, 330
Harpur, Peter, 176–79, 181, 278, 293
Hart, Erik A., 378
Hart, M. Leo, 175
Hawkins, Ross, 450, 452
Heidstra, Robert, 85–86, 263, 296–97
Henry Lee Institute, 412
Hertz, 46
Hew, Randall, 459–60, 474
Hill, Tracy, 46
  Armstrong, Amanda, 46
Hodgman, William, 464, 471–73, 476
Hoffman (doctor.), 320
Hostetler, Barry, 60
Houston Chronicle, 312
Huizenga, Robert, 87, 282
hunting knife, xix
hypothesis, xviii, 478

I

IBARS, 98
If I Did It (Simpson), 368, 434–35
information, xvi–xvii

INDEX

arrest, xvii
conviction, xvii
grand jury, xvii
Institute of Expert Witnesses, 176
intermittent rage disorder, 181, 191, 229, 249, 252. *See also* IRD
International Association for Identification, 176
investigation, xvi–xvii, xix–xx, 43
  calculated methodology, xx
  Internet chat rooms, 43
investigative agency, 11
investigative fields, xv
  crime scene, xv
  forensics, xv
  pathology, xv
investigative reporter, 3
  "never assume, always verify," 3
investigative skills, xxi
investigative technique, 36
  reenactment, 36
investigators, 69
Ippolito, Joey, 43, 46–47, 61
  apartment, 47
IRD, 128, 130
Ito, Lance, 78

J
J. Paul Getty Museum, 12
Jackson, Alan Ladd, 76, 138, 144, 290, 336, 381. *See also* Jackson, Alan.
  grandson of famous actor Alan Ladd, 381
  son of talk-show host Michael Jackson, 381
Jackson, Alan, 90, 92–93, 97, 141–42
Jackson's Farm Restaurant, 141, 144
Jackson's Restaurant, 93, 138, 144, 158, 270, 278, 284, 289, 334–35, 339–40, 345, 348–49, 379,
  now known as Celestino's, 289, 345
  can hold 87 people, not 200, *290*
Java Café, 59
Jekyll and Hyde syndrome, xxii, 124, 127, 241, 432

impulsive control disorder, 127
intermittent explosive disorder (IED), 124, 127, 132, 154
intermittent rage disorder (IRD), 124, 181, 249
Jenner, Kris, 58
Jenney, Doug, 170
Jerrigan, Jerry, 350
Jessie (stylist that knew DeeDee), 233
Jessing, Joe, 350
Jones, Carl, 76, 102, 166, 369, 423
  hired by O. J. to represent Jason, 76
justice, xv–xvi

K
Kaelin, Brian Gerard, 55. *See also* Kaelin, Kato
  automobile pitchman, 55
  cable television talk-show host, 55
  deliveryman, 55
  singing waiter, 55
  stand-up comedian, 55
Kaelin, Kato, 15–17, 54, 57, 82, 145, 261, 295
  covering for O. J., 57
  move into Nicole's condo, 56
  move into Rockingham with O. J., 56
  only person to handle a particular knapsack, 22
Kardashian, Robert, 5, 58, 69, 121, 145, 262, 385
Kathryn (Allen's wife), 50
Kato (Japanese Akita dog), 26, 37, 41, 278
Keane, Dylan, 452
Kelberg, Brian, 83, 87
  Emmy for dramatic use of ruler, 83
Keller, Charles, 125
Kennedy, Maxwell Taylor, 475
  called the display "a cheap bid for attention" in the *Los Angeles Times*, 475
Kennedy, Robert, 475
  clothing when he was murdered, 475
killer, 39

Kim, Danny, 459–60
King, Herman, 43, 45–66, 62, 69–70,
    103, 112, 135, 138, 289
King, Larry, 435
Kirkpatrick, Sidney, 257–58, 269, 272,
    355
Kittay, Burton, 51, 98, 102, 114, 116,
    123, 185–95, 197–98, 204–05,
    208–09, 221, 256, 277, 308–09,
    312
  being used by O. J., 208
  freely discussed to others what was told
    him in confidence, 208
  he wasn't interested in getting involved,
    312
  might have prevented Nicole's and
    Ron's murders, 312
  moved from Santa Monica to Corpus
    Christi, 185
  phone therapy session, 208–09
  running scared when it looked like
    O. J. was going to be arrested, 210
  sessions with the greater Simpson clan,
    208
  shredding files/destroying records, 209
knife, 279, 365–67, 411
  designed to cut and kill, 366–67, 410
  eight-inch chef's boning knife, 275
  replica of a Gerber Mark I, 363, 366
knotted-up ball of paper found in Jason's
    trash, 286
  letter to Jason from one of his
    girlfriends, 286
Koral, Jackie, 412
Kragten, Max, 364–65, 367

L
L. A. Observer, 331, 481
Lange, Tom, 48, 50, 66, 80–81, 88, 146,
    175, 181, 215, 263, 271, 313–14,
    417, 419–20
Lansky, Meyer, 47
  Cent'Anni, 47
LAPD Detective Division, 337
  Jason Simpson was never interviewed
    by LAPD, 337
LAPD investigation, 42, 145, 296
LAPD Parker Center, 6–7
LAPD Police Academy, 51
LAPD, i, ii, xxi–xxii, 3, 6–8, 10, 12,
    16–19, 21, 23, 25, 28–30, 30,
    33–34, 36, 40, 42–43, 50–52, 57,
    61–63, 65, 70, 78–81, 83–88, 90,
    109, 145, 151, 155, 166, 169, 171,
    177, 197, 200, 203–08, 210, 215,
    257–58, 267, 280, 296, 314,
    325–26, 329, 337, 340, 345, 347,
    352, 387, 405, 422–23, 429, 431,
    450, 456, 458, 460–61, 463–64,
    473–76, 483, 489, 492 See also Los
Angeles Police Department.
  Christmas parties, 80
Lee, Henry, xviii, 79, 86, 298, 317–18,
    339, 382, 387, 412–15, 482
legal system, xvi
Lehew, Don, 315, 317, 320, 341, 355
Leno, Jay, 67, 435
Leonard, Dan, 148, 150, 154, 164–165
"Lessons Learned from Famous Cases,"
    xviii
Letterman, David, 435
Levin, Harvey, 441
Lieber, Stanley, 441
limo driver, 16–17, 65–67, 76, 82, 102,
    112, 261
Lockhart, Jack, 471
Los Angeles County, 6
Los Angeles detectives, 262
Los Angeles Observer, 330
Los Angeles Police Department Detective
    Division, 314, 337, 417, 429
Los Angeles Police Department, 281, 298,
    301, 320, 325, 331, 362, 369,
    372–73, 379, 381, 405, 413,
    417–18, 429–31, 464, 471, 473,
    478
Los Angeles Times, 75, 97, 236
luminal testing, 350–51

INDEX

M

Madigan, Lisa, 52
Maria (clerk in the hospital), 104
Markle Symposium speakers, i, 382,
    412–13
  Baden, Michael, 382
  Cornwell, Patricia, 413
  Crier, Catherine, 413
  Dear, Bill, 413
  Dorsey, Charles, 413
  Harper, Al, 413
  Lee, Henry, 413
  Wecht, Cyril, 413
Marshall, Penny, 453
Martin, Steve, 453
McCready, John, xxiv, 450, 452, 455,
    458–61, 474,
McDonald's, 16
McKenna, Pat, 21
McKinney, Laura Hart, 87–88
media, 9
*Medicolegal Investigation of Death:
    Guidelines for the Application of
    Pathology to Crime Invstigation*
    (Spitz), 294
meeting with DeeDee, 245
  Café Tropical, 243–45
Mélisse Restaurant, 281, 284, 301, 328
Merston, Terry, 173, 176, 182, 278
metal box, 363
  containing the knife found, 363
Mezzaluna Trattoria, 21
  cocaine, 21
Michelle (Dr. Courtney's associate), 350
mind-altering drugs, 126
  cocaine, 126
  LSD, 126
Mitchell, Silberberg & Knupp, 147
Momchilov, Larry, i, 169
Moore, Mary Tyler, 453
Morris, Eugene Mercury, 318
Morris, Mercury, 318 *See also* Morris,
    Eugene Mercury
Mulholland Drive, 70
murder weapon, 18, 20

Swiss Army knives, 20
murders of Nicole Simpson and Ron
    Goldman, 444, 451, 454, 472–74,
    476–78
Murdoch, Rupert, 435
  fired Judith Regan and shut down
    Regan Books, 435

N

National Conference of Investigative
    Reporters and Editors, 4
  "How the Gumshoes Do It: Tips from
    Private Eyes," 4
National Enquirer, 137, 219, 228, 230,
    247, 266, 325
NBC, 4
neighbor, 33
Nellany, Dennis, 385
"never assume, always verify," 458
Newman, Karl, 421
NFL Super Bowl of Marlin Fishing, The,
    50
Nicole Brown Foundation, 432
Nicole Brown Simpson (Resnick), 49
Nina (Shipp's wife), 53

O

O. J. Is Innocent and I Can Prove It!
    (Dear), xx, 447
O. J. Simpson murder trial, xvi
OJ Is Guilty, but Not of Murder (Dear),
    329
Orange County, 4, 8, 12, 43, 66
Overlooked Suspect, The (Dear), 450, 454,
    508

P

Parents Magazine, 70
Park, Allan, 57, 82, 145, 261
Parks, Bernard C., 337, 373
Paul Revere Middle School, 15
Pavelic, Bill, 197–98
Pearson, Emma, 136
Pennington, Don, 135
Peratis, Thano, 416, 421

Petrocelli, Daniel, 147–59, 162–66, 224, 319–20
   Triumph of Justice, 319,
Phil Smith Productions, 135
Phipps, Betty, 300, 304–05
photograph, 295
   the rear of Kato's bungalow and the chain-link fence, 295
Pietrantoni, Vic, 372
Playboy, 19
police investigators, xxi, 30
police officers, xviii–xix, 81, 176, 325,
police reports, 27, 123
police, 29, 30, 33–34, 64
polygraph test, 215
Potrero Hill, 44
press, 24
private investigator, xviii, xix, 60, 64, 80, 96, 187, 197, 201–03, 219–20, 238, 317, 328, 376,
Problem of Evidence, A (Bosco), xxiii, 21, 76
   buying drugs and carrying in take-out bag, 21
Prody, Christie Michelle, 446, 448–49
   alcohol dependence, 446
   appeared in the *Inside Edition*, 447
   drug addiction, 446
   gave birth to Madeline, 446
prosecutors, 3
public defender, 3

R

Rachael (Sydney's friend), 23, 28
rage attack, 128
rage disorders, 128
Raging Heart (Weller), 314
Ralph (another stylist that knew DeeDee), 234
Ramos, Carlos, 289–90, 339
Randa, Cathy, 197–98, 208–09, 256, 308, 311
Rather, Dan, i, xxiv–xxv
RC (hired professional cinematographer), 475–76

Re, Donald (attorney), 47
reasons Jason Simpson should be considered a major suspect, 484
reasons that prove O. J. Simpson is innocent, 498
Regan, Judith, 434–35
Reichardt, Christian, 58, 60
Reiner, Carl, 453–54
Reiner, Rob, 453
Reiterate (racehorse), 49
Resnick, Faye, 49, 57, 61–62, 68, 145
   Betty Ford Clinic, 60
   drug abuse, 58
   Exodus House, 60
   Nicole Brown Simpson, 49
   opening Jave Café, 59
Revival Café, 74, 98–100, 130, 147, 165, 216, 290–92, 305–06
Riccio, Thomas J (Tom Riccio), 438–41, 442–43
   Busted, 439–42
   criminal who profited from a crime, 443
Rieders, Frederic, 382, 421, 416
   established Renaissance Foundation, 382
   founder of National Medical Services Lab, 382
Rieders, Michael, 382
   son of Frederic Rieders, 382
Riske, Robert, 80
Riviera Country Club, 15
Robert (suffering from epileptic seizures), 131
Roberts, Waylon, 199
Rockingham, 4, 6, 8, 12, 13–14, 16–18, 22, 30, 41, 46, 50–54, 56, 63, 65–66, 69, 71–74, 78–79, 81–84, 88, 95, 114, 120–21, 131, 136, 144, 149, 150, 156–57, 162–63, 165, 176, 178–80, 188, 191, 205, 211–13, 225, 258–62, 267–68, 287, 296, 388, 445, 448, 456
Roit, Natasha, 147
Roland, Donna, 43, 69, 77, 95, 375

INDEX

Dictaphone, 77
Ron Goldman Foundation for Justice, 436
Rooney, Mickey, 453
Rose Marie, 453
Royal Photographic Society, 176
Run of His Life, The (Toobin), 299

S

Sapia, Danielle, 227, 283, 284, 303
  no longer dating Jason, 284
Scheck, Barry, 82
Schulman, Neil, 204–06
scouting mission, 33
Search for Terry Shaw, 237
search warrant for Jason Simpson, 369,
seizures, 111, 115, 117, 125–27, 131, 182, 191
  grand mal, 127, 249
  petit mal, 127
separately, 480,
Shapiro, Robert, 5, 86, 193, 270, 385, 387,
Shaw, Terry, 234–39, 249, 251, 257, 278
  running into Jason, 242
Sheen, Charlie, 452
Shipp, Ron, 43, 50, 54, 73, 79, 126, 184, 189, 194, 198, 200, 203–04, 208, 216–18, 221, 231–32, 246, 248, 266, 299, 313, 319, 339, 393, 425
  covering for O. J. for an alleged domestic violence, 52
  meeting with O. J., 215
  O. J.'s friend and confidant, 204
  residence, 218
  Simpson camp disowning him, 204
Simpson "Dream Team," 60
Simpson, Aaren La Shone, 358, 482. *See also* Simpson, Aaren
Simpson, Aaren, 13, 70–72, 121–22, 255, 287, 311, 353, 482
  drowning in the family swimming pool in Rockingham, 71
  death, 311
Simpson, Arnelle, 13, 15, 63–66, 68–72,

74–76, 85, 162, 208, 211–12, 227, 248, 256, 279, 314
  alcohol use, 66
  Howard University, 75
  serious emotional problem of adjustment, 72
  University of Colorado, 75
Simpson, Carmelita, 85
Simpson, Eunice, 85
Simpson, Jason Lamar, 100, 138, 163, 165–66, 255, 267, 272, 280, 314, 317, 320, 337, 351, 362, 369, 379, 410, 423–24, 426,
  cleared by Los Angeles Police Department, 379
  is still Bill Dear's major suspect, 351
  Jason Simpson's records, 96, 98
Simpson, Jason, 6, 63–64, 68, 76, 85, 89, 93, 96, 111, 116, 135, 144, 181, 187, 230, 232–35, 238, 270, 272–73, 283, 290, 292, 307, 312–13, 318–20, 325, 327, 330–31, 334, 337–41, 344–45, 347–48, 352–57, 361–63, 367, 369, 372, 376, 380–81, 401–02, 404–05, 410–11, 425–26, 432, 456–58. *See also* Simpson, Jason Lamar
  alcoholism in their family, 126
  aneurysm, 120
  angry and upset, 274
  Army and Navy Academy, 73, 112, 130, 320, 362, 376
  assumed a persona as Dr. Jekyll and Mr. Hyde, 269, 275
  attacked Paul Goldberg, 98–99, 339
  busboy, 67
  checked into psychiatric ward at Cedars-Sinai, 121
  choking Jennifer Green with his bare hands, 273
  cook, 67
  could not work under pressure, 305
  cutting Nicole's throat, 276
  Depakote, 111, 114–16, 119, 122–23
  deposition, 147

depression, 67

didn't like being made out to be a fool, 274

disowned by O. J., 248

documentation that contains evidence of instability, 273

dog hair, 457

driving under the influence of alcohol, 98

drug binge, 66

employment, 74

epileptic behavior, 115

executive chef, 327

fight with former employer Paul Goldberg, 339

fingerprints, 458

former sous chef, 345

"going to rage," 120

had gotten into a problem at the Mélisse Restaurant, 284

had put a box containing his personal possession into the Public Storage Facility, 354

handwriting, 341

hired by a local bistro (Angel's Bistro), 327

interest and affinity he had always felt for Nicole, 269

intermittent rage disorder, 313

irrational behavior, 128, 234

Jeep, 301, 340

juvenile mycological epilepsy, 114

knit cap, 423, 455

made reservation at Jackson's Restaurant for his family, 153

medical condition, 124

medical history, 191

medical information, 127, 146

mental instability, 307

overactive psychomotor activity, 115

overdose on Depakote, 147–48

party at Rockingham, 157

pathological liar, 248, 272

played football, 66

  prep chef at the Revival Café, 99

psychological problem, 66

  source of organic malfunctions in his brain, 125

  epilepsy, 125

  referred to Dr. Kittay after being released from Saint John's psychiatric ward, 312

  refused to talk about the murders with DeeDee, 254

residence on Electric Avenue, 300

  prep chef at the Bravo Cucina Restaurant, 112

sous chef at Jackson's Restaurant, 290

spiderweb of crack in the windshield of his Jeep, 303

stabbing himself in the abdomen twice, 113

stopped taking Depakote, 254

stopped taking Depakote two months before the murders, 268

suicide attempts, 130

  last suicide attempt, 123

taking Depakote to control his rage disorder, 283

textbook example of intermittent explosive disorder, 132

time card, 338–41, 353

to-the-death struggle with Goldman, 273

transfer from Cedars-Sinai to a mental ward at St. John's Hospital, 121

tried to kill Jennifer, 228

turning thirty, 316

undergo psychological testing and therapy, 116

undergone testing and treatment at the UCLA Neuro-Psychiatric Institute, 114

USC, 66–67, 74, 98

used LSD, cocaine, and mushroom that caused "audio hallucinations," 114

walking time bomb, 124

went to Mélisse Restaurant for his last paycheck, 301

young man crying for help, 111

Simpson, Justin, 13, 28, 56, 60, 80, 135, 151, 188, 190, 192, 211, 259, 275

Simpson, Nicole Brown, xv, xvii–iii, xxii, 3, 49, 76. *See also* Simpson, Nicole

Simpson, Nicole, 4, 9, 21, 37, 39, 61–62, 76, 83–85, 103, 107, 120, 122, 144–45, 147, 164, 166, 171, 177, 179–81, 183, 189, 193, 201, 204, 216, 219, 221, 228–29, 238, 257, 262, 271–72, 281, 291, 306–07, 311–314, 326, 328, 329, 331, 334–35, 339, 343–46, 348, 354, 358, 366–69, 372, 375, 379, 380, 382, 385, 387–90, 400–04, 408, 410–12, 414, 416–17, 423, 426, 429, 431,

autopsy, 384

curled in fetal position at the foot of the steps, 261

Ferrari, 28

had sex prior to murder, 80

Jeep Cherokee, 29

physically abused by O. J., 211

pneumonia, 20

residence, 26–38, 32, 36, 39

stomach contents, 83

The Daisy, 12

Simpson, O. J., xvi–xviii, xx, xxiii, xxv, 3–4, 11–12, 18, 40, 43, 55, 64, 76, 79, 83, 88, 145, 148, 166, 170–71, 178–80, 197, 210, 228, 256–57, 260, 262, 266, 279, 293–95, 318, 325, 329, 343–44, 346, 368–69, 381–82, 384, 392–93, 396, 401, 414, 417–18, 420, 423–24, 432, 434, 442–43, 446–47, 472–73, 477–78, 482. *See also* Simpson, Orenthal James

and amphetamines addiction, 45

battle for custody of Jason, 71

beating his son Jason, 157

Bronco, 29

Buffalo Bills, 44

cocaine use, 45

didn't like being embarrassed, 212

didn't want any bad publicity coming out of his house, 213

disposes the knapsack containing the Bruno Magli shoes, 260

doing drugs, 19

drinking, 19

failing polygraph test, 386

family man, 8

felt responsible for Jason's behavior, 268

footprints (Bruno Magli shoe prints), 395

giving up pro football, 71

Heisman trophy–winning halfback, 3

If I Did It, 380, 368

insurance through screen Actors Guild covered Jason's medical bill, 112

letter he had written to Nicole, 158

Lovelock Correctional Facility, 443

martyr rather than a murderer, 68

millionaire celebrity 4

not guilty, 454

obsessive or destructive behavior, 19

plea of insanity, 9

polygraph test, 20

San Francisco 49ers, 55

San Francisco City College, 44

stalking Nicole, 19

suicide letter, 8, 121

television spokesman, 3

trial, 94

trial ended, 445

University of Southern California, 44

vial of blood, 416

voted not guilty, 343

Simpson, Orenthal James, 44

Simpson, Sydney, 13, 15, 23, 28, 56, 60, 275, 354

ski cap, 260

slow-speed car chase, 4, 11–12, 66, 80, 121, 165, 209–10, 215, 258

Smith, Chad, 429

Smith, Phil, 135, 344, 350–52, 384, 400–01, 416, 421, 429, 450, 456,

458, 504

Solano, Carlos, 459–61

Solby, Edward, 300, 304

Spitz, Warner, 294
Medicolegal Investigation of Death: Guidelines for the Application of Pathology to Crime Investigation, 294

Sports Illustrated, 70

St. John's Hospital records, 425
Jason was admitted for grand mal seizures, 425
Jason was admitted to the mental health unit, 425

standard police procedure, 34

Starbucks, 59

State of California Investigative and Intelligence Division, 474

Stevens, Stella, 453–54

Stewart, Chris, 11–12, 14–15, 21–36, 40–42, 69, 79, 89–91, 93–94, 96–97, 112, 131–32, 135, 138–44, 256
Dr. Watson, 11
private investigator, 96

Stockdale, Gretchen, 19, 57

Sucharski, Butch, 45

Sunset Boulevard, 6, 12, 22

suspect, 266–67
history of irrational and violent behavior toward women, 266
intermittent rage disorder, 266
same blood type and genetic characters as O. J., 267

Swiss Army knife, 16, 175–176, 181, 393–94, 402,

T

Taft, Skit, 385

Tate murders, 475
Tate, Debra, 475

technique, 31
enter into the "mind" of the killer, 31

Tedford, William, 182

television reporters, 69

Thompson, Phil, vii, 401, 429, 450–52,

45, 458, 460

Tiffany (Kaelin's daughter), 55

TMZ, 441–42

Tomlin, Lily, 453

Tonight Show, The, 67

Toobin, Jeffrey, 299
Run of His Life, The, 299

trash, 282–83
photocopy of receipts for two particular prescriptions signed by Jason and Danielle Sapia, 283
three empty prescription bottles for 500-mg tablets of Depakote, 282

Triumph of Justice (Petrocelli), 319

truth, 7, 204

tunnel vision, xx, 10, 169, 171, 258, 265

U

UCLA hospital, 114

V

Van Dyke, Dick, 453

Vannatter, Philip, xxi, 7, 66, 80, 88, 146, 175, 181, 215, 263, 271, 313, 384, 406, 417–20

victim of outbursts, 129
friend, 129
lover, 129
parent, 129
spouse, 129

Villanueva, Joe, 42, 504, 45–46, 348, 416

Violence Risk Assessment Guide (VRAG), 426

W

Walker, Lenore, 19

Wanda (Dr. DiMaio's secretary), 400

Washington Times, 333

Weller, Sheila, 314
Raging Heart, 314

Whitley, Marguerite, 13, 44, 66–67, 70–72, 116, 122, 211, 248
blamed Jason for Aaren's death, 122
end of marriage to O. J., 13
physically abused by O. J., 211

INDEX

Wigland, Diane, 459–60, 464
William C. Dear & Associates, 506
Williams, Reagan, 343
Winkler, Henry, 453
Without a Doubt (Clark), 88
Wright, David, 228

Z
Zlomsowitch, Keith, 61–62, 64, 259